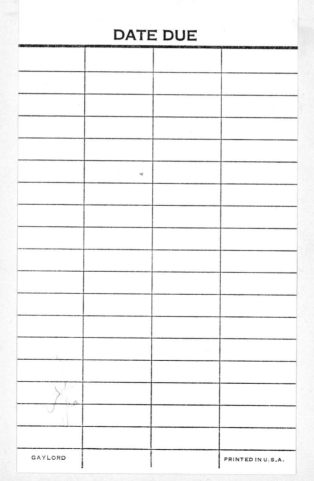

DATE DUE

GAYLORD			PRINTED IN U.S.A.

ALSO BY
Michel del Castillo

THE DISINHERITED
THROUGH THE HOOP

These are Borzoi Books,
published by Alfred A. Knopf, Inc.

Child of Our Time

Child
of Our Time

BY

Michel del Castillo

TRANSLATED FROM THE FRENCH BY

Peter Green

ALFRED A. KNOPF, *New York*

1965

L. C. Catalog card number: 58–10964

© Peter Green, 1958

THIS IS A BORZOI BOOK, PUBLISHED BY ALFRED A. KNOPF, INC.

PUBLISHED OCTOBER 20, 1958
REPRINTED FOUR TIMES
SIXTH PRINTING, SEPTEMBER 1965

Originally published in France as TANGUY: Histoire d'un enfant d'aujourd'hui. © 1957 by René Julliard.

To all my comrades, living or dead

"The world cherishes its filth and
hates having it disturbed."

DOSTOIEVSKI: *Stavrogin's Confession*

PART ONE

Child of Our Time

"The truth, the bitter truth . . ."

DANTON,
quoted by Stendhal

Child of Our Time

I

IT had all begun with the first shot fired in the Spanish Civil War. Of these early years Tanguy retained only a few confused memories. He recalled having seen long motionless queues waiting in front of the shops. There had been bombed and blackened houses and corpses in the streets. There had been women in soldier's uniform who carried guns and stopped passers-by to ask for their papers. Tanguy remembered going to bed hungry and waking to the mournful wail of the sirens. He had wept with terror when he heard the militiamen hammering on the front door that morning, before dawn.

Every evening he listened to his mother broadcasting. She used to say that there was no justice in any good fortune that deprived other people of theirs; and Tanguy believed her, because she never lied. He often cried during her speeches. He did not understand what she was saying, but he knew she was right, because she was his mother.

Often he went to the big public park behind the Prado,

3

with his nurse. He had to stop and raise his clenched fist in salute as they passed the graves of the fallen.

In the park there was a big gun known as the Old Man. At first the Republicans had little knowledge of how to handle it, and the shells it fired fell on their own troops. They had to wait till the arrival of some Russian experts before they could use it properly. Civilians in Madrid came to look at the Old Man; they all felt great affection for it. This gun was the city's defense against the Fascist artillery. During the night when they heard its deep-throated roar answering the distant salvos from the enemy lines, they nearly cried with relief.

Tanguy loved his mother with more intensity than was common with other boys of his age. He had never known his father and felt, vaguely, that his mother was a very lonely woman. So he tried to "be a man" and look after her.

One day the Communists arrested her. Tanguy went to see her in prison. The jail had once been a convent. Its windows were heavily barred, and in front of every door women in uniform stood on guard. Behind the bars he saw his mother with other prisoners. He tried hard not to cry: this would only have increased her suffering. But he heard her explaining to his nurse how each night a group of prisoners was taken away for the *paseo*. Tanguy had no clear idea what this word meant, but he had heard it so often that he guessed his mother was in very grave danger. He burst out sobbing then, and one of the wardresses opened the gate and let him go to her.

Tanguy threw himself into his mother's arms: by now she was in tears as well. He clung to her as if he would never let go. The wardress grabbed him by the legs and pulled as hard as

4

she could, but he still hung on desperately. In the end they were torn apart, and Tanguy returned home feeling as if he had died inside. In his pocket were two little wool dolls which his mother had made for him.

This was a scene he was never to forget.

After a little while his mother was released, and came back to him. But now two strange men who carried guns slept in the hall of their flat. Tanguy was told that they were there to protect his mother, and so he became very fond of them.

Little by little all these memories blurred and faded. These early years left Tanguy with little but a strange feeling of misery, which became more acute as time went on. His genuine recollections began on one cold November night in 1938. Tanguy was five years old at the time.

His mother woke him up in the middle of the night. She held him close to her, kissed him, and told him that they had lost the war and had to leave Madrid. There were tears in her eyes as she said this.

Tanguy was miserable. His mother had been good and kind; she had stood up for poor folk; how could she have "lost the war"? But he said nothing, and let his old nurse dress him. She was crying too. Outside the Old Man still boomed defiance at the Fascist guns.

They left by car for Valencia. Tanguy lay with his head on his mother's breast: he felt at peace there. But a strangely silent atmosphere encompassed him. The grown-ups said little, and when they did it was in low, subdued voices. His mother was crying the whole time. Once she asked the friend who was escorting them whether the Fascists might not cut off their line of retreat and arrest them. Her fears were unfounded, however; they reached Valencia in safety.

There Tanguy and his mother had to find a ship to take them to France. As in Madrid, the guns were thundering away in the town itself and in the neighboring countryside. Thousands of refugees were waiting at the docks, patiently sitting on trunks or bundles of bedding. There were large numbers of women, children, and old people among them, as well as some wounded combatants on stretchers. The quays were crowded with shipping.

It was a long wait. For a whole day Tanguy stood there beside his mother, hungry and tired. But he did not cry. He believed himself to be a man, and men never cried. He stared wretchedly at people who were crying, and who seemed as famished and exhausted as he was.

It was nearly dark before they finally went aboard. Tanguy's mother said good-by to the friend who had accompanied them. She begged him to go on board with them, but he refused. When the anchor was raised he lifted his clenched fist and shouted: "Good luck, comrades! Good-by!" The refugees lining the rail returned his salute and began to sing "*Negras Tormentas*," the famous Republican hymn. But Tanguy hid his face in his mother's dress. He did not want to look at the faintly shining lights which were the lights of his country and would soon be swallowed up in the darkness. His heart was dull and heavy: all round him he heard the sound of sobbing. He did not really understand what had happened, neither the reason for their having lost the war, nor how that loss had been brought about.

2

IT was a long voyage. The ship's cook gave the Spaniards something to eat. The boat was English and the cook was a Negro. Tanguy became his friend and learned a few words of English from him. He would proudly ask the Captain: "How do you do?" The Captain would shake hands with him and answer: "All right, boy. How are you?" But there, since those were the only English words Tanguy knew, the conversation stopped.

The refugees were in good spirits. They talked about France as the land of liberty. Tanguy was fascinated. He had no idea what liberty was; but his mother had assured him that in France there was no war and plenty to eat.

The British boat put in at Oran, and they left it there. Tanguy and his mother strolled through narrow streets full of bad-mannered shopkeepers all talking at once. She bought him a box of lead soldiers, cavalrymen, who wore turbans and brightly colored cloaks.

They spent one night in Oran: they had a beautiful bedroom with a private bath. Tanguy was delighted, and told himself what a fine country France must be. It was on that evening that his mother told him he was French himself, like his father, who had left them some time before the outbreak of the Civil War. She and his father, she said, had held incompatible opinions. She had renounced her social position and traditional family loyalties in order to champion the underprivileged. His father had utterly failed to comprehend her motives. All the same (Tanguy's mother told him) he must be a good boy when they were together again.

"You must behave nicely to him, Tanguy. He is your father. Besides, he can help us. There won't be anyone else there that we can turn to except him—" Her tone changed quickly as she added: "Anyway, he'll be very proud of you. You're as alike as two pins."

Tanguy said nothing. He had no desire to be nice to his father. He knew his father had left his mother in Spain with civil war in the air, and hadn't even wanted her back. He had made no effort to get her out of the country. Tanguy thought his behavior cowardly and disgusting.

They completed the second part of their journey on a French mailboat. It was large, the cabins were comfortable, the service quick and polite. Everyone said please and thank-you. Tanguy told himself that the French were very good-mannered. He was intrigued and flattered by the idea of being French himself, like his father, and wondered what France would be like.

His first impressions were not particularly favorable. Marseilles loomed up through a sheet of rain, an ugly, gray, filthy waterfront. The gendarmes who came aboard were far from polite. They treated the Spaniards like dirt, and took away their money and jewelry. The Spaniards made no protests, but gave up all their possessions in silence. The tourists left the ship. They were well dressed, and porters rushed to relieve them of their gaily labeled luggage. The Spaniards, however, had to stay on board. Soon the quay was thronged with black soldiers carrying guns. When Tanguy asked his mother who they were, she told him they were Senegalese. But she had no more idea of what was happening than he did.

Then suddenly she exclaimed: "There's your father, Tanguy! Look—over there!"

He was a young man, and very tall. He had curly hair and large dark eyes and was very elegantly dressed. He shook hands with Tanguy's mother without seeming to notice Tanguy's presence. Tanguy felt miserable. He realized that this greeting was deliberately cold, that they were not welcome. He was sorry for his mother.

"I take it," his father was saying, "that your money must be worthless now?"

"Very likely, I should think."

"Very appropriate, too. Now you're a real Communist."

She said: "I've already told you I'm not a Communist." Her voice held an unfamiliar weariness which disturbed Tanguy.

"Yet you turn up with all this riffraff—"

Tanguy wanted to cry. He knew that his father was speaking of the Spanish refugees. He felt himself blush, and stole a glance at these gaunt, emaciated men and women who still waited there, uncomplaining.

His father was saying: "I'll try to get you out of here. But I warn you, I haven't got much money myself."

9

Tanguy did not even hear his mother's reply. Loneliness and misery pressed in on him with increasing force. He clung closely to his mother as they went down the ship's gangplank. He still clung to her as he got into his father's car. But before they left the docks, he noticed that the Spanish refugees had been divided into two groups, men on one side, women on the other. Escorted by the Senegalese troops, these groups were marched off from the quay.

"Where are they taking them?" his mother asked.

"To a camp," said his father.

Tanguy felt uneasy. He did not fully understand what his parents were saying. But he guessed from the tone of his mother's voice that this "camp" meant misery for the refugees. His heart ached for them.

Yet after a few minutes a strange feeling of well-being stole over him. It was nice to be in the car. Tanguy loved the smell of gasoline and leather and, above all, his mother's perfume. He sat between his parents and felt happy. They seemed to have forgotten their old quarrels. They were chatting of Paris and their former friends there. Tanguy told himself that he was an ordinary boy again at last, with a mother and father like everyone else. He was proud of his parents: they were both so handsome and clever.

They spent the night in a hotel. Tanguy fell asleep while his parents sat near him and went on talking in low voices. He woke in the middle of the night and was happy because his parents were still there. They were smoking and chatting, all arguments apparently forgotten. The next morning, too, they were still there. It was not a dream.

His mother told him they were going to live in a charming

little town in central France. They would have a house
there and be very happy. His father would come and see
them every week-end. Tanguy was delighted with the idea of
having parents *and* a house. He asked if he could go to school,
and his mother promised him he would.

All the houses in the little town were alike, but theirs was
a short way outside, in the country. There were woods
and green fields all round them. In the evening Tanguy and his
mother went for a walk arm in arm. Tanguy was happy. It
was peaceful here; he had a house; he was going to school.
And he had, besides, a friend and a dog.

The dog's name was Tom. Tanguy had found him wandering
by the roadside. He was a stray: distrustful, and especially
savage with children, because they had made him suffer. Some
hooligans had tied a small tin can full of gunpowder to his
tail and set it off. The poor dog had been badly hurt. From
that day on he was liable to bite any small boy on sight.
Tanguy decided to befriend him. Every day he offered the
dog a lump of sugar. At first the dog refused it. Tanguy had
to put the lump down on the ground and go away. Then the
dog would pounce on it, take it off, and eat it in some safe
corner. But gradually Tom learned to trust Tanguy. Soon he
even let himself be stroked. And then one evening he followed the boy home.

Tanguy brought him in and begged his mother to let him
stay. His mother agreed. Tanguy gave his dog a bath, bought
him a splendid collar, and fed him. Every day Tom waited for
Tanguy at the school gates. At first the other schoolboys
laughed at the dog because it was thin and lame, but soon *it*

became a dog like any other dog: it had found a home and was fed when it was hungry. Tom was devoted to Tanguy. He jumped for joy when his master came home.

Tanguy had also found a friend, a boy with flaming-red hair and a slight cast in one eye. He was nicknamed The Fireman, but Tanguy never called him this. He always referred to him by his Christian name, Robert, and that, no doubt, was why they first became friends.

Tanguy got good reports at school. He learned easily, and it looked as though he would be a brilliant pupil. Robert on the other hand could hardly keep up with the rest of his class. He worked hard, but was slow-witted. Tanguy used to help him with his homework, and he often came to tea at Tanguy's house. Tanguy was pleased because Robert told him that his mother was pretty and his father a "good sort."

Tanguy's father spent his week-ends with them. He used to come down by car. As soon as he arrived they would all three go for a walk down to the river and through the woods. Tanguy used to pick mushrooms or violets. He was delighted to see his parents walking arm in arm behind him. He went running ahead with Tom and threw stones, which the dog proudly found and brought back to him. Tanguy was beginning to love France simply because he was happy. He had forgotten the mutter of the guns, the endless queues at the bakery, the nostalgic wail of sirens in the night.

Nevertheless, things were not going altogether smoothly. His parents had frequent arguments. Sometimes Tanguy was woken up by the sound of their angry voices. Neither of them shouted, but they said horrible things. Tanguy was heartbroken. He did not love his father. He guessed that everything his father said was a lie.

One day an argument was more violent than usual. His mother said: "I don't need your help in bringing up my son. I shall manage very well by myself. I intend to go and work in Clermont."

"I forbid you to go to Clermont," his father replied.

"What right have you to forbid me?"

"What right? Because I say so. I don't want the whole world to know I have a son. You must realize that I want to reshape my life. I have ambitions—"

"You aren't the only person with ambitions. What about me? I want to make a living for myself and my son. To do that I must work. No one can stop me from going where I please—"

"I warn you," said Tanguy's father. "We're getting a little tired of all this Communist scum trickling over the frontier into France. One of these fine days you and your Spanish Socialist'll all wind up in jail, the whole bunch of you."

"Are you threatening me?"

"I'm warning you. Clear out. Take off for America or anywhere you like, but don't let me hear any more of you, or your precious son."

Tanguy's mother said: "I shall go when I choose, and how I choose. You should be ashamed of yourself. But you don't know the meaning of the word shame—"

Tanguy wanted to cry as he listened to this quarrel. He loved his mother more than his father, because he was very young still and had always lived with her. But he was agonized by their estrangement. He had longed to live with both

13

of them but they were always quarreling. They destroyed his happiness.

It was early spring. The near-by woods were bursting out in unfamiliar richness and beauty. They left the house soon after dawn. Tanguy felt as if something had broken inside him. He had helped his mother pack their bags and put them in the car that was to take them to Clermont-Ferrand. Robert had come to say good-by. Tanguy shook hands with him, and climbed into the car next to his mother. She let out the clutch. He turned his head and saw their little house for the last time, half hidden behind the massed lilacs in the garden. Then it vanished. Tom was running along behind the car, his tongue hanging out. Tanguy watched him. Little by little the car drew away from him, but Tom never gave up. He ran and ran, down the middle of the road. Tanguy said nothing. Then, suddenly, he burst out sobbing.

Clermont-Ferrand was as dirty a town as Marseilles. It had many factories in and around it. Tanguy lived with his mother in a small, ill-kept hotel. He waited there for long hours in one tiny room while his mother looked for work. It was not an easy task for her; foreigners had to have a working-permit. They could not get a permit without an offer of employment, and no one would employ them without a permit. To Tanguy this seemed an insoluble problem.

His mother's face after a time showed such plain signs of hopeless fatigue that Tanguy no longer dared to ask her how the day's search had gone. He tried to distract her by talking of other things. He never complained of hunger, though hot meals had become something that belonged to another world.

His mother fed him on sandwiches and fruit. Occasionally she brought him a bottle of Périer water. This, with its sharp, piquant flavor was a special treat.

But every day he found himself missing the little house outside Vichy more. There he had known happiness—a dog, a friend, school life, and every week-end a walk in the woods with his father. He wondered when he would see these things again. He no longer hated his father; at the bottom of his heart he was miserable at not seeing him any more. He realized vaguely that his mother was trying to influence him, to make him share what she called her "just hatred." But Tanguy felt no natural vocation for hate. He missed the Saturday evenings when his father had sat in the big armchair reading the papers. He missed the cigarette smoke, the clatter his mother had made in the kitchen; he could not forget those rare moments of peace when his father had read Hans Christian Andersen aloud to him and he had sat and listened.

Now, in Clermont-Ferrand, the days seemed long and gray to him. He did not dare switch the light on, because the proprietor told them they used it too much. He sat there in the dark watching the crowds come and go in the street. One evening he saw some boy scouts pass by singing. His mother found him in tears. When she asked him why, he told her he wanted to be a boy scout and go off to the woods.

"My poor child, you're far too thin and delicate. You might catch pneumonia and die there. That sort of thing isn't for you."

This reply only increased the dull misery that weighed down on him. What caused his suffering was precisely the fact that he was different from other children, that he didn't have a home with a mother and father who agreed with each other, or at least pretended they did. But such thoughts he shared with no one.

In the end his mother found a job as a shorthand-typist in a big factory. Immediately Tanguy found himself eating better, and the proprietor no longer muttered "Filthy Spaniards!" when his mother and he came downstairs to the hall. Tanguy could even switch on the light and read while he was waiting for his mother to come back from work at half past six.

One day two men came and asked for her. He told them she was at work. They sat down and waited for her to return. Tanguy wondered about these rude men who came uninvited and acted as though they owned the place. He decided to ignore their presence, and went on reading and writing as if nothing had happened.

His mother's surprise was as great as his own. As soon as she came in the two strange men demanded to know her full name. She told it to them, and showed the working-permit she had recently obtained.

One of them said: "You'll have to come along with us, lady."

His mother seemed to have recovered her self-possession. She asked the police officer what they had come for, what was happening?

"They'll tell you down at headquarters. I should pack a bag if I were you. You never know. It might come in handy."

Tanguy's mother got out a small suitcase and put some clothes and other necessities in it. She added a suit and two clean shirts for Tanguy. Then, escorted by the two detectives and her small son, she went down the stairs.

The proprietor watched her pass in the hall. He was a small bald man with glasses. He had been a verger in his youth, and later a professional mourner at funerals; these two occupations had left their mark on him. He stared at them now, full of hatred.

"Filthy foreigners," he muttered to himself, "they're all the same. . . ."

Tanguy flushed. He wanted to hit the man. But he said nothing; he followed his mother out into the street, his eyes fixed straight in front of him. All the passers-by seemed to be staring at them. He wondered what was going to happen to them and whether his father would come to their rescue.

For more than an hour Tanguy waited at police headquarters for his mother to come back. The walls of the waiting-room were covered with posters. Several policemen sat talking quietly in one corner. Tanguy decided that they were decent fellows. After all, they were only doing their duty. At last a door opened, and his mother came over to him. Her face was white.

"Darling, you must try and be very brave. These gentlemen are going to take us to a camp. Someone has denounced us. But you mustn't be afraid, we shall still be together, and while we remain together nothing bad can happen to us."

Tanguy looked at the floor. "But we haven't done anything bad!" he protested.

"I know, Tanguy. That isn't the point."

"Who denounced us?"

"Your father," she said.

With an effort Tanguy held back his tears. At this moment he hated the whole world—his father and mother, the policemen, the hotel proprietor. He hated all grown-ups, because they seemed to hate him, and he was only seven years old.

"It isn't true," he sobbed. "I don't believe it."

"Yes, it's true," his mother said. "The inspector is a Socialist. He told me the whole story."

Tanguy hated his father for his miserable cowardice; but he was even angrier with his mother for admitting this cowardice to him now. She shouldn't have told me, he thought, she has no right to hurt me so bitterly. He bit his lip, picked up the little suitcase, and followed her. The police had handcuffed her, and she tried to hide the handcuffs in the sleeves of her dress.

3

THE concentration camp to which Tanguy and his mother were taken was in the Midi. He had never seen a place remotely like it, and it was very different from anything he had imagined. The camp consisted merely of a few wooden barrack huts, damp and worm-infested, surrounded by a barbed-wire fence.

It was a "special" camp. The bulk of the internees (all of them women) were Jewesses, or political prisoners—a term Tanguy did not understand. He had heard that there were also some "prostitutes," whatever they might be.

The prisoners gave Tanguy and his mother an unpleasant reception. As he went into the "political prisoners" hut, Tanguy saw half-a-dozen pale, thin, haggard faces staring at him. There were jeers and laughs. It was dark in the hut, and the far end was hidden in shadow. Tanguy heard voices there, but he could not see anyone.

"Look at that fur coat!" said one. "We've got a capitalist in here now."

"Don't worry. She won't be here long, by the look of her."

A woman came forward and confronted them. She had hot, feverish eyes, and her hair hung loose down her back. She bowed with exaggerated ceremony and said: "Madame, this is, alas, not the Ritz. But we shall do our utmost to make Madame and her son comfortable. We can offer you a room looking on the garden, with a private bathroom."

There was a burst of coarse, hearty laughter. Tanguy hid his face in his mother's skirt. He had no desire to let these women see him cry. He felt unutterably tired. He thought of Tom, and Robert, and his father, and wondered what he had done to deserve such treatment. After a moment he regained control of himself. He would not give these creatures the satisfaction of making him unhappy.

He followed his mother over to an empty bed-space. There were two bunks, one above the other. His mother put down the suitcase on the lower bunk; Tanguy climbed into the top one and at once fell asleep, fully dressed.

19

. . .

Tanguy retained few clear impressions of the eighteen months they spent in this camp. One day was exactly like the next. They were awakened by the sounds of their fellow prisoners screaming, swearing, or quarreling. Consciousness brought immediate hunger. Hunger was the sharpest, clearest memory Tanguy preserved. All day long he dreamed of food. He lived for the moment when the cooks came in with the big steaming pot. But after swallowing the yellowish liquid, which for want of a better word they called soup, he was hungrier than ever.

Tanguy did not complain. He knew that his mother, too, was desperately hungry. He spent hours stretched out on his bunk. He slept a good deal of the time, yet remained tired and apathetic. His mother sat near him writing. She wrote hundreds of pages. Around her the other prisoners insulted her, and each other, from morning till night.

They hated her. They called her capitalist, bourgeois, class traitor. They jeered at her for reading books or writing. They threatened her. When any breach of barrack discipline took place and the wardress demanded to know who was responsible, they all unanimously named her as the culprit. She was, as a result, punished nearly every day.

All the prisoners were bored and irritable. They passed their day chewing over their hunger, brooding on their captivity. Their nerves raw and frayed, they quarreled for want of anything better to do. They felt themselves forgotten by the world, and the hideous uncertainty of what was to become of them tormented their minds. They were horribly emaciated and swarming with fleas and every kind of vermin.

The wardresses were rather like the women soldiers whom Tanguy vaguely recalled from his Madrid days. Like them, they carried guns. Their habits were gross and vulgar. They were just as bored as the prisoners. That was why they spent the day persecuting their charges: it was their only pastime.

One woman befriended Tanguy and his mother. Her name was Rachel, and she was a big blonde Jewess from Central Europe, with surprisingly blue eyes and a gentle, comforting smile. Tanguy worshipped her. She spoke several foreign languages, and knew an inexhaustible number of wonderful fairy stories. She was also an artist, and did little pen-and-ink sketches on scraps of cardboard. She drew anything that caught her eye: the huts, the cooks serving out soup, the guards at rollcall, the pinewoods beyond the camp. Tanguy spent long hours sitting watching Rachel. He loved to watch her work, to follow the strokes of the pen that re-created the camp in miniature. But Rachel was too kindly an artist. She drew a concentration camp that had no connection with reality. Her barrack huts looked like dollhouses, and the prisoners resembled clever schoolgirls.

Tanguy's mother criticized her for this. "You're far too optimistic, Rachel," she said. "Suppose some paper published your drawings? The editor could say: 'Look what a good time our internees have in their camps.'"

Rachel smiled. "There's a pleasant side to everything," she replied. "It depends on how you look at it. There's some good in everything, too, even a concentration camp. What matters is to know how to see it. You might almost say I was lucky to be here. I managed to escape from a Nazi camp, you know. A Nazi camp is really no joke, believe you me."

One evening Tanguy asked his mother why Rachel was there, what it was she could have done. His mother replied that Rachel was a Jewess, and that the Germans were persecuting the Jews. This made Tanguy very unhappy: he knew Rachel was a kind and generous person.

There were various organizations that sent representatives to the camp with gifts for the prisoners. Most of them were religious. The Protestants distributed parcels to everybody without distinction of race or creed; the Jews brought kosher food for their own people; the Catholics came and said Mass.

The other prisoners took care that Tanguy and his mother were excluded from these charitable donations. Every Saturday Tanguy saw the parcels being passed from hand to hand without ever reaching him. On these occasions he could hardly help crying. But after a while, thanks to Rachel, things changed. She spoke about them to a rabbi, who thereafter brought a big parcel for the boy every week. So once a week now Tanguy could eat chocolate, biscuits, and cheese.

His mother refused to touch anything from these parcels. She pretended not to be hungry, or said she did not feel well. But Tanguy knew that his mother was going without food for his sake, and suffered guilty agonies at the knowledge.

Winter came, a bitter winter with snow. The sky was gray, and air and earth alike were white with whirling snowflakes. Tanguy spent the whole day wrapped in his blanket, chilled to the bone. He snuggled up against his mother or Rachel. Rachel had knitted him a sweater, but the cold was

so intense that even with the sweater his teeth chattered
and he shivered all over.

He had become a sullen and uncommunicative child. His
mother told him he was impossible, and it seemed she was
right. He hardly ever spoke, and he carefully concealed his
innermost thoughts. When he did say anything, it was with a
great effort and as if against his natural inclinations. Yet he
still loved his mother more than anything in the world. For
him she was still the cleverest and most beautiful woman in
existence. But something was lacking: if only she would think
about him a little more, and not spend all her time writing
or talking politics! What good were politics to them? He
dreamed of a little house like the one they had lived in near
Vichy, where he could once more have a dog, and a friend,
and books to read. He would have liked a father, too, and the
chance to get into mischief like other ordinary children.
Instead of which, his life had been spent trailing from town
to town in an atmosphere of hatred and war. Always he
found himself wondering when the war would end and
what peace was really like.

His only respite was when he sat with Rachel and she told
him her marvelous stories. He had seen too much in his short
life to believe in witches and fairies, but he still loved these
tales. For him they meant peace. Rachel, with her gentle
voice, was a wonderful story-teller. She knew just how to
pause at the most pathetic point in her story, so that Tanguy's heart would nearly stop beating. He suffered in sympathy when the Sleeping Beauty lay unconscious, and beamed
with relief and delight when the Prince came to kiss her
awake and marry her. Tanguy needed to believe in these

23

stories. In this imaginary world of marvels he seemed to be in contact with children all over the world. Through Rachel's stories he became a child like other children; and this was the thing which he needed most desperately.

His mother fell ill. She coughed and coughed, and could hardly sleep at night for fear she might choke herself coughing if she lay down flat. She remained propped up in a sitting position, trembling with cold and pain, her forehead bathed in a cold sweat. Tanguy watched her, agonized. He had little idea how to pray, since he had never been taught; but he prayed now every night. He begged God not to take his mother away, and told himself that since he was a child God would certainly hear his prayer. Yet for all his hopes his mother's health deteriorated. One day she was unable to get up. That same evening she was removed to the infirmary. Tanguy heard only one word: "pleurisy." But life had taught him to guess the exact weight of such phrases as soon as they were uttered; and on this occasion the speaker's tone led him to expect the worst. He shifted his few belongings to Rachel's bed-space, and she made him sleep beside her. She soothed him and rocked him in her arms. When he cried and could not sleep at night, she told him such long and wonderful stories that he dropped off before she got to the end.

Twice a week he was allowed to visit his mother in the infirmary. Rachel went there with him. For this special occasion she tidied him up very carefully. He had fine long wavy black hair, which she combed and parted before they set off. The infirmary was a barrack hut, like the rest, but it had

proper beds, instead of the bunks with their straw mattresses, and real sheets and blankets as well.

In one of these beds his mother lay. The whiteness of her face was barely distinguishable from the pillow that framed it. Only her huge dark eyes seemed alive. Tanguy sat down beside her and took her hand. With a great effort she made herself talk to him, and managed to keep smiling as long as he was there. But this sad forced smile only increased Tanguy's dumb misery. When he got back to his own hut he felt desperate. But he said nothing and held back his tears. He was in a very bad state. He found himself shivering when it was quite warm, or sweating when everyone else was frozen.

Some of the women now became much more friendly toward Tanguy. They no longer screamed insults at him or referred to him as a "capitalist." Instead, they greeted him with affectionate smiles and asked him kindly how his mother was getting on. But he liked neither their smiles nor their questions; he stuck close to Rachel. She went on indefatigably with her sketching, turning out sweet little snow-covered barrack huts, which were (no doubt) inhabited by charming dolls.

A wardress called out: "Tanguy! Get your things together. Your mother's going to be transferred to the hospital in Montpellier, and you're going with her. Be ready in half an hour."

Tanguy nodded. He began to pack his few possessions. When he had finished he went over to Rachel. The girl's face was pale, and her eyes red—or so he fancied; certainly her

breast rose and fell with sudden violence. He hesitated, then put his arms round her neck and kissed her.

"Good-by, Rachel. I do love you—you know that, don't you?"

"Yes, Tanguy. I know. Take care of yourself. Be kind to your mama. She isn't very well. You must learn to be a man—"

She broke off, and there was a short silence. At last she smiled at Tanguy tenderly and gave him an envelope.

"Here's a souvenir to remember me by," she said.

"What is it, Rachel?"

"Some of my sketches. When you look at them, you'll think of me."

"I shan't ever forget you, Rachel. You know, deep down I love you nearly as much as Mama."

They said no more. Tanguy took the sketches, picked up his bag, and went out of the hut without looking back. He felt Rachel's beseeching eyes fixed on him, and knew that if he turned his head and looked at her once more he would burst into tears. He climbed into the ambulance and found his mother lying there on a stretcher. The doors were shut behind him. He pressed his nose to the rear window. The camp was blanketed with a thick fall of snow. Behind a window he made out a fluttering handkerchief and guessed it must be Rachel. He wiped away a tear. Then he sat down by his mother, huddled up in one corner. It was very cold.

4

THE nun scrutinized Tanguy closely. She was a big strong woman with green eyes and a boxer's nose. She examined him as she would have examined a bear in the zoo. He stood in the hospital corridor feeling very ill at ease. All around there was a strong smell of ether. He had no idea why the Sister was staring at him in this way. He would have liked to say one short and very effective word to her, but dared not, because she was a nun.

"What do you propose to do?" she asked him. "You can't stay here. Your mother's ill, that's another matter. But you have no right to a hospital bed as well. Haven't you any family?"

Tanguy blushed and stuttered. "No," he said.

"You should say 'No, Sister.'"

"No, Sister. I've only got my mother."

"Are you Jewish?"

He hesitated. "No, Sister."

"Then why are you in a concentration camp?"

"We are Spanish."

The nun appeared to be lost in thought for a moment. Then she raised her eyes and examined him once more. That done, she meditated a little longer.

"Very well," she said at last. "I shall call up the Friars. You will be kept in their college till your mother is better. They will let you come and visit her on Sundays. But you must promise me to behave yourself properly."

"Yes, Sister."

"Good. Now go and say good-by to your mother. Then come back here to me."

Tanguy's mother was in a big ward with a large number of other sick people. Tanguy sat down by her bed and held her hand. She could not move, but she sketched the faintest ghost of a smile. Tanguy smiled too.

"My poor darling," she whispered. "What's going to become of you?"

"The Friars are going to look after me. I shall stay with them. I can come and see you every Sunday."

"Tanguy—" Her voice was becoming weaker.

"Yes, Mama?"

"Be good and work hard in the college. Don't make me worry about you. You've got to help me, Tanguy."

"Yes, Mama."

The college was situated on the outskirts of Montpellier. It was a big gray and black building with barred windows. Tanguy walked through long dark corridors, a Brother leading the way. On the bare walls were numerous huge crucifixes. The spread-eagled Christ-figures loomed threateningly over him, as if their main object was to instill terror. Tanguy and his guide at last came out in a central court that was surrounded by covered cloisters. Here plane trees grew; lights shone in the windows round the courtyard; and he could hear the sound of voices. Tanguy shivered. He felt lost and alone. His first instinct was to escape. But at once he recalled his promise to his mother that he would be good: he had no reason to worry.

28

"A new arrival, Brother Marcel."

Forty heads turned and stared at him. Tanguy, his eyes fixed on the floor, felt the collective force of their curiosity. He was badly dressed and ashamed of it.

"Go and sit down at that desk. I shall give you a test tomorrow. For the time being you can stay at the bottom of the class."

Brother Marcel was an old man with a most compelling eye. He had a long white beard and wore a little black skullcap. His voice was gentle and sweet-sounding. Tanguy decided that Brother Marcel must be a good man and that they would get on very well. Having come to this conclusion, he felt better and looked quickly round the classroom.

A few rows in front of him he noticed a young fair-haired boy. His hair kept falling over his forehead, and he tossed it back with a quick movement of his head. He was dressed in a kind of pinafore with blue and white stripes. His slightly snub nose gave his face a mischievous expression. He turned and winked at Tanguy. Tanguy, astonished and delighted, gave him a faint answering smile.

Life in the college was monotonous but busy. They got up while it was still dark. Then came Mass and early lessons, followed by breakfast, morning classes, and recreation. On Thursday afternoons the boys went for walks in the country or played football.

Tanguy was happy. He had become the best pupil in his class, and Brother Marcel liked him. The old teacher set him up as an example for the others and always spoke in a very pleasant tone to him. The boy that Tanguy had noticed the evening he arrived had become his friend. They sat side by side in class, worked at their exercises together, and were inseparable at meals. Their beds were next to each other in the same dormitory. Tanguy's friend was called Michel. He enjoyed a laugh more than anything. He spent his classes drawing caricatures and paid no attention to what was happening on the blackboard. When he had finished a caricature he nudged Tanguy with his foot and passed it over to him.

They laughed at everything and at nothing. On the Thursday walks they always went together, and if one of their friends tried to join them, Michel sent him packing. They had no secrets from each other. Tanguy had told Michel all about his childhood and his many agonies. Michel pulled his leg and called him funny names. They were devoted to each other, and this devotion was all the stronger because they were still children. Tanguy dreamed of Michel and thought about him day and night. He swore never to be parted from him.

Brother Albert, on the other hand, had little affection for Tanguy. Brother Albert was the almoner. Tanguy, having arrived from a concentration camp, had neither clothes nor money. This annoyed the almoner considerably, and he made no attempt to conceal his feelings in public. Tanguy was ashamed. He told himself it was not his fault if he did not pay for his keep. Nor—since she was so ill—was his mother responsible. Finally a solution was found. Tanguy's grandmother, who lived in Madrid, sent the Brothers a regular allowance. Out of this they bought the child's clothes, shoes, and books, and reimbursed themselves for his living expenses. From this moment Brother Albert's dislike for Tanguy mysteriously vanished.

Every Sunday Tanguy went to see his mother. Her health was steadily improving now, and she was proud of her son for being at the top of his class. Tanguy told her about Michel and Brother Marcel. He was becoming a happy child once more. He loved the college and had a passion for learning. Even better, he had a friend, as he had had at Vichy. Tanguy often wondered why they could not stay hidden in Montpellier till the end of the war. Grandmother sent them enough money to live on. I could stay with Michel, he thought, and go on with my lessons. But he knew that this was beyond his control, however much he longed to remain with Michel and Brother Marcel. He was tired of wandering from place to place with his mother, and found the nomad's life beginning to pall on him. It was no use telling himself that this was not his mother's fault; he was still sick of it.

One Sunday when he arrived at the hospital the hall-porter told him his mother had been taken out of the public ward and put in a private room on the first floor. This news surprised Tanguy considerably. He found his mother in a small, elegantly furnished bedroom with pink wallpaper. There was even a radio on the bedside table. His mother was sitting up in a green bedjacket. Tanguy was so happy to see her there that he began to cry.

"So you like my new home, do you?" his mother asked.

He nodded, still sniffing.

"But you haven't asked how I got it. Well, I'll tell you. There is a very kind nun here in the hospital called Sister Suzanne. She has Republican sympathies and does everything she can to make me comfortable. She got me moved in here.

31

Look—I've even got the radio! And that's not all. You're no longer to live in the college. You'll live here with me, and go to school every day like the other children."

Tanguy was in raptures. Soon his daily life became sheer delight. Every morning he ran off excitedly from the hospital to school, his pockets stuffed with sweets and chocolates for Michel, who adored such things. He would put them inside his friend's desk and wait impatiently to see him open the lid. When Michel's face lit up at the discovery of this treasure trove, Tanguy felt an inexpressible happiness.

In the evening he told his mother the day's events. Then they would listen to the radio together. This was how he came to know the Italian operas. In the still hours of the night, rocked in his mother's arms, he followed the music of Puccini or Verdi. His mother told him the plots of the libretti. Tanguy was especially fond of *La Bohème* and *Madama Butterfly*. He was deeply stirred when he heard Mimi cry just before her death: "Rodolfo, am I beautiful yet?" or when Madama Butterfly told her son: "Go, play! Play!" The latter had a tremendous impact on him. He wondered what would become of him if one day, like Madama Butterfly's son, he was separated from his mother.

Then one week he arrived to find his mother's room in chaos. Half-packed suitcases lay open everywhere; clothes were scattered over the bed and on chairs. His mother was pacing to and fro, nervous and worried.

She said: "Sit down, Tanguy. I have something to tell you."

Tanguy sat down.

32

"The police want to move us back to the camp. This time we might even be sent to Germany. They know I'm better now. They'll be here for me any day now. Sister Suzanne warned me. We've got to get away. If we don't, we'll be killed."

Tanguy said nothing. He still held his textbooks and exercise books under one arm, still clutched the sheaf of reports he had brought to show his mother. He was top in every subject. He stared sadly at these tangible symbols of his freedom.

His mother went on: "I have a good friend in the town, a police inspector. He is on our side. He's managed to get me a valid passport. With that we can get to Marseilles, and from Marseilles to Mexico. In Mexico we'll really be safe for good."

Tanguy made no reply. He had nothing to say; he simply felt tired, disorientated. He wondered if he would have the chance to say good-by to Michel before they left and to tell him what he had never yet said in words: that he loved him.

"This is my plan," his mother was saying. "We'll go and lie low for a few days in a hotel in the town. When the authorities learn of my disappearance, they'll search everywhere for me—but they'll assume I've tried to escape over the border. They'll check the trains and frontier roads. After a fortnight they'll think I've got away, and they'll give up the search. That's when we'll go. But not together. They'll be looking for a woman with a nine-year-old boy. They mustn't find you with me. I'll give you a railway ticket, and you'll go to the station by yourself. Keep an eye out for another little boy or girl with their parents. Get into conversation with them

33

and stick to them when you go through the barrier and board the train. I shall be there too, but we must pretend not to know each other. We'll meet again when we get to Marseilles." She paused, and added: "Your mother's life is in your hands, Tanguy. Will you take care of it well for me?"

Tanguy nodded. Then he asked his mother if he could go and say good-by to Michel. She told him it was impossible. He took a sheet of paper and a pen and scribbled a few words of farewell. "*I shall never forget you,*" he wrote. "*I love you more than I believed possible. Never think of me as far away from you. Wherever you are, I shall be there with you.*"

———

5

TANGUY paused for a moment or two in the station, clutching his ticket firmly in one hand. A steady stream of travelers was moving through the barrier onto the platform. Two gendarmes, one on each side of the barrier, were examining their papers. Tanguy's heart was pounding with nervous excitement. He saw his mother sweep past him without turning her head. She had dyed her hair blond. One of the gendarmes glanced casually at her passport, and then she was through the barrier and lost in the crowd of men and women making for the Marseilles train.

There was no sign of any other children anywhere, and Tanguy began to feel alarmed. Would he be able to get through the barrier? What would happen to him if he missed the train? But after a little while a girl of about six walked past him with her parents. They looked like decent people to Tanguy. He tried to catch the girl's eye. She grinned at him, and he at once joined her.

"Where are you going?" he asked.

"Marseilles," she said. She spoke with a Midi accent. She had two pigtails tied with blue ribbon. Dark eyes, brown hair. A nice smile.

"So am I," Tanguy said.

"You're not from Marseilles yourself, are you?"

"No," he said. "I come from Paris."

"*Paris?*" she repeated, and stared at him in respectful admiration.

"Yes," Tanguy lied, and took her hand. Hand in hand they passed through the barrier, and neither of the gendarmes questioned them. Tanguy felt his heart beating more violently than ever; it seemed as though his chest would burst. At last he took a deep breath and climbed aboard the train. He sat down next to the girl, whose name was Anne-Marie. Her parents asked him where his mother was. He said, vaguely "down the other end," and they stopped bothering about him. They even gave him a piece of candy.

The train began to move. At first it seemed to Tanguy as if the engine were hesitating as to which track it should take, there were so many of them. But soon enough it found the right one. Tanguy stood in the corridor with Anne-Marie and watched telegraph poles, houses, and signal boxes fly past. On the smoke-blackened walls that lined the track

35

mysterious sequences of posters appeared: DUBO DUBON DU-
BONNET.

Tanguy felt sad. Once more he was leaving a town he had
come to love and where he had felt happy; once more he had
been parted from a school and a close friend. He wanted
to cry. Why did they always have to keep moving from
place to place? Why were they always running away? Once
again he decided it must all be because of the war.

The memory of Michel obsessed him. What would Michel
say or think when he opened his letter? Would he understand it? Tanguy recalled the first time they had seen
each other, Michel's first friendly wink. He thought of the
evenings he had spent with his mother in the hospital, when
they shared the little room Sister Suzanne had gotten for
her, and listened to opera together. (Tanguy had always burst into tears at Mimi's death.)

The journey passed off uneventfully. Tanguy found his
mother and had dinner with her in the dining-car. Then,
just before they reached Marseilles, he went back to Anne-
Marie, who was delighted to see him again. Together they
went through the barrier once more, and outside the station
Tanguy said good-by to this little girl who, all unawares,
had preserved his freedom.

Tanguy was getting his bearings in Marseilles. It was as
gray and filthy as he remembered from his first glimpse of the
port, but now he was discovering new aspects of it. His mother
spent her days going around to the consulates in the vain hope
of getting a visa for America; so he was alone for long periods.
They were staying in a small hotel near the Cannebière. The

proprietor was a nice Spaniard who called Tanguy by a Spanish nickname meaning Big Man, and Tanguy was delighted.

While his mother stood in line in consular offices, Tanguy used to wander around the docks. He loved watching the big boats put out to sea, and he envied the smart tourists aboard them. The mournful blasts of their foghorns, the very quays themselves, littered with wastepaper and old banana skins, sharpened his feelings of nostalgia. He stayed there hour after hour, watching the dockers going about their work, fascinated by the fussing tugs and the great cranes that swung up heavy loads of cargo from the holds. He dreamed of a faraway country where there would be no more war, where he could have a friend and a dog and keep them. Michel would come there and join him, he was sure, and they would again be happy together.

In the evenings he went back to the hotel. His mother would arrive discouraged and depressed. She would fling herself into an armchair and lie there exhausted and torpid, like some hibernating animal. On these occasions he felt sorry for her. He would kiss her and tell her he loved her more than anyone in the world; and indeed it was true. She would open her eyes, smile at him, and slowly sit up. Then they would go and have supper in a little restaurant near the docks, and afterwards drop into a movie.

She used to talk to him about America and say it was the one truly peaceful country in the world. But Tanguy no longer believed her. He had been told that France was the land of liberty, but the French had interned him in a concentration camp. He had been told that in France everyone ate well, but he was hungrier than he had been in Madrid in the

37

middle of the Civil War. He had been told that Frenchmen were polite, but a hotel proprietor had called him a "filthy foreigner." He was not quite nine years old, and already there was very little in which he believed.

His only dream now was of a little house with a garden, where he could have a friend and a dog. That was all he asked. He needed peace and quiet, the chance to relax. He had had enough of being treated like a man and being told at all hours of the day that they were in danger and would have to move on. He wanted to stay put. His mother's confidences weighed heavily on his mind. He often felt that a mother had no right to worry her child by telling him of all the dangers they ran. But he also realized that she had no one else to talk to and had to get rid, somehow, of the heavy burden of knowledge she carried with her.

Every morning she went off full of hope because she was going to see "a very kind, important gentleman"; every evening she came back tired and downcast because the "important gentleman" had given her nothing but fine words. They were beginning to despair; and then one day she came home accompanied by the most extraordinary-looking man.

He was a Catalan, and his name was Puigdellivol. He was tall, thin, and nervous, and he had strange blurred eyes, like a drunkard's. He wore a beret and kept it on in Tanguy's mother's presence. Tanguy decided he was a mannerless creature.

"This gentleman is going to help us, Tanguy," his mother said. "Thanks to him, we shall be able to get to London and join the Free French Forces there. He is very kind and very important. He gets Jewish refugees across the Spanish frontier without anyone knowing. He'll take care of us."

"But you can't go back through Spain!" Tanguy said. "The war's over, and you're condemned to death. Franco would have you shot—"

"Darling, you don't understand. I shall have a French passport and travel with a French party. Don't worry. Everything's going to be all right."

Tanguy said no more. Indifference began to creep over him. For a long time now he had accepted whatever came and no longer bothered to ask what it all meant. He knew that generally it had no meaning at all.

"I shall cross the Pyrenees on foot," his mother said. "You will make the journey a week later with this gentleman's wife. You will rejoin me in Madrid."

Tanguy grasped only one single isolated fact: he was going to be separated from his mother. He flung himself into her arms.

"No, Mama, no, please, not that! I'll do anything you want. I've always been brave, haven't I? But don't leave me behind, please! I'll keep up with you over the mountains. I'll make myself tiny and no one will notice me. Please, please don't leave me behind, Mama! If you leave me I'll be so miserable I'll die, I'll kill myself, I swear I'll kill myself—"

His mother had tears in her eyes. She hugged him close to her, and he felt the warmth of her body and the smell of her perfume. He felt as though he were shrinking, till he became so tiny that the misery possessing him was bigger than he was.

"I won't really leave you, my darling," his mother said. "I promise you I won't go away forever. You'll see me again

39

in Madrid, and we'll be happy together as we've always been.
You'll go to school and have friends. You'll see me again. I
promise you."

6

TANGUY stood by the window shaking and sobbing. Something like an iron hand was squeezing him inside and hurting
him terribly. He thought he would die of misery. He had not
yet learned that no one ever dies of misery.

The car that was taking his mother away had just dis-
appeared. She had said good-by too hurriedly. Now he was
alone, and there was no room in his being for anything but
silent suffering. He felt as though he had suddenly become
old. He cried till he thought he had exhausted all capacity
for tears. He would never forget the bitter taste of these
salty tears as they ran down over his lips.

Puigdellivol's house was a little way outside Marseilles, a
suburban villa shut off behind a walled garden. The shutters
were drawn across the windows, and an air of mystery enveloped the place. The house was full of Jews that Puigdellivol had brought from the occupied zone. They arrived for
the most part with neither money nor luggage, with the
yellow star still sewn on their clothes. There were little
groups of them everywhere, in the passages as well as in every
room in the house. They sat on the floor and waited, eating

and sleeping in the same spot. They were forbidden to go out. An unpleasant smell pervaded the whole building.

There was a little bald-headed man there called Cohen who seemed friendly. He was waiting for his wife and children to leave the occupied zone and join him. He had a large map of Europe which he unfolded every evening on the dining-room table and then covered with little flags. He called this "conducting the war."

Tanguy found himself wondering what war really was. Was it the sad wailing of sirens, the lines of people waiting in front of shops, bombed houses, corpses in the streets, and these endless uprootings and separations? Or was it this entertaining game with maps and flags? He could not tell.

One day, when he was sitting watching Mr. Cohen fitting pins into his flags, Puigdellivol came in and told him that his mother had reached her destination safely. Now, said Puigdellivol, Tanguy must get ready to make the trip himself to rejoin her. Tanguy was almost out of his mind with joy. Then Puigdellivol turned to Cohen and said, brusquely: "You'd better get ready to cross the frontier, too. It's no use waiting any longer for your wife and children; they've been arrested in Paris."

The next day Tanguy heard that Cohen had gone mad.

It was August 2, 1942. His birthday was on August 3: he would be nine years old and would celebrate the occasion by setting out to rejoin his mother. That would make it a really wonderful birthday. He went to bed earlier than usual, but took a long time going to sleep because of sheer excitement. He lay there thinking of his mother, imagining the moment

41

when they would be in each others' arms once more. Then, suddenly, a dazzling light lanced through the closed shutters of his bedroom. Terrified, Tanguy screwed up his eyes. He heard a deep voice ordering all the inhabitants to come out in single file, their hands above their heads. A sound of sobbing came from the corridor outside where the Jews were. Tanguy shivered with fright.

Then the same voice came again: "The house is surrounded. We shall shoot anyone who disobeys our orders."

Tanguy got up and went to the window. A group of gendarmes stood in the garden beside two searchlights, which they kept trained on the villa. The Jews emerged one by one, hands above their heads, and lined up outside. Some of them were crying. Cohen was dragged out by his friends like a sleepwalker.

Mme Puigdellivol came into the bedroom. "You'll have to go too," she said; and then: "My poor child!" Tanguy let her dress him, but said nothing. "My poor child!" she whispered, over and over again. "My poor child!"

He went out of the front door with his hands up and his eyes tight shut, forcing himself not to cry. The glare from the searchlights seemed to burn his eyelids. Inside his coat he felt the hard outline of his mother's photograph against his chest. Whatever happened, he would not lose that. A gendarme cuffed him as he passed. "Filthy Yids!" someone said.

Tanguy wanted to tell the gendarmes that he wasn't Jewish. They were Frenchmen, he thought, they would listen to his explanations. But as soon as he opened his mouth one of them roared "Shut your bloody trap!" at him. It was useless.

Through the carriage window Tanguy watched the peaceful countryside of France shape itself and slip out of sight: meadows where cows stood at pasture, smoke coiling up lazily from farm chimneys, sleepy streams slipping between high banks. Tanguy was exhausted. He had become mentally numb, indifferent to his miserable predicament. He was hungry. He wondered where the gendarmes were taking him. Then he decided that none of this mattered, either, that nothing mattered when one was alone and without a mother. On either side of him the Jews nodded and slept. Only Cohen remained awake, a meaningless grin fixed on his face.

The two gendarmes stood outside in the corridor, smoking. Tanguy got up, went out, and asked permission to go to the W.C. One of them accompanied him. As Tanguy was shutting the door, the policeman kicked it open again. Tanguy could not bring himself to do what he wanted with the man watching. He contented himself with urinating and drinking a little water from the tap. It tasted of yellow soap.

He went back to his compartment; the thought struck him that all his childhood had been spent in trains. He remembered one of the nicknames that Michel had given him: Slowcoach. Slowcoach Tanguy. At the thought of his friend misery rose inside him, but he fought back his tears. He wondered when they would "get there"; but as he had no idea where "there" was, he could hardly guess how long the journey would take. He tried to sleep, because he sensed that he would soon need to draw on all his reserves of energy. He thought of his mother, who by now must be awaiting his arrival in Madrid, and vaguely dismissed this disturbing image with the knowledge that it wasn't his fault, anyway.

By now it was nearly dark. The prisoners huddled one against the other. Mme Puigdellivol had wrapped a woolen muffler round Tanguy's neck, and he was dozing fitfully. It was a cold night. The train sped on, relentless and indifferent. At last it began to slow down. Lights appeared through the fog. Tanguy woke up, shivering, and peered through the window. The dimly lit platform was crowded with German troops. Officers hurried to and fro. The men carried packs and rifles. A voice was barking over a loudspeaker. Tanguy heard only the one word, several times repeated: *"Achtung! Achtung!"*

Two German soldiers got into the carriage, and the French gendarmes saluted them. They exchanged cigarettes and shook hands. Tanguy's companions roused themselves. Cohen wanted to get out. He had to get out, he said. His wife was waiting for him on the platform, and besides, the war was over now. His companions on each side of him held him down in his seat.

To Tanguy it seemed as if the train stood waiting there for ever. The officers strolled up and down in their high-peaked caps. Tanguy decided their uniforms were more attractive than French uniforms. Altogether, the Germans looked much nicer. Then, with a slight jolt, the train began to move, and once more slid slowly away into the darkness. Tanguy was hungry. The train was taking him further and further away from his mother. This no longer made him want to cry. All he wanted now was to know where he was.

7

WHEN he woke, Tanguy knew they had reached the end of their journey. He was delighted to find that they were in Paris. He stared eagerly at the seven-story buildings, the rows of chimneys, the long streets crowded with bistros. He was almost happy at the discovery. His mother had told him so much about Paris that he felt as if, through being there, he had somehow found her again. He trotted cheerfully behind the German soldiers, and was the first to get into the truck. Above the houses he spotted the skeletal outline of the Eiffel Tower and the sight made his heart miss a beat. Paris, he whispered to himself. *This is Paris.* He repeated the magic name again and again. He grinned, wondering what his mother would do if she knew he was in Paris.

The prisoners were driven across several squares, and down a wide, tree-lined avenue. As if in a dream Tanguy caught sight of the Arc de Triomphe. He decided that nothing bad could happen to him in Paris. When he got out of the truck with the other prisoners this thought remained to reassure him.

Tanguy lined up against the wall with the rest of them. He did not feel so tired now. He looked about the huge hall where they had been brought with lively interest, and was especially struck by another group of people who were also waiting. Among them was an old, grandmotherly sort of woman. She wore a kerchief on her head in the peasant fashion, and nodded continually, like a mechanical doll. From time to time she paused and stroked her wrinkled cheeks. Then she began to nod again. There was also a handsome young man, extremely well dressed, whose strange expression made Tanguy afraid.

The prisoners were made to stand facing the wall. Behind them two German soldiers marched to and fro, their boots rasping on the floor. On the wall in front of Tanguy was a large poster: it showed a young German infantryman charging to the attack. Under this picture was one extremely long word. Tanguy tried to read it, but couldn't.

The door opened, and the prisoners were ordered to turn round. A tall, thin man had come in. He had almost white hair, and his eyes were green and expressionless. He was not wearing a uniform and he held a sheaf of papers in one hand. In a crisp voice he called out: "All Semites line up on the left!"

Tanguy hesitated. He was not sure what the word "Semite" meant. He caught Mme Puigdellivol's eye. She made a sign to him to stay where he was. He froze. Then, at a sign from the man who had just come in, the soldiers began to make a close examination of those who had not moved over to the left. Tanguy realized that they were opening their flies, and only just stopped himself laughing out loud. All the same, he felt himself blushing as he was subjected to the same scrutiny. He wondered why on earth they were interested in that part of him. Then the soldier shook his head as if to say "Not this one," and went on to the next in line. The young man Tanguy had noticed was dragged out and made to join the group on the left. As he went he shrieked: "I'm not a Jew, Monsieur le Commandant, I swear I'm not a Jew. I had an operation—I'm not Jewish, I swear I'm not Jewish—"

The young man began to struggle frantically. He fell on his knees and tried to fling his arms round the legs of the man who had ordered the inspection. The German stepped back quickly and kicked him full in the face. The young man put his hands to his nose and drew them away all bloody.

Then the German official began to interrogate the prisoners. He asked them their age, profession, and place of birth. The first to be questioned was the old woman. She went on nodding her head and said *"Oui, Monsieur le Commandant"* to everything. He asked her if she had taken in her son two months before. She agreed she had. Then he asked if she had known at the time that her son had escaped from a German concentration camp. Yes, she said, she had known. The man gave an order, and she was taken out.

At last Tanguy's turn came. Nervously he walked forward. The man glanced at him absent-mindedly. Tanguy, like the others, gave his name and age. He described himself as a "student." A smile flickered across the man's face.

"What were you doing in Marseilles with all these Jews?" he asked.

Tanguy hesitated, then said: "I was going to rejoin my mother in Madrid. I am Spanish."

47

The man said nothing for a moment; then he asked abruptly: "What does your mother do? What's her profession?"

"She was a journalist."

"*Was?*" The man's interest was at once aroused. "Is she a political refugee?"

"Yes—"

"Have you been in a camp in France?"

Tanguy admitted it. He felt he had said the wrong thing. But the man gave him no time to invent a story. He shot question after question at him with extraordinary speed.

"Is she trying to get to London?"

Tanguy managed to lie this time. "No," he said. He felt the man's icy stare fixed on him and shut his eyes. He wondered if he was going to be hit.

"How do you know she had no intention of going to London?"

"Because she wanted to get to Mexico."

"In that case, what is she doing in Spain?"

Tanguy hesitated. He stammered: "I don't know—I'm only a child—"

"A remarkably well-informed child. Do you suppose anyone goes to Mexico by way of Madrid?"

"I don't know," Tanguy said hopelessly, and then added: "They wouldn't give her a visa in Marseilles."

There was a short silence. The man said a few words in German, and Tanguy was led off with the other prisoners. They were in a long, gloomy corridor. No one was talking. The handsome young man's nose was still bleeding, and the old woman's head nodded away just as before.

Soon they were all assembled there in the corridor, with the exception of M. Puigdellivol. A German sentry struck a match. The sudden glare dazzled Tanguy. It was at that moment that someone somewhere shrieked: a shrill, long-drawn-out cry, like the howl of a dog, shattering the silence. Two or three minutes passed. Tanguy felt his heart pounding with terror, and dreaded a repetition of this dreadful noise. With the thumb of his right hand he traced the sign of the cross over and over again on his palm. "Please God," he whispered, "don't let him shriek again. Please, please, God. I'm so frightened."

But he had scarcely articulated this prayer when there came a second shriek, quickly followed by a third, a fourth, a fifth. Tanguy choked. He felt as if someone had him by the throat and was trying to strangle him. Sweat broke out under his armpits, and he felt it trickling down his body. His eyes filled with tears. The young man who had been kicked in the face began to cry noisily, and this infuriated Tanguy: he felt that grown-ups had no business to cry in front of children. But when Mme Puigdellivol, too, began to sob, he was sorry and decided that there were occasions on which adult tears were, after all, permissible.

Meanwhile those ghastly shrieks still went on. They became weaker, stopped for a while, then broke out once more, this time mingled with gasps and sobs. Then the voice suddenly became articulate for a moment. It was M. Puigdellivol. He called out to his wife in Catalan. As if she had gone mad, the poor woman threw herself at the door that stood between the prisoners and the room in which they had been interrogated. The sentry caught her by the hair and threw her

49

back among the others again. She made no resistance, but lay there weeping almost inaudibly and murmuring to herself in a low voice.

At length all became quiet; no more tortured shrieks disturbed the prisoners' peace of mind. Tanguy was utterly overcome. The heavy silence pressed in on him. What had happened to Puigdellivol? Then, sharply, he told himself that if he was ever to see his mother again he must stop tormenting his imagination by thinking about the suffering of others. He was immediately ashamed of such a thought. But he had to be tough, he added to himself in self-justification; he had no one left to help him now, no one at all.

The door opened, and once more light dazzled the prisoners. They were hurried out into an inner courtyard where trucks were waiting for them. German soldiers stood on guard everywhere. Mme Puigdellivol gazed desperately at the door behind which her husband was hidden, but there was no sign of him. The truck jerked forward, and the noise of changing gears drowned her last, agonized cry. Tanguy could not hear it; but he saw her stretch out her arms in desperation and understood the meaning of the gesture. It might have been my mother, he thought, and tears sprang to his eyes. He turned up the collar of his coat. Night was coming on, and despite the time of year it was bitterly cold.

Once again Tanguy saw the odd outline of the Eiffel Tower. He had his first sight of the Seine. Its waters were gray, and so smooth that Tanguy could not tell which way they were flowing. Then he reminded himself that this hardly mattered now. But all the same, he thought, I wish I knew whether we were going upstream or down. . . .

. . .

The prisoners were taken to a big covered stadium formerly used for bicycle races. There hundreds, perhaps thousands of other detainees were waiting, crouched on straw like animals. Most of them wore yellow stars with the word JEW inscribed above in black. Tanguy did not look at them. He went over to the "children's group" where there were about fifty youngsters between six and fourteen years old. They were all Jews.

Tanguy sat down in the straw. He felt horribly cold. The fatigue which he had hardly noticed before now spread through his entire body. His strength was deserting him. Like springs too long compressed, his nerves suddenly relaxed. Tears pricked behind his eyeballs, struggling for release. A boy about seven years old, sitting beside Tanguy, gave him an encouraging grin. Tanguy tried hard to smile back, but it was all he could do to choke down his sobs. All the same, he didn't cry.

Now, suddenly, what he had only half understood was driven home to him with appalling clarity. He was absolutely alone. He was going to be treated as though he were a man. He was no longer a child. An enormous lassitude engulfed him. They can't send me away, he told himself. They have no right to. I'm not a Jew; I'm not even French; I'm Spanish. I'll explain to them. They're sure to understand. There must have been a mistake. I'll talk to someone higher up. An official error . . .

The child who had grinned at Tanguy broke in on his thoughts. "Aren't you Jewish?" he asked. He was a small, dark-skinned boy with long hair and feverish eyes. His lips were thick, and he had an ordinary straight nose. Tanguy was surprised at this: he thought all Jews' noses were large and hooked.

"No," Tanguy said in reply, "I'm not a Jew."

"Then what are you doing here?"

Tanguy remained tongue-tied. Finally he mumbled that it was all a mistake.

The little Jew looked at him with some curiosity and Tanguy blushed. But he found nothing else to say, because he didn't, in fact, know what he was doing there.

"What's your name?" he asked the little boy.

"Guy. What's yours?"

"I've got your first name in my first name, listen—Tan-guy."

Guy smiled. He took Tanguy's hand and held it for a moment in his own. Tanguy tried to smile in return, but still couldn't quite manage it. His throat was so tight with misery that he could hardly speak.

"Guy," he said at last, "what are they going to do with us?"

"They're taking us away—transporting us."

"Where to?"

"Germany. We'll be sent to a camp somewhere."

Tanguy stared at the boy in despair. Guy seemed to be indifferent to what happened to him; he spoke in the same way as he would have said "Let's go and play."

"How do you know this?" Tanguy persisted.

"My father said so. He's over there with the grown-ups. My mother and aunt are there, too. We're all going to be transported."

Tanguy could not bring himself to ask any more. He lay

down on the straw. It was quite dark now. Against a huge white wall the sentry's elongated shadow came and went. Small noises broke the stillness—whispering, sniffs, an occasional sob.

Tanguy took his mother's photograph from his pocket. He told himself that perhaps he would never see her again, and his misery grew inside him. Then suddenly he found he could cry. He cried so violently that it felt as if he was tearing something out of his living flesh. He clasped the photograph close to him. "Mama," he whispered, "darling Mama, you know I haven't done anything bad. I don't want to be taken away. I don't want to go to a camp. Mama—"

Slowly his tears ceased to flow. He no longer had the strength even to cry. Deep shudders shook his whole body. His head ached. He tried to sleep, but remained obstinately awake. All night he lay there, alone with his unhappiness, while the sentry's shadow flickered to and fro along the high white wall. Around him all was now quite still.

8

VERY early the following morning they were packed into trucks again and driven off to a big station. Tanguy looked for the clock, determined to know at least what time it was: 6:20. The sky was pale green, faintly flushed with pink as the dawn came up. A fresh breeze blew in his face.

The prisoners disembarked from the trucks in front of the station. All round them stood German soldiers, rifles slung, watching every move. They were lined up and marched into the station. It was a big building, black and filthy, with an unpleasant smell about it. Inside it was nearly dark. Tanguy noticed several inquisitive bystanders peering through the military cordon to get a glimpse of the prisoners. He was ashamed and hung his head. Then he reminded himself that he had done nothing wrong and had no reason to feel shame. Yet, he also told himself, these people had no way of knowing. He kept his eyes on the ground.

The long column moved forward slowly. The grown-ups, both men and women, went in front; the children brought up the rear. Tanguy wanted to get inside the station as quickly as possible to stop people staring at him. But there was nothing he could do about it.

Most of the grown-ups carried bundles or suitcases. Tanguy supposed they must contain a few hurriedly packed clothes, and wondered what use such things would be in a concentration camp. But afterwards he learned that the most precious thing these people had packed in their bags was hope —the hope of adapting themselves to new conditions, of surviving, of beginning life again; the hope that somehow they would get back home; the hope that they would not die. Tanguy thought he was utterly without hope. But he soon changed his mind; he had his mother's photograph.

They were kept waiting for two hours on a filthy, badly paved platform. Some sat down, others chatted together in groups; but mostly they stood in solitary silence. Guy waited with Tanguy, holding his hand.

54

Tanguy stared about him. He noticed an old, white-bearded Jew, dressed in black and wearing a battered old bowler hat. This character was sitting on a pasteboard suitcase and had a napkin tied round his neck. He was eating bread, chewing rhythmically, glancing up from time to time at the sooty, opague glass roof above the platform. His hands were trembling. He saw Tanguy staring at him, smiled, and politely raised his hat. Tanguy suddenly wanted to cry again. He lowered his eyes and went on waiting, patiently.

At last, at 10:00 A.M., the prisoners were herded into a train made up of cattle cars. One of these cars was earmarked for the children, and Tanguy was among the first to board it. The wooden floor had been covered with a layer of straw. Tanguy settled himself close to an air vent, and Guy stayed close beside him. Later that day a faint jolt and grinding of couplings marked the beginning of yet another journey.

Tanguy was miserable during that first night on the train. He had never imagined that memories could be so painful. Each recollection of the few happy moments he had spent in his short life burned itself into his mind. He saw his friends' faces—Michel, Robert, the gravely peaceful features of Brother Marcel. He seemed to catch a whiff of the scent he had smelled in his father's car. He relived every moment of the hours he had spent with his mother in Montpellier. His memories seemed to hammer themselves into his poor head like nails into wood. Time passed slowly. Tanguy began to wonder when—or if—he would ever sleep again.

He propped his chin on his knees, and leaned his head sideways against the wooden wall of the car. In this hunched-up position he peered out furtively from time to time through the air vent, but it was absolutely dark. Only a few faint lights broke the gloom as they passed through each station. He remembered his nickname and began to smile despite himself.

The doors of the car were sealed, and gradually the air inside became unbearable. The children had been cooped up now for forty-eight hours. Outside the atmosphere was humid and heavy; the woodwork of the car steamed gently, and the sodden straw stank of urine. Tanguy began to suffer from fits of giddiness. I'm going to fall, he thought, I'm going to fall. But he was sitting down, and he didn't fall. The blood rushed to his head, and his ears sang. He was shivering with cold, yet at the same time the heat made him sweat. He was suffering wretchedly from thirst, and crying tears of sheer despair and rage. He wanted to get up and bang on the door as hard as he could, but he was too weak to raise himself. In his fury he bit his lips and hands, and the tears ran salt down his cheeks. He swore at the Germans, calling them bastards, which was the worst word he knew. But almost at once he checked himself. It's not their fault, he thought, they can't know what's happening to us. It's a slip-up in the organization. It must be that, I'm sure.

On the third day Tanguy thought he was going out of his mind. His head was aching so horribly that he wanted to scream. His mouth was dry, and his lips stuck together; he could no longer moisten them with saliva. His whole body trembled feverishly. He glanced weakly from time to time toward his air vent, beyond which lay the outside world.

They're going to let us die, he thought. They want to make us die. *I don't want to die. I don't want to die.*

All the children were crying. Some of them were unable to contain themselves any longer and relieved themselves where they lay. The car reeked of urine and excrement. The August sun beat down on the roof, and its heat enveloped them like a fever. Packed tight, side by side, they could not even move. Guy lay beside Tanguy, crying and shivering. Tanguy clasped his damp hand and stroked his long black hair in a mechanical, almost unconscious gesture of affection.

At last, sixty hours after leaving Paris, the train stopped. The doors were unsealed. Tanguy got up, swaying, and climbed out of the truck. On the platform facing him was a long line of S.S. guards, carrying rifles. The prisoners were told they could relieve themselves. In front of the S.S. troops, men, women, and children alike squatted down and emptied their bowels over the edge of the platform. Tanguy found himself almost gasping with pleasure. He would never before have believed that the simple fact of being able to relieve himself could have been the source of such sheer satisfaction. With his left hand he wiped his tear-stained face. He looked around him. The old Jew was down on his haunches too, still wearing his bowler hat. He caught Tanguy's eye and smiled. Everyone was happy. The sky was blue, the sun shone; there was a feeling of renewed life and hope.

One by one the prisoners got up. Two steaming soup kettles were brought out, and the prisoners formed in a long line. Each was given a tin bowl. They were all delighted. They chattered away to each other, joking and laughing and exchanging gossip.

Tanguy had taken his place in the line. He suddenly remembered Guy and ran to find him. Guy was crying. Tanguy tried to pull him to his feet, but Guy lay there, refusing to get up, sobbing and calling for his mother. Tanguy left him abruptly; he was afraid of missing his food. He got back in time, took two tin bowls and presented them to the young uniformed girl who was filling them. She was a pretty blue-eyed brunette and looked kind. Tanguy stretched out the two bowls. The girl said something to him in German. He did not understand, but tried to explain that the second one wasn't for him, but for a sick child. At the sound of the argument an S.S. guard came up. He too was young and good-looking. When Tanguy saw him coming, he was pleased. He thought the S.S. would speak French and understand what was happening. Instead, the man took away the two bowls and knocked him down.

He got up slowly, ashamed and shivering with fright, murmuring his mother's name like a kind of talisman. He began to walk back to the train. But hunger still left him giddy. He had never suffered so much in his life; he thought he was going to die. Never, too, had he felt himself treated with such injustice. He was just about to climb back into his car when he felt a hand on his shoulder. It was the old Jew.

"Is someone ill?" he asked.

Tanguy tried to smile, but burst into a storm of sobbing. The old man stroked his head and said, his gnarled hand cupping the boy's neck: "You mustn't cry. You must be brave. It's your duty to set an example."

Tanguy could control himself no longer. His tears flowed without restraint: he felt he had passed the breaking-point.

"Here," said the old man kindly, "take this," and he held out a big chunk of bread. Then he took a small bottle from his case and slipped it into Tanguy's pocket. "That is water," he said. "Use it sparingly. It's very precious."

Tanguy could not summon up enough strength or self-control to thank the old man. He could neither speak nor stop crying. He climbed into the truck.

The old man said, behind him: "I wanted to tell you one thing more."

Tanguy turned and looked at him.

"If something by any chance should happen to one of the children," the old man said, picking his words carefully, "if there should be—how shall I put it?—an accident, don't let the others cry. It is demoralizing for prisoners to hear their children crying. Make them sing—"

"Sing?" said Tanguy, startled; "sing what?"

"It doesn't matter what. Anything. Don't you know any French songs?"

" '*Au clair de la lune*'?"

"Perfect," said the old Jew. "Nothing could be better."

The train resumed its journey: hour after hour passed, and still they traveled on. As time dragged slowly by one discomfort succeeded another. Hunger and thirst and misery; loneliness, despair, sheer terror. Now Tanguy did not even try to struggle against the agonizing memories that crowded into his mind. He cried without trying to find a reason—much less an excuse—for his tears, like a mechanical doll. Nothing mattered any more, he told himself. Whatever happened, he would never see his mother or Michel again. The monotonous, hammering rhythm of the train numbed his raw misery.

Sometimes he wondered what conditions would be like at the camp, but, again, decided that it didn't matter. "*Whatever happens*," he said to himself, "*they're bound to kill us in the end*." But nevertheless hope refused to be entirely snuffed out. Tanguy still occasionally built some fine castles in Spain. His arrest had been all a mistake; he wasn't Jewish, he had done nothing wrong. The camp commandant would understand his position and release him. He would even apologize.

Poor little Guy was in a bad way. He refused all food and could only swallow a few sips of water. He lay stretched out in the straw, motionless, so pale and thin that he looked dead already. Tanguy stroked his hair. It was soaking wet, as if he had just been for a long walk in the rain.

Outside, the German countryside sped past: quiet fields, tiny picturesque villages, forests of pine. Tanguy decided that Germany was a lovely country and that he would like to explore it. One evening there was such a wonderful sunset that Tanguy felt tears in his eyes again. The meadows and a tiny stream running through them were all tinged crimson with the rays of the dying sun.

Tanguy wondered—the thought nagged at him continually —just *how* such things could happen. Then he looked more closely at the tranquil, sleepy landscape and realized that neither the earth nor the bulk of its human inhabitants knew anything of what was going on. The German peasants who glanced out of their windows at this long freight train would suppose that it carried cattle or munitions, or perhaps agricultural equipment. And even if they had guessed the truth, there was nothing *they* could do about it. Who could help? Who indeed?

At dawn on the fifth day Guy died. Tanguy did not notice at first that his breathing had stopped. Then it occurred to him that Guy was much too quiet. He shook him, and found that his body had already begun to stiffen.

Tanguy had never seen a corpse before. His first instinct was to cry. Then he reflected that tears would accomplish nothing. Guy's eyes were fixed and staring, turned up toward the roof of the car. Tanguy took off his coat and covered the child's face. Having done this, he tried to find some way of taking his mind off the unbelievable fact of death. He stared out at the beautiful countryside rolling past. Inside his chest there seemed to be a strange silent hollowness, an aching void, and he sat very still, as though to move would hurt. He wanted to turn his head and look at a human, living face. But somehow he could not do it. His thin body shook.

Then one of the other children suddenly screamed: "He's dead! That one's dead! I'm frightened!"

Other children caught his fear and began to cry in terror. Tanguy got up. He opened his mouth, but his voice dried in his throat. He made an enormous effort, and somehow began to sing:

> "*Au clair de la lune,*
> *Mon ami Pierrot . . .*"

Several quivering voices began to join in, rather uncertainly. Most of the boys sang badly out of tune.

· · ·

The journey lasted nine days and nights. Guy's body was taken out of the truck on the sixth day. The S.S. left him lying on a siding.

For nine days and nights Tanguy had struggled against thirst, hunger, terror, and despair: worst of all, against his own memories. When the train finally stopped, at dawn on the tenth day, he followed the column of prisoners like a sleepwalker. He no longer felt anything. He no longer had the will to think, or even to hold his head up straight. He was ready to accept whatever came without protest. His only conscious awareness was of being unbelievably old. The knowledge that he was only nine seemed an absurdity.

9

THE camp was more like a pioneer town. It was divided into two cantonments, one of concrete buildings, the other a neatly laid-out group of wooden barrack huts, longer and bigger than those Tanguy had known in France. They were arranged in a grid pattern, with intersecting "streets"; there were even duckboards put down to act as "pavements."

The new arrivals were first of all marched off to the concrete-built cantonment. This consisted of several high blocks, arranged to form a square: administrative offices, quarters for the permanent staff, sickbay and medical stores, and clothing-stores (with one door cryptically labeled DISINFECTION). These four buildings formed the sides of a huge asphalt paradeground.

Here Tanguy stood for more than an hour. He had taken off his clothes as ordered, and waited, stripped, clutching in one hand the soiled, threadbare garments he had worn throughout the journey and in the other the precious photograph of his mother. He wondered if they would let him keep it. Round him the other children were miserably complaining that they were hungry, that they wanted a drink. Wouldn't anyone give them something to eat?

At this point some of the "old hands" turned up—prisoners who had already spent some time in the camp. They announced confidentially that no arrangements had been made to feed or accommodate the new arrivals. But, of course, anyone with a little money or jewelry to spare could have things arranged for him. The offer was eagerly accepted. A gold watch, a ring, a precious trinket would be exchanged for a glass of water or a lump of bread no bigger than a baby's fist. Tanguy had nothing to bargain with. He waited patiently, so tired that he was no longer conscious of either fatigue or hunger. His one desire was to lie down and go to sleep. But things had to be done "through the usual channels"; administrative routine must be observed.

Three hours after his arrival, Tanguy reached the last hurdle, the clothing-stores. Two prisoners stood behind a counter, supervising the issue of prison wear. One of them took the garments Tanguy was clutching. Tanguy held onto his mother's photograph.

"What's that you've got?" asked the man.

Tanguy swallowed, and tried to smile. "My mother," he said.

The man gave Tanguy a quick glance and said softly: "Fair enough." Then he hunted for things that would fit Tanguy; it proved a difficult task. At last he produced a bundle with the air of one who has found what he is looking for.

"There, that'll do you. Won't need altering anywhere. Now pop over there and get your number." Tanguy looked at the uniform; it was the kind reserved for political detainees. The man added: "By the way, better hide that photograph somewhere. Don't say I saw it. I haven't seen anything. Understand?"

Tanguy nodded. He put on the uniform, and found it was too big for him. He tucked the photograph inside, against his chest. Then he went into the office and was given the number 3401. This done, he returned to the courtyard.

"Hey, you—that's right, *you*, you little bastard! Get in this squad here!"

Tanguy joined the group and got into line. An order was barked at them. He saw that the others extended their right arm and touched the shoulder of their immediate neighbor. He did the same. Then the N.C.O. shouted: "Atten-*shun!* Ri-i-ght *turn!* Quick *march!* Left, right, left—*links, recht, links*—"

Tanguy marched as well as he could. He lost the step several times, and had to half run to keep up with the rest. They halted outside two or three barrack huts as they went, shedding a few prisoners at each. Gradually the squad dwindled away. Finally, outside one of the last huts, the N.C.O.

64

told Tanguy to break ranks and report to the barrack orderly.

Tanguy did as he was told. The barrack orderly was a small, skeletal creature with a huge nose and eyes so small that they were hardly discernible at first sight. His skin had a waxy transparency, and he was totally devoid of both eyelashes and eyebrows.

Tanguy went up to him and presented himself. The barrack orderly told him sharply to stand at attention. Tanguy did so. Then the orderly allotted him a straw mattress, and he went into the hut. A long open passage ran down the middle, and on either side were tiers of bunks. The mattresses rested on a few wooden crossbars.

Pale hatchet-faces stared at the child as he passed down between the bunks, some with hate, some with a kind of pity, but most in utter indifference. All the prisoners resembled one another. They were so thin that their faces had lost all individuality. Tanguy could not bear to look at them; it made him feel ill. When he reached the bunk allotted to him, he threw himself down on his mattress and fell asleep instantaneously. But his sleep was shot through with ghastly nightmares, in which the image of his mother always figured.

Tanguy opened his eyes. Someone was telling him to get up. The voice belonged to a handsome young man with blue eyes and rather longer hair than was common among the other prisoners, most of whom had their heads shaved in a close crew cut. He was standing beside Tanguy's bunk, but had to bend nearly double to talk to him.

"Come on, up with you!" he said again.

Tanguy grinned weakly and shook his head. He couldn't

bring himself to get up. His limbs were aching; his head was as heavy as lead and swam dizzily when he tried to move.

"I don't feel well," he complained.

The young man smiled. "No one feels well here. You must get up. They're dishing out soup."

"I can't," Tanguy said, "honestly I can't."

"Listen to me carefully," the young man said. "In this place, if you don't eat the little you're given, you die. Do you understand? We've got to go on living. Everyone wants to give up and die, sometimes. Those are just our moments of weakness. We've got to overcome them."

Tanguy nodded.

"This is an important part of the day. Mealtime, rollcall, propaganda hour. Information, they call it. You'll learn about the incredible number of enemy tanks the *Wehrmacht* has knocked out since last night and all the planes our brave German fighter-pilots have shot down. Isn't that worth getting up for?"

Tanguy smiled again. He felt himself drawn to this strange young man, who now slipped one arm under his neck and helped him to sit up. The gentle gesture reminded Tanguy of his mother.

"Are you French?" the young man asked.

Tanguy nodded. "Are you?"

"Oh no; I'm German."

Tanguy stared at him in astonishment. He had never imagined finding German prisoners in a German concentration camp.

As they came out of the barrack hut a siren wailed three

times. "That's the second warning," the young man said. "We've got to hurry. Lean on me, that's right—put your arm round my shoulders. Come on: left, right, left—" Tanguy found himself grinning despite everything.

The prisoners were streaming onto the paradeground from all quarters. Tanguy walked slowly, leaning on his young guide. The German asked Tanguy his name, and said his own was Gunther. "We're in the same hut. I sleep in the bunk above yours. I'm your neighbor on the next floor, as you might say. If there's anything wrong ever, just knock on the ceiling, one long, three shorts, two longs, and I'll come down and help you."

Tanguy adored his kindly voice. He was so moved by Gunther's considerateness that he felt he would cry. He hardly dared to believe in the good fortune that had befallen him. He shut his eyes and thanked God. Beside him Gunther was giving a running commentary on what was happening.

"Here we are. Now we've got to wait till our beloved commandant shows up. We shall sing *'Die Fahne hoch'* in his honor. He's an old Storm Trooper who has to have his marching-song like the Catholics have their *'Te Deum.'* I'm sorry —perhaps you're a Catholic yourself?"

Tanguy shook his head. To tell the truth, he no longer either knew or cared what he was.

The siren wailed yet again. Tanguy fell in with the rest, on parade. No one was allowed to speak. Some indistinguishable orders were barked out over the loudspeaker. S.S. men hurried to and fro, and N.C.O.'s busied themselves getting the parade in order. At last the commandant appeared. He was a big, heavily built man with an impassive face. The

67

officers greeted him with the Hitler salute. The prisoners struck up the S.A. marching-song:

> *"Die Fahne hoch,*
> *Die Reihen fest geschlossen,*
> *S.A. marschiert*
> *mit einem festen Schritt . . ."*

> ("With flag flying and ranks closed, the Storm Troops march with a firm step . . .")

To Tanguy the time seemed to crawl. And there was still an interminable amount of business ahead. The S.S. guards had to report to their officers; the officers reported to the commandant; finally came the information bulletin, translated into five languages. Tanguy learned that German troops were moving up to besiege Moscow; that the British had sent representatives to sign an armistice with the Führer; that two hundred thousand Russians had been taken prisoner in the last twenty-four hours.

When the parade was over the prisoners returned to their barrack huts for the soup ration. The barrack orderly gave Tanguy a tin bowl and spoon. He joined the line, bowl in hand, to receive a ladleful of reddish liquid and a hunk of black bread. He and Gunther ate this unsavory mess together, sitting on Tanguy's bunk. He felt relaxed in the company of the young German and, listening to his soft, pleasant voice, decided that the camp wouldn't be so bad as long as Gunther was there.

"As you see," Gunther was saying, "it isn't exactly the

Hotel Adlon, but it's better than nothing. Besides, there's nothing like a long fast to make you really appreciate your food. I'm sure that when dear Uncle Adolf kicks the bucket we'll all go into ecstasies over fish and chips."

Evening came: Tanguy had spent almost the whole of his first day in the camp asleep. After curfew everything was quiet; he lay awake for a long time on his straw mattress while the night dragged slowly on. He thought of his mother, and recalled those few happy hours he had spent in Vichy and Montpellier. He wondered what was going to become of him. And then, once again, he told himself that he was only a child, that in any case he wasn't Jewish, and that one day the Germans would realize they had made a mistake. He also thought about Gunther. There were many things that Tanguy didn't understand about Gunther, and others that he avoided trying to explain. But one thing was certain: with Gunther there he felt warm and happy—so happy that he wanted to cry with joy, and could have continued so till he died.

10

THE following day, when the siren went off, Tanguy got up with the rest. Dawn had only just broken. The sky was a greenish-gray, streaked with pink. The air was so fine that

Tanguy felt exhilarated. He shook Gunther awake gently. Gunther yawned and smiled. His eyes were puffy and red-rimmed.

"Where's your bowl?" he asked at once.

"On my mattress."

"Get it."

"Why? Is soup up?"

"No," said Gunther, "no soup yet. But if you leave your possessions lying about they'll be stolen, and then you won't have anything to eat out of."

Tanguy did as he was told. He fastened his spoon and bowl to the string he wore round his waist in lieu of a belt. Then he and Gunther went out of the hut together. He found it hard to walk in the wooden sabots he had been issued; he was not yet accustomed to them.

It was an August morning, full of color and scent. A fresh breeze blew in their faces. All round the camp a vast pine forest grew, and its resinous scent was carried to their nostrils. Tanguy shut his eyes and sniffed ecstatically. He smelled the countless mingled natural odors of field and wood, and decided that Rachel had been right after all. You had to look for the good in everything; it was useless to complain.

There was another interminable parade. The N.C.O.'s buzzed angrily down the ranks. The prisoners raised their arms in salute and shouted "*Heil Hitler!*" But the rollcall was never complete; someone was always missing. Tanguy was exhausted. He would have given anything for these formalities to be done away with. But it was standing orders. Tanguy told himself that, after all, the Germans obviously had to count their prisoners at regular intervals, and the British almost certainly did the same. He tried to think up ways of keeping himself occupied. He had to shout *"Heil Hitler!"* three times before the N.C.O.'s were satisfied. Finally the prisoners were dismissed.

Gunther said: "The fatigue-party N.C.O. is a pal of mine. Come on; I'll ask him to put you on the same job as me."

Tanguy followed Gunther. A few moments later they, together with about twenty other prisoners, were on their way to the lumber yard. They marched along singing *"Die Fahne hoch."* Tanguy didn't know the words, and contented himself with humming the tune. Gunther had told him they all had to sing—or at least move their lips and look as if they did.

The lumber yard was nearly a mile away from the camp. Here Tanguy was given a shovel. They were all set to work digging trenches. No one knew what they were for. A fatigue-party N.C.O. and an S.S. guard supervised the work. Tanguy got down into a trench and copied the others. But he was hardly strong enough to throw his shovelfuls of earth over the lip of the trench. He had to make an enormous effort each time. Then, little by little, he began to work mechanically, almost without noticing it. The S.S. man rolled himself cigarettes and joked with the corporal. They laughed a good deal. Tanguy began to feel exhausted. His arms and legs ached, his hands were sore. He staggered as he raised his shovel, and had to use all his energy to throw the earth clear. Twice in a row he missed his aim, and the heavy black earth rained back over him.

Tanguy looked up and caught Gunther's eye. The young German smiled. Tanguy wiped his sweating forehead and tried to smile back. He felt better. Gunther had the strange power of giving him renewed strength and courage, and despite his fatigue and his aching muscles, Tanguy was happy. It was enough for him to know that Gunther was there and thinking of him.

At last at midday the S.S. guard blew a short blast on his whistle, and the prisoners stopped work. They climbed out of the trenches and sat down to rest. Tanguy spent his break beside Gunther.

"It's tough going at first," Gunther said, "but you get accustomed to it after a while. It's better being out here than in the workshops. Guys who spend their time there are always being accused of sabotage, and that means punishment. Nobody accuses you of anything here. The work's harder, but at least you don't end up in the jug."

Tanguy nodded. He was too exhausted to make any reply. He stared at his reddened hands. Gunther too fell silent, and settled himself down for a rest. It was very quiet now. Then another prisoner strolled over and joined them. He was a tall man, and even more cadaverous than his companions. He had black eyes, and his high bald cranium shone in the sunlight. He spoke a few words to Tanguy in a language that Tanguy had never heard before.

"He's a Russian," Gunther said. "He's telling you that his name is Misha and that he will be your friend."

Tanguy smiled at the Russian and shook hands with him. Misha spoke again; he seemed to be asking a question. Gunther translated.

"He wants to know if it's true that the Americans are only a dozen miles outside Paris and that the German armies have been completely routed? That's the rumor he heard yesterday evening in the latrines. He thinks it must be a new arrival who brought the information."

Tanguy shook his head. "I haven't heard anything like that," he said. "When I passed through Paris there were Germans everywhere. They're occupying half of France. I don't think this rumor about the Americans can be true."

Gunther translated. The Russian seemed very depressed. But presently he smiled again and took his leave of Tanguy.

The soup arrived. Tanguy stretched out his bowl and received the same reddish liquid and another chunk of black bread. He sat down beside Gunther and began to eat.

"Why did they deport you?" the German asked him.

Tanguy hesitated. He never knew how to reply to this question. He told his story as well as he could, and Gunther listened in silence.

"To be quite honest," he said at the end of Tanguy's recital, "once you're in here it doesn't make much difference *why* you're here, or who knows about it."

"What about you, Gunther? What are you doing here?" Tanguy asked.

"Me? I was a young lawyer in Hamburg. The police arrested me. Apparently, as far as I can make out, I was unworthy to take part in the New Germany. So now I must expiate my guilt by toiling for the *Herrenvolk*."

"The who?"

"Oh, nothing. It's just a word they have for the German people."

Tanguy asked him how he came to speak French so fluently.

73

"I studied for a while in Paris. I ought to have stayed there."

"You know Paris well then? It's a nice place, isn't it?"

"I loved Paris," Gunther said. "I used to enjoy loafing along the Left Bank on a spring evening. It's magic then. The old booksellers are dreaming by their stalls, the tramps are asleep, the sky's deepening as night draws on, and there's a wonderful smell in the air. I used to stroll down by the Seine and run my finger-tips over those dusty books and gay prints. The sky was as soft as silk, and the twin towers of Notre-Dame and the steeple of Sainte-Chapelle seemed to slip through it like needles."

Tanguy, too, had his dream of Paris. He knew very well he had only caught a passing glimpse of it. But he had heard so much about this city that he felt he had always known and loved it, ever since he could remember.

The whistle blew again for work to begin once more. Tanguy got up, shook the dust off his trousers, took his shovel, and plunged down to the bottom of his trench. He began to dig again, flinging the earth energetically over his right shoulder, never stopping.

The hours dragged by, and slowly the sun sank toward the horizon. Shadows lengthened, and still the prisoners toiled on. Tanguy had fits of giddiness. Sometimes the blood would rush to his head, leaving him limp and trembling. His arms and shoulders ached horribly. He could not help crying a little, out of sheer rage, when he looked at the S.S. guard lounging about and joking with the corporal. He swore at them under his breath. Then he told himself that it wasn't their fault, it was all part of the regulations.

Slowly time passed. Tanguy began to wonder if they would be made to go on working till it was completely dark. He felt at the end of his tether. He could hardly keep on his feet now, and shot beseeching glances at Gunther, who smiled back at him sympathetically. At last the siren gave the signal and the prisoners put down the tools; they had been out at work for more than ten hours.

At this moment Tanguy felt everything going round, and had to clutch the edge of the trench to prevent himself falling. His eyes filled with tears. He no longer had the strength to climb out by himself. Gunther came over to him, and without saying a word hoisted him up. Tanguy uttered no word of thanks to his friend; his throat was thick with choking sobs. He fell in with the rest of the squad, and they marched off, singing as they went. Tanguy found himself singing too.

The parade was even longer than usual. They had to wait for the squads from the workshops, and those who had been on domestic fatigues, who were at least twenty minutes late. The various groups marched on to the paradeground in close order, singing as they came. Some of them were badly footsore, and supported by their comrades; others looked, to Tanguy, as if they had fainted. These wretched creatures were held up under the armpits and dragged along like puppets with all their strings cut.

The commandant appeared. The N.C.O.'s reported to the

75

S.S. guards; the S.S. reported to their officers; the officers reported to the commandant. Then the roll was called. Those men whom Tanguy had supposed to have fainted were released and fell to the ground like sacks. They were dead. The N.C.O.'s came up to each in turn, gave them a good kick to be quite sure, and marked them "deceased" on their nominal rolls.

Tanguy hardly dared to believe his eyes. Then he began to find himself accepting the incredible. He was all but indifferent to the sight of these corpses lying about the parade-ground. He thought of little Guy, who had died in a cattle car, and had been left on a siding by the S.S. It's war, he thought. The purpose of war is to kill men. But why should it kill children?

When the rollcall was over, the prisoners got their usual ration of good news. They learned that the *Wehrmacht* had captured a Russian town. When this was announced the N.C.O.'s cheered, and the prisoners prudently imitated them. Then the order was given to sing the "*Die Fahne hoch.*" But someone sang out of tune and the commandant was cross; so they had to start all over again.

Tanguy thought he would go out of his mind. He wanted to lie down in peace, like the men who already lay sprawled on the asphalt. He was so tired that he could hardly control his reactions. When the song was finished, and the prisoners dismissed, he slowly followed Gunther. They did not speak, but took their place, silently, in the line for bread and soup. Tanguy did not so much as open his mouth when he learned that their N.C.O. had punished the whole of the barrack hut by withdrawing its bread ration—simply because the man who had sung out of tune happened to sleep there. Tanguy swallowed his soup and then sat for a little while before curfew, enjoying the calm summer evening, watching the sky and the near-by forest turn smoky red as the sun went down. The forest filled him with nostalgic longing; he thought how wonderful it would be to wander through it on such an evening as this.

He went in for the late night rollcall, which was taken in the hut by the barrack orderly. Then he slipped out to the latrines.

These were housed in a hut the same size as the rest and consisted simply of a long plank pierced with holes at regular intervals. A prisoner was squatting on almost every hole. A latrine orderly was stationed by the doorway. Tanguy chose his hole and squatted like the rest. Someone whispered his name quietly. A prisoner he had never seen before made a sign to him. Tanguy shifted to the next hole without attracting attention.

"Got any money?" the man whispered.

"No."

"What hut are you?"

"Number 12."

"Tell them that if they want bread, I've got some. They'll find me here tomorrow. And tell them I've learned that the English have landed in North Africa and Rommel's finished. I got that from a Boche." The prisoner was silent for a moment. Then he added, in an even softer whisper: "You the French kid?"

"Yes."

"How come they've put you in with the 'politicals'?"

77

"I don't know," Tanguy said.

"Your dad a Communist?"

"No."

"Good. Not that it matters. I'm French too—Alsatian, rather, but it comes to the same thing. Where are you from?"

Tanguy hesitated, and finally said: "Paris."

"Got here last night, eh?"

"Yes."

"How are things in Paris?" the man asked.

"Pretty bad."

"Don't worry. Things'll take a turn for the better soon. It won't be like 1914 this time. I swear we won't forget so quickly when this show's over. Were there a lot of you kids?"

"About fifty. Nearly all Jewish."

"Yes," said the Alsatian, "I saw them. Any die?"

"One. His name was Guy. He was only seven—"

"Were his parents on the same train?"

"Yes."

The latrine orderly shouted: "Hey, you down there, when you've quite finished talking—"

Tanguy lowered his head, afraid of being punished. He tried to get up and go, but his neighbor signed to him to stay. Then he called out in a loud, confident voice: "Orderly!"

"What is it?"

"Come here!"

"What do you want?"

"Come here and I'll tell you. Something to your advantage."

The orderly (who was a prisoner himself) came up to the Alsatian and bent down toward him.

"Well, what is it?"

"I've got some bread for you."

"How much do you want? Anyway, I haven't any money."

"That doesn't matter. I'll let you have some on credit. You can pay me when you get some money."

The orderly said: "Show me the bread."

The Alsatian took out of his pocket a hunk of black bread about the size of his hand. He held it out to the latrine orderly, who asked the price.

"Five marks."

"Are you out of your senses?"

"Why should I be? You don't know the risks I ran in getting hold of the stuff. And anyway, you've got to pay extra for getting it on credit."

"All right then. It's a deal."

"Good. Now, go away and eat your bread and let me talk to this boy for a bit. He's telling me some important news he's brought in from Paris."

"You know talking's forbidden in here," the orderly said.

"So what? No one can hear us."

"I'm responsible for the latrines. I've got to—"

"I know, I know. You're a loyal little bureaucrat. Now shove off and leave us in peace. I promise you we won't be long."

The orderly wandered off. Tanguy grinned, and the Alsatian grinned back.

"My name's Antoine Desprez," he said. "What's yours?"

"Tanguy."

"That's not a *name*, is it?"

"It is, really."

"All right, no offense. Where are you working?"

"At the lumber yard."

"Digging trenches?"

"That's right."

"You must be crazy. You'll kill yourself at that game. I'll see that you're transferred to the wool-carding shop. The N.C.O. in charge is a pal of mine."

Tanguy hesitated. Then he said: "I'd really rather stay where I am. I like working in the open air—"

"So it's true. You have got a crush on the pianist."

Tanguy didn't understand this remark. He said nothing.

"The young German, you know. The one who plays for the S.S. every Saturday evening. That's your friend, isn't it?"

"I don't know," stammered Tanguy. "His name's Gunther—"

"Then it's the same one, all right. I've got nothing personal against him, mind you. I just don't like the Boches. Even when they happen to be on our side, I always get the feeling it's an accident, and that there's nothing they'd like better than to demolish us. That's only my opinion, of course."

Tanguy said nothing; there was nothing to say. It made no difference to him whether Gunther was German, Belgian, or Chinese, so long as he was kind and gentle—and Gunther most certainly was.

"None of the N.C.O.'s been onto you yet?"

"Onto me? What do you mean?"

"Had you on the mat. If they haven't, you ought to watch out. They've been getting bored lately. They're looking for trouble. All right, *mon petit*, don't worry. I'm in Hut

No. 10. If something goes wrong, or there's anything you need, just say the word. I'll be happy to help you."

Tanguy got up and said good-by. He liked the Alsatian too: he was nice. But it struck Tanguy that, instead of making fine speeches, it would have been more to the point if he had offered Tanguy a piece of his bread. Then he blushed at the thought. The man must have worked hard to get that bread. It had cost him a lot in exertion and risk. He had no right to give it away as a present.

Stretched on his mattress, hands folded behind his head, Tanguy thought about his past life. He felt desperately unhappy. He thought of his mother, and of his father who had disowned and betrayed him, and wondered why he hadn't been treated like other children and what he had done to be different from them. He was drained of all energy: he would never, he thought, be able to stand up to this back-breaking work, day after day, practically without food. He was so famished he had stomach cramps. It's all because I haven't had a chance to talk to the commandant, Tanguy decided miserably. If I had managed to have a word with him, he would certainly have understood my position. He would have had me released— Tanguy began to weep tears not of misery but of surrender, the tears shed by those who no longer have any control over their fate.

THE days passed in their immutable routine: the morning siren, the long-drawn-out parades, the marching and singing of *"Die Fahne hoch,"* the ten hours' exhausting labor in the trenches, the march back, rollcall, evening parade, it was always the same. Tanguy was permanently tired. A numb torpor had seeped into his body and invaded his very soul. He hardly talked at all. He dragged himself like an automaton to paradeground or work, put up with going to bed without bread, no longer even displayed any inner symptoms beyond his control. He behaved as though he were under the influence of a powerful soporific. He was stupefied.

Gunther was his one prop. The young man had become absolutely essential to Tanguy. To feel his presence acted as a kind of balm to his tired nerves. He loved watching his friend's face as Gunther talked to him of Paris. He felt secure when Gunther was near. He loved him with a kind of utter despair. He never questioned the reason or nature of his affection: he simply loved. There were no words to turn this love into a myth; it manifested itself by eloquent acts and gestures, which all served to bring the two of them yet closer together. Tanguy clung to his friend with the ultimate intensity of one who has lost everything throughout his existence and now has nothing left to lose but life itself.

The other prisoners, on the contrary, disliked Gunther intensely. They insulted him, hit him when they got the chance, and rigged framed charges against him to try and get him extra fatigue details. Gunther never answered them or defended himself. Tanguy sobbed with rage at the sight. He hated these men who conspired against Gunther. He hated anyone who did not love his, Tanguy's, friend.

One day out at the lumber yard, about the time of the midday meal, the S.S. guard called Gunther over. While they were talking the soup was served out. Tanguy took Gunther's ration and put it beside his own. A prisoner came up, grabbed Gunther's bowl, and pissed in it. All the rest burst out laughing.

Tanguy was speechless, overcome. He stared at the bowl in a bewildered way. Gunther came back, sniffed at his soup, guessed what had happened, and threw it away. Tanguy sat there crying helplessly into his own soup. But while he was in the middle of it he caught an expression on Gunther's face that he would never be able to forget: a mixture of weariness, inner conflict, and sheer animal hunger.

"Here," he said, "have mine, Gunther."

Gunther smiled; the mask was in place again. "Certainly not, Tanguy. I'm quite all right as I am. You need soup more than I do."

Tanguy looked him straight in the eyes. "Please, Gunther. I want you to have my soup. I insist."

Gunther hesitated. In the end he took the bowl and began to swallow its contents. Then the other prisoners began to shout and make a disturbance. The N.C.O. came over.

"What's going on here?"

"It's that German bastard. He made the kid give him his soup. The boy's far too thin already. He'll be ill if he doesn't take care—"

"*I* gave him the soup!" Tanguy shouted furiously. "I *wanted* him to have it!"

The N.C.O. turned to Gunther. "What have *you* got to say about it?" he asked.

Gunther said not a word; simply stared at the ground in silence.

"The boy's telling the truth," said the Russian, Misha. "He did give him the soup—"

"Shut up, you bloody fool," hissed another prisoner, and then, to the corporal: "He gave it to him because the German made him. Every night he cajoles the kid into giving him his bread or his soup. It's not the first time it's happened."

"He's lying," Tanguy howled, "it's all lies! I swear it's not true. It's the other way round—Gunther often gives *me* bread—"

"That'll do," roared the corporal in disgust. "Shut up, the lot of you. I'm sick of your squabbling. As for you two, you can both bring me your bread ration for a week. That way no one'll give any bread to anybody. Come on, now. Back to work!"

Tanguy thought he must have misunderstood. He tried to protest that he hadn't done anything, but the corporal told him to shut his trap and get on with his digging.

Tanguy got down into the trench without saying another word, heavy-hearted, miserable, and exhausted. He could not bring himself to look at his companions, he was so overflowing with hate and distrust of them. He began to work, swallowing his resentment, behaving as if nothing was different. When the evening siren sounded he marched back to camp with the rest.

84

All the same, he cried after he had given his bread ration to the corporal. He knew very well that the corporal would sell it that evening in the latrines. Tanguy felt his bread had been stolen. It was a coward's trick to pick on a child like that. He went to bed, and here Gunther found him. When he saw his friend Tanguy burst into tears. He hid his face in his pillow and cried his heart out. "They've no right to do it!" he sobbed, "they've no right!"

Gunther ran his long fingers comfortingly through the child's hair and called him pet names in German, which Tanguy always loved.

"Cheer up, my *kleiner schwartzer Fürst* [Little Black Prince]. Don't cry. These are very unhappy people. When you are very unhappy, it's easy to become malicious. You must try to understand them. I'm a German, and they are prisoners in a German camp. It's only natural that they should react in that way. They're so desperately weak, poor creatures."

"But I'm unhappy, Gunther—so are you, and we don't behave like that. They have no right to do such things. I hate them. I hate them—"

The young German said passionately: "No, Tanguy. Don't hate. Never hate. Hate is a sickness, a horrible disease. Because you have suffered, you must learn to understand and forgive. Leave hate to those who are too weak to love."

Tanguy was in the last stages of exhaustion, and so famished that his belly ached. He felt a heavy dragging sensation in the pit of his stomach, as if he had swallowed a large stone.

Gunther got up and said: "All right now?"

Tanguy nodded.

"Good. I'm going to play this evening. It's several months since the commandant asked me last."

"Play? Play what?"

"The piano," Gunther said. "It's the commandant's birthday. I'm to give him a recital. Guests have been invited."

"You are a pianist?"

"Certainly. When I was very young I wanted to become a concert pianist. I even got a scholarship to the Conservatory. But in the end I chose law instead."

"Does the commandant like the piano too?"

"He has a passion for music. Especially Chopin. Tonight I'm going to play him five of the best nocturnes."

Tanguy said: "Do you *like* playing for the Germans?"

Gunther smiled.

"I am German myself," he replied. "Besides, it makes no difference to me who my audience may be. I love music, and music knows no frontiers."

Someone shook his shoulder gently, and Tanguy woke up. He opened his eyes and made out Gunther's shadow in the darkness. Gunther put a finger on his lips, and then sat down on Tanguy's bunk. Without saying a word he opened the parcel he carried and displayed its contents to Tanguy: bread, two oranges, a bar of chocolate, two bananas, a packet of biscuits, and a thick slice of fruit pie.

"I didn't want to raise your hopes in advance," he whispered. "I wasn't sure that I'd get anything this time. You wouldn't have been able to sleep, and you'd have been terribly disappointed if I'd come back empty-handed. Look: I got all this by playing Chopin. Who says musicians starve? Now, we'll divide it into two equal halves, and eat the lot here and now—all except the biscuits, that is. I shall barter them for some meat in the latrines tomorrow. There's nothing like a little meat to put you on your feet again. Come on, let's eat."

For the first time in his life, Tanguy was crying with sheer hunger. He stared at the food which Gunther had spread out on his bunk, yet could hardly believe it, let alone bring himself to touch it. For three months he had seen neither an orange nor a banana: merely to look at them now amazed him. He wondered what oranges would taste like.

Finally he stammered: "I can't—these things aren't for me —they were given to you. I don't want them—"

"You don't want them? Look, Tanguy: you're going to eat your orange, your piece of bread, your banana, and half that piece of pie, whether you like it or not. That's an order. We'll celebrate the commandant's birthday together."

Tanguy did as he was told. While he was eating he began to feel happy—so happy, indeed, that he could not imagine himself ever feeling happier. He smiled lovingly at Gunther, who was telling him between mouthfuls what the concert had been like. But Tanguy hardly heard him. His hands were trembling with emotion. He tried to control himself and eat slowly; but it was impossible. He darted scared glances round the hut, telling himself that he must hurry up and finish before anyone else woke up. If the others saw them they would complain that Tanguy and Gunther were trading on the black market behind their backs.

When the last crumb was eaten, Tanguy was beaming with joy. He drew a deep breath, but no words would come.

87

Finally he threw himself into Gunther's arms, murmuring inarticulately that he loved him, he loved him as much as his own mother, perhaps even more, he loved him, he loved him.

Gunther received this declaration of affection with quiet contentment. Then he wiped his hands and climbed up into the top bunk. Tanguy took a long time to fall asleep.

12

WINTER drew on, heralded by heavy rain. The earth became thick gluey mud. Black clouds piled up in the sky, and the near-by forest seemed to grow visibly darker. The rain fell continuously, day after day, and soaked everyone to the bone. It was accompanied by frequent gales.

Now the morning siren got the prisoners out of their bunks while it was still dark. They dragged themselves outside in their threadbare uniforms (no capes or winter coats had been issued) and stood shivering in the rain and wind for more than an hour, while rollcall was taken. These parades went on longer and longer every day. Prisoners died from the cold every night, but their corpses had to be dragged on to the paradeground for rollcall; the N.C.O.'s wanted to satisfy themselves that the men were really dead. The commandant had news bulletins and march music relayed through the loudspeakers.

Tanguy wrapped his arms about himself and jumped up and down to stop his limbs from going numb. He was wet through, and his thin undernourished body trembled with cold. He had no underclothes and the rain trickled down his bare skin. He had a bad cough. Yet he no longer cried or complained; he knew such things were useless. He had even got used to the sight of corpses. You had to get used to anything, he thought. Even to death.

The squad working out in the trenches had hoped that with the onset of the rains they would be transferred elsewhere. They were told that German soldiers were fighting in the mud and snow of Russia without complaining. The work went on, but now it became refined torture.

On the first day Tanguy struggled despairingly; after that he imitated the others and took the line of least resistance. Bent double, they spooned away at the brown liquid slush which formed the bottom of the trench. Most of it streamed off the shovel again. The work had become completely useless; they repeated mechanically actions which now had neither meaning nor purpose. To the exhaustion of physical exertion was added the fury of absolute futility.

For the first weeks of the rainy season Tanguy thought he would never last out without dying or going mad. He thought of his mother, and told himself he would never see her again. But gradually he learned that dying is not always so easy, and that there is something worse than outright death: to die a little every day, imperceptibly.

The S.S. guard and the corporal in charge of their work party had made the prisoners build them a kind of small wooden cabin, and here they spent the day gossiping or playing cards. Sometimes they would light a fire, and when he looked up from his work Tanguy could see the two men warming their hands and feet. And all the time the prisoners endured rain, wind, and bitter cold, as the mud churned up over their ankles and the canker of despair ate away at their hearts.

During the midday break they were forbidden to come near the fire. They had to stay out in the icy mud and warm their hands on their bowls while they swallowed a few mouthfuls of soup. Sometimes, too, the cooks took their time on the way, and the soup reached them almost stone-cold. On these occasions Tanguy ate in silence, and afterwards he and Gunther would huddle together in an effort to keep warm. They chafed each others' hands, blew on their fingers and then rubbed them vigorously to make the blood circulate. Then work began again. The siren sounded at five o'clock, when it was already dark.

After the rains it began to freeze. Snow fell in the first week of November. The sky had a wonderful, unearthly light in it and shone as white as the snow-blanketed landscape. Even the pine forest was blotted out beneath a thick layer of whirling flakes. The air was clear and icy: the cold sharpened, cut like a razor. Ears turned first red, then blue, and finally froze. Tanguy's hands and feet were badly frostbitten: they hurt so much that for a fortnight he could hardly sleep. Then the sores cracked open and began to fester. Gunther managed to scrounge up some old rags, with which he bandaged Tanguy's hands as well as he could. Even so, Tanguy could hardly use his fingers at all, and to use a shovel was almost unbearable agony.

Soon after the first snows the prisoners lined up at the clothing-store for the distribution of overcoats. This time the orderly in charge was a big jolly Pole. Tanguy caught his fancy; he gave the boy a red knitted balaclava as well as an overcoat, and so Tanguy was able to protect his ears. The coat was far too big and he had to turn up the sleeves. Gunther found him an amusing spectacle.

"You know what you remind me of?" he said. Tanguy shook his head. "A Chinese mandarin, something like that. Those two little ear-flaps, and that huge coat, with your hands lost in the sleeves—you look really impressive!"

Tanguy couldn't help laughing, though he felt far from cheerful.

"Well, we're completely fitted out now," Gunther went on. "If anyone dies in future it won't be our dear commandant's fault, especially since he's most graciously provided his guests with coats of so exotic a cut. Confound tradition! Why shouldn't we prisoners set our own fashions? We might even organize a mannequin parade."

To this suggestion Tanguy found no adequate reply.

When winter arrived in earnest, the work in the trenches was cut short. The working-party was split up and allotted to various "cleaning-fatigues." Every morning they marched to the nearest village and cleared the paths that ran from the school to the station, from the station to the church. It was a pleasant, countrified place. All the houses were attractive little chalets, each with its own garden, very different from the townhouses that Tanguy knew. The inhabitants watched the prisoners march past with some curiosity. The children behaved cruelly to them while they were sweeping away the snow. They threw stones at them, and called them "filthy Russians."

Tanguy wanted to tell these children that he wasn't Russian and therefore they shouldn't throw stones at him. Then it occurred to him that even the fact of being Russian wasn't an automatic reason for such violent behavior.

One day they changed their tactics and bombarded him with huge snowballs, so hard that on several occasions he stumbled and fell under their impact. The S.S. guard and the corporal slapped each other on the back and roared with laughter. The children, stimulated by such appreciation, redoubled their efforts. When Tanguy tried to stand up, a snowball struck him full in the face. While he lay on the ground the children pelted him with more snowballs and shouted *"Schweinhund!"* at him. It was the word Tanguy heard more than any other there.

He made no further attempt to get up, but lay in the snow and let the children have their fun. He was still lying there when he heard a woman's voice being raised in his defense. At once the children stopped what they were doing. Tanguy got up, shaking the snow from his neck and coat. A few yards in front of him stood a woman of about fifty, wearing a flowered dress, a navy-blue coat, and a black hat. She was big and white-haired, with a warm, friendly expression. Tanguy took off his balaclava and smiled his thanks at her: he was happy again now. The woman asked the S.S.

guard something, and he nodded. Then she rummaged in the basket she carried on her arm and held out to Tanguy a hunk of bread and a big apple. Tanguy did not dare to come any closer to her, so she walked forward toward him. But gradually he edged away from her, muttering *"Danke schön, gnädige Frau. Danke—"*

The woman smiled encouragingly. She pressed the bread and apple upon him, whispering *"Bitte,"* in a coaxing voice.

The S.S. guard came over and told Tanguy sharply to take the present. Tanguy did so, and thanked the lady all over again. He was on the point of bursting into tears, and kept glancing in a scared way at the corporal, who was watching the scene with a sentimental eye. The lady leaned down and stroked his battered head.

"What is your name?" she asked, in German.

"Tanguy, *gnädige Frau.*"

"Tanguy? That's a nice name. How old are you?"

"Ten, *gnädige Frau.*"

"Ten?" She thought for a moment. "Are you Jewish?" Tanguy shook his head. "No, *gnädige Frau.*"

Then the lady went away. Tanguy hardly dared touch the things she had given him. He watched her go as one might watch one's last hope vanishing. He would have liked to tell her that he was innocent; that he was neither a Russian, nor a Communist, nor even French. He ought to have made her understand that there had been a mistake—definitely the whole thing was due to a mistake.

"Come on," said the corporal; "eat what she's given you! Or would you like me to dish it out to the others?"

Tanguy began to eat. He swallowed the bread quickly, and

choked on several mouthfuls. Half of it he palmed and hid inside his shirt for Gunther. All the time he was thinking of the things he should have said to the lady. He knew she would have understood. It wouldn't have been any use, though, he thought. There's nothing she could do. Orders are orders. It's an official matter.

He glanced up and saw Misha staring at him in a kind of dumb stupor, which reminded him of his dog Tom. He walked over to Misha and, while the corporal and the S.S. guard were busy talking, gave him a piece of bread. Misha nodded and beamed delightedly: he looked just like a dog that has been thrown a bone. He swallowed the bread in two gulps and thanked Tanguy again.

Tanguy returned to his work in some distress. He knew that Russian prisoners were treated worse even than the Jews; that the N.C.O.'s had orders to beat them up; that they only got one ration of bread a day and were dying, one by one, of starvation and maltreatment. It isn't my fault, he thought stubbornly. It really isn't my fault. I'm not responsible for them. But all the same he felt a guilty shame because of the extra suffering that the Russians had to endure. That was why he felt affection for Misha: because Misha was so much the more unfortunate.

Neither the N.C.O.'s nor the prisoners themselves, for the most part, had any sympathy with the Russians. They were isolated completely from the rest of the camp. The German civilian population, even the children, spoke of all Russians as though they were monsters or plague-carriers. Tanguy found himself liking them for their generosity and simple good humor. He was fond of listening to their sad, nostalgic folksongs: they used to sing till the curfew, packed like animals in their barrack huts, and Tanguy was profoundly moved by their deep, melancholy voices.

That evening he hid the piece of bread which he had saved under Gunther's coverlet and waited impatiently for the young German to climb into bed. At last Gunther did so, and almost at once came down again and clasped Tanguy's hand.

"Thank you," he said.

"Don't thank me. Thank the kind German lady who gave it to me."

Gunther said nothing for a moment. Then he observed seriously: "Don't bear a grudge against those children who hurt you. They only did what they had been taught to do. They're unkind because they were brought up to be unkind. The sad thing is that it's such children who will be tomorrow's generation, the generation to whom we should look for a better world."

Tanguy did not answer. He just looked at Gunther and then clasped his hand firmly. "I know, Gunther," he said at last; "I know. After all, it's my generation too."

The temperature dropped steadily further below zero, and snow continued to fall. A biting east wind blew through the camp, and the timber of the barrack huts began to crack. Work out of doors had to be suspended. But the parades still took place regularly. Morning and evening the prisoners had to stand at attention on the big paradeground. The N.C.O.'s strutted up and down the ranks. Someone was always missing. Sometimes the rollcall took as long as an hour and a half.

Prisoners occasionally fainted in the ranks, and were brought round with cuffs and kicks. The S.S. guards were particularly addicted to this sport. One of them was a nineteen-year-old youth, the commandant's son. He had invented what he called a "quick recipe" for reviving prisoners who passed out: he used to slap their face and legs with a napkin soaked in icy cold water.

Tanguy was by now beyond resentment. He regarded all these things as if they had formed permanent features of his life from the beginning. He hardly ever thought about his past life now, and his recollections of it were fading, leaving nothing behind but a kind of gap in his emotional make-up, together with a secret nostalgia for a lost paradise which had never really existed.

He had abandoned all hopes of one day regaining his freedom. He knew that total war engulfed children, women, and old men just as much as those actually engaged in fighting; and his only defenses against death lay in his emaciated body and the enormous affection he felt for Gunther. He had passed into a world entirely different from the one in which he was born. In this camp neither good nor evil, happiness or sorrow meant anything at all: the one object was survival. Tanguy learned to regard every moment wrested from death as a tremendous victory. He learned to speak sparingly; his most ordinary actions and gestures became clothed in new, almost symbolic meaning. These gestures were, in fact, the public affirmation of his continued existence as an individual.

The barracks were unheated, and the temperature continued to fall. What with cold, boredom, hunger, and brooding on their past misfortunes the prisoners nearly went insane. They spent their time brawling and insulting each other. Personal possessions such as bowls, spoons, and blankets suddenly began to disappear in unprecedented numbers. Every heart nursed suspicion, and fear sat in every face. At night every prisoner slept clutching to him the few objects that had been issued to him by the authorities. Severe penalties were inflicted on anyone who lost one of these pieces of government property.

Every Saturday there was a general inspection at which the prisoners' kits were checked. In the morning the barracks were thick with insults, mutual accusations, blasphemous obscenities, and the occasional fight, all of which served as an excuse to the N.C.O.'s to hand out extra punishment drill. Sometimes the victims were kept standing at attention for hours at a time in a howling blizzard; sometimes they were deprived of their bread ration, or forced to eat their soup cold. The prisoners would see the big soup kettles brought in steaming hot, and were then kept standing at attention in front of them till the contents were on the point of freezing.

Frantically Tanguy asked himself whether the spring would ever return and put an end to this hell. He spent his time snuggled up against Gunther, trembling with fright as much as cold, watching in fascination while the German made dolls and sailboats and even flowers for him out of scraps of paper. They were the permanent scapegoats of their hut. Sometimes the other prisoners would form a ring round them and shout insults at them, or kick them. On these occasions Tanguy clung despairingly to Gunther's arm. Gunther himself never reacted to these attacks. He endured the vilest insults without protest. The filthiest insinuations never stirred him out of his carefully cultivated indifference. Afterwards, when their tormentors had retired to their own bunks, he would say quietly: "It isn't their fault, Tanguy. The poisonous atmosphere of this place is driving them crazy. We shall end up cutting each others' throats if we're all cooped up here much longer."

The freezing cold decimated the prisoners. Even during the summer and autumn there had been daily deaths. But during that winter death stalked from hut to hut like a contagious plague. Every morning there were seven or eight corpses in each block. The authorities instituted what became known as the "undertakers' fatigue." Two prisoners were detailed to remove the bodies from the barrack huts, undress them, put them in a special tent set aside as a mortuary, and take their bedding to be fumigated. Every evening, after the news bulletin, a rickety cart with a starved old nag between the shafts pulled up at this makeshift morgue to collect the cadavers. From his hut Tanguy could see the two "undertakers" pick up a corpse by feet and armpits, swing it a couple of times to gain momentum, and toss it over the tailboard of the cart. This operation was repeated as many times as was necessary. Then the cart lurched off, loaded with sprawling corpses that made Tanguy think of marionettes.

From shocked astonishment Tanguy proceeded by easy degrees to cool indifference. He ceased to wonder how he preserved his sanity. He even amused himself by counting the daily tally; the average was thirty-five, with the Russians leading by several lengths. They only occupied two barrack huts, but each of these produced ten or twelve corpses every day.

Tanguy heard after a while that Misha too had died: a Jewish prisoner gave him the news one evening in the latrines. He also told him that the Germans had invented a terrible new secret weapon that would crush the Americans and Russians in a matter of weeks.

Tanguy went back to his hut and sat with his nose glued to the window, watching the undertakers' fatigue moving in and out of the mortuary tent by the main gate. He thought sadly of Misha, and turned up his coat collar, shivering. He swallowed and blinked. Then he shrugged his shoulders. We shall all die, he thought. One after the other. The whole lot of us. They won't leave a single one alive. And then, with this new weapon of theirs, they'll turn the whole world into a German empire.

He reflected that the Germans had perhaps already destroyed Paris. He remembered the day when he had seen the Eiffel Tower for the first time, from a German truck, and shortly after that had passed by the tranquil, apparently unmoving waters of the Seine.

What had become of Mme Puigdellivol? The women had been taken to another camp, further off. What about the handsome young man? Or the old Jew with the bowler hat? Tanguy had failed to find him among the Jews in the camp. Perhaps all these, too, had died?

CHRISTMAS 1942.

It was a Christmas that Tanguy was never to forget, a brief truce created out of concerted hope in that world of silence and death. A few days beforehand the prisoners began to scrub out their barrack huts and decorate them with pine branches and colored paper garlands. They even tacked up Christmas messages on the doors.

Then it was Christmas Day.

The evening inspection was shorter than usual, and the commandant wished the prisoners a happy Christmas. Then the loudspeakers began to braodcast carols. The soup had potato-peelings floating in it and was less reddish in color than usual. Everyone agreed that the bread ration had been increased a little.

The atmosphere in the camp was completely transformed. Even those who most habitually quarreled and insulted each other now spoke in friendly tones. They gave each other cigarette butts that they had bought in the latrines, and inquired after their companions' health. They even behaved kindly to Gunther; and one of them who had always shown himself particularly hostile to the young German went so far as to shake hands with him.

In the endless sea of hatred which formed their lives this day stood out, a peaceful island. The prisoners lay on their bunks and dreamed of their own countries and homes, of other, prewar Christmases. For this one evening they felt themselves in touch once more with the rest of the world; and they knew instinctively that the linking thread was hope. Hope for a more just and better world; hope for true peace to men of good will; above all, the hope of spending future Christmases in their own homes again, and becoming men once more.

"*Stille Nacht, heilige Nacht*"—all over the world, they knew, in countless different tongues, this carol was being sung and heard; and everywhere men dreamed of this same peace promised to men of good will.

Tanguy, too, lay and dreamed. He felt surging up in him an infinite nostalgia for every Christmas he had never known: the Christmas Days he should have spent in the peaceful company of his family, with a beautiful glittering Christmas tree. He felt in himself the collective nostalgia of all children who, without parents and without love, still dream of the Christmas season. The unspoken yearning of children everywhere stirred in him: those that Dickens portrayed in his *Christmas Carol*, all orphans and charity boys and every one, boy or girl, that had never known true affection. He felt in his innermost heart what all these poor deprived creatures felt: the lack of any happy memories.

Gunther came over to Tanguy's bunk. His face, in the dim evening light, seemed more fine-drawn and beautiful than ever, Tanguy thought. Gunther smiled at him and wished him a happy Christmas.

"Happy Christmas, Gunther."

"Look," Gunther said, "I've brought you a present. Not much, but all I could find. Let it be a token of my affection for you."

101

Tanguy tried to smile his thanks, but instead he found himself blushing and stammering and very close to tears. Clumsily he opened the parcel. It contained a book: Tolstoy's *Resurrection*.

He thanked Gunther in a choking voice.

Gunther was standing over him, and Tanguy still stared at his face by the faint light of the winter moon. The child's emotions were violently aroused, and yet he could find nothing to say to express his gratitude, though there was much he wanted to tell Gunther. He sat there on his bunk in an agony of indecision, clasping his present in both hands. He was so happy that it hurt.

"Tanguy—there's something I wanted to say to you—"

"Yes?" Tanguy asked eagerly.

Gunther seemed to hesitate. Then, in a nervous voice, he said: "If something . . . happens to me one day, get up on my bunk and pry up the nearest board. Under it you will find a tiny gold medallion. I was wearing it on the day of my arrest. It belonged to my mother. I bequeath it to you."

"But what do you think is going to happen to you?"

"I don't know. It doesn't matter, anyway. Happy Christmas!"

"Happy Christmas, Gunther. And—you know—"

"I know. And now," Gunther said, in a different voice, "now I'm going to give the staff my Christmas recital. You're going to hear it too. The commandant has decided that prisoners are entitled to some music tonight. The curfew is being put back two hours. I'm going to play a Mozart sonata which'll be wasted on the S.S.—but at least

I'll have the satisfaction of knowing that you'll be in the audience."

"Thank you, Gunther—that makes it a real Christmas for me."

"Perhaps Christmas has more true reality here than anywhere else," the German said. "Here that dream of hope and love, the Christmas spirit, has more solemn undertones than the free world knows, or cares to know."

Tanguy was silent for a moment, and examined his book, deeply moved. The words for which he fumbled would not come; they suddenly seemed to have lost any meaning. Doggedly he returned to the attack.

"Gunther—"

"M'm?"

"It's the first Christmas I've had—in my whole life—with decorations, and someone giving me a present. You know?"

"I know."

"All the same, I'm glad to have spent it with you. I shall never forget tonight."

"Others will forget for you. Christmas will go back to being a mere orgy—getting drunk on beer or champagne, expensive dinners, theaters, promiscuousness. There will be very few for whom Christmas will still symbolize a living hope: the hope of that peace which is sworn to those who earn it. But perhaps mankind will never earn it."

Tanguy lay in his bunk and listened to Gunther's playing over the loudspeaker. He felt as he had felt when, a tiny child, he had listened to his mother broadcasting for the Reds in

Spain. Gunther's interpretation and re-creation of his chosen pieces seemed to come from another world. Tanguy pictured his long fingers fluttering up and down the keyboard while his eyes stared into space, absorbed. He felt that through the medium of this music, with its melancholy serenity, Gunther was trying to impart some essential truth to his young mind—something so beautiful that words were inadequate to express it, and only music would suffice. He listened with rapt attention. All was forgotten: his hunger, the fear he had felt during the past few weeks, his frostbitten hands, the whole wretchedness of his ruined childhood.

In the silent, sleeping barracks Tanguy sensed the secret thoughts, collective and individual, of his companions. He knew which prisoners were reliving their moments of former happiness, and which, like himself, must be regretting the happiness they might have had if life had not denied it to them. He felt them dreaming, as he dreamed, of a world without wars, concentration camps, hatred, or betrayal. And perhaps, he thought, on some remote station platform other children now traveling to other camps must be dreaming of the happier Christmases they had once known.

When Gunther's recital was over, the commandant had records of Wagner relayed over the loudspeakers. Tanguy knew the *Tannhaüser* overture, but it was the first time he had heard it played in the camp. He listened with intense pleasure. Gunther had once explained the libretto to him, and now in his mind's eye he seemed to see the Pilgrim's Chorus moving across a huge, brightly lit stage.

Presently Gunther came back, carrying his usual booty. Tanguy sat on his bed in happy anticipation while Gunther meticulously divided the bread, chocolate, and orange he had been given. Then the two friends ate their Christmas dinner in silence, while the music played on, penetrating to every corner of the camp, feeding the nostalgic dreams which all prisoners cherish.

14

DURING 1943 the prisoners were to learn that man's capacity for the scientific extermination of his own kind is capable of the most frightful refinements. They thought they had reached the limits of their endurance, and then learned that endurance knows no limits, and human misery can be infinitely extended.

A whole series of catastrophes struck the camp. The first was the arrival of two new convoys of prisoners. By now Tanguy and his companions had been put back to outdoor work. When they were marching back to camp one evening they learned that the rollcall that night would be taken in the huts, and there would be no general parade. The convoy consisted of Polish Jews. Their journey must have been longer than Tanguy's, or at any rate tougher: the barrack square was thick with corpses, plainly visible from the huts. They looked like men who had fallen asleep in an exhausted stupor.

Those who were still alive stood there in the courtyard

stark naked, as Tanguy had once done. The boy stared unhappily at these poor sheeplike creatures huddling together,
stripped of their human individuality. Hands clasped under
armpits, they stood in a shivering line outside the door
marked DISINFECTION. They must have already been through
the barber's hands, since their heads had been shaven. Their
skulls gleamed in the pale, overclouded moonlight. Watching
them, Tanguy thought how men in the same moment of
stress always tended to make exactly the same gestures.

The initial problem was to find billets for them. The
barrack orderlies, however, ordered the occupants of the huts
to come inside and shut the doors. Tanguy obeyed. Then
the little waxy-skinned man who was orderly for their hut
proceeded to bolt the door himself, although it was not yet
curfew time. A few moments later the first appeals for help
were made to them.

A voice outside called: "Have you got any mattresses?"
No answer. "For pity's sake, answer me! In the name of
heaven—"

The barrack orderly said through the closed door: "Are
you Jewish?"

"Yes."

"We're full up here. This hut is reserved for 'politicals.'
You'll have to go down there—huts 9, 10, and 11."

"We have," the man said. "They're full up themselves.
We managed to billet one or two men on them, but they've
no more spare bunks. Look, it's only for one night. We've
got children with us—they're going to die of cold. For
God's sake let some of our children in—"

"Full up," repeated the barrack orderly.

Tanguy lay on his bunk and shivered. Every word the Jewish suppliant outside uttered went home to him with terrible force. He trembled with fright. It's criminal, he thought. They can't do such a thing to children. But he had spent all day out working in the trenches, and even at this moment could hardly keep his eyes open.

"Let us in," the voice called. "For God's sake, let us in." Someone began hammering with increasing violence on the barrack-hut door.

"I've already told you this isn't a Jews' barrack. We're political prisoners here. Besides, we haven't any spare room."

"Let us see, then. One of us can come in and make sure things are as you say. The children can sleep on the floor. They don't need beds. We've marched on foot for nearly a fortnight. Many of us have died. For pity's sake, let us come in and see for ourselves."

"I tell you there's no room," the barrack orderly shouted. "Go away. Leave us alone. We've been working all day, and we haven't got any spare room for Jews. Go and see the Russians. Maybe they'll find you something."

"The Russians have taken some of us in. They're sleeping four or five to a bunk. Why can't you do the same?"

"*What?* Don't make me throw up. Now for God's sake move on and leave us in peace."

This extraordinary dialogue burned itself into Tanguy's mind, and confused him. He found it hard to believe in the reality of what he had heard. But what could he have done? He wanted to get up and protest. But he knew that if he so much as opened his mouth the barrack orderly and his mates would beat him up or get him punished. So he remained lying on his bunk, eyes wide open, heart beating violently. He had a dull headache. There was nothing he could do.

Outside the knocking and shouting increased. Then there was silence, broken only by wailing sobs. Gradually these too faded away. Tanguy, wrapped in his blanket, thought of them crouched in the open, poor devils, with no more protection than their threadbare garments afforded them. He pictured them, grouped round the hut, shivering with cold. In the end he stopped thinking altogether. It was useless, he told himself. Yet he found it difficult to sleep; he felt as though he had a touch of fever. I mustn't get ill, he whispered. Whatever happens, I mustn't get ill.

The following day, when the occupants of barrack hut No. 12 emerged for the morning rollcall, they found the bodies of more than thirty Jews outside. These poor wretches had crawled as close to the hut as possible in the hope of catching a little warmth from it. Some were still clutching the window ledges to which they had desperately clung the night before. The bitter cold had caught and frozen them in their final gesture of self-preservation.

Tanguy looked at these bodies for a long moment. He looked at them as though he had never seen dead men before. To him, it appeared that they had died stretching out their arms to him as he lay inside, warm and asleep. He felt partially responsible for their deaths. For a long time he remained motionless. He was very tired, and a sudden need for sleep spread through his body. Then he blinked his eyes, stifled a couple of enormous yawns, and walked across to the paradeground. On the way he heard the barrack orderly defending himself with noisy self-justification.

"It was us or them," the little man was saying. "Anyway, they were only Jews."

A voice somewhere said: "We would be better dead instead of them. A pity we're not."

Tanguy turned round, recognizing Gunther's intonation. The German was even paler than usual. His voice was harsh and weary.

"What do you mean?" the barrack orderly shouted.

"I mean that at least then I should have had the pleasure of knowing that you were dying with me."

The barrack orderly's eyes lit up. He looked pleased rather than otherwise. "Threatening to kill me, eh? You all heard him. I've got witnesses, my friend. You're going to explain yourself to the corporal—"

"Oh no," someone else broke in. "You've got it wrong. *You* threatened to kill *him*. Plenty of witnesses for that."

The speaker was a Czech. He had the reputation of being a Communist, and had never liked Gunther, which made this sudden defense of him all the more surprising to Tanguy. He stared at the Czech, not understanding what was going on. The Czech looked coolly indifferent. His hands were thrust into his pockets, and he strolled along without looking at anyone. His voice, too, was unheated as he went on: "Besides, we all saw you selling bread and meat on the black market yesterday evening."

"Who, me?" screamed the barrack orderly. "You're making it all up. I've never traded on the black market. I only do my duty as orderly in charge. You're lying, you're lying! I know very well you're lying. I can see your little game. You want to get me demoted. Well, you won't do it. You're nothing but a filthy Red. No one'll listen to you. But they'll listen to me all right when I tell them how you distribute propaganda in the latrines—"

"But it's not a question of my unsupported word," the Czech said. "Ask Mathias, he'll tell you. Mathias isn't a Communist. Isn't it true, Mathias, that our barrack orderly is a black marketeer and has just threatened to kill me?"

Mathias was an Italian. He always swore he had no idea why he had been interned. He spent his time shouting slogans such as *"Viva il Duce! Long live Benito Mussolini!"* But even so the Germans would not release him. He was a stunted, sickly little man, as dark-complexioned as Tanguy, with black eyes. The other prisoners suspected him of being a Jew, a charge he rebutted with some vigor and accounts, to those who would listen, of how he made his First Communion.

"Per la Santa Madonna!" he swore, "I hear everything. He make-a da threat. *Per il Papa!* He sell-a on da black market. I see him. I see everything—"

"It isn't true," the orderly shouted frantically. "You're lying, Mathias, you filthy Yid. You want to destroy me, that's it. You're all against me—"

"Me?" Mathias said, blankly. *"Per la Santa Madonna!"* He looked at Tanguy. "Ask the *bambino*. Is innocent child. He will tell-a truth."

The barrack orderly was deathly pale. It was plain from his expression that he was in a sweating panic. He shot a desperate glance at Tanguy.

"You know it isn't true, don't you? You know they're lying. You're not going to tell lies too—not a nice boy like you—"

Tanguy hesitated, and closed his eyes. He thought of the bolted barrack doors, with those wretched Jews clawing at them and slowly freezing to death. He looked at Gunther, and saw his face set in a stern mask of condemnation.

"Yes," Tanguy said, "it's true what they say. You did threaten to kill that man. You are a black marketeer."

The morning rollcall took place a few moments later, and took rather longer than usual. As their N.C.O. came down the ranks to inspect them, Mathias stepped forward and whispered something in his ear. Shortly afterwards two S.S. guards dragged the little barrack orderly from the ranks and frog-marched him across the paradeground to the courtyard wall. There was absolute silence. Then the orderly began to struggle and swear and accuse the Czech, Mathias, and Tanguy of having framed up a charge with the sole object of destroying him. He kept on shouting over and over again that he was innocent.

The S.S. guards drew their pistols and fired. The body slumped down against the wall. Mathias was appointed barrack orderly in the dead man's place. Then the prisoners listened to the daily news bulletin, which was followed by a catastrophic announcement: in future they would get bread at only one meal a day.

As he marched off to work Tanguy realized that he had become a murderer.

. . .

A few days later a second convoy of prisoners arrived. Jews and political internees assembled together in a confused mass on the barrack square. As before, an incredible number of starved corpses were left lying there. The new arrivals were as emaciated as the old hands. A few days' traveling had been enough to make them as much like walking skeletons as the long-term prisoners.

They had to find billets somewhere, but the huts were full to overflowing. Tanguy now moved up to Gunther's bunk; and even so they shared it with a third prisoner, one of the new arrivals. With three sleepers crammed onto two narrow planks, it was impossible for any of them to stretch out in comfort. They decided to take turns, and thus Tanguy spent half the night sleeping upright. This he found sheer agony. His back and legs ached. He developed a thick cough in his chest, so that when he breathed the air bubbled raucously through his lungs like boiling water. Damp sweat sprang out on his forehead and back. He could not stir without waking the other two, and so kept absolutely motionless. Sometimes his limbs went numb, and the returning circulation hurt him so much that tears came to his eyes.

Despite this he knew that whatever happened he had no right to deprive his companions of sleep. So he choked back his sobs and tried to concentrate on something quite different in an effort to forget his sufferings. When at last he dropped off to sleep it was only to be woken up again an hour or so later, and told it was his turn to lie down. The following morning his limbs would be stiff, his eyes red and swollen. But there was nothing to be done about it, and he did not complain.

Even Gunther was weakening under the strain: he became taciturn, irritable, and withdrawn. A queer silence brooded over the camp, which presaged little good for the future. It was as if the prisoners had learned to fight their increased sufferings by enduring them with this terrible dumb patience.

Some highly improbable rumors gained currency in the latrines. One evening Tanguy met Desprez, who told him that the commandant has received orders to "exterminate" his prisoners. Others claimed that the Germans could no longer afford to feed so many internees and had decided to let them die of hunger. As these rumors passed from mouth to mouth they became fantastically exaggerated, and created a strange nervous tension among the prisoners: they no longer knew what to expect or believe. The newcomers said the war was beginning to go badly for the Germans, and that the *Wehrmacht* had had some serious reversals in Russia. Others again were confident that the Russians were in Poland and the Allies in Italy. Because one or two prison trains had been bombed, a rumor spread that the main German towns had been reduced to vast cemeteries.

Tanguy, for his part, listened but remained indifferent. One half of his mind believed the stories, the other dismissed them. What mattered to him was to stay alive. If the Allies did win the war and he were dead, it would still be a defeat as far as he was concerned. For this reason he was far more interested in rumors concerning the future of the camp itself than those which dealt with events outside.

His hunger took on a compulsive animal quality, and he was no longer capable of analyzing his own feelings. His whole conscious being was transformed into one vast unsatisfied appetite. Belly, head, eyes, and back all ached: hunger had crept into every corner of his body. Day and night he dreamed of food, nourishment, anything to put in his mouth.

15

TANGUY had had ample time in which to become accustomed to the presence of death. He had seen it lurking around the Russian barracks, the big tent at the camp gates, and accompanying each fresh draft of prisoners. But suddenly his fear of death increased; for death ceased to be a thief in the night, but installed itself openly among them. Every morning piles of bodies lay outside the barrack doors. The rickety old cart had to be replaced by a big truck, rather like those used by a sanitation department. Everywhere death became an immediate and pressing reality. Something like a panic fear of dying spread through the camp, and men began to doubt whether they were in fact alive.

Dying became of all acts the easiest and simplest, yet the one which provoked still the most frantic resistance. Out in the trenches one prisoner suddenly collapsed and lay where he fell. Another keeled over on the paradeground. Someone in a barrack hut apparently slipped on the floor, but failed to get up again, ever. A new and grisly sport now began: the death hunt. No one mentioned dying. Bodies were whisked out of sight with uncanny speed, and at the same time a kind of cynical gallows-humor became popular. At night some prisoners would make a tour from bunk to bunk and touch their companions on the forehead "just to see if they were still alive." The dead were stripped before they were even cold. All their possessions vanished—bowls, spoons, private papers. It was less important what you got than that you should make some gesture against this terror of death which haunted those who survived. People began to die of fear as hitherto they had died of starvation or illness. It seemed a natural process.

This fatal contagion merely served to stimulate the N.C.O.'s and S.S. guards into a kind of necrophilic frenzy. They campaigned zealously for death, and became its living auxiliaries. They knew that to deprive a hut of bread altogether for three days would reap them a rich harvest of corpses, and they did not stint themselves. Terror stalked through the camp. Those who still lived asked how they happened to be alive, as though it were a miracle.

Tanguy shared this catching fear of death. He no longer dared to look at a corpse. When, after rollcall, the truck came to remove the day's casualties, he flung himself trembling on to his bunk. He hardly dared even to let himself fall asleep. The least attack of giddiness set his heart pounding with fright. He no longer thought "I'm going to fall," but "I'm going to die." The result was a desperate struggle against a plague which spared no one and always struck without warning.

Presently a really unbelievable rumor spread from hut to hut. Tanguy dared not think of it as true. There was a big oven being built near the administrative block, and some prisoners asserted that the authorities intended to use it for burning the old and therefore useless prisoners, so as to make room for younger ones whose work would be more productive. But Tanguy could not believe such a thing. He sided with those who maintained that the oven was a perfectly ordinary baker's oven for making the camp's bread, and that the plan was to get the prisoners to do their baking themselves.

Soon the camp learned the truth: this oven was for the incineration of corpses. From this moment death took on extra terror, as though being incinerated somehow gave the victim extra agony. The prisoners watched the smoke coil slowly from the oven's small chimney, terrified and fascinated. A change in the wind sometimes blew this smoke down among them.

So time passed by. Tanguy worked ten hours a day without fail, still digging those long trenches with the rest of his squad. He had become so weak that he had to be half carried back afterwards. Since he could no longer raise shovelfuls of earth, his fellow workers put him on to light work with a pick, which was more difficult for the N.C.O. to check.

The day's work was followed by the same interminable parade, which got longer and more complicated as time went on. Each group was obliged to carry back its own dead.

Tanguy could not remember afterwards when he first learned of the existence of the death chambers. One convoy of Jews had had immediately on arrival half its effective strength sent off "to the showers." They did not come back, and a few days later the prisoners found out just what these "showers" really were. The news was broken in the latrines and flew around the whole camp in a single evening. That night they knew that death had finally won, and no one dared any longer to pit himself against it. Soon they all came to accept the departure at night "for an unknown destination." But they no longer slept. They lay in a conscious stupor, one ear alert, anxious not to be taken by surprise. That was the one intolerable thing.

About two or three o'clock in the morning the door of the barrack hut would open, and reveal two S.S. guards standing outside, guns in hand. The barrack orderly would go from bunk to bunk waking those prisoners who were on the list. Not all of them, unhappily, knew how to go to their deaths without fuss; and there were some frightful scenes. The majority, however, left quietly enough. They shook hands with a few of their friends and vanished into the night.

Tanguy knew he could never haved faced death with dignity. At the least sound he shot upright and sat trembling on the edge of the bunk. Not even Gunther could reassure him, and indeed Tanguy was becoming very short-tempered with his friend. He had reached the point where he could no longer respond to Gunther's conversation, and existed as little else but a meager handful of flesh and trembling bones.

The N.C.O.'s had at last found a way to break the prisoners' spirits by sheer terrorization. They used to burst in noisily in the middle of the night and wake them up unexpectedly.

"Well, well," they would say, "you look quite scared, don't you? Come on, we're going to inspect you."

At this point Tanguy would burst into tears. One day he had a real *crise de nerfs* and took several days to recover.

Toward the end of 1943 leakages of information began to occur in the administrative offices. Those whose names figured on the fatal lists could thus be warned, indirectly, of what was in store for them. When a friend came up and asked, very kindly, where someone was from, and whether he was married or had a family, everyone knew that the person thus questioned had little time left to live.

It was about the same period that the camp underwent its first air raids. In the middle of the night the sirens would sound, and be followed by searchlight beams probing the sky. A few moments later a wave of aircraft would pass overhead: the noise of their engines made the huts creak and tremble as if about to collapse. Then followed the heavy detonations made by high-explosive bombs. On the outward journey the aircraft engines labored hesitantly, but returning they sounded as though released from a dragging weight. At some point on the horizon there would appear a lurid red glow that went on unchecked.

The first major bombing-raid that Tanguy experienced took place in December 1943. He had never been so scared in his life. Nothing, he thought, could be worse than the sad wailing of those sirens, or the sinister whistle of falling bombs. Several planes were shot down near the camp with their bomb load still aboard, and they blew up as they hit the ground. Tanguy felt as though an earthquake were about to engulf him. Cold and frightened, he yet found himself thinking of those women and children who must at that moment be huddled in cellars, as scared as he was and, like him, praying to gods in whom they did not believe.

But on the majority of the prisoners the raids had a quite

different effect: they provoked a frenetic outburst of joy. In all the huts they began singing national songs and anthems: the *"Marseillaise,"* the *"Internationale"* for the Russians, even some Jewish hymns of praise. Prisoners embraced each other, shook their fists in vague threats. Some were actually weeping with happiness.

"They're ours!" they shouted. "They're here at last! It's really true—"

The familiar, long-suppressed cries went up: "Long live liberty!" "Down with Fascism!" Someone shouted optimistically: "We have won the war!"

Tanguy, who was lying on his bunk with Gunther, asked the German if he thought this was true. Gunther shrugged his shoulders indifferently.

"In a war," he said, "there are neither conquerors nor vanquished: only victims."

The following day the prisoners were collectively punished for their demonstration: three days without their evening meal, on the grounds that they had "lowered the morale of foreign volunteer workers." During these three days the truck made two trips, and the oven chimney smoked continuously.

What with the air raids, the nocturnal irruptions of the N.C.O.'s, and the genuine removal of prisoners in the small hours "for an unknown destination," the nights had become one long nightmare. Tanguy lay awake listening and jumped at the least sound, even when he thought he was asleep. He could never lose contact completely with the brutal reality of the outside world. No one who has not experienced them, in any Nazi camp during 1943, can imagine what those nights were like. No one who has not known the experience can imagine what the victims felt when the barrack orderly drew near each bed in turn, list in hand. No one can imagine what it is really like to spend every moment in expectation of death. Each new day may be the fatal day, and time draws out in a slow agony.

They were back from the day's work. The evening rollcall was over, and the prisoners had had their soup. The sentries were dozing on their high watchtowers. The evening sky was pale and clear; the oven chimney smoked steadily; night hovered hesitantly on the horizon. Tanguy lay stretched out on his bunk, trying to snatch a little sleep before Gunther and his other bedfellow came in and made it necessary for him to sit upright. He felt exhausted and apathetic. Now as often before he felt the temptation to let go completely and never get up again. Death was beginning to seem like a blessed release to him; and indeed for many of the prisoners it could not have been anything else. Only Gunther still had the power to get him up each morning, though they often quarreled. Tanguy actually bit him once, and Gunther in response had boxed his ears.

Gunther came in at last and climbed onto the bunk. Tanguy suddenly felt his heart wrung by the German's appearance. He was terribly pale: drained, ashen. In this colorless mask his reddened eyes were prominent and unmistakable. He had obviously been crying, a thing Tanguy had never known him do before. The boy shivered, and dared not question him. He felt a lump form in his throat, but swallowed, and said nothing, merely waited.

120

Gunther clasped his hand and held it tightly. Then he tried to say something, but his voice failed. At last he got control of himself.

"Tanguy," he began, "promise me one thing—"

"What?"

"Promise me that whatever happens, you'll make a really heroic effort to get yourself up in the mornings and go to meals and work. Promise me you won't stay in the hut. Even if I wasn't here any more. Even if you felt really ill and desperate."

Tanguy felt colder and colder as he listened. His eyes were blurred, he could find nothing to say. A vast lassitude crept over him, and a kind of deathly torpor enveloped his spirit.

"Will you promise?" Gunther persisted.

"Yes."

"Thank you." Gunther paused. Then he said: "I would like to give you this. Guard it carefully. It's all I possess. I'm offering it to you because it's the only object of value that still belongs to me."

It was the tiny gold medallion, with a long thin chain of the same metal. Gunther put it into Tanguy's hand, and the boy stared at it for a long time. Then he swallowed, and looked around him. What was there to hold onto now? He could not believe that any child could suffer so much and still live. Finally he threw himself into Gunther's arms. But what could he say? There were no adequate words. Yet he felt the pressing need to say something, to put his feelings into concrete form.

"Gunther," he stammered, "I love you. I love you more than the whole world. I've been horrible to you these last few days, and yet you've always been kind to me. Still, I always loved you, even when I was terrible to you. It was just that I was afraid of dying, and I simply couldn't go on. But I do love you. I'm still a child, yet I've grown old. I know too much—" He broke off for a moment, then said: "Gunther, why are there wars? Why do people want war?"

"But who *does* want war, Tanguy? The man in the street? Stupid unreasoning people and patriotism goes to their heads because the newspapers know just how to stir up their enthusiasm? No, war is like some contagious disease. We say 'that's war' fatalistically, just as in the Middle Ages they used to shrug their shoulders at the plague. Nobody wants war, but war is there all the same. We are at its mercy. We never discover its horrors except by experience; and then it is too late."

Neither Tanguy nor Gunther could sleep that night. They lay there hand in hand, ears pricked for each tiny sound that broke the silence. The hut was in almost total darkness. The third man who shared their bunk was asleep. He was so emaciated that his body was almost invisible under his coat and blanket. Time dragged on, slow and inexorable. Tanguy hardly knew whether he was alive or not. What Gunther had told him had evoked a choking misery, too violent for him or anyone to bear. He was so numb with shock that he could not even cry. He made no effort to understand what was happening, or talk about it; he simply lay there and waited, as one might wait for a train. The night seemed endless, and it was cold in the hut. Tanguy sat there, wrapped in his blanket, a fold of it over his head like a cowl. In that agonizing stillness he heard his teeth chattering. It was like the vibration of a window when bombers pass overhead. Round him other prisoners were coughing and groaning, but all these sounds seemed to fade away to nothing in the immensity of that autumn night.

About midnight the *Alert* went, and the raid lasted for three quarters of an hour. The prisoners did not even wake up. They had become used to the noise of bombs and anti-aircraft guns. The hut was lit up by searchlights probing the darkness for enemy planes. Then, suddenly, it became as bright as daylight: flares were being dropped. From a distance this kind of raid looks like an outsize firework display, and has a kind of beauty.

But Tanguy made no move, merely gripped Gunther's hand more tightly in a silent, distressed appeal. Gunther gave an answering squeeze. At last the *All Clear* went, and everything became still once more. Tanguy dozed, and the hours began to slip by more quickly. Suddenly he sat up, startled. The hut door was open, and Tanguy saw two black uniformed figures standing there, just distinguishable against the outer darkness, guns pointing into the hut. Mathias switched on his tiny flashlight.

Gunther did not wait to be summoned. He took off his blanket and wrapped it round Tanguy. Then he gave the child a long kiss on the forehead, and walked toward the door. He was deathly pale and looked taller than usual. Mathias did not seem surprised to see him there. They shook hands.

Other prisoners were getting up as well. Some were still half asleep. Tanguy saw the Czech going past toward the door. Someone else began screaming: "Not tonight! I swear I'll go tomorrow, but not tonight, not tonight—" An S.S. guard went across to him, and the screams stopped. Then they all went out, and the door shut behind them.

Tanguy found himself on his feet without knowing how. He went across to the window and pressed his nose against the frost-rimmed pane. Here and there groups of prisoners were being marched off to the administrative buildings, handcuffed in pairs, with armed guards following close at their heels. Tanguy spotted Gunther's tall silhouette.

Suddenly the blanket Gunther had wrapped round Tanguy's shoulders was torn off him, and he heard a voice muttering: "Give me that. The German promised it to me."

Tanguy said nothing. The other prisoner gave a fierce tug, and Tanguy dropped the little medallion, which he had still been holding. The prisoner pounced on it.

"What's this?" he asked.

"A medallion. Gunther gave it to me to remember him by."

"Oh no, it belongs to me. I'm his heir. I've got a witness—"

"He asked me to keep it in memory of him," Tanguy protested in a tired voice. "You know very well it's mine. Please—"

"No, it's mine, it's mine—"

Tanguy went back to his bunk. There were only two of them to share it now. Dawn was breaking, and gray light showed through the barrack windows. The siren wailed, and the first hymns were relayed over the loudspeakers. Tanguy shivered and got up again. Mathias shook his hand silently, and Tanguy thanked him. Those who had died during the night lay in the doorway. The furnace chimney showed signs of life: a thin thread of smoke was spiraling up into the sky.

PART TWO

Shattered Illusions

"It must be hard to live with nothing
but one's knowledge and memories,
deprived of all hope."

ALBERT CAMUS: *La Peste*

Shattered Illusions

I

TANGUY sat in the train, his forehead pressed against the carriage window, and watched the German countryside slip past. He had not yet completely recovered his sight; but thanks to a special pair of glasses, he was beginning to distinguish objects with reasonable clarity. Sadly he considered this war-scarred landscape. Everywhere there were ruins, and long lines of refugees fleeing from the Russian Zone, clutching their scanty possessions. Everywhere he recognized the same dumb, anonymous crowd that had no real understanding of this immense disaster which had overwhelmed them. Every half-shattered station along the line swarmed with them, thrown back before the tide of the Russian advance. Skeletal children ran up to the train and stretched out sticklike arms to travelers who themselves had come from concentration camps. They ran after the train when it was pulling out, crying: *"Ein Stück Brot, bitte! Brot! Brot!"* ("A piece of bread, please! Bread! Bread!") The ex-prisoners gave them little, and sometimes even shouted insults at them.

127

Tanguy said nothing. He had distributed the contents of his Red Cross parcel as they left Berlin. Now there was nothing left for him to do but contemplate an endless panorama of suffering and destruction. He could not even weep for it: he felt spiritually and emotionally empty. Gunther's last words haunted him: *"In war there are neither conquerors nor vanquished: only victims."*

He thought, yet again, of the young German: indeed, his mind was constantly on Gunther. It was something deeper than an obsession; it was the loss of a part of himself. He tried to turn his mind to other things, but failed. He thought of the last months he had passed in the camp, days spent struggling against almost certain death. He remembered the final week before the liberation, when he lay on his bunk, indifferent, waiting for death, though the guns of freedom were thundering closer and closer. He had a vague recollection of a mysterious hand that pushed bowls of soup at him and saved him from dying; and then there had been the accident, though how it had happened he did not know. He thought of the moment at which he had lost his sight.

Then he recalled the delirious joy of liberation, the Russian soldiers who hugged him while he cried helplessly. Finally, he thought of the moving memorial service. As the youngest prisoner he had put a floral wreath on the site of the gaschamber, while all those left in the camp stood round and paid a last tribute to their dead comrades. Then the camp guards were shot, standing where Tanguy had placed the wreath, after being tried by a jury of seven ex-prisoners. Already it all seemed immeasurably distant to Tanguy. Now he was heading for Paris—this would be his second visit

—and Spain, which he was about to rediscover after seven years' absence. He had left Madrid at the age of five one cold night in 1938; he was returning in the summer of 1945, and how many years older was he?

The train reached the French frontier. Tanguy had a confused impression of an excited crowd shouting and waving flags and streamers. A band struck up the *"Marseillaise."* Tanguy's eyes were aching. He got up as the train stopped— no longer in Germany, not yet in France—stirred by the thrilling notes of the anthem. But already the mayor of the first French village across the border was beginning his speech.

He began by saying what a moving occasion it was, and welcomed the exiles home in the name of their grateful country. "You may well have thought," he went on, his voice throbbing with emotion, "that France had forgotten you. In the name of every Frenchman, I can reassure you that you were, all of you, constantly in our thoughts. Today, as we welcome you back, we feel deeply shocked by your sufferings. We want to help you forget your unhappy memories—"

Tanguy sobbed quietly as he thought of Gunther and Misha and all those who were no longer there to hear these words. Who would remember them? The mayor's voice orated on: "We have conquered Fascism. Now our task is to build a better and a juster world—" Tanguy looked about him at the skull-like faces, the cripples on their stretchers. Were these half-dead creatures *conquerors?* He paid no further attention to the mayor's speech.

. . .

They reached Paris at midmorning. As soon as the train drew into the Gare d'Orsay they were greeted by a shouting, cheering crowd. Red Cross workers came bustling around the prisoners, treating them like spoiled children. Tanguy got out of the train. Then he saw a long line of women standing motionless on the platform, holding out photographs toward the returning deportees. Under each photograph was written a name and profession. Paul Levy-Strauss, 46, architect. Jean Marleau, 26, barrister. Silently Tanguy moved down the line, past each mute and uncomplaining proclamation of despair. He left the station without saying a word, escorted by a social worker. His only thought was to go back to his grandmother in Madrid. He was given two days' rest in Paris before beginning his journey again, and spent them sightseeing around the Arc de Triomphe and the Champs-Elysées, this time under more favorable conditions.

The Red Cross official who had been entrusted with Tanguy's repatriation took him to a certain Mme Lucienne, who ran a family *pension* in San Sebastian. She was an elegant old lady with white hair and kindly eyes, who welcomed Tanguy and made much of him. She knew very well without being told that he had much to forget; so she left him to himself, sparing him any questions that might have worried or irritated him. Tanguy was grateful for such kindness and tact. Some of his memories, those especially which were too raw and fresh still, he told her; and she listened patiently to his stumbling confidences without showing the least sign of boredom.

On his first evening in San Sebastian Tanguy went out for

a walk around the town. He was dazzled by the brightness of it all—the glittering street lamps, the magical flashing neon signs. He loitered along, gazing in one shop window after another, unable to believe that so many *things* still existed in the world. He grinned ecstatically at the sight of all the food-stuffs on display, telling himself that peace had come at last, and everything was going to be different now. He was going to be able to *live*.

He reached the beach known as La Concha, because of the seashells there. The light from the lamps was reflected in the water, and the moon scattered scraps of silver paper over the sea. White foam swept gently over the rocks as the waves rolled in. Tanguy was entranced. He climbed down onto the beach and walked along the sand, laughing out loud from utter happiness. He was so filled with happiness that he felt almost as though he would die of it.

Then he took a deep breath and turned back toward the *pension*. In the quiet night his footsteps echoed behind him. For the first time since his liberation, Tanguy really felt himself to be free. Spain and the sea had achieved this, and he blessed them for it.

Mme Lucienne was waiting for him in the drawing-room, reading a magazine. A small table lamp spread its subdued light around her, and softened her aged features. She smiled as he came in.

"How was the walk?" she asked.

"Lovely. I went along the river—I don't know what its name is—and the tide was coming in. There are some fine bridges across to the other side, aren't there? I went to La Concha, too. The sea was beautiful."

"What a lot you've seen! You'll know San Sebastian better than I do soon. It's a pretty town, isn't it?"

Tanguy nodded. "I love it. I saw all the shops, too. They've got everything there—hams, sausages, cheese, lovely clothes, everything! And there are so many lights everywhere!"

"Yes. The war has been over a long time here."

They sat in silence for a moment. Then Mme Lucienne showed him a letter in its envelope.

"I've got some news for you," she said. "Your grandmother doesn't live in Madrid any longer. She's moved to Barcelona, so that's where you'll be going—to rejoin her. She seems to be a very wealthy and distinguished lady. Does she know you're coming?"

"No."

"Well, in that case, you're going to stay here another week. The Red Cross has paid me for your board. You can spend your time getting to know the town a bit better and putting on a little weight. You look like nothing on earth at the moment."

Tanguy blushed and hung his head.

"Cheer up," said Mme Lucienne, "it's all arranged. Now off to bed with you. I'll undress you and tell you a story before you go to sleep."

Tanguy smiled. He found it funny that Mme Lucienne wanted to help put him to bed. He was twelve years old, and no one had ever helped him to go to bed before. All the same, he let her do it. When he was tucked in she told him a story. His mind was running on the sea, and he hardly heard a word she was saying.

At last she stopped, kissed him good-night, and said, with

her hand on the switch: "Would you rather I left one light on?"

He nodded, smiling. She bent over him and whispered softly: "What you have to do now is make yourself forget everything nasty you've seen. Two things to concentrate on —getting lots of sleep and putting on weight. All right?"

"All right," Tanguy said.

Tanguy lowered the carriage window and looked out at Mme Lucienne, who remained standing on the platform. She was wearing a gray dress and a little black hat, and seemed upset by his departure. He had spent the extra week with her, exploring, boating, wandering around the old port. He had even gone to the movies with her. Now he was leaving, and was on his way to find his grandmother in Barcelona. He had written to her, but so far no reply had come.

He put on a brave smile and shook Mme Lucienne's hand yet again. The whistle blew.

"Write to me!" she called. He nodded.

As the train sped on Tanguy stared, fascinated, at this vast, sun-scorched landscape with its ever-widening horizons. He told himself that this was *his* country, the land of his birth, and felt proud to belong to it. He looked at the rough, bare uplands and felt a thrill of excitement run through him. He sat in the corner of a first-class compartment, dressed in fine new clothes; several newspapers and magazines rested on his knees, but he had not even opened them. All he could think of was the wonderful fact that all his troubles were at last over, that peace had come in the end. He was going to begin a new life in peace and happiness. He tried, vainly, to picture his grandmother. Then, tired of thinking, he let himself be rocked by the rhythm of the train, and made no further effort to analyze his thoughts.

Tanguy stopped outside the block of flats and asked the concierge, a small, dark fat woman, whether this was where Mme de Bayos lived. The concierge was a voluble mine of information.

"Mme de Bayos?" she said, "but she's dead! She died three years ago. She lived on the second floor, in fact she owned the block. It's been taken over by a big company now—" She broke off, and said in a different voice: "Look, who are you? What do you want?"

Tanguy tried to summon up a smile. He felt very tired, and his one desire was to go to sleep. He hardly knew what was happening.

"Nothing," he said, "I want nothing."

"Are you related to her?"

"I'm her grandson."

"The one who was in the concentration camp?"

"Yes," he said.

"Holy saints! The poor old lady! How she must be suffering now! If you only knew how much she told me about you! Everybody discussed you, you were our main topic of conversation here— Do come in for a minute. I'd be so pleased if you would. Come in and lie down, get a little rest."

Tanguy followed her. He heard little of what she was saying, but he liked hearing her talk. More than anything else in the world he needed to give himself at least the appearance of no longer being alone. He went into the concierge's cubbyhole and sank down in a chair. The concierge sat across from him and held his hands while she talked.

"I was in service with your grandmother in Madrid. I saw you born—you were a sweet little baby, you know. My father was concierge in your grandfather's townhouse there. He was a real man, your grandpa was, really distinguished. Oh, you come from a good family, all right, make no mistake about that. He was the richest, most handsome, most intelligent man in Madrid, I reckon. Ah, the parties he gave! Enormous parties—and what money my Dad made in tips! There were two flunkeys at the door to announce the guests— But you're crying—what on earth are you crying about? Holy God, the suffering you must have gone through out there! It was all your mother's fault. Politics! Politics! A lot of good her politics did her. Now, now, cheer up, or you'll have me crying too. To see you in such a state as this, though, who ever would have dreamed it, dear God? Your grandfather would have died of shame if he'd foreseen that one day his grandson would come and cry in his concierge's lap. *Santa Maria del Pilar!*"

"It doesn't matter," Tanguy said. "I'm all right now. Have you any news of my mother?"

"She passed through in 1942 with a French convoy, on her way to join the British. She'd dyed her hair. But since then we've heard nothing. Absolutely nothing. You poor child— what can I do for you?"

"Nothing, thank you," Tanguy said. "Nothing at all."

But he was wondering in an agonized way just what he was to do himself. He had become a kind of foreigner in his own country, with no known destination and no one to turn to. He had no point of contact with the distinguished family whose splendor this concierge boasted of; he no longer belonged to it. He sat there opposite the fat little woman, twisting his fingers nervously and wondering what to do.

"If I was you," she said, "I'd go to the police. They'll take care of you some way or other—they can't let you wander about the streets. Would you like me to come with you?"

"No, thank you. It's very kind of you to offer to, all the same. Good-by."

"Good-by, young sir. God knows I feel bad seeing you left on your own like this—"

"Thank you," Tanguy said, and walked slowly out of the building without looking back. He was scarcely even surprised by what had happened. He strolled across well-laid-out boulevards and thought what fun it would have been to explore Barcelona. Then he made his way to a police station. He had to wait sitting on a bench for hours. Beside him an old man was delousing himself. Whenever he found a particularly big louse he gave a disgusting little cluck of satisfaction.

2

THE DUMOS ORPHANAGE AND REFORMATORY, Tanguy read. He clutched his little green case more tightly. The policeman with him rang the bell. The peephole in the middle of the heavy door was opened, and a pale face appeared.

"What do you want?"

"I've got a new one for you."

"What about the admission order?"

"Here it is." The policeman handed it over, and the door opened. Tanguy found himself facing a monk in a black habit, a small, thin man with expressionless eyes. He dismissed the policeman brusquely, and beckoned Tanguy to follow him. Tanguy did so, and found himself in a cramped little office with a window that looked out over a vast tree-filled park. The Brother sat down at a typewriter, and Tanguy told him his name, age, and the names of his parents.

"What was your last address?"

Tanguy hesitated, then said: "San Sebastian."

"How long did you reside there."

"A week."

"And your address before that?"

"A concentration camp in Germany."

The Brother raised his dull eyes and stared at Tanguy, who at once sensed his hostility, and tried to find a cause for it.

"Are you Jewish?" the Brother asked.

"No."

"Communist?"

Tanguy felt strongly tempted to grin at this, but merely said "No" again.

"Then why were you interned?"

"There was a war on," said Tanguy, disgusted. He could think of no better answer. All these questions were making him impatient, and he began to wonder what they implied.

"You're not in France now," the man in the cassock said. His voice was flat and dull. "We give your kind of scum some discipline here. You'll stick to the rules if you know what's good for you. Otherwise—"

He left the threat hanging in mid-air. Tanguy remained unmoved. He picked up his case and followed the Brother across the park, and up a big flight of steps. The Center stood at the top. Tanguy walked in miserable silence. The noise of the city outside sounded dead and muffled, as if heard in a dream.

They came out in a big square treeless courtyard, surrounded by Spanish-style benches. Children were seated on these benches or standing about talking. They all had their heads close-shaven and wore the same uniform—khaki shorts and a collarless shirt, with espadrilles on their feet. The Brother stopped at the entrance to the courtyard. Two heavily built boys stood there, each with a stick in their hand.

"Here's a new arrival," said the Brother. "Have him taken down to the barber and shaved."

"What dormitory is he going to?"

"B. 11."

Tanguy watched his hair fall under the razor. The barber was a very thin boy, with yellowish eyes and the wary look of a hunted animal.

"Are you the German?" he asked suddenly.

"I've come from Germany, if that's what you mean. I'm not German myself."

"What have you got in that green case?"

"Clothes, a few books—"

"Nothing to eat?"

"Well yes—some fruit and bread and a little condensed milk—"

"What kind of fruit?"

"Bananas and oranges, and one or two tangerines."

"Dibs on the skins."

"What?"

"I said, dibs on the skins."

"What do you mean?"

"I mean that I've spoken for those skins first. You can't give them to anyone else. Understand?"

"You eat the skins?" Tanguy asked.

"Of course. They're very nourishing. Orange skins have lots of Vitamin B in them. Tangerines are even better. They use them to make vitamin pills. Think of it—vitamins in tangerine skins! Funny, isn't it?"

There was a short silence. The "barber" had finished his job. Tanguy got up, smiled, and stretched out his hand to this thin boy who had just shaved his skull bare.

"My name's Tanguy," he said.

"Mine's Antonio Maderas. But everyone calls me The P."

"Why?"

"Because I have—" and the boy said something that sounded like "P-lipsy."

"What's that?"

"Attacks. Fits. I faint, and fall down and bite my lips, and mess myself. You know?"

"Of course. Epilepsy. I have had attacks too, I still have them. But not epilepsy, something else."

The P. stared at Tanguy admiringly. "What a lot you know!" he said.

Tanguy shook his head.

"Do you know how to write?"

"Why, yes."

"Would you write a letter for me? It's to my sister. She's in another Training Center. She sent me a letter, but I don't know how to answer it."

"You mean you can't write?"

"No."

"Can't anyone write here?" Tanguy asked.

"Brother Rouge's secretary can, but you have to bribe him. I haven't got any family, so no one sends me parcels. I haven't anything to give away except my rations, and I don't want to do that. You've got to eat to live in this place, especially if you're ill."

"I'll write your letter for you."

"You're a nice guy," The P. said, gratefully. He hesitated, then added: "Would you like to be my friend?"

"Why shouldn't I?"

"I mean, would you like to go halves over everything?"

"I don't understand," Tanguy said.

"I give you half of everything I get, and you do the same for me."

Tanguy considered this. He watched The P. as he packed away the scissors and clippers; and thought about his illness.

"I don't get any parcels," The P. repeated. "Since I'm the barber, the delinquents give me something to eat every Thursday—that's when I trim them. But no one wants to go halves with me. It's only the delinquents who go halves anyway. The orphans never share anything, they haven't got anything to share. But it's nice to go halves with somebody. It makes you feel less lonely. Understand?"

"Of course I do. I'll go halves with you, if you like."

"Shake on it?"

"All right." Tanguy, smiling, shook hands with The P. "Now spit on the ground and say: 'The first one who breaks his promise is a traitor.'"

Tanguy did so. His new friend's eyes gleamed in a most extraordinary way, and he began to chatter wildly and irrelevantly about anything that came into his head. At last he said: "You have to go to the clothing-store now. Take the food out of your case. I'll keep it for you. The chaps in the clothing-store would confiscate it. You'll find me here after you're through with them."

Tanguy did as his friend suggested. When he had drawn his new clothing-allotment he came back to the courtyard and found The P. waiting as he had promised. They found a quiet corner, sat down, and began to eat. The P. had a curious way of dealing with oranges. First he sucked the juice out of them; then, when they were dry, he tore them open, folded them double, and ate them skin and all, as though they were sandwiches. Tanguy could not bring himself to eat the skins, so The P. had them all. They sat and stuffed themselves in silence. Gradually some of the other children gathered round. They said nothing; merely stretched out their hands. At last one of them addressed Tanguy.

"If you give me something, I'll let you have something back on Thursday."

Tanguy looked at the boy who was about fifteen, with heavily lined features that made him seem twice his age. He wore an expression that Tanguy interpreted as indifference but was, in fact, contempt.

141

"Here," said Tanguy, and held out a piece of bread. The P. stopped him with an abrupt gesture.

"Don't give him anything," he said. "You'll never get it back. He's a dirty cheat. He says the same thing to everyone, but he never gives away a thing."

"I don't mind. I'm not giving it to him because I want something back in exchange, but because he's hungry."

A voice called out: "I'm hungry, too!" Others joined in the chorus: "I'm starving!" "I'm an orphan!" "I'm a charity boy—no one sends me anything."

Tanguy got up. The clutching, outstretched hands made him feel sick; and the expressions on the faces stirred up far too many unpleasant memories. He kept what few scraps of food he had left and walked away. The children followed him, pleading and cajoling, asking for a piece of bread, only a little piece, or, as a last resort, the skins from the fruit.

It was Sunday. Tanguy would not have realized the fact unless The P. had told him. That was why the children were hanging about the courtyard all day. Leisure merely made them conscious of their hunger. They talked about food, and women, and freedom. They could be divided into two categories: "Charity Boys" and "Court Orders." The first were orphans or children of delinquent parents. The second were themselves juvenile delinquents, sent to the Training Center as a punishment. After six months or perhaps a year of "corrective training" they were released. They called it getting their ticket. Orphans and delinquents lived together and led exactly the same type of existence.

The P. pointed out to Tanguy a beautiful, very delicate little boy who had murdered his father. Tanguy found this hard to believe. The youthful parricide's name was Firmin. He would spend his entire adolescence in the Center, and afterwards be transferred to prison. He was sixteen, and had an enchantingly angelic smile. It was impossible to believe there was anything inherently wicked about him. Tanguy went over and spoke to him.

"Why do we have to spend all day in the courtyard?" he asked, as an excuse for getting into conversation. The boy was standing alone, very much on the defensive. When he heard this question, his eyes glittered like a snake's.

"Have I asked you what time it is?"

Tanguy hardly knew what to reply: he stammered: "I'm sorry. I was only trying to be nice. Really I didn't mean to annoy you—"

"Oh, you didn't?"

"No, really I didn't."

"In that case be really nice and f— off."

And as Tanguy still hesitated, Firmin repeated: "I told you to f— off! Don't you understand *anything*?"

Tanguy went away miserably to find The P. He would have liked to make some kind of contact with Firmin, and could not understand why Firmin had refused his overtures. Then he decided that he, Tanguy, must have looked silly. All new arrivals, anywhere, look silly.

Life in the Center was regulated by the Brother's whistle. The commands given by this instrument had to be obeyed with instantaneous alacrity. After each blast the Brother would add: "Last boy in line gets two days without pudding!" or "Last boy up, three days without bread!" The boys fell over each other in their hurry. The ones at the rear scrimmaged and fought and dug their elbows in each other. Once lined up they were forbidden to talk. They had to fold their arms and keep a yard's distance apart from the boy in front and the one behind. Between these silent files were stationed the squad leaders, mostly convicted juvenile delinquents. The Brothers chose the strongest young toughs they could find: squad leaders were empowered to punish the rank and file—for instance, by striking them or docking their rations. The boys were as much at their mercy as they were at the Brothers'. The squad leaders were the only boys who were allowed to have an ordinary haircut instead of the weekly shave.

There were various types of punishment employed. One favorite consisted of being deprived of bread for a week, and having to eat all meals during that period on one's knees. Another involved doubling around the courtyard. This was known as the Relay Race. The Brother and the squad leaders placed themselves at strategic points around the courtyard and made those undergoing punishment run fast and avoid cutting corners. As they passed by they were slashed about the legs with supple chestnut-switches. In addition to this, those who were on punishment drill were deprived of their parcels, and the squad leaders ate the contents instead. For this reason the squad leaders kept a sharp look-out for any misdemeanor, and issued punishments with the sole intention of getting hold of their victims' parcels.

The Center was well guarded. Every gate or door had its sentry, and high walls stood between the boys and freedom. In addition, the Brothers had devised a kind of whipping-boy system which turned all their charges into potential sneaks and stoolpigeons. Every boy had two others "responsible" for him and they were severely punished if their "ward" scaled, or attempted to scale the wall.

Despite all these precautions, however, several boys did succeed in getting away, though they were almost always recaptured. Sometimes they were brought in by the police several days after their break. When this happened they were publicly flogged. In the evening the Brothers would take the fugitive and set him with his face to the courtyard wall, his wrists pinioned by big staples set in the brickwork for that purpose. Then they proceeded to flog him. In the silent dormitories the other boys could hear the horrible shrieks of the victims enduring this treatment. They howled like wounded animals, yet the howls were interspersed with childish sobbing. Sometimes, too, if the fugitive had been a delinquent, he would hurl frightful and obscene insults at his tormentors. With each oath the Brother's fury would increase. Blows would rain on the boy's head and legs, sometimes even on his genitals. If the cane broke, the Brother would kick his victim, or beat him with clenched fists. Brother Antonin had actually torn off a boy's ear; Brother Armando had, in another case, brought on a cerebral hemorrhage which nearly cost the victim his life.

Tanguy kept quiet, not daring to surrender completely to the feelings of horror and despair that rose in him at such outrages. He shut his eyes and tried to sleep. But it was impossible; the floggings took place in the cloister immediately beneath the dormitories. From their beds the boys could hear the Brother's hoarse panting and distinguish clearly every curse, every sob uttered by his victim. Some of the older

145

hands kept statistics. The record was held by Brother Rouge: two hundred and ten strokes.

3

THE boys slept on mattresses laid out on the floor, two to a mattress. They only had one blanket between the two of them, and slept in their clothes. During the night the bigger of the two would pull the blanket off his companion. Tanguy was lucky; he shared his mattress with a sound sleeper.

Nevertheless he found it hard to sleep. He lay awake for long hours, his mind running feverishly over both his past and his present existence. He had never felt hatred before in his life; but he found himself hating these Brothers with incredible intensity. Indeed, the violence of his feelings terrified him. He knew that if he had had the strength he would have strangled every one of these cassocked monsters with his bare hands. He would not have felt one shred of pity for them.

Tanguy was familiar enough with the rigors of concentration camps; but they were a product of wartime conditions. When the Germans murdered their prisoners they were at least faithful to their own terrible principles. They showed some consistency in their sadism. But these Brothers went to Mass every morning, and even made the boys act as acolytes.

They had the effrontery to expound the Gospels to them, and Tanguy detested this revolting hypocrisy. Sometimes in chapel he wanted to shout his disgust aloud. He asked himself how they dared behave in this way, why they did not die of shame. Yet Tanguy had learned never to be surprised by anything. He contented himself, as a gesture, by never communing at Mass. He was not going to play the Brothers' own game. Most of the boys took Communion every morning to get in their good books. Some of these had never made their First Communion, others did not even know if they had been baptized.

Tanguy had once more lost all hope. In Germany he had clung to the belief that with peace he would return to a better life, and this belief had sustained him till the end. Now he had no more hope for the future: the peace had come, and brought with it a world still more unjust than what had gone before. Tanguy went on living like an automaton; he had lost all urge to survive, his only activity was the storing up of hatred, a hatred so vast that it threatened to engulf him.

The Brothers kept the boys in constant terror of the whistle which ruled their lives. They did not even get them up at a fixed, regular hour in the morning, but tried, on the contrary, to catch them out by calculated irregularity. They would tiptoe into the dormitory; and then a long, sudden blast on the whistle would jerk the wretched sleepers out of bed, shivering with fear and cold.

"Last boy in the showers, a week without bread and recess!"

The boys jostled each other in frantic haste. Sometimes one of them, in the general confusion, would forget his towel; but he never dared go back for it in case he was caught.

The morning shower was an institution which gave the Brothers peculiar pleasure. At the first blast of the whistle the boys stripped in a dark corridor, lit only by two skylights. There they waited, naked, hugging their arms round themselves. At the second blast of the whistle one lot would proceed to the showers, while the rest waited in the chill dawn air, their teeth chattering.

Once under the shower, they had to stand there while icy water hissed down over them, not moving till the Brother gave them the word. They had to make a show of soaping themselves as well. The Brother strolled along between the cubicles with a strap in one hand. The showers had no doors, and he would, without warning, use the strap on any boy he chose. It left purplish welts on their wet skin, hurting excruciatingly, bringing tears to the eyes. The Brother tried to strike the most sensitive parts of the anatomy, especially the ears and calves. The victims howled with pain, while the Brothers laughed heartily.

"You wet little hen! What a sight you are!" they would say. "Come on, soap yourself properly. What about your ears?" (Another slash with the strap here.) "Come on, now, hurry up! *Soap your ears!*"

When this happened to him, Tanguy could only concentrate all the hate and contempt he felt in his expression. One day Brother Rouge managed to hit his ear with the strap. Tears sprang instantaneously to Tanguy's eyes, but he pretended to have felt nothing. Brother Rouge had had no reason to hit him at all; he had simply done it to amuse himself, shouting "Hurry up!" as he wielded the strap.

Tanguy kept on at exactly the same speed. He took a private

pleasure in defying Brother Rouge, who was a young, lame bespectacled man, and almost illiterate. These Brothers were never ordained priests; their order was entirely recruited among the lowest social classes, and the majority of them entered it for much the same reasons as certain other young men had joined the S.S.—as an outlet for their overwhelmingly brutal instincts. Tanguy had no liking for Brother Rouge, and the feeling was fully reciprocated.

"I told you to hurry up!" Brother Rouge said, and the strap curled round Tanguy's knees. Tanguy had to make a vast effort of self-control to prevent himself yelling out loud. He felt himself flush, then go pale, but did not budge.

"Are you trying to make a fool of me?"

Blows rained down on the boy. Tanguy dropped the scrap of soap he was holding, slipped on it, and fell. His forehead struck the floor. He put up his hand to his head and drew it away covered with blood. Brother Rouge was cursing angrily and incoherently.

"Bastard! Little shit! Want to be obstinate, eh? I'll teach you to be obstinate, you filthy little turd, you bolshie Communist! Don't believe in God, eh? Play your devil's tricks, would you? *Shit!*"

Each epithet was accompanied by another stroke of the strap, and Brother Rouge was by now out of breath. Tanguy lay there, half-choking, tears starring his eyes as the strap seared his jerking body. But he did not cry. On the contrary, a kind of monstrous pleasure filled him. He fed on this display of rage, and felt himself the stronger of the two. He knew that the Brother, in the depths of his heart, was afraid of him, and that this fear was directly responsible for his hatred.

149

Suddenly such an uprush of loathing possessed Tanguy that it dizzied him. He got up, his face livid under its bloodstains, his body striped with purplish welts, and faced the Brother.

"You'd like to kill me, wouldn't you?" he shouted. "Go on. Kill me. What's stopping you? Your Christ? Your Christian charity? Well, say something, can't you? You know what I think of you, and it scares you stiff. If anyone here's a shit it's you, and that goes for the rest of you as well. Untouchable, protected shits, a pack of thieves and murderers who go to Mass every morning—"

Brother Rouge recoiled, the blood draining from his face. Then he advanced on Tanguy once more, and instinctively the boy threw up his hands to protect himself. Blows rained on his naked body, and a sudden pain shot through his head, numbing him. Finally, a violent kick in the kidneys made him lose consciousness.

He spent five days in the infirmary. When he was discharged he still had a lump on his skull and bruises all over his body. When Brother Rouge saw him reappear, he at once ordered him to double round the courtyard till further orders. Tanguy did as he was told. For the first two or three times round it was not too bad, but slowly he felt himself turning giddy, and the walls quivered as he looked at them. Hunger tore at his guts, and sweat ran down his forehead and trickled under his armpits. But still he ran on, gritting his teeth, determined not to faint. Despite himself he trembled violently every time he passed the Brother, who stood there with a stick in his hand.

Yet, for some reason, he did not strike Tanguy, whose

punishments were indeed impressive enough already. He was condemned to eat all meals on his knees for a month; to go without bread for a week; and to kneel for an hour before going to bed, also for a month. In consequence his whole existence became a kind of embodied punishment, and yet this left him curiously indifferent. He suffered, certainly, but his suffering was eclipsed by hatred. Often he asked himself why he had been born, whether he would not do better to kill himself. But he knew he would never have the courage. He bore his new troubles without uttering a word of protest. He wanted neither help nor sympathy from anybody. He tore up the one photograph he possessed of his mother, and this gesture took on a symbolic significance for him.

As for The P., he and Tanguy were no longer "going halves." In fact, all The P. had wanted was to get his hands on some of the food Tanguy brought in as a new arrival. Still, Tanguy bore no grudge against him; he was a poor creature, sick and starved and more to be pitied than anything else. Tanguy was almost glad to be rid of him, since at the moment he had no desire for friends or even chance conversation. He only wanted to be left alone.

After the incident in the showers the squad leaders were watching him all the time, and Tanguy knew it. He made considerable efforts not to give them any excuse to punish him. He observed all the rules, and was perpetually alert for trouble. He knew they were trying to make life as hellish for him as they could, and was ready to protect himself in any way open to him. Sometimes he was overcome by exhaustion and indifference, most often when he was thinking about Gunther. At night, while the other boys slept, Tanguy knelt

on the floor, absorbed by his recollections of the one person
he had truly loved. He remembered every feature, every
gesture, almost every word Gunther had ever spoken to him.
With these memories a heavy weight seemed to penetrate
him, and he bowed his shoulders beneath an invisible burden.
His struggle seemed meaningless. What reason had he for
staying alive?

Gunther.

On the evening before his death Gunther had put into his
hand the one object of value he still possessed; they had
passed that last night waiting for the end that, agonizingly,
was delayed for many long hours; and then another prisoner
had snatched from Tanguy's grasp the only souvenir he could
ever hope to retain of his closest friend.

Tanguy no longer cried; he would never cry again. There
were times when he felt misery tighten his throat or stab at
his heart, and then he thought he was going to burst into
tears. But no tears came. Tanguy had exhausted his capacity
for crying, just as he had drained away his reservoir of hope.
There was no room left in his heart for anything but hatred
and rebellion. He detested everyone with fine impartiality.
He obliterated the past from his mind, and even wiped away
all memories of his mother's love because he did not wish to
see in her the enmity that he saw in all others—all but one, and
he no longer existed.

4

THE boys spent their day in workshops situated in the left wing of the building. These were leased by private businessmen, who found in the Center an admirable source of cheap and efficient labor. Furthermore, since the bulk of the inmates were minors, these "employers" only had to pay the Brothers a nominal daily wage for their services. The boys themselves got no money except a weekly five pesetas as "pocket money."

Tanguy was sent to join the polishers. This was the most unpleasant job of all, and was generally reserved for those undergoing punishment or would-be fugitives. The polishing was done in a cellar, where twenty boys worked under the orders of a foreman and a working-squad leader. Their job was to burnish pieces of metal. The machine-driven cylindrical brushes which did the polishing revolved at a dizzying speed, and gave off a revolting smell which turned Tanguy's stomach. Nearly all polishers, sooner or later, became seriously ill. They were in the cellar from 8:30 to 12:30 and 3:00 till 8:00 in the evening. During that time they were forbidden to talk or go to the lavatory, or even interrupt their work.

Tanguy's finger-tips were burned by the turning brushes and the heat of the worked metal. He tied one handkerchief round his head and another over his mouth. He worked in silence and tried to think of nothing all day long. He hated the Brothers with such intensity that he felt almost happy in the workshop, where at least he was left alone, and no demands

153

were made upon him except the exertion of his negligible strength and a certain degree of concentration.

This work had another great advantage as far as he was concerned: it stopped him brooding over his past. This was very necessary. Tanguy stupefied himself with fatigue in the way that other people do with wine. He tried to drive all memory of his brief past, all sad recollections of one beloved face, clean out of his mind. He never talked to anybody. His workmates decided he was an odd customer; the less perceptive ones told everyone he was off his head, a theory which Tanguy regarded with indifference.

The foreman was a kindly man called Mateo: tough, heftily built, with a square head and large black eyes. He had little liking for either the Brothers or his employers, and for this reason showed himself very willing to do the boys a good turn. He would cuff the squad leaders on the slightest pretext: to him they symbolized the Brothers' tyrannous regime. Mateo was a strong man, and when he hit anyone, he hit them very hard. He used to remark that the squad leaders were all little quislings, the Brothers were plain bastards, and the employers slave-drivers. He made no attempt to conceal his opinions, and proclaimed openly that he was a "liberal." The apotheosis of his liberalism would have been to murder every monk in the place if he got the chance.

Mateo was fond of Tanguy. He often sent him out on errands, to deliver pieces of polished metal or collect scrap. He used to wink at him and say: "If they keep you waiting at the other end we'll just have to put up with it, won't we?"

In this way Tanguy managed to get an occasional breather. He would lock himself in the lavatory and smoke the cigarettes he rolled from Mateo's butts. He had to keep on the *qui vive* while he smoked, and take care to clear the air afterwards. But those few moments alone with his cigarette, in the silence of the deserted courtyard (broken only by the distant rumble of machine-looms, stamping-presses, and polishers) gave him a real feeling of freedom.

Every day Mateo brought with him what he called his dinner. He ate it at 10:30 A.M. When he opened the packet he would call over one of the boys working under him and give him half of it. He made him eat it there and then. This done, he would turn to the squad leader, laughing, and say: "Tell *that* to bloody Brother What's-his-name. Do your duty, boy! Go on, tell him, and by God I'll flatten your face for you."

Mateo knew very well that the squad leader would not have the nerve to report the incident. Everyone, to some degree, admired Mateo, and there was no arguing with his strength.

Tanguy's "employer" was a very tall man, who wore perfume, and whose fingers were loaded with rings. He was always impeccably shaved and dressed, and spent much of his time nosing round the workshops because of an obsessional fear that the young delinquents might commit acts of sabotage. It was seldom, however, that he came down to visit the polishers: the cellar smelled too unpleasant. When he did turn up, he generally looked disturbed. He would smile nervously at the boys, but no one smiled back. He was simply ignored. To save face he would pick up one of the polished pieces and pretend to examine it carefully. Everyone knew he was scared of the polishers. The boys called him the *Gula,* which is Catalan for miser or greedyguts.

One morning, while Tanguy was at work, the emergency

siren sounded. The boys rushed out and soon learned what had happened. Someone working at a stamping-press had made a false movement. A piece of metal had jammed in the matrix, and he had tried to remove it by hand. Accidentally, perhaps through fatigue, he had touched the release gear; and the three-ton press had fallen with all its force on the poor child's hand. His agonized shrieks for his mother rang through the building.

Outside in the small courtyard by the workshops all the boys waited, their faces strained with anxiety. Then an ambulance arrived, and two male nurses in white smocks got out. They went into the stamping-shop, and a moment later the boy's screams stopped. He was carried out on a stretcher, his face ashy-white; he looked as though he were asleep. Tanguy had never seen a face so entirely colorless. There was an ominous silence as he passed, a silence heavy with unspoken thoughts. The ambulance roared off with a great wailing of sirens.

The *Gula* was there, with a doctor, the stamping-shop squad leader, Brother Rouge, and several of the boys. Tanguy went over to the group.

"He must have made the wrong movement," Brother Rouge was saying.

"Yes, yes, of course," the *Gula* said, vaguely. "Of course."

"It's a terrible business," said Brother Rouge.

"Appalling," said the squad leader, not to be outdone.

"Yes, yes, indeed," said the *Gula*, who seemed to be unwilling to admit what had happened.

"Was the boy in good health?" the doctor asked.

"Excellent," said Brother Rouge. "He was running around the courtyard last night."

Tanguy's temples throbbed. He was sunk in shame and disgust; he felt as though his head was going to burst.

"That's a lie!" he shouted. His teeth chattered as he spoke, and he was trembling with rage.

Every head turned in his direction. Brother Rouge became purple with rage. "Go back to your workshop!" he hissed at Tanguy, and to the doctor: "Don't pay any attention to him. He's a Communist. He was in a German concentration camp—"

"You're scared, aren't you?" Tanguy shouted. "You're afraid the doctor might learn the truth. Well, I'm going to tell him the truth, even if you kill me for it, even if you cut me in little bits!"

Brother Rouge turned furiously on the squad leader.

"Manolo," he said, "take this hysterical creature back to the polishing-shop."

With a violent gesture Tanguy threw off the hand that was about to descend on him. He dodged away quickly, saying: "Don't touch me! You disgust me! You disgust me!"

The doctor said: "Let him speak. He obviously has something to tell us."

He was a small, pale, bald man with glasses, who wore a well-cut gray suit and carried a leather briefcase. His words struck Brother Rouge and the squad leader dumb with astonishment. A silence grew and spread, with Tanguy as its center. He stood there, tears in his eyes, chest heaving with emotion.

157

"Speak up," said the doctor, not unkindly. "What's your name?"

"Tanguy."

"Do you promise to tell us the truth, and nothing but the truth?"

"Yes."

"You're not afraid to tell the truth?"

"Yes," Tanguy said. "Yes, I am afraid."

"Then why tell it?"

Tanguy hesitated. How could he have told this doctor that, since he was alone in the world, he had very little to lose by speaking up? How could he have said that when you have lost all hope of a just world you find courage to tell the truth by that very fact? How could he explain that when everything in which you believe has crumbled away men no longer have the power to terrify you, even though you may be only thirteen years old? In the end Tanguy merely said: "I don't care what happens. It's all the same to me."

"Are you a delinquent?"

"No."

"Why are you here, then?"

"I'm an orphan."

"Good. Well, what have you to say?"

"Don't take any notice of him!" screamed Brother Rouge. "He's a Communist. He'll make up a pack of lies. You can't listen to him—he's a Communist, I tell you!"

The doctor turned and stared at the Brother.

"How do you know he is a Communist?"

"The Germans interned him in one of their camps—"

"How old was he at the time?"

"Ten or eleven, I suppose."

"A Communist at eleven?" The doctor looked searchingly at the monk, who was stammering incoherent phrases to himself.

"He doesn't believe in God," he got out at length, "he holds nothing sacred—"

The doctor's expression changed to something very near contemptuous disgust. He remained silent for a long moment. At last he said: "How do you know all this?"

"He doesn't take Communion," said Brother Rouge.

"If he was in another place, he might act otherwise," the doctor replied. Then he turned to Tanguy, looked searchingly into his eyes, and said: "Now: talk."

Tanguy was sobbing. His first burst of indignation had ebbed away, leaving nothing but inarticulate exhaustion. With a tremendous effort he pulled himself together and spoke.

"The boy's name was Antonio Fuentès Mazos," he said. "He was fifteen and a half. He used to work on plastics—it was a much easier job. Last week he wanted to smuggle a letter out to his family to say he was starving and half frozen. He wanted his mother to send him a proper bedcover. I know that was what he said in his letter, because Fuentès can't write and I wrote his letter for him.

"He arranged to give this letter to a squad leader who he thought was a good friend of his. He'd promised this guy his weekly pocket money for a month to smuggle it out. The squad leader was going into the town and had promised to mail the letter for him. But instead he squealed on Fuentès, and the night before last Fuentès was flogged as a result. We could hear the flogging from our domitory, and we counted

159

the strokes. He got a hundred and ten. His back was all bruised and swollen. I saw it yesterday.

"Why did I see it? My comrades always ask me to help them here when anything's the matter. They think I know everything because I can read and write. I deal with their boils and cuts. I dressed Fuentès' back as well as I could, and rubbed a little oil on it as well. Fuentès told me he was having trouble with his eyesight, but unfortunately I couldn't do anything about that. He hasn't had anything to eat for two days as a punishment. For two days he has had to go on his knees in the dormitory, the refectory, everywhere.

"Brother Rouge told you he was running yesterday evening in the courtyard. He was; but he was running what we call the Relay Race. Do you know what that is? Brother Rouge and the squad leader who gave him the punishment stood in opposite corners of the court and lashed him round the legs with a long thin leather strap as he went past. We call that strap the Prairie Oyster because it revives your energy. Finally, Brother Rouge had Fuentès shifted from the plastics section to the stamping-press. The rest you know."

There was a long silence. Tanguy wiped his eyes dry. He had delivered this monologue in a neutral, emotionless voice. He felt detached from the whole episode, as he did also from the personal risk he was running. He knew in his bones that nothing worse could happen to him than what he had already endured; he knew, too, that it was extremely difficult to kill a child.

"Thank you," said the doctor. His voice was bleak and expressionless. "I shall now go and examine the boy and see whether he bears the marks you have suggested he should.

I shall also have his eyes tested. Unfortunately your unsupported testimony is not sufficient. I shall need a second witness to give your statement legal validity. Could you find such a witness for me?"

Tanguy considered this. Mentally he went through several names, but finally said: "I don't think so. They are all too scared."

"I understand. A pity."

A voice said: "I will be your second witness."

Tanguy turned round. It was Firmin, the sixteen-year-old parricide. He stared at Brother Rouge with a vicious smile of hatred that pulled down the corners of his mouth.

"Everything Tanguy has said is true," he confirmed. "What he hasn't told you is that he himself has been undergoing punishment for a month, and hasn't eaten bread for a week. He hasn't told you half the truth—"

Mateo, the foreman, broke in at this point. "I can support his story up to a point. I have heard the boys in my workshop discussing the case of young Fuentès, and what they said agrees with this lad's account."

The doctor said: "Your evidence is very important. You are an unprejudiced witness—you're not involved in the affair yourself. Your evidence is absolutely vital, be assured of that."

Brother Rouge exploded. "But everybody knows this fellow is a liberal!" he exclaimed. "He never goes to church—he doesn't even observe Easter—"

TANGUY was neither flogged nor punished for his out-spokenness. He was disconcerted by the silence which sur-rounded the affair. Brother Rouge now made a show of ig-noring his existence. Life went on as if nothing had happened. Fuentès came back after a while with his arm amputated, and was excused from all work. He told Tanguy that a doctor had come and questioned him and examined his back and legs. Tanguy began to wonder how the whole business would turn out in the end, and decided the Brothers must have got a fright. But all his theories foundered on a conspiracy of silence. The authorities pretended that Tanguy did not exist. This suited him very well; his only fear was that one day they would begin to take notice of him again.

Days turned into weeks, and weeks into months, with an endless round of work, chapel, meals, and recreation. Each day was almost identical to the one before and only a single clear memory remained to Tanguy: hunger. Hunger was the sovereign power in this tiny enclosed world, a tearing, animal hunger. The boys spent their leisure in talking about food and swopping imaginary menus. They only got two meals a day: they never ate meat or fish; instead they made do with a Catalan dish called *farinetas*, a kind of barley mash. At mid-day they got a tangerine and a hunk of bread; in the evening, bread alone. This bread was certainly not made with wheat. It was yellowish, tacky stuff, and was only palatable if ac-companied by copious draughts of water. The Brothers themselves had their own private kitchen, and enjoyed three courses at every meal: hors d'œuvre, fish, and meat. They had cakes and pastries baked for them, and Tanguy got an occasional glimpse of well-filled dishes. The smell of meat cooking was alone enough to give the boys stomach-aches.

The refectory was a vast hall. The tables were marble-topped, and the benches fixed to the floor. The kitchen orderly went down between them serving out *farinetas*, followed by two boys wheeling the big cauldron known as the "fish-pond." Each boy on the inside bench had to hold out his own mess-tin and that of the boy sitting opposite him. The ration was one full ladleful to each mess-tin, and catching it was a skilled occupation. The orderly hurried along and dished out the food as fast as he could, and it was necessary to do some clever juggling with the mess-tin so as not to lose a drop. Sometimes, when the orderly passed a boy he disliked, he deliberately burned his fingers with a splash of hot *farinetas*, thus making him drop his mess-tin. Then the orderly would rap him over the head with his ladle and leave him without any food at all.

There was a black market in food. Those who were sent parcels resold part of the food they contained. Tanguy always spent some of his Saturday pocket money in this way. One day he bought a piece of cheese, an odd make with bluish veins in it: "a French cheese," he was informed. He hid it away in his shirt to eat that evening. The idea of eating French cheese tickled his fancy. He told himself that this cheese symbolized liberty.

That night he waited till his bedfellow was asleep before producing his booty. This time he wanted to share it with no one else. He ate it slowly to prolong the pleasure it gave him, delighted at the thought that it was French cheese he was eating. He even ate the silver paper in which it was wrapped: The P. had told him that silver paper contained elements of Vitamin C. He told himself that, after all, silver paper wasn't so bad; you only needed to get used to it.

The "delinquents" got their parcels every Thursday. When Thursday came, Tanguy took a large sheet of paper and made a kind of bag out of it. Then he went round angling for a bargain. Sometimes the owners of parcels became irritated and said "No" to everyone. Generally they were agreeable to Tanguy, though, since he knew how to write and they all to some degree made use of him. More particularly, he was the one who gave them some kind of first-aid. So they gave him little pieces of bread, or half a dozen raisins, or perhaps a quarter of an orange. He collected the skins very carefully: he had got used to eating them, and was now even somewhat addicted to their flavor. But banana skins he still found it a little difficult to get down.

On Thursday evening those who had received parcels did not eat their *farinetas*, but passed it on to the orphans who had no one to send them anything from outside. So every Thursday Tanguy gobbled up five or six helpings of this barley mash. It always made him ill, generally with stomach-ache and colic. Yet he could not bring himself to refuse it when it was offered. He sweated as he ate it. He became as red as a lobster and swelled up like a balloon. Sometimes he felt disgusted with himself in the very act of eating. He told himself it was shameful to stuff his belly in this way with his comrades' leavings. But he had already learned the hard way that human dignity cuts very little ice under the pressure of certain abnormal conditions, and that it is better in the long run to stay alive, whatever the cost.

Another unpleasant memory Tanguy retained of the Center was its "recreations." Games were compulsory. The boys were divided into teams, and each team had its own playground. There were also "games leaders." The boys were made to play a kind of tag: the team was split into two "sides," and the playground marked off with two chalk lines. They tossed for ends, and one side took the top end, one the bottom. The captain of the team at the bottom end threw the ball to his opposite number, who then ran toward the other side and tried to hit one of its members as hard as he could. The game consisted in feinting and scoring "hits" on the one hand, and dodging the attacks on the other. If the player with the ball hit his adversary, the victim was "dead"; if he missed, he was out of the game himself.

The games leaders took advantage of this game to work off their personal grudges. They tried to hit their enemies either in the face or the kidneys. The balls were hard and solid, and a knock from one of them was extremely painful. Tanguy became expert in the art of dodging, being both nimble and nervous. Yet, even so, he hated the game, which sometimes brought tears to his eyes. The Brothers gave them only five or six minutes of recess in a full hour's "recreation." This was known as the "rest." During it long lines formed outside the lavatories, since it was forbidden to relieve oneself in the middle of a game. If by any chance some outside stranger paid the Center a visit, they had to pretend to enjoy playing games enormously—laugh, run fast, "put some life into it," and whip up the appearance of enthusiasm. Tanguy hated this kind of hypocrisy. He watched his exhausted, half-starved companions forcing themselves to laugh or cheer, and despised them for it.

To hate is a difficult accomplishment to learn; but Tanguy learned it at the Center. His natural inclinations were toward the affectionate; yet now he became solitary, misanthropic, and taciturn. He avoided close contact with his comrades, and only felt really at ease stupefying himself with hard work in the polishing-shop. Here he found his bearings again; his nerves unwound themselves and his features relaxed. He could even smile at his fellow workers. He was happy when Mateo sent him out to collect scrap metal, and he could shut himself in the lavatory and smoke a cigarette; he always thanked Mateo for this favor.

Tanguy learned more at the Center, especially with regard to sex. It was hardly surprising that these boys, being deprived of all feminine company, satisfied themselves with homosexual practices. Many of them changed beds at night while the rest kept a look-out. But what made these activities particularly repulsive was the shameless cynicism with which the delinquents flaunted their proclivities. They would make sniggering jokes about various boys' physical peculiarities, look their companions up and down with sidelong glances, and publicly praise the charms of their latest favorite.

The squad leaders did not even have to make approaches to the object of their desires: they simply commanded them. When two squad leaders took a fancy to the same boy, they played cards for him. The boy himself had no say in the matter.

The Brothers themselves had their "favorites," who constituted a kind of intermediary class between the rank and file and the squad leaders. They avoided much of the normal discipline, did not have their heads shaved, got food from the Brothers' private kitchen, were allowed to wander round the park, and, finally, were excused from working-parties.

Sometimes there were unpleasant incidents. The Brothers chose their "favorites" chiefly from Division A, which consisted of the youngest boys, between eight and thirteen. Sometimes things went very wrong, and the resultant scandals had to be hushed up as well as possible.

Once again Tanguy began to feel he was going out of his mind. This ubiquitous atmosphere of frenzied sexuality was a frightful strain on his nerves. His own budding virility was constantly needled by the talk that went on all around him. Wherever he went it was the same; he felt himself engulfed in a sea of absolute animality. He wept with rage at the feeling that in a physical sense he was becoming enslaved by his own urges, and his mind revolted against such a surrender. But the only answer he could see was to struggle against the urge and discipline himself.

6

THE Center was celebrating. The Bishop was going to come and lay the first stone of a new dormitory wing. The boys had had a new clothing-issue and had scrubbed themselves in the showers; but this time the Brothers had not beaten them. A strange febrile excitement flickered through the buildings and gathered in the courtyard. The Bishop was due to arrive at 10:30. A smell of potatoes and roasting meat had spread into every room in the place, and it gave Tanguy a belly-ache. The boys had been given special instructions to line the Bishop's path on his arrival and shout "Long live our Bishop! Long live the Pope!" At 9:15 they were already in place, standing there waiting with arms folded, their new clothes chafing them. One piece of news created a sensation: they were going to get two courses at dinner, first soup and then meat with potatoes. There was even to be dessert. Everyone became excited. But it was a hot, heavy, humid day, and by 11:30 the Bishop had still not arrived. The boys were tired of standing in the hot sun.

At last, at 12:15, the Bishop appeared. Three black cars climbed the lane which led to the college. The Bishop was in the second. Immediately the boys began to cheer him, and the Pope and Mother Church as well. He was a short, thickset little prelate, with a full-blooded complexion and expressionless green eyes. He scrambled awkwardly out of the car, hitching up his cassock as he did so. He wore purple gloves, and on one finger, over the glove, a huge amethyst ring. His small, puffy hands matched the rest of him. As soon as he had struggled free from the car, he began to make the sign of the Cross in the air in front of him. He walked with deliberate and leisurely dignity, bestowing condescending smiles on the boys as he passed. They cheered and clapped louder than ever.

Meanwhile several Brothers had rushed obsequiously forward and helped him off with his purple cope. They arrayed him in his pontifical habit, put the miter on his head and the crozier in his hand. The Bishop stood still while all this was going on, rather like a mannequin. When his vestments were on, he stalked over to the foundations of the new building and sprinkled holy water over them, chanting in Latin as he did so. As a final gesture he gave one of the biggest stones a tiny tap with a small hammer, and at this all the Brothers applauded. The boys promptly did the same. The Bishop held up his hand for silence.

"Beloved children," he began, "the loyalty which you have demonstrated to the pastor of this happy and generous city of Barcelona touches us deeply—" and at this point he launched into a long speech in praise of Barcelona and the generous benefactors it had produced, with a passing reference to the distinguished history of the Catholic Church in Catalonia "—a Church very close to His heart." Then he turned to the Center and the Brothers themselves—"those splendid monks who care for your bodies and souls alike. They turn you into men, h'r'm, perhaps, shall we say, a little against your will? Of course they sometimes have to beat you, and of course you resent it." He coughed. "Indeed, even crude metal would resent the blacksmith's stroke if it

169

were articulate; yet how proud it would become once it had
been forged into some object of beauty and value! And the
same, beloved children, is true of yourselves. . . ."

Tanguy listened in silence, wondering if the Bishop were
not perhaps having a little joke at their expense. But he
appeared to be quite serious. Tanguy felt sick with disgust.

When they all trooped into the refectory they were astonished to see china plates on the tables, each with a piece of
bread, an orange, and a tangerine on it. On every table there
stood two carafes of red wine. They sat down and began
applauding the cooks, who now brought in two huge cook-
ing-pots, one full of soup and the other of meat and potatoes.
Tanguy could trust neither his eyes nor his palate. He
had eaten his orange (skin and all) and now there was meat
to follow! Unconsciously he rubbed his hands.

The Bishop made a brief appearance in the refectory.
He tasted the food being served out and raised his arms to
heaven as if in ecstatic praise of its quality. The boys cheered
this little display. The Bishop was surrounded by well-dressed
gentlemen whose faces were fixed in permanent unctuous
smiles. Tanguy felt that if the truth were told there was very
little to make all this fuss over; but, not wishing to get into
a bad temper, he turned his mind to other things.

"It's disgusting," Firmin said.

Since their first unfortunate encounter Firmin had never
addressed Tanguy directly, and Tanguy was surprised at this
sudden remark.

"They make me sick," Firmin went on. "Did you see the
swine, with his great fat belly and his rings? That thing a

servant of Christ? Christ certainly feeds his servants well!"

"And us too, you know," Tanguy said. "Thanks to the Bishop we've eaten meat today. I've been here for three years, and that's the first time I've ever had meat."

Tanguy was not over-anxious to reveal his own private thoughts; he had learned to be suspicious of everyone and everything, and was very much on his guard.

Firmin said: "I'd rather have eaten barley mash and not seen a disgusting display like that. Don't you realize he didn't care two damns about us?"

"Why do you say that?"

"*Why?* For God's sake! That stuff about pig-iron, or whatever it was, *enjoying* being forged! Did you swallow that? It was too big a lump altogether. So was he, for that matter. He knows damned well what goes on here—not all of it, but a good deal. And he approves of it, can't you see? That finishes him as far as I'm concerned. Understand?"

"Yes," Tanguy said.

"Is that all it means to you?"

"No."

There was a silence. Firmin stood with his back resting against the wall, warming himself in the sun. Most of the other boys were doing the same. Some of them were eating; most of them were simply drowsing in the sunlight. Tanguy watched Firmin from the corner of one eye. The young murderer was scratching patterns with his foot on the dusty ground of the courtyard.

Presently, in a low voice, he said: "I'm thinking of going over the wall."

Tanguy's heart stood still. For a long time he had nursed

171

the same crazy idea. But all he said was: "They're sure to catch you."

"That's a risk that's got to be taken. If you don't take risks you don't get anywhere."

"It might be possible to get out of here," Tanguy said, "but what would you do then? No, they're bound to recapture you."

"Perhaps. But even if I only manage to spend three months at liberty, that's something they can never take away."

"They'll flog you for it, you know."

"You don't say. I've had some floggings in my time. I'm past feeling them any more."

Still Tanguy did not dare to reveal his own desires. But he felt now that Firmin was someone on whom he could rely. He made a tentative opening.

"It'd certainly be wonderful to be free again," he said.

Firmin looked at him and said: "You're a charity kid, aren't you?"

Tanguy nodded.

"You're nowhere near getting your ticket yet. You have to wait till you're twenty-one."

"I know that."

"How old are you now?"

"Sixteen."

"Only five years to go."

"It's a long time."

"If you want it to be," Firmin said.

Tanguy shivered with fear. He knew now that the thing had to be done, but still could not find the way. He looked at Firmin's classically beautiful face—the big greenish eyes

172

with their long lashes, the straight Greek nose, the full red lips. When Firmin smiled, he showed white and perfect teeth. He was tall and slender, and his beauty gave his face a certain feminine quality. But, in fact, there was in Firmin's character an extraordinary and dominant masculine streak.

Tanguy said: "Is it true that you killed your father?"

"Yes, it's true."

"Why did you do it?"

"He got on my nerves. He was always blubbing. Every time he had a skinful he came to look for me, and sniveled a lot of nonsense—'Firmin, my boy, my dear boy, you're my sole support! Give your old Dad a little money, boy, just a little'—and one day I felt I'd had enough of it."

Tanguy looked at the ground. He felt a tide of misery creeping through him. He tried, in vain, to ignore it.

"How long have you been here?" he asked.

"Oh, years."

"What did you do before the—accident?"

"I was pretty well off in a way. I knew I was attractive. My mother had always told me how good-looking I was. There are plenty of people who like good-looking boys—"

"But didn't you find that revolting?" Tanguy said.

"Of course I did, but no more revolting than anything else. Do you think it's fun to work as an unskilled laborer in a glass factory or a textile plant? Do you think it's fun being a stevedore?"

"You mean you—did things—with women? For money?"

Firmin grinned and nodded. "Not only women," he said.

Tanguy found difficulty in replying to this. He tried in vain to think of some friendly comment, realizing that Firmin

173

must have had an absolutely wretched childhood, but what he said in the end was: "Did you make a lot of money?"

"It varied. It wasn't always easy. The evenings were all right. Sometimes I was the only one in the family bringing in any money, though. That made it pretty rough."

Tanguy said: "Why wouldn't you speak to me the first day we met?"

"Oh, you were one of the Charity boys. They're nearly all bastards. Most of them end up spying for the Brothers. Besides, you had a parcel. I don't like it thought that I'm ready to be anyone's pal if they've got a parcel. That's a favorite dodge here. You saw The P. in action, didn't you? He works that trick with every new arrival—'going halves,' that crap. He helps them eat their food, and then fades out of their lives."

"And why are you talking to me now?"

Firmin said: "Because no one sends you parcels. And because you're a decent fellow."

No compliment could have pleased Tanguy more; he blushed with pleasure. But as he was about to ask Firmin another question he heard his name being called, and found out, to his great surprise, that he had a visitor. Wondering who it could be, he went off to the college parlor and was confronted with the little doctor he had talked to about Fuentès. They shook hands, and Tanguy sat down.

The doctor said: "I was determined to see you. You behaved very bravely after that deplorable accident which cost your friend his arm. Thanks to you, I was able to establish proof as to responsibility in the affair." He paused, and looked at Tanguy. "Unfortunately," he went on, "the inquest which I asked for has been canceled. I have received an official notification to that effect. I'm sorry, but there's nothing more I can do."

Tanguy smiled bitterly. "I understand," he said.

"There is something else I want to tell you. You don't belong here. If you can find some means of getting to Madrid, go and call on the Society for the Protection of Minors. This society runs some excellent Centers where you could study. I thought a note of introduction might not come amiss. Here it is. It's addressed to a lady who is a very old friend of mine, and at present holds the position of secretary to the society. She could help you a good deal."

Tanguy shook the little doctor's hand and carefully put the letter away. "Thank you," he said.

"It was no trouble," the doctor said. "Whenever I come to this place I feel morally guilty. Do you know what I mean? I'm being as frank with you as I can. You *must* get out of here somehow."

"I shall do my best."

"I wish you luck, then. If you get to Madrid I know you will find yourself in good hands. You have suffered a great deal, I think."

"A little," said Tanguy, after a moment.

"Yes, I can see that. Good-by, and once more, good luck."

Tanguy went back to the courtyard. He decided that there must be something more than mere coincidence about the doctor's visit following so immediately on his conversation with Firmin. He felt tempted to talk of Providence, but dis-

liked this word because the Brothers were very fond of mis-
applying it. He found Firmin where he had left him.

"Firmin," he said excitedly, "would you like me to come
with you when you make your break?"

"Surely I would. What's got into you all of a sudden,
though?"

Tanguy told Firmin about the doctor. Then he asked him
if he had a plan. Firmin said he had.

"What sort of a plan? For when?"

"For tonight. We've got to take advantage of the Bishop's
visit. The squad leaders are all half drunk—they finished up
the wine. It's a unique chance. Now, listen—"

Firmin spoke in a level, neutral voice. He never looked
directly at Tanguy while he was talking, and scarcely moved
his lips.

"You often get these attacks of yours, don't you?" he asked.

Tanguy nodded.

"What do they do with you when that happens?"

"They take me to the infirmary."

"Could you pretend to have a seizure—put on an act for
them? It'd be bound to work. If they're used to your having
real ones they won't suspect a fake."

"All right. I'll try."

Firmin said: "You'll fix it so that you 'pass out' between
The P. and me. We'll hoist you up and carry you. I'll make
sure that it's The P. who helps me. He's got privileges, and
the squad leaders trust him. They'll simply tell us to cart you
off to the infirmary. When we're the other side of the park I
shall say I'm tired, and we'll put you down for a moment.
Then I'll get out my knife and threaten to kill The P. if he

makes a sound. We'll tie him up and leave him behind a tree. Then—over the wall we go!"

"Fair enough. But what'll you do if the squad leader tells you to put me down and sends someone else instead of you?"

"Nothing. No harm'll be done, except that you'll have the trouble of faking up a nervous attack. We'll just have to wait for another opportunity. But my guess is that the whole thing'll go off according to plan."

"Right," Tanguy said. "Where's The P. now?"

"Up at the far end of the wall, digesting his dinner by the look of it."

"I'll go over now."

"Better let me go first," Firmin said.

Tanguy's heart was beating fiercely. He watched Firmin strolling slowly toward The P., and waited a moment or two before following him. When he was almost abreast of Firmin he swayed and collapsed on the ground. He fell on a stone, and a sharp stab of pain ran through his back. He heard Firmin shouting "Give me a hand, P.! It's Tanguy—he's had another attack!"

Hands gripped Tanguy by armpits and ankles and lifted him off the ground. Whoever had his legs nearly let him drop again. He felt himself being carried to the end of the courtyard. Here his rescuers stopped. A voice asked what the matter was.

"The Boche. He had another attack."

"Not *again?* Oh, take him away to the infirmary, then. With any luck he'll kick the bucket this time. I'm tired of all these seizures of his."

Scared, Tanguy shut his eyes tightly, and wondered what would happen if The P. began to shout for help, or if a Brother saw them from his window.

"Wait a bit," he heard Firmin say, "I'm exhausted. Let's have a breather. Put him down."

Tanguy opened his eyes just as Firmin's knife flicked out, its point at The P.'s throat. He sprang to his feet, and Firmin tossed him a hank of stout cord.

"Tie his hands behind his back. Hobble his ankles. That's fine."

While this was going on The P. was babbling at Firmin in a frightened voice: "W-what are you going to do? You can't kill me—you're not going to kill me, say you're not! You mustn't go over the wall, *please!* If you do I shall be punished. . . . I'm ill, you can't do this to me—"

"Aw, knock it off," Firmin said.

"Is that everything?" Tanguy asked him.

"Wait a minute. I don't want him to shout the place down."

Firmin produced a much-chewed India-rubber ball from his pocket and stuffed it into The P.'s mouth.

"*So* sorry, dear boy," he said. "An emergency, you know."

Tanguy took to his heels, with Firmin close behind him. When they reached the wall Firmin helped Tanguy to scramble up on top of it.

"I can't jump, Firmin," Tanguy said desperately. "I'm afraid."

"You've *got* to."

"I can't. I'm going to break my leg. I'm scared."

"Land on your toes and bounce up like a ball. Off you go, now!"

Tanguy shut his eyes and jumped. When he hit the ground his whole body jarred. He felt his legs cautiously: no bones broken. Firmin jumped down and landed beside him. The street was deserted; dusk was falling. The two friends scampered off as though every policeman in Spain were at their heels. At last they paused, out of breath. Tanguy gulped in great mouthfuls of the air of freedom, half crying, half laughing. They crossed a main street as a streetcar passed by. Groups of people stood around on the sidewalks. The air was fresh and clean, and smelled of pharmacies and fried food.

7

THEY left the city by one of the Tibidabo roads, panting and worn out. Every time they saw a uniform, they hid. When the coast was clear they struggled on again as fast as they could. They ran in step, not talking and hardly ever stopping to rest. Soon they were in the open countryside, among kitchen gardens and orchards. It was nearly dark: the sky was still clear, but dusk had already obscured the landscape. At last they slackened their pace.

"They must be at evening service now," Firmin said.

Tanguy nodded. "They're bound to be looking for us. The P.'s in for an extra-special flogging, I should think."

"That won't do him any harm. Dirty little sneak—serve him right."

Tanguy was hungry. He stared into the orchards on either side of the road. But there were still a good many peasants working there, filling their handcarts with fruit. They wore big straw hats and black corduroy trousers.

"How are we going to feed ourselves?" he asked Firmin.

"I was just thinking about that. We'll beg some fruit off one of these men."

"I wouldn't have the nerve to. I'd feel ashamed."

"*Ashamed?* I suppose you wouldn't be ashamed of starving to death? All right, then. Wait here for me, by the roadside. If you see a police patrol, hide in that field somewhere."

Tanguy nodded, and sat down beside the road in the shadow of a big plane tree. Several cars purred past, their headlights shining. The air was as soft as silk, and heavy with sweet summer scents. Voices rose from the surrounding fields, and an atmosphere of almost majestic peacefulness enveloped the boy. I am free, he told himself. Free. Free. His eyes blurred with emotion. He sat and watched dusk spread peacefully over the countryside. He was so moved that he wanted to pray; yet to whom should he address his prayers? It was not the Good Lord, but Firmin who had saved him. And Firmin was most certainly not God.

He sat there and waited for a long time, and even began to wonder whether Firmin had not deserted him. Then he told himself that Firmin was a man, a real man, and that real men always keep their word. Firmin had promised to come back; one simply had to wait for him. And a few minutes later, sure enough, he reappeared, a wide grin on his face and his shirt bulging with booty.

"Well?" Tanguy asked him.

"I helped an old guy to load his barrow. He gave me a loaf, some apples, a can of sardines, half a liter of red wine, and twenty-five pesetas."

"How on earth did you manage that?"

"I told him my little brother was sick."

"Did he believe you?" Tanguy asked.

"Of course he did; why shouldn't he? Besides, it's true in a way. You *are* sick—with hunger."

They both burst out laughing. Then they resumed their march. They were hardly more than three miles outside the town, but it might have been thirty or forty, so deeply wrapped in peace was the countryside. They munched the apples as they walked. They sang, skipped along, almost dancing with pleasure and relief.

Firmin tossed an apple core into the hedge and said, laughing: "If The P. were here he'd be after that like a shot."

"Poor P. Do you think Brother Rouge will have flogged him by now?"

"Not a doubt of it. He'll get every stroke the old swine would have liked to give us."

"Why does that please you so, Firmin? After all, he's sick—"

"So what? It's not my fault if he's sick. He's a sneak, a spy. He makes it his business to lick the Brothers' feet and smile like a virtuous little saint. You can have bad luck without being a lickspittle. Nothing excuses that."

They reached a crossroads with a signpost. One of its arms simply read: TO THE SEA—300 YARDS.

"Just the thing," Firmin said. "On the road there's always

the chance of being picked up by a police patrol. We'll spend the night on the beach."

Night had fallen. Under the bright, sharp light of a full moon the sand shone like old gold, and on the surface of the water a path of white glittering flakes stretched away, it seemed, to some enchanted kingdom. Everything was quiet: over everything hung a profound and impressive stillness, only accentuated by the regular booming explosion of breakers against the rocks. Lights winked out along the coast, and seagulls swooped overhead with their melancholy *yap-yap-yap*. A sea breeze stirred the pine woods and set up a faint sighing sound that persisted in the background of their consciousness.

They walked on in silence along the sand. Tanguy felt a sudden desire to kneel down and kiss the seaweed that lay strewn about the beach. His heart was beating wildly with excitement. Firmin, too, seemed preoccupied; he walked along with a completely bemused expression, his breath coming fast. They stopped, looked at each other, and smiled. Tanguy took Firmin's hand.

"It's wonderful, isn't it?" he said.

Firmin nodded.

"That's what freedom means: being able to look at the sea."

There was another silence. Firmin beckoned Tanguy to follow him. They clambered over a scatter of rocks where the cliff ran straight down into the water, and stopped in front of a kind of grotto. Its floor was still littered with paper and empty bottles, which seemed to suggest that couples might have spent the night there. They sat down and ate their bread and sardines. Outside the silver-flaked sea surged up against the rocks' dark immobility: two forces nobly balanced against each other. Above them the stars shone out; and far and near the countryside lay locked in sleep.

The two boys sat awake for a long time. Tanguy told Firmin the whole story of his childhood. He talked about his mother, and all his secret longings—a happy and peaceful home, friends, a dog of his own. Firmin heard him out in silence. Then he said: "Do you believe your mother's still alive?"

"Of course."

"Why should you suppose so?"

"She wasn't in any great danger where she was going."

"What would you do if you found her again? How would you feel?"

Tanguy hesitated, then shrugged. "I don't know," he admitted. "A lot's happened to me since I saw her last."

"I understand that," Firmin said. "My mother loved me very much. She was a very simple woman, but she was my mother and nothing else. She adored me; she never questioned my actions. She was a very simple woman—very *humble*, if you see what I mean."

"Yes, I see."

"She always dressed in black, and never wore make-up. She only lived to look after us. When my father came home drunk he used to beat her. One day I picked up an iron bar and threatened him with it. My mother cried out to me— 'Firmin,' she screamed, 'you're not going to kill him, are you? You're not going to become a murderer? Not that, Firmin, you mustn't! You mustn't blame your father, he's just been

183

unfortunate—!' My mother was a saint, a real saint. She lived for nothing but her family. She died in the hospital of cancer. Her last words to me were: 'Firmin, be kind to your father. He's so lonely.' "

Firmin broke off at this point, and stared at his hands, as if he could still see on them some trace of his murdered father's blood. Then he went on in a low, hopeless voice: "If she could see me now, and know what lies in front of me! One reformatory after another, and then prison. She always used to say what a good boy I was. I had a kind heart, she said."

"And who ever said you haven't a kind heart?"

"The judges. They were astounded at what they called my 'insensibility and general predilection for evil.' "

Tanguy thought for a moment. Then he said: "I used to adore my mother. She was so beautiful, and so clever! I shall always remember one night when she was going to the Casino. She was wearing a black evening dress. I was in my cot and watched her get ready. Suddenly I said to her: 'You're as lovely as a fairy,' and she turned round, astonished. It somehow hurts me to think that for seven years she's been living a free, independent life—talking, laughing, drinking, dancing—while I was interned in Germany, or even when I was at the Center, under the Brothers. I used to love her so much, Firmin! I tell myself she must have forgotten me. Not completely, perhaps. But she must have rearranged her life, become used to my absence. She may even think I'm dead."

"That would hardly be her fault. For all you know she may be thinking of you. Who can tell?"

"Thinking isn't everything. When she left me at Mar-

184

seilles—" Tanguy swallowed. "Would your mother have done that?"

"Never."

"That's what I wanted you to say. You see, my mother loved Humanity, Fraternity, Liberty, all the capital letters; so she couldn't be overbothered with mere *people* around her."

"What about your father?"

"Oh, him! I hardly ever think about him. He left us almost immediately after I was born. He was a poor sort of fish—rather like yours, by the sound of it, except that he didn't drink. He spent his time looking for wealthy women, profitable jobs and deals—you know. I don't think he was malicious, not very malicious, anyway; but he certainly was a coward."

They fell silent again. The sea burst and roared against the rocks, and the moon climbed slowly in the sky. The wind had fallen, but the lights still twinkled along the coastline.

"It must be horrible not to know what to think about your mother," Firmin said at length, abstractedly.

"Yes. You feel you can't really trust anyone or anything ever again."

Soon they fell asleep, and the sea's rhythm lulled them as they slept through their first night of freedom.

The following morning they took to the road again, and pushed on till midday. It was beautiful weather, and everything glowed cheerfully in the sunlight. They amused each other by exchanging stories about the Center. Then a truck-driver picked them up and gave them a lift into Sitgès. He was a jolly man who, like them, had very little time for priests. They all sat and joked in his driving-cab, and he gave them both cigarettes and waved good-by when he dropped them.

Sitgès turned out to be a small but fashionable seaside resort. The tiny narrow streets were full of half-naked bathers, with very white skins. Firmin went into a small shop and bought some food to eat on the beach. After their meal they left Sitgès behind them and went for a swim in a deserted bay further up the coast. Once again they spent the night on the beach.

Next morning Firmin took Tanguy back into Sitgès, to the railway station. They spent some time there. Tanguy had no idea as yet why Firmin had taken him there, but carefully refrained from asking him questions: he left all decisions in his hands.

About noon a freight train came in and pulled up where they were standing. Then Firmin turned to Tanguy and said: "Listen carefully. You're going to get aboard this train and travel in it as far as Madrid. You *must* get to Madrid. I know it's hard for us to separate, but the police will find it far easier to catch us if we stick together. I'm a convicted murderer, and my description must have been circulated to every police station in the country. You'll be able to get through by yourself."

Tanguy felt as though he were choking. He gestured nervously, then stammered: "Not yet, Firmin! I can't leave you yet—tomorrow, if you must, but not now. We were so happy together, and besides, I'm scared at the idea of being on my own."

186

"No. It's got to be *now*. Otherwise we'll never manage it. This is the right moment."

"I can't do it. The police are bound to catch me."

"No they won't," Firmin said confidently.

"I don't know how to ride a freight train without being seen—"

"Don't worry, you'll find out. Now, you're going to get into this brakeman's look-out—that's right, the one in front of you. You're going to sit still and keep mum. It may be a long trip, but there's nothing much to be afraid of. Look—do you see? The car's got MADRID chalked on it. It's a through train."

The departure bell shrilled out, and Firmin stood up.

"Come on, get aboard!" he said.

"No, tomorrow, if you insist—"

"Now," Firmin said, and gave Tanguy a great shove up and through the door of the wagon.

Tanguy climbed up into the brakeman's look-out. It was very narrow: too narrow to lie down in, so he sat on the floor, in a miserable stupor at being left alone in the world once more. He was convinced that his fate was always to be alone, always to lose what he loved. A draft blew down his back, and the train moved out of the station. Tanguy rested his forehead on his knees. He did not cry, but felt an aching hollow emptiness inside him. He was sad for Firmin as well as himself: Firmin was now all alone too, and deserved love and friendship as much as anybody.

Soon he stopped thinking altogether. The little cabin was narrow and badly ventilated, and became quite warm inside after a while. The train rattled on all day without stopping, and Tanguy fell asleep just as it was getting dark. He woke

187

up in the middle of the night and realized that they were now halted somewhere. He got up and peered out: it was a small wayside station. A Civil Guard sat on a bench, smoking a cigarette, muffled up in his cloak. The station clock said 4:10. Trainmen with lanterns were strolling down the tracks past the freight cars. The night air was cold and clean.

Tanguy settled down to sleep again. When he woke once more the train had still not moved, and he wondered if this was as far as it was going. He glanced out to make sure: still the same station. He had no idea where he was, since his field of vision was not wide enough to include the station name-board. The clock now said 6.10 A.M. Once again Tanguy composed himself for a nap, but a few moments later, with a slight jerk, the train began to move again. Tanguy gave a sigh of relief, and his mood at once brightened. He decided that life was, after all, an enjoyable business, and no hardship was as bad as it seemed at the time. Dawn glowed in the sky, and a light morning mist hung in the air. The light had an astonishing clarity about it. Then the sun rose, and slowly it grew warmer.

8

TANGUY reached Madrid in the early hours of the morning. He slipped through the barrier at the terminal without any trouble, and made his way out into the city.

The size and opulence of Madrid staggered him, with its huge, beautifully planned blocks of flats, its bronze equestrian statues, its wide tree-flanked boulevards and ruler-straight streets. The roads were crowded with traffic, and Tanguy had to take some care to avoid being run over. He made his way up by the Prado, along Alcalà Street to the Public Park. There he stood for a while, gazing into the lake, pleased with the idea of having been born in so splendid a city. The people of Madrid seemed very friendly. They had a way of walking and speaking which struck Tanguy as the very height of urban sophistication.

He noticed that passers-by were glancing curiously in his direction and some loafers actually began to laugh at him. Wondering what was so funny about his appearance, Tanguy walked over to an automatic weighing-machine and looked into the mirror. A grimy, black face with long tangled hair stared back at him. He saw a small fountain playing among the trees, and washed his face in its water. This at once restored his confidence; he could mingle with the world again and excite no notice.

He decided to go and see the house where he was born. He threaded his way through streets named after great artists —Velasquez, Goya. He stopped in front of a small townhouse, whose well-proportioned façade hinted at an architectural style more French than Spanish. He smiled to himself, amused to think that he was the grandson of the man who had lived in this house, a man who owned vast estates and countless houses all over Spain. Then he shrugged his shoulders and walked on. Before he handed himself over to the Society for the Protection of Minors he wanted to see a little more of his native city.

He went back down Alcalà Street, through the Puerta del Sol to the Gran Via, and walked the whole length of the Castellana, enchanted by everything he saw around him. The streets were crowded, and that too made him feel more comfortable, since the crowd seemed essentially friendly, a barrier against his loneliness. At last, when he began to feel weary, he decided to call on the lady to whom he had his letter of introduction.

She was a very thin, very tall woman, gray-haired, and wearing a black costume of decidedly mannish cut. Her small black eyes darted about restlessly, and she wore no make-up. The nearest approach to jewelry was a gold medallion that hung round her neck. She read the letter through twice, carefully, and then stared at Tanguy, as if trying to equate what she saw with what she had read. Then she asked him a series of questions, and these he answered with some care, since she often asked him the same thing in different terms, and there were some things he had no desire to mention or discuss. Finally she asked him if he believed in God.

Tanguy had no idea how to answer this question. In fact he was by no means sure whether he believed in God or not. God left him absolutely indifferent, and he never knew how to deal with the problem. After a pause the lady said that she was going to send him to see a man who was a saint, a true saint, she repeated. Tanguy merely felt relief that she was willing to do *something* about him.

That same evening he found himself in a train again, destined for Andalusia. In the same compartment were some other children, happy and cheerful enough to judge by their behavior, and a nice man of about forty who seemed to be in charge of them.

Tanguy yawned. He had got accustomed to being shuttled about from one existence to another, and at the moment felt comparatively peaceful. But he still thought anxiously about Firmin. Had the police arrested him? Tanguy recollected their first free night together, in the grotto by the beach. A tear welled up in each eye. He felt them trickle down his nose, and drip off it. One of the children called out: "Look, sir, he's crying!"

The man took Tanguy's hand and said to him, in a kind, gentle voice: "There's no need for you to cry. You're going to a very good college indeed. The Jesuits run it. They'll make a fine man of you, you'll see!"

Tanguy smiled, and suddenly felt immensely tired. Again his mind turned back to Firmin. What would become of him? What would the authorities do to him? He began to wonder if a world could ever exist in which children were loved and protected. Then he leaned his head back against the cushions and dozed off. Toward midnight the other children woke him up to show him the Sierra Morena, with its sheer rocky pinnacles seemingly suspended between earth and sky. It was an impressive sight; but Tanguy gave it one quick nostalgic glance and instantly fell asleep again, completely exhausted.

9

FATHER PARDO was a lean man with a most penetrating gaze, in which intelligence and understanding seemed blended in equal proportions. He had gray hair, and was beginning to go bald. His age Tanguy put somewhere between forty and forty-five. He wore glasses, and rubbed his eyes with one hand every time he took his glasses off. It seemed a kind of automatic tic.

Tanguy had been shown into Father Pardo's study at five in the afternoon. It was now half past eight, and he was still there, talking as he had never talked in his life before, opening his heart completely. From the first moment of their meeting this man had inspired an unquestioning trust in him. Tanguy felt from his expression alone that here, for the first time, was a man who would understand him. He told Father Pardo about everything, down to the most intimate details, as though he were in the confessional: his father and mother and early disappointments, the monstrous piece of bad luck which had led to his being deported, the story of Gunther, life in the Rehabilitation Center, his escape with Firmin.

The Jesuit listened with patient attentiveness. Occasionally he interposed a comment or asked a question—on the organization of the camps, for example. But for the most part he remained silent, while Tanguy talked on, nervous and voluble, his sentences tumbling over each other, each successive phrase relieving a little more of the heavy burden he had carried for so long. He felt as though he were becoming another person, simply because this priest was willing to listen to him.

The study was a tiny room, with little furniture in it but an oak table loaded with books, one upright chair, and one armchair. In one corner was a prie-dieu and above it, on the wall, a crucifix; in the other an articulated skeleton on a stand. Facing Father Pardo, behind Tanguy's back, was a narrow open window, and through this one caught a glimpse of olive-clad hillsides, and beyond them the snow-capped ridges of the Sierra Magina.

At last Tanguy stopped talking. The Father smiled: an odd smile, the smile of a man who deliberately conceals his sensibilities, and makes a practice of disciplining the natural impulses of his heart.

"Here," he said, "there are neither walls nor guards. You will be completely free. If one day you wished to leave us, no one would try to stop you by force. Until you find a place of your own again, I would like you to think of this house as your home. We are not here to punish you or chase you around, but to help you to the best of our ability."

Father Pardo paused for a moment, then went on. "It won't be entirely plain sailing for you. The children here have no idea of the kind of problems you have had to face. Their only troubles are the run-of-the-mill ones that are as old as Andalusia itself. They are rough in their manners, though not malicious. You, I think, will find them a little childish. You know, the thing that really puts years on people is saying good-by to friends or places. The more partings you endure during your life, the quicker you grow old. Growing old means leaving something or somebody.

"You will feel old among these other boys. They won't understand you right away. They'll find you a little odd. When that happens, and things aren't going too well, come here, to my study. Treat it as you would the confessional if you were a believer. We will always find something to talk about. We will be quite alone, too—except for Philiston—" and here Father Pardo pointed at the skeleton.

"Philiston? I don't understand."

"My dear boy, he's my greatest friend. I bought him in my third year at medical school. I was studying in Granada, and I wasn't very well off. My father was a doctor himself, and had fourteen children, so I had to watch my expenses. I used to study anatomy with a friend of mine, and one day he offered me the chance of buying Philiston cheap. I was so delighted the night I got him that I took him to bed with me—"

Tanguy shuddered. Father Pardo raised one eyebrow in amusement.

"Dear me," he said, "you mustn't be afraid of Philiston. He's a charming creature, and his discretion is absolute. How many living human beings could you say that of?"

Tanguy smiled. When he left Father Pardo's study for the refectory, he felt happy and replete. He took a deep breath: peace flowed over him. Only the church bells of Ubeda, ringing and hammering, disturbed the calm evening air.

The college was a fine modern building, built on a height overlooking a valley full of olive groves. On a clear night you could see the lights of Jaén in the distance.

Tanguy had a room to himself. Its furniture was plain but

sufficient: a bed, a chair, a worktable, shelves for books, and in one corner a washbasin with a mirror above it. Tanguy loved working in this room when the whole college was quiet. His window looked out on the Sierra Magina. When he woke in the morning, the first thing that met his eye was this majestic snow-topped mountain, ringed with its purplish mist. It looked near enough for him to reach out and touch it with one hand, although it was in fact nearly twenty miles away.

From his first day there Tanguy experienced a happiness such as he had never even dreamed of. A feverish urge for work seized him. Despite his hardships, he had found the means to read a great deal; but his learning was like that of most self-taught people, patchy and unsystematic. In the college he found something he had always lacked hitherto: first-rate teachers.

They were not monks, and indeed Father Pardo had deliberately avoided instructors of this kind. Most of them were young graduates preparing doctoral theses. The four Jesuits resident in the college restricted themselves to teaching religion, moral ethics, theology, and philosophy—with the exception, that is, of Father Pardo himself, who lectured on anatomy, botany, organic chemistry, and Greek!

These teachers were friendly and easily approachable. Most of them were excellent at their job, and equally devoted to their pupils and the college as a whole. All of them, in varying degrees, realized the vital mission they were carrying out on the children's behalf. They assisted Father Pardo to the height of their several abilities; but they were never less than remarkably efficient.

Tanguy had an unusual geography master, who conducted extremely lively and interesting classes. He had a series of "blank maps" on which rivers, mountains, and towns appeared without their names. The boys soon learned their way about these maps. This master's name was Don Francisco; he was exceptionally kind to Tanguy, who responded by doing very well in geography.

Spanish literature was taught by one Don Armando. It was to him that Tanguy owed his taste for classical severity of form and language, and it was he, too, who supervised Tanguy's first serious reading. They began with Cervantes, Lope de Vega, Quevedo, and Calderón, then passed on to Azorin (Tanguy's particular favorite), Pío Baroja, and Unamuno. Don Armando was a small blue-eyed man whose eyebrows met in the middle. He came from Galicia, in the north, and was doing research on the influence of German romanticism on the evolution of Spanish literature in the nineteenth century. He was a man of vast learning and most delicate taste, and Tanguy loved talking with him. The other boys did not take so kindly to him since he was extremely caustic in his reports and showed great severity in correcting essays. Tanguy long remembered the comments scrawled over the margins of his own exercise books in that energetic handwriting: *Useless! Platitude! Give metaphors a rest for a bit!*

There was also Don Isman, who taught French—dry, nervous, intelligent yet weak-willed, and generous to Tanguy in the matter of marks. There was Don José Aguilde, a mathematician with the very rare gift of combining excellent scholarship and an ability to make his pupils actually enthusiastic about algebra. Among the rest the master Tanguy liked least at first was Don Santos. He was kind and gentle enough, but he labored under the handicap of teaching Latin and Greek, neither of which Tanguy had ever studied before. For Tanguy was suddenly plunged in among boys who had been familiar with declensions and neuter nouns since they could walk, and suffered agonies when he had to translate Latin in class. He did everything he could to avoid it. Don Santos had, into the bargain, developed an extremely polite way of inviting him to perform: "Come now," he would say, "shall we take a look at Cicero's speech against Catiline?"

Long afterwards Tanguy still recalled the voice of this unusual man, who had the patience to rebuild Tanguy's grounding in the humanities almost from scratch. One day Don Santos told him that in future he was to come for extra coaching in the classics every evening during the art period, because he thought that Latin and Greek would be of more use to Tanguy than drawing or music.

Every evening, then, Tanguy would go and find old Don Santos in the masters' library. Here he would spend more than an hour sweating over declensions and conjugations. Soon, by this method, he found himself capable of translating Caesar with reasonable facility; and later he moved on to Cicero, who came as a revelation to him. Don Santos knew how to give Tanguy a taste for history. Before starting work on one of Cicero's speeches, he would sketch in the entire historical background, and this gave new meaning to the text, so that the whole story at once sprang to life. At the end of four months Tanguy had overtaken his fellow pupils; but the evening lessons still continued. Don Santos would preen himself, saying he would turn Tanguy into a Latinist yet, and they both would laugh.

Soon Tanguy began to read Ovid, who at once took first place in his affections among the classic authors. He knew long passages of the *Tristia* by heart, and was fond of declaiming them as he paced up and down his room. If he ever felt miserable or depressed, this was a better remedy than any kindly encouragement from other people. His second favorite was Virgil. Tanguy's taste was formed and influenced by these two old masters, and he was never to shake himself free from them. Don Santos had shown him the most infallible way to escape from the here-and-now: by acquiring a taste for enduring and immortal works of literature.

Another characteristic feature of college teaching was the system of "team projects," to which Father Pardo attached great importance. The boys were divided into "research teams" to study some specific problem which was given them. Their rule was always to co-operate fully with each other. Father Pardo abolished rank and seniority from these teams. There was no master or "team leader"; only a so-called "philosopher," whose job was to make a synthesis of the team's work—to collect each individual's evidence and to correlate the various aspects of the subject into a homogeneous whole. Every Thursday one team was chosen to demonstrate the results of their researches in front of the faculty. At these meetings the Fathers and other masters would challenge them with searching questions and intellectual problems which required some notice before they could be discussed. Some of them were so difficult as to provoke disagreement and arguments among the masters themselves.

But Father Pardo always had the last word; everyone turned to him as the final arbiter. His instructors spoke of his formidable erudition, and certainly he had a prodigious memory. He moved with equal assurance in the fields of history, chemistry, literature, and natural science. They might well wonder how one human brain could absorb so much diverse knowledge and—an even greater wonder—digest it into a coherent whole.

10

THE boys at the college never called Father Pardo by his full name: he was simply "Father," and the title acquired symbolic significance. They laughed at his absent-mindedness and made jokes about his phenomenal memory. But they loved him deeply and had absolute confidence in him. The tough cases cried like babies when Father had them in for a dressing-down. One word of criticism from him was enough to make a boy completely miserable. They knew that his integrity and sense of justice were inflexible, and that he yet combined them with an almost superhuman generosity. They were not deceived when he roared at them—a trick he sometimes overdid—nor by his terrible frown. They *knew* he loved them, just as he was aware of their childish affection in return.

Father Pardo was not a saint in the strict sense. But he was a real man, which is almost as rare. The college was *his* college, the product of his energy, devotion, intelligence, and (last but not least) his faith. Father Pardo had laid the foundations of that faith when—already a Doctor of Medicine and Philosophy—he became a theological student. He was over thirty when he decided to enter the Society of Jesus. Later he became obsessed by the miserable conditions prevailing in Andalusia, which were exacerbated by a soaring birthrate. Families with nothing to eat had anything up to a dozen children, and the children were hungry from the day they were born. When they reached the age of ten they went to work on the estates of the big landlords.

Father Pardo saw it all, and had a private dream. He wanted schools—modern, well-lit, airy schools in which children would feel at home, and where they would be taught entirely free. To make his dream come true involved a long and unrelenting struggle with the authorities. His colleagues referred to him as a mere Utopian idealist; but his Jesuit superiors gave him a free hand. He began by wheedling a disused school-building out of the municipal council of Andujar: this was the first step toward the fulfillment of his dream. He gathered a nucleus of poor children there, fed them and taught them. He turned one room into a chapel and said Mass there. He only asked the children to repeat the one prayer: "Sacred Heart of Jesus, I put my trust in You!"

Tanguy had made friends with one of Father's earliest pupils, a boy called Gabriel Almonzas, and it was from him that he heard these stories of the school's foundation. Sometimes, Almonzas said, Father would telephone from Madrid in the middle of the night, saying he was having trouble with the Ministry of Finance. He told the masters to say Mass, and ask the boys to pray for him in relays till he phoned again. Day and night the children repeated the same prayer, tirelessly, over and over, while at the other end of the line a man struggled against government bureaucrats, fighting to win these children the right to develop into men.

Slowly the dream was realized. Schools were opened at Andujar, Las Carolinas, Linarès, Puerto de Santa Maria, finally in Ubeda. Big, roomy buildings rose on virgin soil, and Father, when asked how it had happened, simply said: "Providence and your prayers were responsible." The boys trusted him to see them through. Sometimes in the difficult days after the end of the Civil War, provisions ran out. No one knew how fresh supplies were to be obtained. Then Father would gather the school together and tell them the situation. "I have complete confidence in you," he would conclude. I know that if you all pray sincerely, things will turn out for the best."

And then the boys would kneel down in front of the Host, and day and night the building would hum with endless relays of prayers, while Father Pardo scoured the area in his truck. When he returned, the truck would be loaded with jars of oil and sacks of potatoes. He liked to say that the college was a perpetual miracle; Tanguy felt that the real miracle lay in Father's own courage, energy, and rectitude.

For the children the college was *their* home, and they always spoke of it so. They were as involved in its management as Father Pardo himself; they always knew how full or empty the reserves were.

The Ubeda Center was actually divided into two colleges. Up at the top stood the college, properly so called; down below was the technical college. Father Pardo took boys of all ages and types. Those who were qualified to study at a higher level entered the main college; the rest trained as skilled craftsmen, in workshops equipped with all the most modern machine tools. Each chose the trade that suited him best: they were turned into highly specialized technicians, since such skills were hard to find in Andalusia, and Father Pardo aimed to make them a cadre with which to fill the gap. There was no social difference between "workers" and "scholars"; they were all equally attached to the college.

Tanguy had never before come in contact with, or even known real charity. But Father Pardo was charity personified. He expended on every person he met all the care and love of which they stood in need. He did not care to prod into their consciences; "the important thing, always" he used to say, "is to give," and he himself followed this precept at every hour of every day. He was always there, ready to help even before he had been asked for anything. There was no element of complacency or prurient curiosity in his readiness to listen to confidences. If someone needed to talk, he let them talk. They could joke if they wanted to; and some came to his study for a good cry, just as they would have done with their mother. Father Pardo said to Tanguy one day:

"Charity is not a virtue: it only exists in action."

It was true that he himself was action incarnate: he thought practically, in terms of action, and in his mind notion and action were indissolubly linked by the invisible bond of charity. He had little time for scrupulous consciences and tortured souls. One day when Tanguy confessed that he spent a good deal of time wondering whether or not he believed in God, Father was very short with him.

"Leave all this rubbish alone!" he said severely. "Eat, sleep, play, work, don't tell lies, be decent to your friends and loyal to your society. When you have done all these things, and over and above them feel able to show love for your neighbor by deed as well as word, then—not before—you can ask yourself whether you believe in God. Most of us Christians behave in a very un-Christian way as soon as we're asked to give away a thousand pesetas or so. It's a slender faith which so depends on one's wallet. What's really important is to know how to give away not one's spare cash but one's basic necessities."

Tanguy's life followed its well-marked course of study, leisure amusements, and meals. He had put on nearly 14 pounds in weight: Father weighed him regularly and noted the least change. His hair had grown out to a decent length again, and he wore good clothes.

On Thursdays the boys went for a walk, two by two, crocodile-fashion, either to Baeza or down the valley to a deserted farm they had christened The Chateau. Here they played games, fooled around, or sat arguing.

Tanguy had acquired some close friends, among them a boy

from Cadiz, called Manolo, a natural clown who had his neighbors in fits of laughter even in church. He was small and dark, with long curly hair that fell into his eyes, and a wry, twinkling expression. He also had a strong Andalusian accent. Don Armando was always scolding him for not writing the s's at the ends of words, and for mixing up s and z.

"What do you *do* with your s's?" Don Armando asked him.

"Swallow them, I s'pose. Not my fault really, sir. I write Andalusian, not Castilian. The Academy tells us that our language should be written as it's pronounced. That's just what I do."

"Your pronunciation is very bad, then, Manolo."

"*Bad?* I know *Castilians* say that, but surely not *you*, Don Armando? As far as I'm concerned the real Spain is Andalusia."

Father Pardo was very fond of Manolo, who indeed exemplified his dictum that the boys were mischievous but never malicious. Tanguy knew that he was an orphan and one of Father's first recruits, picked up in a Seville back street. Manolo at that time was a shoeshine boy. He was seven years old.

There was also Platero, a big boy with a passion for football. He spent much time arguing with Manolo, whose only sporting interests were centered on the bullring. Manolo always referred to him as the Dried Cod, and he retaliated by calling Manolo Monsieur Zi-Zi, because of his Andalusian accent.

Then there was Josselin, a very gentle boy who had been ill for a long time and had a passion for the movies. He was also devoted to music, and Tanguy spent long hours with him, shut in the library, listening to records. Father Pardo had a vast collection, which included practically the entire works of Beethoven, Mozart, and Bach. When they came out of the library, in a kind of musical seventh heaven, Manolo would shout: "Pray silence for Beethoven & Co.! They've just been listening to that highbrow work '*La Vaca Lechera!*'"—a popular peasant song about milking a cow.

Manolo, Platero, Josselin, and Tanguy were inseparable; they went everywhere together. The other boys nicknamed them the Four Musketeers, which Manolo parodied as the Four Mosquitoes.

On Sunday afternoons the boys were free to do what they pleased, and this produced never-ending arguments between the four friends. Josselin wanted to sit and listen to music; Platero wanted to watch a football match; Manolo was all for a long country walk, and Tanguy for the movies. But every Sunday the argument was resolved by the same compromise: they all four went to watch football during the afternoon, and afterwards, about seven o'clock, took in a movie.

Tanguy always took pleasure in putting on his Sunday best: he polished his shoes, knotted his tie with especial care, and combed a neat parting into his hair. Then he went to draw his weekly allowance of five pesetas from Father Pardo, a privilege he shared with all the orphans. There was a movie theater in the town that showed very old films and only cost two pesetas. With the remaining three Tanguy bought sweets or sometimes a couple of cigarettes, which he smoked in the lounge W.C.

The movie house was a regular flea-bag, about as old as the films it showed. There were always four or five break-downs every performance, which were greeted with endless whistles and catcalls. Manolo was adept at this particular game: he produced a piercing street vendor's whistle by putting two fingers in his mouth, and the noise he made silenced everybody else. Josselin was unashamedly senti-mental. When the two leading characters in the film embraced, he uttered little romantic ohs and ahs of sympathy. Manolo, on the other hand, was quite liable to jeer at the screen. "All right, all right," he would call out, "we know what happens next!"

One Sunday Father Pardo took several boys to Linarès, to see the famous bullfighter Manolete; Father was an en-thusiastic *aficionado*. Manolo was delighted to be asked; Platero affected a scholarly distaste for the bullring, but nevertheless was so worked up that he was the first one ready to go; as for Tanguy, it was his first *corrida* and he was beside himself with excitement. Three days beforehand Fa-ther had begun to explain to him the symbolic meaning that lay behind the formal gestures and all the ritual that go to make up a *Fiesta*. He lent him books and old lithographs, and sketched out the classical "passes" for him. Finally he assured him that Manolete was "the greatest matador of them all."

Tanguy was full of anticipation; but unhappily his first *corrida* was Manolete's last. The bullfighter's death came as a shock to the whole college; it was a kind of personal disaster. Father Pardo celebrated a Solemn Mass for the repose of Manolete's soul, and in his sermon described him as "the

last representative of the great Spanish bullfighting tradition."

Though their pleasure had been a little dashed by this tragic
incident, the privileged few who had accompanied Father to
the *corrida* soon were busy playing at matadors, making elaborate passes with their shirts and describing Manolete's fatal
accident to their friends. This supplied a topic of conversation
for more than a month, as they all spoke of Manolete's great
courage and peerless technique, using the same phraseology as
Father Pardo.

Tanguy, who had wondered if it was really orthodox to
celebrate Masses for dead bullfighters, had another liturgical
surprise a few weeks later.

There was a model farm on the college estate, for the
benefit of those who wished to study agriculture, which supported a sizable quantity of livestock—chickens, rabbits, cows
and so forth. It had first-rate equipment, and was run by a
Dutchman. One day one of the cows, known as Louise, became ill. Father Pardo promptly celebrated a series of Masses
to dissuade the Almighty from depriving the college of
Louise's milk! For six days "scholars" and "workers" gathered round the poor animal, who seemed somewhat alarmed
by this sudden increase in her popularity. Certainly for a week
everyone was almost morbidly concerned with her health.
Rumors about her temperature and insomnia flew round;
even her appetite was eagerly discussed. A newcomer might
have been forgiven for supposing that Louise was at the least
a Spanish Infanta.

11

EASTER was approaching; it was over eight months since Tanguy had first arrived at Ubeda. He was working overtime preparing for the end-of-term examinations. He was already top of his class in all subjects for the term; but he wanted to get really high marks in the term papers, because he knew that would please Father Pardo, and he would have done anything in his power to please him. He did most of his work in his room; sometimes Platero and Manolo joined him there, and they would test each other.

At the same time Tanguy was not at all well. He frequently broke out in a cold sweat. At night he was afraid to lie down flat, because this produced bouts of coughing that nearly choked him. He lost his appetite. One evening, in the middle of one of his worst paroxysms of coughing, the door opened and Father Pardo came in.

"Not feeling too well?"

"I'm all right. It isn't anything. Just a cough."

"So I heard," Father observed, and put one hand on Tanguy's forehead. "You've got a fever, young man," he said at once.

"No—I'm just a bit hot—"

"Hot, hot? The nights are far from warm now, and we've got the high Sierra practically on our doorstep. No: you've got a fever, and that's that."

"You really think so?"

"I shall know for certain in a moment. Lie down and wrap

yourself up well while I go and get a thermometer."

Presently he came back and put the thermometer into Tanguy's mouth. He stood staring out over the countryside while Tanguy lay there and let the mercury rise, his eyes fixed on the lean black silhouette framed in his narrow window.

Father took out the thermometer and looked at it.

"Well?" Tanguy asked. Father nodded.

"Let me see—"

"You've got fever all right, my boy—a fairly heavy fever, at that. Right. We'll try and diagnose it. I shall ask you one or two questions and you must try to answer them exactly. Do you get fits of shivering?"

"Yes."

"Are they short spasms, at irregular intervals?"

"No. They go on for a long time."

"Excellent. Have you had a nosebleed within the last few days?"

"Yes. One yesterday and another the day before."

"Ah. You have sweating, migraines, aches in your body—have you vomited at all?"

"No."

"Do you feel a distinct pain in any part of your body?"

"Yes—here, in my left side."

"Right. I shall now go and get one of my little toys, and listen to what's going on in that old chest of yours. After that we'll take you over to the infirmary."

Father went over Tanguy with a stethoscope, made him cough, asked him some more questions, and then wrapped him up in a blanket and carried him in his arms to the infirmary, which was on the same floor of the building. The white-clad infirmary Sister helped him put Tanguy to bed, and Tanguy relaxed and let them do everything. He felt warm and comfortable. He watched Father Pardo coming and going and felt reassured: Tanguy's confidence in him was absolute. He was still shivering, however, and snuggled down deeper into the bed. When he stretched out his feet they encountered a hotwater bottle. He smiled. It was nice to be ill and be looked after and coddled. If he had had parents, he thought, they would certainly have looked after him in the same way.

Father Pardo came back with a tray of instruments and prepared to give him an injection.

"Now," he said, "we're just going to prick you a little—"

Tanguy smiled and held out his arm, as Father made the injection with practiced skill. Then he gave Tanguy a gentle tap on the forehead, and said: "You've got a nasty bug, my boy. But we'll get you well in a while. You've got to be reasonable and help us, that's all. Sister Marie-Madeleine is going to look after you. If there's anything you need, just ask her. She's going to make you a big pitcherful of orange juice, and I want you to drink as much of it as you can. Tomorrow morning I'll bring some really fascinating apparatus to photograph your insides with. We're going to find out just what's going on under your ribs."

Tanguy said: "You mean I won't be able to take my exams?"

"Of course not. You're going to spend at least a month in here—first to get you better, and after that to give you a chance to convalesce."

For a fortnight Tanguy was seriously ill. The pain in his side was more acute every day, and his cough became increasingly congested. Whenever he opened his eyes he found either Father Pardo or Sister Marie-Madeleine there with him. Sister Marie-Madeleine had dark, kindly eyes, and in her white habit she made Tanguy think of a fairy. Father Pardo simply stood at his bedside, erect, unmoving, a smile on his face to which Tanguy tried to respond.

"We can't have our invalid on his back till Easter," he would say. "Sister Marie-Madeleine is going to make you a really enormous Easter cake."

Tanguy was happy now. He felt as light as a feather and had an immense desire for sleep. When he woke it was enough for him to see that he was not alone, that *they* were there near him. As soon as he opened his eyes Sister poured out a little orange juice and made him drink it, supporting his head with one arm. Tanguy found this a pleasant sensation: it was wonderful, he thought, to have genuine affection bestowed on you. He no longer troubled his head about his family or anyone else. Father Pardo was there, and that was the one really important thing.

After a while Tanguy began to take a little nourishment again. His cough became less violent, and the fever fell. He still stayed in bed, but was able to talk with Sister and Father Pardo, who often joined him at meal time to make sure that he ate enough. This amused Tanguy. When he had had enough, he smiled cajolingly at Father; but Father never weakened. He fixed the convalescent with his famous frown and made him finish his food to the last mouthful.

Indeed, Tanguy had never eaten better in his life. Chicken broth and chicken breast, milk, fine pastries, eggs beaten up in wine—Sister served all such delicacies to him on a tray, sometimes garnished with a few flowers as well. Tanguy felt better every day. Outside spring was ripening into summer: hardly any snow was left now on the peaks of the Sierra Magina.

Lying in bed, Tanguy learned to distinguish all the various sounds of college life, a pastime which gave him much pleasure. He knew what his friends were doing from the noise alone. Another interesting thing was the fact that the church-bells in the town were never rung simultaneously. One lot began as the other finished. Tanguy came to recognize them all by their tone and *timbre*, and could always tell which church they belonged to.

Soon, however, he began to feel bored. His only distraction (and indeed, his only true pleasure) were the visits of Father Pardo, who came very day at the same time, after morning recess. As he sat beside Tanguy and chatted with him, his incredible range of knowledge never failed to delight and astonish Tanguy. He knew hundreds of fascinating anecdotes from every period of history, and recounted them in so vivid a fashion that he gave the impression of having been an eye-witness to everything he described. Every day they tackled a different subject: history, philosophy, music, politics, all were discussed in turn. Father's opinions were always unpredictable, and full of human warmth. He never made *a priori* judgments. He took a proposition, examined it, analyzed it, turned it around in all directions. Often he came to no firm conclusion at all, but satisfied himself with his attempt to reach a better understanding of his subject.

One evening, when they were discussing education and all

the problems of teaching, Father suddenly asked Tanguy whether he ever thought about his family.

"Yes—sometimes," Tanguy said.

"Would you like to see your father again?"

Tanguy shrugged his shoulders indifferently.

"I don't know. I'm happy here."

"Truly happy?"

"Yes."

"It gives me great pleasure to hear you say that. We are all very fond of you, you know; your teachers and fellow pupils, Sister, the other Fathers, all of us."

Father broke off at this point, and then went on in a flat, tired voice: "Personally, I have often wished that I could restrict myself to one single person in order to be able to help him properly. I would have dearly loved to offer you more than I have. But despite everything this is a college. What you needed was a home, a proper home; and I, alas, have to attend to all of you. There are too many who have no other home than this house. I have to make an effort to give them the belief that what they have here is a real home—even if the belief is nothing but an illusion."

Tanguy made no reply. He could have told Father Pardo that it was thanks to this illusion that he, Tanguy, had regained hope and happiness; that for the first time in his life someone had behaved to him as a father or mother should; that only since coming to Ubeda had he learned how to laugh and really enjoy himself. But he said nothing.

"On the basis of what you told me," Father Pardo went on, "I have made some inquiries to see if I could trace your parents. I have just had a letter giving me your father's address. Here it is. Would you like to write to him?"

Tanguy glanced at the letter; a few bare typed lines. He read it. The beating of his heart suddenly quickened. Father held out a little identity-card photograph to him.

"I went with this address to the French Consulate in Madrid," he said. "They promised to write to your father, and I asked them to forward his reply. But you could, I think, write to him yourself, independently. They gave me this photograph in the Consulate. It's of your father. He was about twenty-five or so when it was taken."

Tanguy looked at the photograph. The face he saw told him nothing. He searched his memory for any recollection of his father, but only muddled images emerged. He felt a strong, unanalyzed emotion take hold of him. He took Father Pardo's hand and kissed it.

"Thank you," he said.

Father looked sadly at him for a moment, and opened his mouth as if to say more, but finally changed his mind.

That same evening Tanguy wrote to his father. He was determined to write in French, and made several mistakes in grammar and syntax. He hoped that his father would realize that he had forgotten a good deal of his French, and appreciate his friendly intentions. That night he lay awake for a long time before finally dropping off to sleep.

A month later he came out of the infirmary and returned to his old class. He did not find it too difficult making up the ground he had lost. Everybody was glad to see him back. His teachers shook him affectionately by the hand; his friends gave him prodigious slaps on the back. It was only now that he learned how critically ill he had been, and how one night Father Pardo had said a Mass for him, and the entire college had prayed in the chapel for his recovery, till morning, "scholars" and "workers" alike. Tanguy was so moved when he heard this that he could say nothing; and tears sprang to his eyes.

12

TANGUY awaited his father's reply with some impatience. But the days went by, and still no letter came. This made him miserable. He had written to his father that since his mother had abandoned him in France, he was now alone in the world. He failed to understand how his father could disregard such an appeal. He had announced to all his friends that his father was alive, and that Father Pardo had found out his whereabouts and address. He let them know that he was waiting for a letter, and they were all delighted on his behalf. But now, whenever one of them asked if he had heard from his father yet, Tanguy's face darkened.

He had led a truly happy life for so long now that the possibility of living with his own father, as other children did, no longer seemed alien or remote. He had envisioned it as something real; so now he indulged in wonderful dreams to preserve the sense of reality. When he was forced to admit that his father was taking a long time over replying, his private explanation was that his father would turn up at the college without warning, just to give him a surprise. Tanguy pictured this meeting in every detail. A car would arrive. Tanguy would be sent for, fall into his father's arms, and burst into tears.

But time passed, and still no letter came. Once more Tanguy knew the meaning of utter misery. At night all those events in his past which he had vainly tried to forget loomed in front of him. He tried to work out why his father was indifferent to what had become of him. He thought about his mother, too: those long-ago days in Vichy, when they had made a home together. Such memories as this tortured him, and he found himself clenching his hands whenever his mind turned to her. He could not understand why she, too, had made no effort to find him again.

Tanguy passed his second-year examinations with remarkable distinction, obtaining a special commendation in every subject. The night after prize-giving he sat in his room staring at the diplomas and medals which littered his bed, sad because he had no family to share his triumph. Once again he felt loneliness pressing in on him, and only found peace in Father Pardo's company. There, in the little study, sitting beside Philiston (that model of discretion) Tanguy could open his heart. He paid Father frequent visits, and they would sit chatting for hours, Tanguy nervously loquacious, Father the attentive listener.

"It's hard to grow out of the parent myth," Father said to him one day. "It's the illusion which all children cherish most tenaciously. Even here. You know, I often have cases of boys who have been deserted by their mother or thrown out by their father, who cling to the legend with a kind of fierce despair."

"I know. But what else can a child cling to?"

"Very little, that's true. I was going to say God. But on the whole people who talk like that have no real idea of what they mean. Even for adults God alone is not enough."

Tanguy said: "When I was in that camp the memory of my mother often kept me going. Especially right at the end. I was tempted to give up—to just lie on my mattress and never move again. Then I told myself I had to go on, if only to see her once more."

"You had Gunther, too."

"Yes; I had Gunther. But after his death I had no one to take his place."

Father did not reply to this. He took off his glasses and rubbed his eyes; he looked tired. An earthy, evening smell drifted in through the open window.

At last he said: "The parents are the real obstacle every teacher has to face. They don't understand their children. They often hardly love them. They do everything wrong. But—but they *are* the child's parents. To the child they are like gods, and he will often go straight to his own destruction at their hands with eyes wide open."

"I think of them somewhat differently. What I need is stability and order. Do you see what I mean?"

"Not quite."

"I mean—well, everything I've ever had has always been shattered, impermanent. I'd like to impose some kind of pat-

217

tern on this chaotic existence. If I don't I shall go mad. This is the only way I shall ever find peace, by working myself into an established pattern, by finding my own niche in society and my own locale."

Tanguy broke off for a moment, then resumed: "You see, when I was at that orphanage, I often used to say that my mother was dead; I even invented circumstantial details about her death, though my account varied from one telling to the next—I couldn't even be bothered to lie well. But the necessity behind the lie was compulsive. *I had to kill her*—"

"I understand," Father Pardo said. "But remember, Tanguy, that neither order nor peace belong to this world—not even the relative degree of order which you need. There are things about your mother and father which you will never understand. Parents are human beings, you know. And all human beings are incomprehensible."

"I often tell myself that. All the same, I still need to know more than I do. Have you any idea what vast efforts I've made to bring myself to forgive them? I'm eighteen now. I was only nine when they began to destroy my life. They destroyed even my most basic hopes. I don't want to have anything to do with them. But—do you understand?—*I want them to see me as I am.*"

"I understand."

"It's not because of bitterness. I have none. All I want is to stand in front of them and let them see my face."

"My poor child," said Father Pardo, "you would be the only one a penny the worse for the experience. *They* wouldn't lift an eyebrow."

"The day I arrived in Barcelona to see my grandmother,

the concierge talked quite a bit about my mother's life in Spain after her return. She was happy, she laughed a lot, the concierge said. That was in 1942. I often wanted to forget or explain those words somehow, but I never had the courage. She had just lost me—she had just left me in the hands of strangers. She knew how wretchedly unhappy I was. I can't help feeling, underneath, that she was laughing *about me*."

Father did not answer; he was playing with a paper-knife. He looked at Tanguy, his eyes full of sadness and compassion, gestured with one hand, and said: "Have you written to the Consulate?"

"Yes. I—I just can't stand it any longer. I want to go to France, at all costs. It's something stronger than me—"

"That's obvious."

"But the people at the Consulate say that if no one is willing to take responsibility for me in France, or guarantee me a home, they can do nothing for me. I've told them I'm French, but that makes no difference at all, as far as I can see."

"What are you going to do, then?" Father asked.

Tanguy hesitated, his eyes gazing through the window at the rows of olive trees. The olive is the tree of unhappiness and abnormality. It resembles man in the way it is all twisted and knotted back on itself, as though racked by some evil secret. Like man, too, it clings fiercely to dry and sterile soil. Like man it only bears small fruit, for all its misfortunes.

"I shall leave here," Tanguy said at last.

"Where will you go?"

"Madrid first of all. I shall go to the Consulate there and see what the situation is."

"And then?"

"Get as close to the frontier as possible."

There was a silence: Tanguy dared not look at Father Pardo when he had said this. The priest had once more removed his glasses and was rubbing his half-closed eyes wearily.

"You are making a mistake," he said. "But it's one I should make in your place. I can offer you only my prayers, though I fear they will be of little use to you. I shall tell Sister in the linen store to find you another suit, a shirt or two, and a fresh pair of shoes. I'll buy you a ticket for Madrid, and you can start tomorrow evening."

Tanguy kissed Father Pardo's hand. Then, after a moment's hesitation, he went down on his knees. It was a custom in the college to give a blessing to those about to leave. Father placed both hands on Tanguy's head, and blessed him in his calm voice. Tanguy rose to his feet, heavy-hearted. He knew instinctively that Father was as upset as he was, and had no wish to add to his suffering; so he went down quickly into the courtyard, without looking back. Here the four Sisters in charge of the kitchens, the linen store, and the infirmary were waiting to say good-by to him. After them came Manolo, Platero, and Josselin.

Finally Tanguy got into the college car, took a last quick glance back, and saw Father Pardo, standing motionless behind a window. He shut his eyes. The car slid away, through fields lined with olives, their loaded branches gleaming in the moonlight. He reached Baeza station just in time to catch his train—an express that was full. Tanguy stood for a while in the corridor, then sat down on his suitcase. He wondered when the train was due to arrive in Madrid, but had forgotten to check this point in the timetable. He tried to think of something to distract his mind, and failed. He sat there and let his mind become an absolute blank.

13

IN Madrid Tanguy lodged as the guest of a monastic house to which Father Pardo had given him a letter of introduction. The house itself was near the big public park, and Tanguy had to walk only across the gardens to reach the French Consulate, a journey he made nearly every day.

There was a pleasant, elderly lady there called Mme Bérard. She was petite and white-haired, and still used make-up. She behaved in a most friendly way to Tanguy, and addressed him as "young man." Tanguy felt reassured by the sight of her, and reached the Consulate in a comparatively calm state of mind because he knew Mme Bérard was there. She seemed extremely touched by his predicament. To prove that the Consulate was taking the matter seriously and doing something about it, she showed him a thick file containing several dozen letters that had gone to and fro between the Ministry of Foreign Affairs in Paris and the French Consulate in Madrid. She told him that nothing more could be done, as far as she could see. Then he argued more and more insistently that they had to let him back into France. He even offered to join the army. It seemed to him that, since he was, after all, French, no one had the right to keep him out once they realized this. But Mme Bérard, with infinite patience, tried to make him understand that he had to have somewhere to go to. One day, when she was feeling more intimate than usual, she said to him quietly: "You know, my dear, your father is something of a bore. His refusal to reply to any of our letters seems to us both obstinate and irksome. All the same, I hope you succeed in getting back to France somehow."

When he left the Consulate Tanguy went for a walk in the park. He felt limp and exhausted. He was fond of strolling through the Rosary, where the barrel-organists played old Madrid dances. He stared at the children's nurses in their blue uniforms and white bibs. Sometimes he walked as far as the lake, where young men and their girls paddled about in canoes. When they got them out in deep water the boys would snatch kisses from the girls, a sight which amused Tanguy. He smiled and decided that life was fun after all.

Two months passed in these futile negotiations, and at last he realized that he would either have to give up and go back to the college, or else find some kind of a job. He foresaw the questions he would be asked by his friends if he went back, and made up his mind to look for work.

First of all he went to say good-by to Mme Bérard, sad at the thought that he would not see her again. He thanked her effusively for all she had done, and apologized for the trouble he had caused her. Mme Bérard was distressed at his going; she was sorry she hadn't done more for him, she said, but no one could force Tanguy's father to act against his inclinations. Tanguy said he understood, and smiled, and walked out of the place where he had spent so many long hours trying to rediscover his identity.

Since work was hard to find in Madrid, Tanguy had decided to go to Barcelona. He was sorry to leave Madrid, and even sorrier when at the end of his train journey Barcelona turned out to be an ugly, dirty town. Then he told himself that getting work was what mattered at the moment; and though he loved Madrid, he would find employment far more easily in a dirty industrial city than anywhere else.

Nevertheless, it was not so easy as he had imagined. Everywhere he applied, the employers looked down their noses at him. Tanguy had to remind himself that there was nothing to be ashamed of in wanting to find work. He read the "Help Wanted" columns in the daily press from end to end. He bought the papers early in the morning, and ran all the way to the addresses they gave. He was always told to make a written application, or come back in a week's time. He came to know what "come back in a week" really meant, but never was sure if he would be alive in a week or not.

He sat for long hours in smelly waiting-rooms. Here other job-hunters sat on the benches unrolling cigarette butts and making fresh cigarettes with the tobacco from them. They coughed incessantly, hawking and spitting on the floor. Tanguy would sit and listen, through this medley, to the deadened sounds of city life that seeped in from outside. After about two or three hours an employee of the firm would pin a little notice on the door which simply said: "No more vacancies." At that everybody would get up and slouch out patiently.

Tanguy used to go down to the port and watch the big mail-steamers, with names such as *El Cabo de Hormos* or *El Cabo de Buena Esperanza*. He would squat down on the edge of the quay and stare at the filthy water, with its floating jetsam of banana skins and rotten oranges. He indulged in curious daydreams: his spirit seemed to detach itself from his body and go adventuring in fabulous countries of the imagination. His physical desires had become a constant torment, and he often spent all night wandering through the streets like a soul in agony. The morning after one of these sleepless nights he had a furry mouth and cold misery in his heart: he felt himself somehow diminished.

His money had run out; he slept under park benches, and lived on fruit which he earned by unloading trucks in the market. Sometimes he got a tip as well, and then he was able to drink a hot *café au lait*. On two occasions he even made enough to go to the movies, a place that he particularly welcomed for its warmth and dark enveloping security.

But days passed into weeks, and still Tanguy found no work. One day he reminded himself that he could always commit suicide, but such an idea at once appeared absurd: who would benefit by his death? It was better to continue the struggle.

He would wander down the Ramblas, a bright pattern of flowers and hurrying people, or loiter in the Plaza de Cataluña; sometimes he even went as far as El Paralelo, his eyes fixed on the human tide surging past him, a tide in which he felt lost and solitary. Would any of these passers-by, he wondered, have understood him, had any of them ever found themselves in a comparable situation? He wanted to ask them this point-blank. Their faces intrigued him; he wanted to rip open their skulls and read the thoughts concealed within. Unyielding, ubiquitous, they continued their brisk to-and-fro activities, indifferent to his dilemma.

At last he was told, one day, that he was to be signed on in a cement factory at Vallcarca, a town in the Sitgès area just outside Barcelona. A ten minutes' train journey took him there.

14

THE factory was in itself almost a small town. Half a mile away there were the yards and the workshops with their big furnaces that blazed night and day, and never went out. Beyond all these lay the port, with its private flotilla of cargo vessels that were the company's property.

The factory proper was built in a small valley entirely surrounded by hills. The tall belching chimneys were framed in a setting of high pine-clad mountain slopes. The one road out led to the sea, where the company maintained a port and a recreation beach. On the far side of the mountains, along the coast, lay Sitgès, the elegant resort which Tanguy had already visited. The factory was laid out, like a planned town, with straight roads, all running parallel to each other, and included living quarters for employees. Houses and workshops alike were smothered in a fine white dust that looked like snow.

Tanguy reached the factory about ten o'clock in the morning and went first to the administration-building, where he found a door labeled EMPLOYMENT OFFICE. In the waiting-room he joined about twenty other men, among them a youth of sixteen. Yet this mere boy looked older than Tanguy, so ravaged was his face by misery and the battle for survival. Tanguy greeted the others and went and sat down in a corner. No one returned his "good morning." He sat there and waited. The workmen chatted and laughed together. At last, about midday, the door opened. One by one the workmen went in and came out with a piece of paper in their hand. They seemed satisfied enough. Tanguy wondered if he, too, would get such a chance. When his turn came he went into the office, and found himself in front of a white-haired man of medium height, with gray eyes and a very red complexion. He wore an excellently cut suit.

This man stared at Tanguy and asked if he had ever held a job previously. Tanguy shook his head.

"Have you any papers?"

"Here they are." Tanguy passed over the certificate Father Pardo had given him. It declared that he was honest, well-read, and spoke several languages. It added that he had done a two-year course of studies equivalent to the final two years of the baccalauréat, and that this course had been undertaken at the college of which he, Father Pardo, had the honor to be principal.

The man sat in thought for a moment, looked curiously

226

at Tanguy, and asked him whether he spoke French and English. Tanguy said he did.

"Then why are you looking for manual labor? You could have got a job as a secretary or private clerk in Barcelona, surely?"

"I've tried already. I found nothing."

"I see. The work is hard here—" he stared hard into Tanguy's face as he said this. "It's man's work."

"I'll do the best I can."

"To be absolutely frank, you don't look built for heavy labor."

Tanguy said: "I shall do whatever I have to do."

There was a pause. The man scribbled a few words on a piece of paper.

"I'll take you on trial. If you show yourself satisfactory over a period of three months, I'll have you assigned to the company's insurance office. You'll begin work on Monday at the yards. Chico will take you. Find him on Monday morning. He'll tell you what you have to do."

Tanguy felt as though he could fling his arms round the man's neck. But he merely smiled and thanked him.

He went out of the office in high spirits, practically skipping along. Someone asked him if he had got a job, and he showed them the piece of paper. They congratulated him. It was Saturday; so Tanguy had two days of freedom before him. He found the road down to the beach and went for a swim. The only thing separating the beach from the port was a jetty. The water was thick with oil discharged by the cargo boats. The sun was shining. Tanguy stretched himself out on

227

the sand: the sea was so dazzling that it hurt his eyes to look at it, points of light and white-flecked waves in an expanse of blue. The mountainside rose behind him, a purplish blue, except where in its flank a huge white scar was visible.

Cement.

Occasionally the silence was broken by the factory siren, which seemed to be continually summoning or dismissing the workers. Those released from work came and stretched out on the beach, covered with white dust. Some ran up and down the beach or went splashing into the sea. Above, on the Sitgès-Barcelona road, a stream of expensive cars (mostly belonging to tourists) passed by all day.

Tanguy had to find lodgings. He was given the address of a widow called Sebastiana, who had a room to let, and went there. Sebastiana had been born in Estremadura. She was a strong, thick-set, independent woman, with a wicked temper and a rough manner of speech. She had very little time for her neighbors, declaring them a pack of idle busybodies. She never went to church, and put up her shutters when a religious procession passed by. The workers loved her, and always grinned when her name was mentioned. Her husband had been killed in the factory. For thirty years she had known no other horizons than those of the narrow, dust-impregnated valley. Her life was regulated by the factory siren. Forthright herself, she detested sentimentality in others.

Tanguy was impressed by her blunt demeanor. She stood in front of him, hands on hips, in an aggressively respectable black dress. Her hair was done up in a bun, and there was an ageless quality about her. She stared him up and down with her black eyes and then said sharply: "Cat got your tongue?"

"I—er—I wanted to know if you had a room—"

"Yes, I have got a room. What of it?"

"A room to let, I mean."

"H'm. What part of the country are you from?"

"Madrid."

"Not so good," the Widow Sebastiana said. "People in Madrid are too fond of getting married. What are you doing here?"

"I'm starting work on Monday."

"Where?"

"In the yards."

"What's your family do?"

"I have no family," Tanguy said.

The Widow Sebastiana paused in her interrogation and looked at Tanguy more closely. Tanguy was beginning to wonder where all these questions were leading. He waited.

"No father or mother?" she asked.

"No." He had no desire to explain the whole story to everyone he met.

"Very well, then. Come on up, I'll show you your room."

The apartments let to the factory-workers were all identical; on each floor there were two separate rooms with a common lobby, which the tenants had to go down a flight of steps to reach. A small paved courtyard, not more than ten feet by twelve, had been laid down in front of the main entrance, and abutted on similar courtyards belonging to the apartment houses on either side. There seemed to be no windows in the rooms. The courtyard and the partition-walls were whitewashed. The furniture was cheap but scrupulously clean and well polished.

"This is the only room I have," Sebastiana said. "But it doesn't matter; they're all alike."

"Yes, so I see. How much do you charge?"

"What for?"

"The room."

"There's no fixed rent. You give me all your earnings. I'll fix that up with them myself, in fact. You've got to eat and have proper clothes. Men need to smoke, as well. Then there's the movies, but I shouldn't waste your time or money on *that*. Now, go and listen to the radio for a while and I'll cook the dinner. Do you like eggs?"

Tanguy nodded. He sank down into a chair, and took out his copy of the *Tristia* from his small suitcase. He read several favorite passages, and then combed the dial trying to find a program of classical music. Finally he hit on a German station which was broadcasting a Brandenburg Concerto.

Sebastiana came in, a plate in one hand piled high with eggs and fried potatoes. She looked a little worried. She put down Tanguy's meal, sat down herself, and said: "So you like Strauss, I see."

It took Tanguy a moment to realize that for Sebastiana there were only two sorts of music: popular Spanish dance-tunes and Strauss. Everything she couldn't understand was in the Strauss category. And as Spanish dances were the only tunes she understood, almost all music, for her, was by Strauss.

"Yes," Tanguy said (having worked the problem out), "yes, I do."

"And you read German, too."

"Oh, that! No, that's Latin."

230

Sebastiana looked at him distrustfully. "You're not a priest, are you?" she asked.

"No, no. This is secular Latin, nothing to do with religion. It's a poet called Ovid."

"Oh."

She sat quietly for a moment, watching him eat.

"Why have you come here?" she said at length.

"To work."

"But this is no place for someone like you!"

"Why not?"

"Nobody reads—what d'you call him?—Ovid, here. They read, oh, quite different things—"

When Tanguy had finished his meal, Sebastiana took him by the arm, and they went for a walk together down the main road. She stared at him with vast admiration. Suddenly she blurted out in a low voice: "I would have loved to have a son as handsome and intelligent as you."

Tanguy was moved by this impulsive remark; he felt its sincerity. He turned to her, smiling, and ran his hand once, quickly, over her gray hair. Then they resumed their walk. The factory chimneys still belched smoke, and a reddish glow was spread across the night sky. Close by the sea was roaring in against the cliffs. Down in one of those natural grottoes Tanguy had spent what he thought then was his first night of freedom. He smiled at the recollection: he had grown up a good deal since.

15

ON Monday Tanguy went out to the yards, and presented himself to Chico, his foreman, a big Catalan with a cheerful face. They got on well with each other from the start. Chico showed Tanguy his duties; the work was not too demanding, and he could take a rest occasionally.

From seven in the morning till seven at night, with an hour off for his midday meal, Tanguy rode standing, as a kind of guard, in the narrow-gauge train that transported the raw cement from the yard to the factory. Here the train passed beneath the tall cylindrical furnaces which were refining the cement at high temperatures. The workmen said they were the best furnaces of their kind in Europe, but Tanguy knew nothing of such matters. He was happy simply to be making a living. He was proud of his job, and worked hard at it. He did everything with meticulous care, as though the factory had been his own personal property.

He was delighted when someone told him that everything was going well, or that cargo-vessels were waiting for delivery of sacks. He took a lively interest in factory organization and the increase of productivity. But one day he stopped and asked himself why he was taking all this trouble. No one took any notice of him. It was no less than his desserts if the workshop hand grinned patronizingly at him when he went past in his little train. Then he realized that in this huge factory, belching fire into the night, he was a mere nothing.

His work had no meaning at all except to prevent him dying of hunger.

There was, to be sure, the managing-director's office, remote in some Olympian eminence; but Tanguy had never laid eyes on either the managing-director or his office. The managing-director, in fact, was something of a myth. He was a man who talked on the telephone, who had a secretary —perhaps two or even three secretaries; who could dismiss him, Tanguy, without the slightest argument.

Tanguy wondered how the men in this place could go on living such a slavish existence. He simply could not understand, however hard he tried, what made them accept it all, why they toiled there day after day without even having seen their own managing-director. Then he discovered one simple but vital truth: they were acclimatized to it all. Acclimatized. That was the word. Acclimatized to their wretched life, acclimatized to having nothing more than the meanest and most immediate hopes. The whole week they lived for Sunday, laboring on in the hope of buying a dress for their little girl or a table for the dining-room. They were satisfied with being men only on the week-end, when they bathed at the beach or went to the factory movie theater. They used to say they didn't go into Sitgès, because if they did the gentry would be obliged to move elsewhere. Tanguy was astounded by their servility; he could not stomach their docile animal patience. After his own desperate struggle for independence he told himself that these men could have no idea of their own strength, or their capacity for fighting oppression.

Little by little the factory swallowed up their individuality.

The superintendent was a German, and the workers spat on the floor whenever his name was mentioned; but that was the limit of their self-assertiveness. This German had introduced a series of new rules which made their life even more intolerable than it had been hitherto. Workers' children, for example, were not permitted under any pretext to seek employment elsewhere. They were tied up in advance by an agreement with the company. If their parents sent them to work in Barcelona, then the parents themselves lost their job or were evicted from their wretched lodgings.

In order to cut the cost of wages, the German had made contracts with the state to supply a part of his labor force. Freight trains arrived at the factory, full of ill-clad and starving Murciens, who had traveled in sealed trucks under a collective passport. They were forbidden to leave the cars during the hours of daylight. The managing-director then "offered" them a contract of employment which, for Murciens, represented generosity. Then the board of directors would publish an announcement that declared that employers and workers had *unanimously* agreed to reduce the scale of wages by so much "in view of the fall in the cost of living."

Tanguy earned 18 pesetas a day. He worked two hours overtime, and these were paid at the rate of 3.65 pesetas. This meant that on the average he earned 25 pesetas a day. The maximum wage-scale rose to 32, overtime included. The foremen got about 40. Moreover, the cost of living, far from falling, rose continually, and Sebastiana was hard put to make both ends meet, and Tanguy knew it. On Thursday she had to buy on credit at the co-operative store by pledging Saturday's paycheck.

Despite everything Tanguy was pleased on Saturdays when he got his little blue envelope, and only too glad to hand it over to Sebastiana. She had bought him (on credit again) a sports jacket and a red tie. On Saturday, after leaving the factory, he washed himself under the tap in the courtyard, put on his jacket, and went off whistling to find his friend José, whom he nicknamed Pepe. Together they would take the train into Sitgès, and go to a café Pepe knew, where they would have several drinks and listen to *flamenco*. Then they would go to the movies.

But Monday came around again, and Tanguy went back to the factory. Every day he became a little more exhausted. In the evenings he had a return of his long bouts of feverish shivering, accompanied by headaches and coughing. He could not lie down flat without beginning to choke. The cement dust irritated his throat; it tasted like sand. His palate was coated with the stuff. When he coughed, Sebastiana came into his room, wrapped a woolen shawl round his shoulders, and sat down on his bed, stroking his hair and patting him gently on the back.

Tanguy was suffering acutely. Besides his physical fatigue, which increased daily, he began to feel the utter despair of someone who sees himself turning into a mere beast of burden. He was gradually being sucked into the miserable quicksands of resignation: he was coming to *accept* his wretched lot, and this was the one thing he was determined to avoid. Between two fits of coughing he suddenly burst into tears. Sebastiana whispered comforting words to him in her gruff voice, and he came to the conclusion that at nineteen one isn't so grown up after all.

His face grew paler and paler, his features more worn and drawn. He lost his appetite. He spent his evenings writing letters to everyone he could think of—the French Consul and his father leading the list. No reply ever came. Every day he trudged off to the factory while it was still dark, and stayed there for twelve hours. He wore a handkerchief over his mouth to avoid swallowing the dust that pervaded the factory, but this was useless. When he returned home he was covered with a white floury crust from head to foot. It was useless to try and spit the stuff out; it was *in* him.

Soon he had to do as the others did and sign on for a night shift. The rates were higher, 5 pesetas an hour. After the hours of day-work came three hours on the night-shift. The work consisted in loading the cargo boats, stacking sacks of cement in the holds. It was a back-breaking job. As the cranes dropped the sacks in the hold, they sent up clouds of dust. The workers had protective masks, but even so their eyes stung horribly, and they coughed all the time. Two men lifted each sack as it came and stacked it. They had to work fast. The sacks fell at mathematically spaced intervals, and if you gave up for a bit the labor became sheer agony.

One of Tanguy's companions on this shift was called Alejandro. He was a big fellow of about thirty-five, with a lined face. His wife too worked in the factory. He did fourteen hours a day, she did ten. He only had one fear: that the night-shift might one day be stopped.

Tanguy began to lose all hope; he felt himself sliding into despair. His final efforts to make contact with his family had met a blank wall of silence. He had written to his father and said he was ill. No reply. This, indeed, did not worry

Tanguy unduly. It was not so much his father that he was trying to reach as the soil of France. Tanguy still believed some of the things he had been told as a child, among them that France was the country of liberty, equality, and fraternity, where there were neither rich nor poor. One made a decent living there. It was true, as Tanguy admitted, that his first experience of a concentration camp had been in France; that the police who had handed him over to the Germans were French, and so, indeed, was his father. But he told himself that all this was under wartime conditions, and that now he was bound to discover the real France, the France that had greeted him on his return from Germany, the France of the Revolution.

At night, when he could not sleep, he listened to radio programs from Paris, and waited for the end of the transmission simply to hear the *"Marseillaise,"* which brought tears of emotion to his eyes. He was sure that once he got back to France he would at last gain the peace of which he dreamed so long.

Then, in the middle of the night, Sebastiana would wake him to go on late shift. She hardly needed to touch him; he woke as men wake who have in the past had frightful awakenings. He jumped out of bed at the least noise. Sebastiana cut him a slice of bread which he dipped in oil and ate. He used to cut a tomato in two and eat it as he walked to the docks. Every day there was the same struggle against resignation and apathy. Every day he had to make the same superhuman effort to keep going.

SEBASTIANA was devoted to Tanguy, in a silent, inarticulate way. She watched over him and took care of him. Every day, during the midday break, everyone saw her arrive with "the kid's" dinner. She had a half-hour's walk each way to bring him his food, but she was determined he must get something hot inside him. She always managed to get something which she considered a "luxury"—a slice of ham, perhaps, or a little cheese. She arrived proudly carrying her bundle and sat on a big stone, in the shade, beside Tanguy. Other workers used to have jokes at her expense, and tell her she was "past the age for that kind of thing." She let them talk, and did not even take the trouble to reply. She was desolated at seeing Tanguy so ill and dejected, and she continued to look after him with extraordinary tenderness.

She spent a great deal of time finding classical music for him in the radio programs, pretending to adore Bach and Beethoven. In the evening, after Tanguy had come home, they would sit before dinner in the little courtyard and chat. When he was reading the paper or listening to music, she sat quietly, without moving or speaking.

They never expressed their affection openly. Sebastiana's love remained dumb; like Gunther, she never gave external reality to her tender feelings except through the unimpeachable eloquence of her actual behavior. She lived for Tanguy as she would have lived for her own son, watched over him while he slept, took care of his clothes, gave him

the kind of food he liked best (as far as she could), and tried
to find amusements for him. On Sundays they sometimes
picnicked on the beach, well away from the crowd.

He told her about everything. She listened in silence and
smiled at him tenderly. All her understanding came from her
heart, for she was the maternal instinct personified. Tanguy,
on his part, loved and admired her because she was fair and
honest. He loved her uncalculating generosity and her tranquil expression. She was sensible rather than clever, but she
almost always knew what was right.

Six months after Tanguy began work in the factory a
rumor spread among the workers that there was going to be
a strike in Barcelona. The excuse was this: Parliament had
voted a 10 per cent rise on all salaries and wages "on account
of the increased cost of living." Seven months later this increase had by no means been universally enforced. The various
branches of industry were taking concerted action, and
the students were only too ready to join them. Plenty of
shopkeepers were ready to put up their shutters at the
first hint of trouble.

So far the cement factory had had nothing more dangerous
than a few secret meetings. Some were all for the strike and
declared that no especial risk was involved by joining it;
others were certain that the risks were considerable, and no
particular purpose would be served by such action. The two
sides argued on volubly day after day. The national radio
launched a full-scale propaganda counter-attack, accusing
"Communist or Jewish elements" of trying to foment dis-
turbances, and every day repeating their *ad hoc* slogan: "Hold

the *pass* against the Reds!" Tanguy knew very well that the workers cared very little about Communism, and that all they were interested in was getting better wages, and therefore better food: perhaps, too, in working shorter hours.

Loudspeaker systems were installed throughout the factory, and filled the air by turns with promises and threats, blowing hot or cold according to the management's mood. Nobody paid any attention to this stuff. What did alarm the bolder spirits were the trainloads of armed police and Civil Guards, armed with sub-machine guns, that began to arrive with monotonous regularity. Were they going to shoot? Would there be incidents? This was what everyone wanted to know. Tanguy watched this display of force in silence. He had never taken part in a strike, and hardly knew what it meant. Nevertheless, he attended the meeting of the strike committee.

The workers argued for a long time. They took a vote on a show of hands. Some claimed that a strike would be tantamount to suicide. Alejandro got up on the platform and claimed that the employers were going to abolish overtime and take other serious decisions of a similar nature. Chico got the most attentive hearing. He had worked in the factory for twenty-six years and was far from being a hothead. He too thought that the strike was an act of despair, the "last ditch stand of an army whose cause is lost," and refused to believe that such extreme steps were necessary. He would have supported lightning strikes in different sectors of industry, which might have had some real effect. But he felt, also, that they had no right to leave their comrades of

Barcelona in the lurch simply because the management had shown their teeth.

This speech received loud applause. Another worker wanted to know what steps they could take to avoid "incidents." Chico took up this point. He thought the "bloated pluto-crats" were trying to provoke incidents in order to have an easier excuse for crushing the strike, and stopping demon-strations. The best thing to do, he thought, was to make the women go on a protest march: no one would open fire on them.

At this point a confused hubbub arose. Most of the men firmly believed that a woman's proper place was in the kitchen; she had no business meddling with politics. Chico shouted back that this was not a matter of politics but bread, and women knew the meaning of hunger as well as men did. What was more, a large proportion of the women actually worked in the factory.

In the end the strike was approved by an overwhelming majority. The factory would shut down, and strike pickets would be posted to prevent blacklegs going back to work. The workers would assemble in the biggest square in Barce-lona and stage a protest march with their city comrades. They would take great care to avoid all "incidents" and would not respond to any provocation—except verbally, of course.

The day fixed for the strike arrived, and Tanguy put on his best clothes as though he were going to a party. All the other workers did the same. He set off down the street with Sebastiana on his arm. She was delighted by the whole business, and kept declaring to anyone who cared to listen that the workers were at last beginning to use their heads. The strike committee had "confiscated" all the factory trucks, and it was in these that they traveled to Barcelona. Each truck carried a placard which read: WE WANT BREAD. On one the message was altered, and read: WE WANT TO LIVE. This slogan stirred Tanguy deeply. He knew the utter misery of these men, who were risking their livelihood in order to express their will to live. The urge for life must be immensely strong, he thought, if those who have never really lived at all persist in affirming their right to.

They found Barcelona in a state of armed emergency. The streets were packed with idle spectators, and police squads armed with sub-machine guns lined the pavements, exchanging insults with the workers, who called them every name under the sun but carefully refrained from any kind of physical gesture. When a worker got excited and tried to break ranks, his comrades pulled him back into line again. At last the procession reached the big square. Tanguy had never seen such a vast mass meeting in his life. There were thousands and thousands of people assembled there, men, women and children alike, chatting and joking among themselves. The men were in shirtsleeves. In the fashionable streets around the square all the shutters were up and barred.

About eleven o'clock the procession got under way again. It spread right across the roadway and covered both pavements, and was so long that anyone in the middle could see neither the beginning nor the end. It was a vast human wave, sluggishly rolling toward the docks. The police watched it pass, but made no effort to stop it. Slowly the air became hotter.

Tanguy was suddenly struck by the potential strength of these men. There they were, marching shoulder to shoulder, and nothing could stop their advance except the docks and the harbor beyond them. They were the strong ones. All of them at this moment became aware of their own strength and, more still, of their collective powers as a group. Tanguy realized that the myth of the "management" only really existed because they wanted it. And it was at this same moment that a wave of depression swept over him. He was acutely aware of being different from them, of "not belonging." He was afraid of the force which they symbolized. Listening to their wild laughter, their threats and insults, he knew in agony that one day these men would stream out into the streets again, not calmly this time but hot for blood. And when that day came, there would once more be neither conquerors nor conquered, but only victims.

About one o'clock, the hottest part of the day, Tanguy reached the Ramblas. It was then that a new rumor spread from group to group: soldiers were driving the streetcars. Everyone speculated anxiously on what this meant. Eventually the order was passed to close ranks and not give way. The workers continued their advance. Then came the grinding, metallic sound of a streetcar moving up the Ramblas toward the procession. Neither the streetcar nor the marching workers gave way: it was a queer, silent duel of wills. Finally the procession won; the streetcar pulled up barely a couple of yards in front of the leading ranks, which were composed entirely of women. A huge, raucous, barely human shout went up: "*We have won, comrades!*"

For two days everything was quiet in the factory. The personnel went back to work as usual. But something was different. Sebastiana said to Tanguy: "They have realized that they hold the whip hand. Sooner or later today's strike will turn into a real disaster for the scum. It's always fatal for them when the workers learn their own strength, and realize there's more of them. It won't happen immediately, but the wheels have begun to turn. Nothing will stop it now. Getting it going is the really difficult part."

Tanguy made no reply to this. He went on with his daily work, coughing and spitting. He wondered if one day there would be an end of it all, and could not see the use of such things as strikes; nothing essential seemed to have been changed. But on the second day after the strike he learned that seventy-two men had been let off. He went over to the typed notice of dismissals and found his own name on it. He asked himself why they should pick on him, of all people; what had he done? Then he shrugged his shoulders; he had become almost indifferent to this kind of thing by now. He was unhappy for Sebastiana's sake. But when he got home Sebastiana was not there: she had been taken off by the Civil Guard. Tanguy found out from a neighbor that she had taken a leading part in inciting the women to strike with the men.

He went back to Barcelona and tried by every means he knew to find out what had become of her. But he could not discover even where she was being held. When he finally gave up the search he sold his new suit, his one overcoat, and a watch that Father Pardo had given him as a farewell present. He had made up his mind to risk everything on one desperate chance.

He boarded a train for San Sebastian, exhausted, feverish and shivering, but driven on by one determined idea, to get into France by any means he could.

17

IT had been raining ceaselessly for five days. Tanguy lay in bed with the big window open, lulled by the monotonous drumming of water on the roof and ground. It was a soft, gentle, cozy sound, like the rustle of a woman's dress.

Tanguy felt himself getting weaker from lack of food. He had eaten nothing for two days except a small bag of sweets. He lay stretched out on his bed, trying to pull his thoughts into some coherent pattern. Sometimes he got up, but when he did the blood rushed to his head and his legs began to tremble worse than ever. He was not even hungry any longer.

The room he had rented was on the seventh story. His window looked out on a terrace with a panoramic view of San Sebastian, the bay, and the surrounding countryside.

Tanguy thought it would be very pleasant to be sitting out on this terrace in hot weather, with a glass of lemonade. Then he grimaced, because he actually disliked lemonade; what he needed was a Cinzano, or a gin-sling full of crushed ice.

The room was covered with neutral-tinted wallpaper. One night Tanguy had spotted some bedbugs crawling over his blankets, so he took to sleeping in his clothes to avoid being bitten, and left his light on to make himself feel less lonely. His room was paid in advance for a week, but he realized that he could not stay there indefinitely without eating. The idea crossed his mind of going to call on the woman who had befriended him seven years before, Mme Lucienne. But this at once made him blush with shame. I haven't sunk to begging yet, he told the empty room. Then he began to listen to the rain again. It kept him company.

Every evening he went to the station to watch the departure of the little electric train that ran to the frontier. He had no more money left, otherwise he would have boarded it himself. It's the nearest I can get to France, he said to himself over and over again, like a talisman.

He suddenly wondered what would become of him in Paris if there were no one to meet him at the station. He smiled wryly: in all probability he would never manage to get out of Spain. Besides, if things went wrong, he could always find work there. He honestly believed that in Paris everyone worked, and could find jobs easily.

He studied train timetables, and worked out which services

were the quickest, and how often they ran. It was something to amuse himself with.

One day while he was thus engaged a young man sat down beside him on the station bench and got into conversation with him. He began by grumbling about the weather: this rain had been going on for far too long, and there had been an excessively dry spell before it. There was a likelihood of floods, besides serious damage to the crops. Tanguy had not paid much attention to this particular problem, though he vaguely remembered having read something about it in the papers. His new acquaintance looked worried: it would be extremely awkward for him, he said, if the floods made the rail and road connections with the frontier impassable. Tanguy asked him if he knew Biarritz, and the young man said yes, he went there every day on business.

As they walked back into the town together, Tanguy told the young man about himself, leaving out several of the more incredible details. The young man, whose name was Ricardo, smiled to put him at his ease, and Tanguy was grateful to him for this encouragement. Ricardo agreed that it was a difficult business, getting across the frontier, but that there was just a chance that he, Ricardo, might be of some assistance. But what would Tanguy do when he *had* crossed the frontier? How would he get from Hendaye to Paris without any money? This was a problem that had never occurred to Tanguy. The one thing he had concentrated on was getting into France. He believed that this squiggly red line drawn on the map was the one thing that stood between him and the peace and happiness for which he craved. Now he began to see that there were many other obstacles, but that if he tried to forestall them all, he might reach a point where he never left his room or even his bed. He had to make a start somewhere.

Ricardo invited him to come home with him and stay for dinner. Tanguy accepted gladly: he felt an almost physical need to stay close to Ricardo. He clung desperately to the young man's vitality and confidence. He felt soothed and comforted by this kindly person, in whose voice he read nothing but warmth and simple affection. The whole relationship struck him as quite normal.

After a bath and a change of clothes, Tanguy brushed his hair and examined himself in the mirror: he looked very thin and pale. Nevertheless he felt a vast sense of well-being spread through him. He went down and had a very pleasant dinner with his new friend. At first he was too exhausted to appreciate what he was eating. By the end of the meal his head was swimming a little.

"I've drunk too much," he said solemnly. "It must have been because I mixed the wines. Yes, that's what it was."

Ricardo went on talking away cheerfully. He explained that he had in his possession a number of passes, signed by the Commissioner of Police in San Sebastian, authorizing him to cross into France for two-day trips. With one of these cards Tanguy would get across the frontier the following morning. Suddenly Ricardo looked hard at him and said: "Is it all true, honestly?"

"Is all what true?"

248

"All this stuff about your childhood and your father and these Jesuit priests, and the rest of it. Do you *really* want to find your father? Is that *really* your reason for crossing the frontier?"

"Why, of course."

Ricardo was silent for a moment. Then he went on, in a quiet, serious voice: "When I was a little boy, I believed everybody. Even the priests. Little by little life has taught me not to believe anyone. I swore I'd never be had for a sucker again. Despite all that, something tells me you're not lying. I shall pay for your journey to Paris. You can repay me at your leisure."

Tanguy felt his throat tighten with emotion. He thanked Ricardo awkwardly.

"No, it's fair enough. We all have to help one another. One day you'll be in a position to do me a good turn. You never know, do you?"

He came close to Tanguy and rested a hand lightly on each of the boy's shoulders: then, with a lover's tenderness, slid them down and under his coat. Tanguy's mind went whirling: Ricardo was still murmuring words to him, but he did not hear them. He was thinking: so that's what the bastard wanted all the time, simply to take advantage of my position. That's why he invited me to dinner, and promised to pay my fare! Then he stopped thinking, realizing that there must be more to it than this single motive. His suspicions might well be unjust. The young man could easily have acted on the spur of the moment, and simply be taking advantage of a propitious moment. Tanguy still felt that

249

when a moment or two earlier Ricardo had spoken with such generosity he was sincere in what he said; and, indeed, that he was sincere now, as well.

Tanguy wanted to find words to express his feelings. His mind turned suddenly to the rain, the bedbugs, the horrible loneliness he had experienced during the last few days. Despite everything, would it be better, in the long run, to stay? And at that he gave up trying to think altogether. Only the feeling of misery remained, because he felt in his bones that what he was doing was wrong.

PART THREE

The Two Worlds

The Two Worlds

I

RICARDO had kept his promise. Tanguy sat in the corner of his compartment watching the French countryside slip past him. After eight hours the rain had stopped, and a watery sun shone through the clouds, revealing green pastureland and neat hedges. The sight moved Tanguy with nostalgia: this was the land he had known as a child, and so often despairingly recalled. Eagerly he examined the rich, fertile panorama spread out in front of him, though his eyes were blurred with tears.

He shivered: he was still very weak. There was a continual pain in his throat. Suddenly, for no apparent reason, he felt like lying down and crying his eyes out. He felt exhausted and broken. Everything terrified him. He wondered whether his father had received the telegram he had sent him and whether he would be at the station to meet him; then shrugged this off as unimportant, and once more glued his nose to the window. He was trying to establish some kind of relationship between France and Spain, but found it impossible.

Spain, he thought, is the desert. The desert is infinite. What is really astonishing in Spain is the strange relationship between man and the countryside. It is right that Spain should be the land of fanatics, mystics, and idealists. Quixote and Pancha would both die of misery among these nicely hedged green fields, with their civilized garden walls.

He got up, suddenly nervous. Would the French police search the train, or ask to examine all passports? Ricardo had assured him that nothing of the sort was liable to happen after Bordeaux. But they had not yet reached Bordeaux. Supposing something of the sort happened, and he was caught, what would they do with him? No one would believe him, or even listen to his story. Besides, he was so badly dressed.

He went into the W.C., took out the few scraps of paper which might have established his identity, and tore them into bits. This way, he thought, they won't know where I've come from. They won't even be able to tell that I'm Spanish.

He put away his wallet and came out of the W.C. relieved partially at least of his anxiety. He went back to his window seat and let himself be lulled by the monotonous rhythm of the train's wheels, his memory wandering over the crowded past weeks. It was cold, and he felt the tightening in his throat again. The past still weighed on his mind; he carried it about with him and had no idea of how to exorcise it. He shut his eyes and suddenly remembered Sebastiana; she must be in prison, perhaps thinking of him and weeping. Then, once again, he asked himself what he would do if his father was not at the station to meet him. What could he do other than he had always done—resign himself to the inevitable, find some way out of the immediate predicament? He had become accustomed to impossible situations.

No awkward incidents disturbed his daydream; he hardly even noticed when the long autumn afternoon faded into dusk, and the first suburban lights winked out. He was asleep. But as they drew into Paris he woke up and smiled to himself. He found it rather funny that this should be his third visit to Paris, and yet that he should still not have really *seen* the city at all. All he knew about it was that the Champs-Elysées ran from the Place de l'Etoile to the Place de la Concorde, and that if you followed the river you came to Notre-Dame.

He got up, took down his little green case from the rack, and went back to the W.C. He observed that in France the trains were cleaner; probably, he decided, because they were electric. But he had a weakness for those good old Spanish trains which kept no timetable except that dictated by the driver's fancy. Tanguy looked at himself in the mirror, took out a comb that Sebastiana had given him, and combed his long hair back. Then he washed his hands and face, and gave his jacket a brush-down. He was wearing an old suit which Father Pardo had had made for him, and which was now dyed black. It was too tight for him. Not my fault, he told himself.

He was just going out of the W.C. when he remembered an occasion in his childhood: a French policeman had made him leave the door open while he satisfied his needs. This recollec tion depressed him again. Then the train ground to a stand-still, and Tanguy got out, clutching his suitcase.

The station looked enormous to him. He walked toward the barrier, throwing agonized glances about him, suddenly afraid. He was dreading the moment when (in all probability) he would find himself alone in a vast unknown city. He began to think he never ought to have left Spain; but it was too late now. A great human tide was swirling sluggishly to-ward the exit. Tanguy felt he wanted to stop one of these men and speak to him. Among these anonymous faces there must be someone who had known war, hunger, loneliness, and despair. They would listen to him, surely? He felt a desperate need to talk to *someone*, to say what had happened to him. But no one would believe his story. They would either think him mad, or presume him to be importuning them. All these men around him had forgotten the past; they would never want to listen to so improbable a story. The war had been over for years. How was it possible that in 1953 a young man had still not escaped from its clutches?

Tanguy gave his ticket to the collector, and walked out into a big courtyard filled with cars; he had never seen so many at one time before. He stood there astonished, gazing at the illuminated signs, the brilliant street lamps, the red carrots marking the tobacconists' shops. He stood still, scared. He knew he should pluck up courage and plunge out into the street, but he remained rooted there. He had given up all hope of his father being at the station to meet him. The last travelers were straggling out with their relatives or friends. People were kissing and exchanging embraces all round him. Tanguy wondered where he should go. He had three hundred francs left. Could he have supper on three hundred francs? Then it occurred to him that it was too late for supper.

A tall, balding man bent down toward him (this movement obviously cost him an effort) and asked him if he was looking for someone. When Tanguy nodded the man said: "Are you young M. Legrand?"

Astonished, Tanguy agreed that he was, and stared at the man in some perplexity. The man, guessing the meaning of this look, at once added: "No, don't worry, I'm not your father! He's just coming. He was waiting for you on the platform. He's been cursing you for not turning up. Now, put your suitcase down. He won't be long. Did you have a good trip?"

"Yes, thank you."

Tanguy stood there, waiting. His heart was beating so violently that he thought he was going to faint. This, he told himself, is not exactly the moment to faint. Distinctly not. He imagined it as a scene from a novel: a father and his son looking for each other on a station platform like a pair of strangers. Then he came to the conclusion that his whole life had been pure fiction, nothing more, and fiction of the sort that not even Jules Verne would have dared to put his name to.

"There he is now," the man said.

A stranger was approaching them. He must have been between forty-five and fifty, and his sparse hair was beginning to turn white. He was wearing a dark gray overcoat and walked with his shoulders hunched. His complexion was as dark as a Spaniard's, his nose short and straight, and his lips very full. But the first thing one noticed about him was his eyes: huge, dark, liquid eyes that shone like a crow's wing in the sun. His hands, in contrast to all this, were powerful and rather clumsy, the hands of a manual worker.

Tanguy watched him, with some emotion. His father, quite suddenly, had become old. For Tanguy his father's face was unconsciously fixed in the image of what he had been fifteen years before, when he used to visit Tanguy and his mother in Vichy. But time had passed, and now his father was an old man. The thought distressed Tanguy.

"So it's you, is it?" he said, in a brusque, disagreeable voice. Once again, Tanguy had the sensation of not being exactly welcome.

"Y-yes."

"Good. Come on, we must go and talk somewhere. You can leave your suitcase in the car. What have you got in it, by the way?"

"A little dirty linen—"

"*Dirty?*"

"Yes—that is, I—" He gave up. They all three got into a big black car. His father was fiddling nervously with a bunch of keys.

"I should be very interested to know what made you decide to come here. Oh, I realize you must have thought, I've got a father, why not go and find him again?—but why *now*, in particular?"

Tanguy tried to explain his reasons to his father, who seemed anxious to know every detail, and was particularly curious about Tanguy's mother. How did they come to be separated? he wanted to know. Tanguy made up his mind to say nothing, or at least as little as possible; and, besides, there was comparatively little that he did know. But his father insisted, and Tanguy had to get out of this impasse as best he could. He was tired of talking. Every instinct in him cried out that his father's attitude toward him was steeped in contempt, and that he was absolutely not to be trusted in any way. This was a man who spoke, in every sense, with his lips only, just as when he shook hands he only offered you the tips of his fingers.

He took Tanguy to Montparnasse, and the man who had spoken to him first came with them. They sat down on the terrace of the Rotonde. Tanguy asked for a small brandy. While he drank it he was subjected to a fresh interrogation. Inside the café an orchestra was playing "The Blue Danube," and his father still went on fiddling with his keys. These noises set Tanguy's teeth on edge, and he would have given anything on earth to make them stop. He shut his eyes and went on talking as best he could. His father was smiling in a falsely unself-conscious manner. Inside, a woman in a very low-cut evening dress was beginning to sing something about "shovelfuls of—" Tanguy didn't hear exactly what, but decided it was probably kisses.

"You haven't any papers, then?" his father was saying.

"No."

His father turned and glanced at their companion, as if to call him to witness that everything was exactly as he had predicted. Then he looked his son up and down with infinite distaste and said: "You look just like some lousy little light-fingered street-arab."

259

Tanguy flushed. He would have liked to reply that after a week of near-starvation, lonely and miserable, it was hardly to be wondered at if he looked a little odd and disheveled. He might also have added that it would have occurred to no one except his father that Tanguy would come back nicely dressed and with all his papers in order. He might have said that most starving men in rags are less dishonest than many others with fat bellies and testimonials from the right people tucked away in their wallets. Testimonials, like food, are to be bought; but honesty and honor are neither for sale nor for purchase. But how much of this would his father have understood? Almost nothing. He sat looking at Tanguy now with plainly visible antipathy, and Tanguy felt sick at heart. He had reached the limit of his physical endurance, and felt nothing but relief when his father announced that he was going to take him to a hotel and call for him the following morning at eleven o'clock.

2

THE following morning his father actually arrived on time. He was dressed in a smart black pin-stripe suit which accentuated his height. He was freshly shaven and had a languid air about him. Tanguy found him extremely good-looking.

Once more he took his son to the Rotonde, this time to

the inside part of the café. At this time of the morning no orchestra was playing, and the place was empty except for two lovers locked in an apparently endless embrace. Tanguy approved of the lovers, and their evident pleasure gave him pleasure too. Nevertheless he listened carefully to what his father was saying: he had produced a file of letters, and was trying to prove with their help that his mother was responsible for all Tanguy's troubles. At this point Tanguy tried to remove his conscious mind altogether: he found this man's behavior extremely vulgar, and told himself that no Spaniard would ever have conducted himself in such a fashion. His mind went flitting back to the country he had so recently left.

"I don't want to run down your mother to you," his father was saying, "but I don't, equally, want you to get the impression that I'm some kind of monster. If I didn't reply to your letters, it was because I was convinced that they were more or less dictated by your mother. When you were a child, and your mother and I separated, I wanted to take you with me. But she refused to let you go: so I told her that I never wanted to hear your name mentioned again. Besides, I—er— thought you had become, h'm, some kind of, ah, *workman*. But I see you have an educated look about you—"

Tanguy felt a strong temptation to laugh. What would this incredible man have made of him if he had turned out to be one-eyed, mad, or criminal? Then he reflected that, after all, it is only natural for an intelligent man to desire well-educated sons.

"I propose to give you a chance, as the English are so fond of saying. I am going to try and help you. How, I'm not quite sure yet. I'm not a very rich man, and I work very hard for what I have. But I think I can arrange something for you—"

Tanguy hardly heard a word of what his father was saying; his mind was elsewhere. Occasionally he said "yes." His father was beginning to discuss his mother again. Suddenly Tanguy felt himself blushing from utter shame. He was ashamed for the man sitting facing him, who seemed incapable of blushing or feeling shame at all. What his father had said that so astonished Tanguy was: "Besides, I can't even be sure you *are* my son. Your mother was a pretty hot little piece in those days."

This remark stank of falsehood, the kind of lie that was deliberately calculated to hurt. But Tanguy remained outwardly unruffled. He was blushing, indeed: blushing for a man who dared to speak in this way without being struck dead for it. But on reflection he decided that his father's motive was to be found in cowardice rather than malice. His father carried an aura of cowardice about with him. Tanguy had only to take one look at him to identify it. His eyes flickered furtively away from you, his hands were soft and nervous, his speech stilted, his manners falsely protective. Tanguy began to feel sorry for him.

Tanguy had lunch in a self-service cafeteria in the Avenue George V. He was glad to be alone in Paris. He finished his meal quickly and walked back to the Place de la Concorde, where he stood for a while in silent admiration; then he went back up the Champs-Elysées. The leaves were turning yellow; the air was misty, but a rather watery sun struggled through it to warm the heart. Tanguy smiled wistfully; how wonderful it would have been if Sebastiana had been able to see him in Paris, actually on the Champs-Elysées!

At three o'clock he went down to the tearoom in the Colisée, where he was supposed to meet his father again. This time his father was late. Tanguy had ordered himself a coffee; he felt more at ease. There was a pleasant atmosphere about the place; here the orchestra played soft, muted music. Tanguy promised himself another visit to the Colisée.

Once again his father returned to the subject of his mother. Tanguy paid no attention to what he was saying. He felt in a pleasant mood and had no desire to be hurt unnecessarily. He went over his father's characteristics with minute accuracy and tried to analyze just what reaction the word "father" evoked in him. But it seemed merely to leave him indifferent.

"I wanted to say—there is something else I have to tell you—" His father, he suddenly noticed, was visibly embarrassed. Tanguy was curious to know why, and concentrated his attention on his father's nervous ramblings. At last his father came out with the fact that he had remarried. He had married a charming woman, with two grown-up children, and they had a very happy home. . . .

Tanguy bore him no resentment for this. His only concern was at not knowing his stepmother. Then his father, in a still more strained and formal voice, announced that he was tired of dragging Tanguy round cafés, and was going to take him home to tea.

I'm going to have tea in my own home, Tanguy thought. But the phrase had an unpleasant taste about it, the excitement fell somehow flat.

Before being taken "home," Tanguy had to pass through the hands of a hairdresser and men's haberdasher in turn. He began to notice a subtle change in his father's attitude toward him. He now seemed quite pleased to be able to take an interest in his son, and to buy him things. He kept an eye on the way Tanguy's hair was cut, and went so far as to say that they both had the same hair, you couldn't help noticing it. Tanguy realized then that his father must have retained, somewhere in the depths of his conscience, the memory of this son who, from time to time, wrote him imploring and agonized letters. He was touched by this discovery. He would have liked to kiss this man, his father, and say that, yes, he loved him; that he, his father, was not the only one responsible for his son's mishaps. The whole thing had been a horrible stroke of bad luck which simply had to be forgotten: there had been the war, the occupation, successive waves of destruction—no, his father could not be saddled with the entire responsibility, perhaps not even with the greatest part of it. Besides, Tanguy felt no ill-will toward him. He bore no grudge against him or anyone: he was simply tired and wanted rest, a chance to recover and begin life over again.

When he was ushered into his father's house he was taken back by the beautiful furniture in the drawing-room: he had never seen anything to compare with it, even in the movies. Sensibly, he sat waiting in an armchair while his father went to look for his stepmother. He felt somewhat embarrassed.

A door opened and his stepmother came in. She was a tall, svelte woman, who carried herself with considerable elegance. Her eyes were green and her hair was blond and she was very well-dressed, with a kind of expensive simplicity. She grasped both of Tanguy's hands and stammered some kind of greeting: there were tears in her eyes. Tanguy wondered *why* she was crying. She told him she would try to love him and be kind to him. Then she wiped her eyes and explained that all the furniture consisted of genuine antiques, made by famous craftsmen. . . .

They both found themselves a little embarrassed in the other's presence. Tanguy felt somewhat relieved when his father came back, and told him to go and have a bath. Tanguy, delighted, did as he was told. When he emerged from the bathroom he felt relaxed and almost as good as new. His father smiled at him, and they all three had tea together in front of the fire. The misery which had haunted him at San Sebastian and throughout his journey now melted away. He ceased to think about anything. His stepmother introduced him to the maid, Marie, an Alsatian girl who looked kind and warm-hearted. She cried more than any member of the family, and was sniffing quietly all evening.

Tanguy also met his stepmother's daughter, a woman of about thirty called Jeannette, whom he found both pretty and pleasant. She had recently been widowed, and Tanguy felt a great deal of sympathy for her. She gave him an overcoat which had belonged to her husband, and a package of cigarettes. She carefully explained to him that he was almost exactly the same height as her husband had been. Tanguy smiled, touched at the knowledge of how much effort it must have cost her to make him this present. He found himself wishing he had had a big sister like her.

Since there was a shortage of beds in the house, it had been arranged that Tanguy was to sleep in a near-by hotel, but take his meals with the family. In the evening he and his father went for a walk together with the dog, a whining bad-tempered brute, who conceived a sulky dislike for Tanguy, which Tanguy fully reciprocated. For the first time since his arrival in Paris, Tanguy found himself chatting with his father without any sense of constraint. They talked of all sorts of things: Spain, Granada, the sunsets over the Sierra Nevada. Tanguy went to bed happy.

3

THIS easing of the relationship between father and son increased during the days that followed. There were moments of real intimacy between them, when they sat for long hours talking in the drawing-room, their chairs drawn up to the fire, exchanging memories of Spain.

Tanguy's father was a queer mixture of middle-class prejudice and simple humanity. At one level he was a conscious rationalist, a faithful disciple of Descartes. He claimed to investigate events and their causes with a slightly cynical precision of method. But he was also capable of understanding and extracting that intimate poetic essence latent in both objects and living beings: he was passionately in love with nature. Every Sunday they would drive out to the forests near Paris, and go for long walks, their feet crunching over the dead leaves, the smell of damp earth in their nostrils. Tanguy's father was *en rapport* with the countryside. He went into raptures over the vivid colors of the trees, or he would stop to admire some little ivy-clad country cottage with an old-fashioned tiled roof. He was fond of stopping in country inns and talking hunting, fishing, or even the weather with the local people. He instinctively knew just the right tone in which to address each one of them. But he had another side to his nature which baffled Tanguy. He was easily dazzled by surface appearances, and considered financial success the sole criterion of real value. This meant that he loathed and despised the poor, and looked on himself as belonging to a world apart.

This inconsistency of outlook tended to disturb their relationship. Whenever Tanguy felt that they were beginning to reach a point of real intimacy, something would come between them at the very moment of their closest *rapprochement*. Tanguy could never quite work out what this "something" was; perhaps the past.

When they talked simply, without artifice, they found much common ground. It seemed that both father and son tended to like things and people "for what they were." They would smile at the same gestures and make excuses for the same bad habits. They shared a common contempt for theatrical behavior and public ballyhoo, for all pretentious intellectualism that seeks to dispense with the element of humanity. They both had a knack of seeing through bombastic grandiloquence to the underlying petty fatuity it concealed, and shared an acute eye for the emptiness of inflated speeches. They loved the variegated humanity of a city street, and felt equally friendly toward tramp or lovers.

What really united Tanguy and his father was their complete lack of accepted morality. They looked on the everyday world with a natural sympathy which set them on the side of the lover against the puritan, and turned them to the happiness of the here-and-now rather than abstract speculations about Happiness, capital H. Neither of them was disposed to judge the world. They simply loved it because they found it good; neither of them had any time for a hypothetical hereafter in Time or Space, constructed as an emollient for death, but without any consultation with the dead. The world might not be the best of all possible worlds, but it was well worth having, with its procession of small pleasures and miseries. Tanguy had learned this philosophy the hard way; but as for his father?—the question hung unanswered in midair.

They were fond of street songs, and laughed at the Parisian street boys. They would cheerfully have exchanged every general in the world, medals, brass hat, and all, for a verminous but philosophical old tramp. They shared a love of the simplest kind of liberty, which consists in being able to say "Balls!" to anyone you dislike. Their position in life could be summed up as opposition to any kind of -ism. They had unbounded confidence in mankind; not because they thought men naturally good, but because they knew them capable of doing good things. Both father and son were anticlerical and antimilitary: another bond which united them.

But there was yet another aspect of his father's character which Tanguy found hard to understand: his proneness to misplaced and absurd bursts of snobbishness, his scathing verdicts on people whom he did not know, but who had the great misfortune of not coming of a "decent family." It was such small, petty, essentially mean things which stood between father and son still.

Tanguy knew very well that if his father had ever been inside a penal camp he would have soon learned that birth means nothing. He would have learned to love men for what they are and not what they seem to be. He would have applied to human beings the general theory that he held about life. Tanguy suspected that his father's sympathetic attitude to life was largely a pose, and this led him to wonder just what was pose and what sincerity: the sneering allusions to a woman's lowly origins, or the familiar chitchat with tramps.

This pinpointed the essential difference between them. For Tanguy, the whole world was "well born," cats and dogs included. He refused to accept the restrictions imposed by a narrow world which talked about good breeding and antique furniture. Tanguy was not "well bred" in this sense. He felt a closer sympathy with the sufferers than the happy ones; his place was instinctively with the victims. He supported the strikers against the forces of authority, the deserter against the military court that tries him, the guttersnipe against the policeman.

He would have found it hard to analyze such sentiments; but at least he had learned that the barrier separating the guttersnipe from the honest citizen is not a particularly high one. He had learned many things that he had no intention of forgetting. He knew that to deny the long lines of silent, downtrodden creatures who had been with him all his life would be to deny himself, and to deny also everything that had helped him to struggle through: in particular, the devotion he had sworn to these humbly born men and women whose only weapons against authority are their patience and resignation.

There were, too, some terrible misunderstandings. Tanguy, for instance, sometimes retired into a complete silence, having lived so long alone with himself that he found it difficult to live a social life and join in conversations that bored him. His father imagined that this withdrawal implied criticism and was a kind of tacit condemnation on Tanguy's part of all his father's past mistakes. There were one or two scenes, and a wall of hostility began to rise once more between these two people who, at bottom, loved one another despite their faults —perhaps even because of them. They found it hard to stand each other's presence at times.

Besides, Tanguy was thinking about his mother.

Then, one day, his father told him that his mother was alive, that he had seen her in Paris.

"But that's impossible!" Tanguy cried. "She would have come to see you, if only to ask for news of me!"

"No, I think not. She is afraid of me. She thinks it was I who denounced her and had her interned in a concentration camp."

Tanguy was silent. All the old misery came flowing back;

it was in vain that he had tried to forget it. It sprang up of itself, unbidden.

"And that is not true?" Tanguy asked.

"Not exactly. The police did ask me for—er—certain information—"

Tanguy felt sorry for his father, though he was still far from completely understanding him: there was so little he lacked to make him a real man. Tanguy was ashamed for him; he felt that it must be hard to renounce, day after day, a part of one's real nature.

"Besides," his father went on, "I don't advise her to come annoying me. She'd get a very nasty shock if she tried anything like that: I only have to say the word to get her interned again."

Tanguy said nothing; he could think of no adequate words. He was not surprised at his mother being alive; he was even expecting her to be living in Paris. But what lay behind his father's barely concealed threats? He stared at his hands. He had always pictured this moment when he would find his mother again. Now that it seemed about to happen, he dreaded it. A strange malaise spread through him; he would dearly have loved to postpone this fatal moment a little longer.

"Perhaps," he stammered, "perhaps it wasn't really her you saw?"

"Don't be silly. When you have lived ten or eleven years with a woman, you can at least recognize her when you see her again."

"Ye-es. I suppose so."

Tanguy looked at his father. This man had denounced his wife and his child, had had them interned, yet here he still was, making further threats. Tanguy shivered. It struck him that neither war, occupation, bombing, or hunger had wrought any change in some men. They remained in every respect what they had been; they had not progressed a step from their position in 1938; they were still full of their small hatreds and small ambitions. The world they represented was dead; yet in its death throes it still clung with ferocious determination to life. Tanguy knew very well that this world was a dead world; yet what could replace it?

"She must surely have got into trouble with the police," his father was saying. "Especially when you consider her political record—"

Once again Tanguy felt afraid. Would this man be capable of repeating what he had done once already? Had he the kind of mentality that would let him send his own wife and child into exile and imprisonment *for a second time?* Tanguy knew, instinctively, that he was capable of such an act, though he was by no means a malicious man. What he was was a coward, and he had that special cruelty shared by cowards and all those who lack the courage to die for an idea. Tanguy pitied him: he was a man greatly to be pitied.

_____

4

TANGUY'S father had two brothers, of whom the elder was called Norbert. He was a tall, well-built, athletic man with large brown kindly eyes and hair already white. In his youth he had been a great gambler, and had kept from those early days his love of danger and hazard. He had made a love-match with a woman who was neither of his nationality nor his religion, and his family had made him pay dearly for what they referred to as his misalliance. His brothers and sisters had ignored his existence for years. No one had reached out a helping hand to him even when he was in the severest straits. For many long months he had lived from hand to mouth in a little seaside resort in Normandy, often going without food. He scoured the neighborhood for green apples, which his wife cooked. He wrote despairing letters to his brothers and his mother, all of whom refused to open their doors to the pariah.

Norbert had had a son who died soon after birth; yet he had no more acquired a legacy of hatred from his long years of solitary struggling against fate than had Tanguy from his time in prison. What instead he had done was learn to judge human beings at their true worth. Often he remained silent; there were many things that his experience entitled him to say, but which he preferred to leave unsaid.

Norbert was fond of Tanguy. He had summed him up in a flash at their first meeting, but had no wish to appear to meddle in his brother's affairs. Nevertheless, Norbert showed considerable affection to his nephew. He respected his personality (without always understanding it) and let the boy follow his own inclinations. He had had the passion for gambling and its calculated risks, and had suffered as a result. Perhaps that was why he watched Tanguy as he would have observed the thoroughbred racehorse. He was wondering how a young man so mistreated by life, so rebellious against "established traditions," would finally turn out. He was letting the boy make his own choice, and had already decided to help him, whatever the cost, without asking anything in return.

Nita, his wife, was a tall, slender, attractive blonde, with a faintly retroussé nose and eyes of a clear sea-blue. Her gestures and smile conveyed something of the impalpable misty charm of that remote northern country from which she came. She spoke French with a light, lilting accent.

She had known Tanguy when he was only five; in fact, she had at once offered to look after him as soon as his parents separated. She had seen, with her intuitive sense, just what the boy's life might become when his parents were divided by such irreconcilable hatred. No one had listened to her; she had always been thought of as "the foreigner," the misfit in the nest. Her husband's family had never let her in. She knew very well that They had little love for her, but felt no need of Their approval in order to follow her own bent; that was why, in her heart, she ignored them.

Tanguy loved his uncle and aunt. They had prejudices, no doubt of that; but they knew when to forget about them. He adored their plain, airy, sun-filled house, and was delighted to sit with them and talk the day away. Hardship had drawn this married couple more closely together, and Tanguy knew that they loved one another deeply. The security he found with them—which was built, not on antiques but real love and affection—soothed him immensely. This was the reason for his frequent visits. They tried to convince him that, despite everything, his father loved him.

Despite this, Tanguy found living in his father's company progressively more difficult. Quarrels would erupt on the least excuse. With clumsy, treacherous malice this despicable creature was trying to spoil his son's most precious possessions: his memories.

One day a scene developed from the most absurd beginnings, but quickly blew up into a situation of unusual violence. Some years previously Norbert had taken an interest in a little girl from a poor part of the city whose mother was ill with tuberculosis, and whose own lungs were slightly infected. He had taken this little girl, Monique, into his own home, and thus given her two years' training and a share in his family life. Thanks to Norbert she had got a job as a secretary with a publishing-house. She had sworn eternal gratitude to the man responsible for her rescue, and Norbert in his turn had a very soft spot for his little protégée. One day he had the idea of introducing Monique to Tanguy, who was imprudent enough to mention the suggestion at home.

"But you can't think of such a thing!" his father exclaimed angrily. "You can't go out with a little servant girl like that!"

Tanguy said: "First, there is no question of her being what you call a servant girl; secondly, I shall go out with who I please; and thirdly, I shall enjoy her company a good deal more than that of plenty of people in our world."

His father turned to his wife and said: "Look at this impertinent little guttersnipe, daring to answer his father back! I should have left him to starve to death. I was under no obligation to go and pick him up at the station, but I went. I brought him back to my own home, and made a gentleman of him, and look at the result!"

"Albert, calm yourself," his wife said. "This child can't possibly *understand*. He's always lived with impossible people. You mustn't forget he's had to mix with workmen—

possibly even criminals. You've got to be patient and make allowances. He'll change."

Tanguy got up, pale, his heart beating frantically. Despite himself there were tears in his eyes. For the first time since his arrival he was determined to get off his chest everything he had carefully repressed for so long.

Did they consider themselves better than any workmen they had known? he asked them. They were not. They were hardly worthy to pull a worker's shoes off. Here was a man who had denounced his wife, who boasted he had reformed thanks to an influential mistress, who ran away when the first shots were fired. How could he, how dared he set himself up against real men? He had never even done his normal duty toward his son: how could he face men such as Father Pardo or women such as Sebastiana? How dared he insult people who had a hundred times his virtue and courage?

"Look at yourself," Tanguy shouted, "look at yourself, with your period furniture and your well-connected wife! Where has it brought you? To the point where your own son insults you and calls you a coward. The nastiest sort of coward, the kind of creature that intrigues in back alleys and hasn't even the courage of his own convictions. You hoped we were both dead and buried, and that you'd never hear of either of us again. You made a big mistake there. If you want to get rid of your guilty shame it isn't enough to go to the Vichy secret police and denounce your wife and child; your guilt and shame will pursue you, and all those who shared your crimes—who signed deportation orders, who sent men to their death and then turned up after the liberation wearing the Free French brassard.

276

"You have deceived no one. You have been allowed to go on living because already life is harder for you to endure than death. I loathe and despise you. Every person I've met in my whole life was worth more than you, because each was more of a man than you are. No, you've never had the courage of your acts and you never will. Shall I tell you what you are? Not even—not even a shit in a silk stocking, but a silk stocking sunk in a dungheap. It's too late now to get rid of all the stinking filth. It'll choke you. You'll choke to death in your own foulness. And you won't even have a dutiful son to close your great greedy eyes.

"I don't hate you. You spend your time saying how much I hate you, but why *should* I hate you? It's because of what I suffered, and those others who suffered as I did, that I've managed to get clear of all your stinking shit. All that is ultimately due to you, and I almost can feel grateful to you for it. Men like you have no business to be fathers. Being a father isn't just a matter of—of having balls and knowing what to do with them. Being a father is something much more difficult than that. Being a son is difficult, too. No; you are nothing, simply nothing. All I feel for you is pity, infinite pity."

Sweat was streaming down Tanguy's forehead. He paused, lips tight with disgust, face pale and mottled. His father had changed color several times during this tirade. Now he jumped up and began hitting his son, blind with rage, screaming insults as he did so: "Bastard! Little shit! I made a gentleman of you. I took you into my own home. This is the end of it. Out into the gutter with you! Go and find your equals, your Sebastiana and your damned workers! I knew it. I al·

ways knew it. You've got it in the blood. You're a Red, that's what you are! A shit of a Red!"

A blow of his fist caught Tanguy full on the ear, and the boy collapsed on the ground, in the throes of one of the worst seizures he had ever experienced. When he recovered consciousness his father was standing beside him, wringing his hands. The maid was placing cloths soaked in vinegar on his forehead. Tanguy rose to his feet, staggering. Without saying a word, he stumbled across to his cupboard, took out the few possessions he kept there, and left the house. Everyone watched him go without saying a word.

Outside it was a beautiful spring afternoon. Tanguy went straight to his uncle's house. Norbert was astonished at the sight of his nephew's bruised and swollen face. Tanguy tried to smile, but his ear was in the most angonizing pain. His uncle took him straight to a doctor, who diagnosed otitis, and prescribed drops to ease the pain. Then his uncle took him home, and Tanguy collapsed into an armchair. His aunt came over to him and stroked his hair.

"Do you know, darling," she said, "that you've already slept once in the bed you're having tonight?"

"Surely not. When was that?"

"At the time you were living in that little house near Vichy. You remember that, don't you?"

"Of course," Tanguy said.

"You were on a journey, your mother and you, and you stayed with us for a time. Have you forgotten?"

"I remember a little. . . . Does that mean this is my *fourth* visit to Paris?"

"That's right. You were very tiny. It was before the war.

278

Your mother wanted to emigrate to Mexico, you know. That was before they took you off to that camp." Then, in a softer voice, Nita added: "You were terribly badly behaved then! You used to raise your fist in a Communist salute, and call people comrade."

"Honestly?"

"Oh, yes."

"That's funny," Tanguy said, thoughtfully. "You imagine you remember everything. But there's always something that eludes you. I never even knew I had an uncle. If I had, I should have written to you from Spain."

Nita was following her own train of thought. "One day," she said, "your mother had gone out, and you and I were alone in the house together. I was working in the kitchen. You came in very softly, walked up to me, put your arms round my neck and said: 'You know, Auntie Nita, I love you a lot. I'd love to live in a nice clean house like yours.'"

Tanguy smiled; he had already forgotten how much his bruises were aching. He clasped his aunt's hands in both of his. The setting sun lit up the room. His uncle was sitting near him reading the paper. He was grinning wickedly to himself because he had bought a lottery ticket without his wife knowing. He had, on the other hand, told Tanguy; and this harmless conspiracy gave him much pleasure. He winked at his nephew, and Tanguy winked back. From the street came the sound of automobile horns, in an ever-increasing cacophony. Tanguy felt completely at peace now. He leaned back and closed his eyes, and felt Nita's hands placed gently on his burning forehead. He lay quite still.

5

IN the spring of 1955, on the evening before Mother's Day, Tanguy once more met his own mother, after thirteen years. It was an unhappy occasion. Each of them had pursued their own individual road, and when they came together again neither of them was the same person. The war might not have changed some people; but it had certainly changed them.

They completely failed to understand each other. She was still full of hatred, still believed unflinchingly in the absolute justice of her cause. For her, the world could still be divided into two camps: comrades and bastards. The bastards were all those who were not on her side. Tanguy, on the other hand, simply did not believe in a world thus split into two opposing camps. He had no desire to hate. Perhaps he was an idealist, perhaps he was shrewder than she was; but he still persisted in his fierce, almost desperate love for mankind and life itself. Because he had learned the value of his brother's blood, he could not bring himself to spill a single drop of it, even in order to build the best of all possible worlds. His world meant the world of here and now. There were people such as Sebastiana, Firmin, or Father Pardo; there might even be another Gunther. As long as people of this sort existed, he would always feel at home in this world. As for those others, he would avoid them and leave them to themselves, facing only each other.

His mother tried to demonstrate that all the responsibility for his unhappy life rested on his father's shoulders. She tried to convince him that he should cherish a righteous, a dedicated hatred against his father. Tanguy replied that in his view no hatred could properly be called righteous. She accused him of opportunism because he was not "committed." He replied that he had no idea what this meant, nor did he care. He wanted nothing to do with "parties" or "class struggles." They separated without even a wrench, in the way that railway lines branch off from each other and follow their different courses.

And what is to become of Tanguy now? Let us leave him in the street he loves, among those whom he knows and trusts. Let us leave him to do as he will, and not seek to strip his last illusions from him. It would be pleasant to leave him with God; but we are by no means sure ourselves that God exists. So we will leave him alone with his obstinate, indestructible love for a country that has never knowingly given him anything. Our only parting hope is that he will find new friends such as Sebastiana or Father Pardo to reach out a helping hand to him. Then he will smile, and be satisfied. Perhaps he will even come to find life the wonder and delight it should be; who knows?

Paris, October 1954—Madrid, July 1956.

Michel del Castillo was born in Madrid on August 3, 1933. His father, like Tanguy's, was French, and his mother was a Spanish journalist whose Republicanism forced them to flee Franco Spain. In France they were interned as political refugees in a concentration camp in Lozère. When the Nazis entered this territory, Michel del Castillo was separated from his mother and taken to Germany, where he spent the rest of the war. At the end of the war Michel del Castillo was sent back to Spain, only to be placed for several years in an orphanage and delinquents' home. After his escape he spent two rewarding years in a Jesuit school in Ubeda.

Just after his twentieth birthday Michel del Castillo made his way to Paris, where he was admitted to the Sorbonne and began to write *Child of Our Time*.

A Note on the Type

The text of this book was set on the Linotype in a face called JANSON, a recutting made direct from type cast from matrices made about 1700. Anton Janson, a Dutchman who worked at Leipzig in this period, and for whom the modern version of the type was named, is now thought not to have been responsible for its design, which is, however, probably of Dutch origin, although the matrices have been in Germany for many years. The type is an excellent example of the influential and sturdy Dutch types that prevailed in England prior to the development by William Caslon of his own designs, which he evolved from these Dutch faces. The Dutch, in their turn, had been influenced by Garamond in France. The general tone of Janson, however, is darker than Garamond and has a sturdiness and substance quite different from its predecessors. The book was composed, printed and bound by H. Wolff, New York. Designed by George Salter.

"All this stuff about your childhood and your father and these Jesuit priests, and the rest of it. Do you *really* want to find your father? Is that *really* your reason for crossing the frontier?"

"Why, of course."

Ricardo was silent for a moment. Then he went on, in a quiet, serious voice: "When I was a little boy, I believed everybody. Even the priests. Little by little life has taught me not to believe anyone. I swore I'd never be had for a sucker again. Despite all that, something tells me you're not lying. I shall pay for your journey to Paris. You can repay me at your leisure."

Tanguy felt his throat tighten with emotion. He thanked Ricardo awkwardly.

"No, it's fair enough. We all have to help one another. One day you'll be in a position to do me a good turn. You never know, do you?"

He came close to Tanguy and rested a hand lightly on each of the boy's shoulders: then, with a lover's tenderness, slid them down and under his coat. Tanguy's mind went whirling: Ricardo was still murmuring words to him, but he did not hear them. He was thinking: so that's what the bastard wanted all the time, simply to take advantage of my position. That's why he invited me to dinner, and promised to pay my fare! Then he stopped thinking, realizing that there must be more to it than this single motive. His suspicions might well be unjust. The young man could easily have acted on the spur of the moment, and simply be taking advantage of a propitious moment. Tanguy still felt that

The Comic Spirit of
Eighteenth-Century Novels

Kennikat Press
National University Publications
Literary Criticism Series

General Editor
John E. Becker
Fairleigh Dickinson University

SUSAN G. AUTY

THE COMIC SPIRIT
OF EIGHTEENTH-CENTURY
NOVELS

National University Publications
KENNIKAT PRESS • 1975
Port Washington, N.Y. • London

823.03
Au 9c
99560
Jan. 1977

With love and mirth,
for my husband

Manufactured in the United States of America

Published by
Kennikat Press Corp.
Port Washington, N.Y./London

Library of Congress Cataloging in Publication Data

Auty, Susan G
    The comic spirit of eighteenth-century novels.

    (National university publications) (Literary
criticism series)
    Bibliography: p.
    Includes index.
    1. English fiction—18th century—History and
criticism. 2. Comic, The. I. Title.
PR858.C63A8   823'.03   75-34314
ISBN 0-8046-9120-7

CONTENTS

This work owes much to the ideas and encouragement of B. L. Reid of Mount Holyoke College and J. S. Cunningham of the University of York, England, and to the stimulating direction and suggestions of Patricia Bruckmann, George Falle and Kenneth MacLean of the University of Toronto. I am also pleased to be able to acknowledge the generosity of the Canada Council for the Arts and Sciences.

The Comic Spirit of
Eighteenth-Century Novels

INTRODUCTION

The comic novels of the mid-eighteenth century, like all comic works, have a built-in resistance to critical girdles. Thus the recent attempts to give shape to the "new species of writing" (that is, novels written in the manner of Fielding) by linking the works structurally and spiritually to the long and eminent tradition of satire have been only partially success-ful in accounting for the distinguishing character of these novels. Ronald Paulson, in his broad study of the satiric elements in eighteenth-century novels, is careful to qualify his assertions concerning the importance of satire with a reminder that it is "not *the* key to the meaning or essence of the major novels examined."[1] Nevertheless, his focus gives undue emphasis to the corrective material at the expense of the mirth that a-rises from the satiric incidents. More misleading, however, is Melvyn New's recent study of *Tristram Shandy*, which examines the novel from the exclusive viewpoint of satire. Like the many critics who assume the importance of satire in Smollett's novels because they have looked to the teller's personality and background rather than trusting their own responses to the tales, New distorts the tone of *Tristram Shandy* by pre-judging Sterne's intentions and mood (which probably changed with each writing day). The vestigial remains of satire are undoubtedly pres-ent and undoubtedly affect the various incidents and portraits within the expansive whole, as do the foreshadowing hints of sentimentalism which formed the basis of many earlier critical studies. But the very expansiveness which allows so many diverse elements to be coordinated within the work is the distinguishing feature of *Tristram Shandy* and the other novels of this period which at once prevents critical categorization and accounts for their mirthful comedy.

The roominess of the new form, which proved flexible enough to accommodate the elaborate plot of *Tom Jones* on the one hand and the undisciplined wanderings of *Tristram Shandy* on the other (not to mention the intensive analysis of Clarissa's experiences) encouraged the particularly domestic narratives that so often give rise to humorous comedy. The comprehensive account of a portion of life, or in Smollett's phrase, "a large, diffus'd picture of life," usually includes enough simply extraneous material to put even serious occurrences into perspective, the objective perspective of comedy. Indeed, Richardson, with the help of such characters as Anna Howe and Belford, could have turned *Clarissa* into an ordinary domestic comedy at almost any point in the narrative, but of course he chose not to do so.

That domestic or nonsatiric comedy has never been adequately defined, although its spirit has been frequently appreciated, is because it is no more definable than is ordinary life; laughter, like life, is a commonly shared experience, but the way one goes about explaining what is laughable or what is life is never the same for any of the sharers. However, a convenient identification of the comic spirit, especially as it contrasts to the satiric mode, is provided in a recent philosophical study of laughter: "Nor is the truest comedy bitter satire or crass realism. Far from casting slanderous aspersions on human nature or leaving a bad taste in the mouth, it gives us hope for our kind, a sense of the doggedly upstanding, unquenchable spirit of the absurd human animal with all his weaknesses."[2] An appreciation of the doggedness of everyday living and the doggedness of human beings in facing everyday life is what is meant by the label "comedy" in the present work, which seeks to show that this appreciation is what the novels of the "new species" are about, much more than they are about the evils of society or individuals. In the particular accounts of human doggedness and human absurdity lies the source of the mirthfulness, a comic quality that contributes far more to the longevity of these works than the incidental satire or didacticism which is more easily identified by critics.

In the opening chapter of this study, the shift from satire to "amiable" humor during the eighteenth century, which has been carefully

documented by Stuart Tave, is reviewed. The influence of liberal attitudes on literary forms is discussed with reference to the changes in subject and style that were taking place. The particular suitability of the
new novel form to the new temperament is suggested as a factor in its
rise at this time. The flexibility and breadth which the novel has to assign motives and describe extenuating circumstances, in contrast to more
succinct forms, would be appreciated by readers who put good-nature
above wit. In turn, the popularity of the good-natured novels corrobo-
rates the spread of the benevolent temper, and suggests a reason for the
characteristic cheerfulness of the "new species"—the growing concern
with the mental health of the nation as exemplified by its preoccupation
and increasing distaste for the spleen. The determination, voiced aloud
by Smollett and Sterne and present by inference in the works of many
other writers, to be against the spleen, against anger and gall, seems to
have contributed a self-conscious gaiety to the tone of these works. It
is argued that so pervasive is the insistence on lightheartedness and the
maintenance of a comic perspective that bits of satire and political ha-
rangue which remain are put into a context whereby they lose their effectiveness for anything but the arousal of amiable laughter. The dispute
then is one about tone, and its object is to insist on the need for considering the effect of a whole work when interpreting its parts.

The term "antisplenetic" is derived to describe the characteristic tone
of the novels of the mid-eighteenth century. The rest of the study examines the extent to which an underlying antisplenetic attitude has affected
the characterization, plot, and style of these works. An analysis of *Tom
Jones* and some of the novels, both well-known and forgotten, which
were modeled on Fielding's new species is followed by a look at the
more spirited—some would say coarser—less plot-oriented novels of
Smollett and Sterne. *Peregrine Pickle* and *Humphry Clinker* have been
chosen as representative of Smollett's range and antisplenetic tendencies.

CHAPTER ONE

FRESH STREAMS OF MIRTH
IN SOCIETY AND LITERATURE

Moved by the liberal spirit which breathed through England in the early part of the eighteenth century, the spirit which allowed Addison to assume in 1711 that it was "infinitely more honourable to be a Good-natured Man, than a Wit,"[1] comedy began to eschew the example of its traditional bedfellow, the spleen (disease), and to imitate instead the beneficial operations of the spleen (bodily organ), which was thought to act against ill-nature in the manner described by Dr. William Stukeley:

As the vein was to draw or convey this melancholy to the spleen, the artery by fresh streams of pure blood coming to it in so plentiful a manner, was by degrees to concoct and clarifie it therein, till at length it was fit to be admitted into the mass again. ... As the *atra bilis* created anger and melancholy, so the spleen which was to purge it off render'd us cheerful and alert.[2]

Comic writers began to see quirks of character not as splenetic emanations, tell-tale signs of a "redundancy" of melancholy with which the spleen was unable to cope, but as splendid evidence of the liberty granted to every Englishman, the liberty to be an oddball. The humorist came to be regarded as one who aroused harmless amusement in others rather than one who suffered from a dangerously unbalanced temperament.

The comic spirit itself was being redefined, or in the phrase of E.N.

Hooker "wrenched loose from satire,"[3] in the years that stretched between *A Tale of A Tub* and *Tristram Shandy,* the earlier work being a kind of warning signal against the careless gaiety of the later one. The association between comedy and satire, so close as to make them seem indistinguishable at times, may be traced to the beginnings of comedy and to the form it has most often taken on stage since the writers of New Comedy first stylized the Old. That comic pieces were at one time no more than lampoons of well-known figures may be surmised from Aristotle's remark that Crates was the first Athenian poet to "drop the Comedy of invective and frame stories of a general and non-personal nature, in other words, Fables or Plots."[4] These fables or plots, however, were no less satirically motivated than were the simple invectives, for the phallic rituals which gave occasion to comic productions were corrective in intent, performed in order to purge disease and evil and to restore the health of the land. Moreover, lampoons did not simply disappear, nor were they necessarily confined only to the vigorous comments of the chorus on behalf of the author in the parabasis. When events demanded it, Aristophanes did not shrink from honing his wit to its finest cutting edge and applying it relentlessly throughout the play: thus Cleon was transformed into a sausage-seller and paid-magistrates were turned into wasps.

While generalizing their victims into stock characters—the *miles gloriosus,* the *senex*—the Romans retained the edge and evoked laughter that was primarily (unlike Aristophanes') a mark of scorn, carrying with it a criticism of society: admirable oddballs, such as Trygaeus, who harnessed his pet beetle to ride to heaven and conduct peace negotiations, no longer claimed the hearts of the audience while directing their minds to the public matter. The private individual comes to be in most comic works a symptom of the public disorder, as even Falstaff is, though his amiable qualities became as notable as his figure when eighteenth-century critics endowed him with the rights and privileges of a humorist.

The Tale Teller follows in a direct line of descent from the *alazon,* the impostor, the public outrage. To Swift, his chaos is a malevolent growth which must be isolated and uprooted, just as to Locke, the mind's habit of associating ideas is a disease which has the same root as madness causing similarly dangerous confusion if unchecked by reason.[5] But like Sterne's recalcitrant work, which turns the mind's weakness into its most appealing characteristic, the *Tale* undermines Swift's assumptions about

7

disorderly expression. Beverle Houston, in an unpublished thesis, sees the effectiveness of the *Tale*'s parodic structure as a sign that "the qualities of modernity he attacked had already so influenced the shape of literature that the traditional principles and practices Swift wished to reaffirm were no longer viable even for him."[6] Indeed, the religious fable provoked all the indignation that would have been more properly directed at the unbalanced Teller. Yet if one does not look upon the activities of dunces as a threat to art, to civilization or, more immediately, to one's own reputation, it is an easy matter to cast an indulgent eye upon them. Thus like most readers, William Wotton, whom Swift allowed to bring up only mud from the Helicon in *The Battle of the Books,* accepted the mock-modernity with equanimity and devoted most of his critical remarks to exposing "the Mischief of the Ludicrous Allegory": like most readers, he failed to see the moral connection between the Teller and his Tale.[7] This blindness is explained by the fact that the Teller was simply not very remarkable; the symptoms of individualism which so appalled Swift were so familiar as to be unworthy of comment by the time the work was published. The range of acceptable human behavior (and with it that of stylistic license) was in the process of being greatly extended; at the same time, the natural targets of satire were becoming immune to the slings and arrows of ridicule.

Less than half a century passes between Swift's attempts to root out irresponsible eccentricity and Corbyn Morris's celebration of similar behavior. In this time, "cosmic Toryism" (in Basil Willey's phrase) gives way to the more flexible notions of the Whigs, moral philosophers such as Hutcheson and Hartley continue the investigations that were begun by Locke into the workings of the human mind, and laughter changes from being an expression of chastisement to being one of tolerance and acceptance. By mid-century the comic action no longer charged and sentenced; it cherished and rewarded by calling upon the audience to love the malefactor in spite of his refusal to fit into the orderly niches of approved patterns. Stuart Tave summarizes the changes in attitude which made satire seem suddenly improper:

The reaction against satire, a powerful force within the most vigorously satirical period of English literature, was a rejection of the basic satirical assumptions of clear and fixed standards, cosmic, social and moral, against which the aberrations of man are measured with a just severity.

The reaction was, on its strong side, the substitution of a more historical interpretation of life, one in which particular persons, motives and circumstances, explanations, light and shade, were valid and necessary considerations that preceded judgment; and when all these were weighed in the balance, the result was more often forgiveness than condemnation, Christian mercy than strict justice, or even loving acceptance of human weakness and irrationality as an element of the universal scheme.[8]

Coupled with a growing appreciation of English liberty, the liberty which according to Congreve guaranteed that he who would have a maypole should have a maypole,[9] this attention to the uniqueness of the individual fostered the gap that was discovered to exist between the ridiculous and the simply risible. The distinction between the contemptible and the "altogether pleasant," to which Lord Kames first gave clear expression as late as 1762, was implied much earlier in the century by Hutcheson, who argued that the Hobbesian notion of laughter as an expression of "sudden glory" was ungenerous and misleading, for it excluded the possibility of a parody based on an admirable original and encouraged mirth at what is most appropriately productive of pain or sympathy: "If we observe an object in pain while we are at ease, we are in greater danger of weeping than laughing; and yet here is occasion for Hobbes' sudden joy. It must be a very merry state in which a fine gentleman is, when well-dressed in his coach, he passes our streets, where he will see so many ragged beggars and porters and chairmen sweating at their labour, on every side of him."[10]

The arena of the contemptible had been significantly eroded as early as 1690 when Locke published *An Essay Concerning Human Understanding,* a document which contributed forcefully, especially through the persuasive medium of the *Spectator* papers, to the climate of toleration that pervaded the early eighteenth century. The revolutionary denial of innate ideas and immutable moral truths contained therein carried with it a plea for open-mindedness and generosity towards men of differing opinions:

We should do well to commiserate our mutual ignorance, and endeavour to remove it in all the gentle and fair ways of information; and not instantly treat others ill, as obstinate and perverse, because they will not renounce their own, and receive our opinions, or at least those we would force upon them, when it is more than probable that we are no less ob-

9

stinate in not embracing some of theirs. For where is the man that has incontestable evidence of the truth of all that he holds, or of the falsehood of all that he condemns.[11]

The apparent offender against order and reason was not to be condemned out of hand nor his ideas ridiculed simply on the grounds of their being contrary to one's own. Indeed, in his famous chapter on the association of ideas included in the fourth edition of the *Essay*, published in 1700, Locke virtually absolved rational man of most of the responsibility for his perverseness, that is, his individual variations in thought and action that naturally appear perverse to all those who have not been exposed to the same impressions and thus have not formed the same ideas. His suggestion that the mind was inevitably influenced by "gangs" of ideas which quite involuntarily fixed themselves to other ideas in the shadowy regions of the consciousness implied that most contemptible actions were committed in extenuating circumstances. After Locke, one could no longer blame a Walter Shandy for the mismanagement of his son's childhood.

The extent to which new notions of acceptability and liberty, granting the individual the right to flourish in his own way, guided the comic tastes of the eighteenth century may be inferred from Corbyn Morris's 1744 essay on "standards of wit, humour, raillery, satire and ridicule." Humor, which is associated with the risible, the admirable, is preferred to wit, which is devoted to ridicule and mockery. Wit, as defined by Morris, is "the LUSTRE resulting from the *quick* ELUCIDATION of one subject, by a *just* and *unexpected* ARRANGEMENT of it with another subject"; it is an art which arouses admiration. But humor, being derived "from the *Foibles,* and whimsical *Oddities* of *Persons* in real life, which flow rather from their *Inconsistencies,* and *Weakness,* than from TRUTH and GOOD SENSE," is more interesting than wit; it is "more apt to affect our passions," to "justly commend our fondness and love." Whereas wit thrives on "severity, bitterness and satire," humor is most often concerned with the "worthy amiable sentiments of the heart." So much does Morris value the display of human oddities and foibles, that he considers the humorist to be the sign of a nation's health. Such an individual, according to him, "flourishes only in a Land of *Freedom,* and when *that* ceases he dies too, the last and noblest *Weed* of the Soil of *Liberty.*"[12]

England, with its liberating climate, had started nurturing hearty specimens of the "noble weed" by the end of the seventeenth century, as is indicated merely by the need Swift felt to present his mocking variety and by the calm reception of one whose imagination was "exceedingly disposed to run away with his reason." If Sterne was not directly influenced by the works and accounts of these early humorists, he could not help being aware of the license claimed by some of his predecessors, who let their imaginations take the reins and guide the course of their actions and thoughts to wherever fancy and whim should lead them. John Dunton's 1691 work is well-named *A Voyage Round the World; or, A Pocket-Library*, for the author rambles through wide-ranging topics following only the logic of his wandering imagination:

From henceforward Reader, don't expect I shou'd give *every distinct Ramble* a distinct Chapter, for truly I can't afford it any longer; for the Chapters being heavy things, and the Rambles brisk *little airy Creatures,* the last run away so fast, and scamper about at such a mad rate, that the first, do what they can, can't keep pace with 'em, being besides a great many, one still *begetting another,* and running all *different ways* from one another.[13]

Obviously reveling in his own extravagance, Dunton digresses from his digressive rambles:

[D]on't let the reader trouble me with so many impertinent *objections,* for that unavoidably leads a Man into *Digressions* from the main subject, and then these *Digressions* lead a Man into further *Digressions,* for *Error is infinite,* and the longer you wander in a wrong Path, my shoes to yours, the further you go from the right, if they are opposite one t'other: Not but that *Digressions* are so far from being always a fault, that they are indeed often pardonable, and sometimes a *great Beauty* to any discourse. ... *I love a Digression,* I must confess with all my Heart, because 'tis so like a *Ramble*—but all this while what's *Digression* to *Westminster.*[14]

Had Dunton made any observations of human nature that were worthy of the easy humor he displays throughout his odd little work, we might well bestow upon him some of the praise that is now reserved for Sterne. He had the generous attitude towards human shortcomings, his own and others', which distinguish the great makers of mirthful comedy, but his rambles lead no further than to Westminster or to dull and repetitive bits of nonsense, which fail to promote the easiness of heart that gives value to the escapades of a free-ranging imagination.

The longevity of the *Spectator* papers rests precisely on its free-ranging manner, not unrelated to Dunton's, and on its own good-natured strong-mindedness which it helped to make respectable in the figure of Sir Roger de Coverley. Whereas each essay may stand on its own as a little satire, a little sermon, the character of the work as a whole is appealingly disjointed. It lacks the urgency of satire or sermon, being rather a collection of coffee-house conversations and having the same comforting effect as such chats. Indeed, while lamenting that "it must be chiefly owing to the great Depravity of Manners in these loose and degenerate Times, that such worthy Performances have produc'd no better Effects," Sir Richard Blackmore values the *Spectator* and *Tatler* as much for "the just and generous Sentiments, the fertile Invention, the Variety of Subjects," which they show, as for "the Surprizing Turns of Wit and Facetious Imagination, the genteel Satire, the purity and propriety of the Words and the Beauty and Dignity of the Diction."[15] Thus while preserving the standards of moral expression—purity, propriety, and dignity—with which Dryden, Swift, and Pope brought satire to its moments of greatest eloquence, Addison and Steele, by shifting to a more casual mode, contributed to the very relaxation of those standards which made serious satire seem out of place in the coming years. C.S. Lewis accurately describes the difference between the two styles of instruction: "A satiric portrait by Pope or Swift is like a thunderclap; the Addisonian method is more like the slow operations of ordinary nature, loosening stones, blunting outlines, modifying a whole landscape with 'silent overgrowings.' "[16] Both have the improvement of mankind as their primary concern but the Spectator adjusts his method to ease the sting of his lesson and to give the benefit of the doubt. Indeed, his satire ceases to be satiric in effect because he provides a context against which the offenders may be viewed to their advantage, implying that a man may be worthy in spite of his faults.

Ordinary characters, picked from among those who frequent the various places of social gathering, serve in the *Spectator* as models of decorum by virtue of their good-nature rather than their sinlessness: Sir Roger de Coverley himself is "rather beloved than esteemed" and one has the sense that if he were suddenly to become estimable he would no longer be lovable. Rakes, of course, had been appealing to audiences throughout the Restoration period; Horner and Dorimant were never spurned by the crowd for their offences against society. But Sir Roger is no enacter of secret desires, no purger of frustrations; he is simply a quirky gentleman, out of step with the times but hardly ever out of temper. It is the grace and ease with which he carries his quirks, whether political or social, that makes him so endearing.

Even before the ordinary gentleman, distinguished only by his particular manifestations of human weakness, began to dominate the pages of comic works, the rake on stage was quietly giving way (nudged slightly by Collier's *Short View* published in 1698) to his more temperate cousin, the good-natured man of fashion. However witty Mirabell may be, his character as a suitor worthy of Millamant is never compromised, for his wit is never at the expense of his love and thus never has the unpleasant tone of Dorimant's. The growing preference for the reformed rake, the romantic rather than satanic hero, may be traced progressively through the works of Farquhar, who has been accused frequently of "killing" Restoration comedy and leaving it to expire in the arms of sentimentalism. If he is to be identified as the one delivering the death-blow, the applause of the audience must be held responsible for having dictated the harsh command: the popular reception in 1699 of the urbane but sensitive hero of *The Constant Couple,* Sir Harry Wildair, who "turn[s] all Passion to Gaiety of Humour, by which he chuses rather to rejoice his Friends, than be hated by any,"[17] is attested by the sequel which Farquhar saw fit to present two years later and by the successive softening of heroes in the plays that followed, his own and others'.

The gentlemen in his last plays still behave like full-bred gentlemen: Plume in *The Recruiting Officer* still begets sons like any man who has any claims to "gentility"; Aimwell in *The Beaux' Stratagem* does not intend to fall in love with Dorinda. But Plume, who—true to his name —acts with panache, looks after Molly right away, giving her a "husband" and an allowance; Aimwell goes so far as to confess his rakish plot to his beloved Dorinda, risking her wrath and thus her fortune by this act of unusual openheartedness. Such human kindliness, however, need not snuff out the possibility of spirited conversation. The exchange between Plume and his roguish sergeant concerning the not-very-surprising results of his intrigue with Molly shows Farquhar's ability to combine liveliness and sensibility:

Kite: You remember your old Friend *Molly* at the *Castle?*
Plume: She's not with Child, I hope.
Kite: No, no Sir;—She was brought to Bed Yesterday.
Plume: Kite, you must father the Child.[18]

It was the assumption that genuine expressions of sensibility had to be somberly spoken, that truly sapped Restoration comedy of its spirit in the early eighteenth century and explains both the absence of eccentric humorists in the genteel comedies of this period and the short-lived popularity of these works. Those that are reprinted today are generally ones by playwrights such as Hugh Kelly, who did not resist the impulse to satirize gently the very sentiments they were at the same time hoping to arouse.[19] Until Goldsmith rescued the dying "art" from the grip of pathetic emotion, mirthful laughter did not benefit on the nonburlesque stage from the encouragement of the new liberal attitudes. Though Farquhar moved stage comedy out of the drawing room into the "provinces," very much as Fielding later moved his novels onto the road in order to offer a more comprehensive view of humanity, he failed to attract any followers until Goldsmith, half a century later. The consciously liberal attitudes had, it would seem, one stultifying side-effect, which retarded the development of the humorist and the expansion of comic territory in the theater in the intervening years: one might be so solicitous of human feelings as to avoid laughing even good-naturedly at the evidence of human uniqueness, avoid all reference to the harmless oddity and innocent grotesquerie everywhere apparent; affection and sympathy might seem to be properly shown only by tears. In the Preface to *The Foundling,* presented in 1747, the author is commended for his gentleness, showing as Allardyce Nicoll notes "the power of sentimentalism by this date":

> Intent to fix, and emulous to please
> The Happy Sense of these politer Days,
> He forms a Model of a virtuous sort,
> And gives you more of Moral than of Sport;
> He rather aims to draw the melting Sigh,
> Or steal the pitying Tear from Beauty's Eye;
> To touch the Strings, that humanize our Kind,
> Man's sweetest Strain, the Musick of the Mind.[20]

Goldsmith had no desire to conform to the politeness of the age and doubted that morality or delicacy had anything to do with the comedies that were filling the theaters. In his "Essay on the Theatre, or A Comparison between Laughing and Sentimental Comedy," he offers a simple "receipt" (in the manner of Pope's for an epic poem) for making a sentimental comedy, contending that the ease with which they are written explains their prevalence over the "true" comedy: "It is only sufficient to raise the Characters a little, to deck out the Hero with a Ribband, or give the Heroine a Title; then to put an Insipid Dialogue, without Character or Humour, into their mouths, give them mighty good hearts, very fine cloaths, furnish a new sett of Scenes, make a Pathetic Scene or two, with a sprinkling of tender melancholy Conversation through the whole, and there is no doubt but all the Ladies will cry, and all the Gentlemen applaud."[21] The "ease" of following such a recipe lies in the unreality of the ingredients: the authors do not have to account for the contradictions that are inherent in human nature, actively exerting opposing influences on every human action.

It is their failure to deal with genuine people, their failure to dramatize the comic complexities of motives, which make "sentimental" comedies inevitably spiritless. One cannot be cheered by benevolence if the good person is too good to be true or has undergone a sudden conversion from evil without due process of nature. One simply stares in disbelief at the fictitious possibility of unmitigated goodness, while the rehabilitating possibility of worthy foolishness or foolish worthiness goes unconsidered. Goldsmith ends his essay on a note of ominous prophecy: "It is not easy to recover an art when once lost; and it will be but a just punishment, that when, by our being too fastidious, we have banished Humour from the Stage, we should ourselves be deprived of the art of laughing." His prophecy is really hindsight: if it were not for the custom of attaching farcical afterpieces to plays and the efforts of the burlesque writers (until the Licencing Act of 1737 cramped their style), the especially hearty laughter that is heard in places of public gathering, the laughter that takes into account the cause for mirth of all those around would scarcely have been heard in the eighteenth century; not until 1768 did the "low" bailiffs interrupt the decorous action of Goldsmith's *Good-Natured Man* arousing the wrath of those who had come to the theater to weep for the reclamation of a weak mortal in fine clothes.

But laughter fortunately survived in the timely farces of Samuel Foote and more thoughtfully in the energetic burlesques. Many of these works may be looked upon as the offspring of Restoration comedy, mocking modes of public rather than private expression, aiming darts at the form of heroic drama rather than at heroes. Nicoll is sufficiently impressed by their wit to consider them, especially *The Beggar's Opera,* among "the

15

best and brightest things which the age of Anne and that of the Georges have given us."[22] Indeed, *The Beggar's Opera* is a satire in the best Scriblerian tradition: it has the form of a work composed by Pope's harlot muse of Italian opera, who minces past her nine legitimate sisters in *The Dunciad*, addressing them "in quaint Recitativo, 'O Cara, Cara'." Yet the tempering spirit which melted conventional comedy into a sighing mass had the effect of humanizing the burlesque of this period into true comedy. The songs and dances of *The Beggar's Opera*, while mocking Italian stage styles and reflecting on English society, make the plight of Macheath's "wives"at once funny and poignant: their fears and griefs are undercut by the lyrics of their songs and at the same time the contrast between the facts of the plot and the romantic melodies emphasizes the realities upon which the plot is based. Lucy's predicament, arising from having genuine emotions in a depraved and hardened world in which conventions and artifice pass for love, is well expressed in her song to her father:

> When young at the bar you first taught me to score,
> And bid me be free with my lips, and no more;
> I was kiss'd by the Parson, the Squire, and the Sot,
> When the guest was departed, the kiss was forgot.
> But his kiss was so sweet, and so closely he prest,
> That I languished and pin'd till I granted the rest.[23]

Gay's oblique vision is directed quite forcefully upon the pressures of Lucy's "education," but the image of Lucy's weakness for Macheath elevates the verse from satire into drama. The drama in turn, while flirting with the tragic implications of Lucy's ruined life, remains firmly in the comic mode, held down by the rhymes and the flippant air of the song —"I was kiss'd by the Parson, the Squire, and the Sot."

In the same way, the beggar's plan to hang Macheath in accordance with "strict poetical justice" is rejected by the player, who insists on a comic catastrophe. Gay's satirical intention is supposedly "to comply with the taste of the town," but the satire is not what makes the happy ending ultimately the more appropriate of the two: the integrity of the play is preserved only by the comic reprieve, for civil justice has no real bearing on the offences of Macheath and Peachum or of any other characters in the play, who are representative of the human race before they are criminals. Their crimes are not against specific laws, for the milking of a country is shown to be not very different from the milking of a coach; if one hangs the highwayman, one must hang the prime minister as well. Poetic justice must therefore be sacrificed to what in the play's terms is true justice: Macheath suffers a wife for a punishment. The play ends with another song and a dance, reaffirming its sportive air of acceptance rather than accusation.

The extent to which satire in the early eighteenth century was gradually slipping into amiable comedy, refusing more and more to incriminate mankind for falling into the traps of pride or greed or lust that his own nature sets for him, has been masked, according to E.N. Hooker, by "the greatness of Pope and Swift, who waged eternal warfare upon dunces, quacks, enthusiasts, venal subjects of all sorts, beating down the enemy with every weapon, from mirth to irony to withering scorn."[24] Yet symbolic of the changing outlook, as Hooker notes, is the difference in preference between Dryden, "whose tastes in satire drew him close to Juvenal and vehement indignation," and Pope, "who despite his addiction to malice and satire, found a congenial spirit in Horace, the bard of good nature and raillery."[25]

Pope's addiction may be seen to be not so deep as his reputation, based upon his associations with Swift and the caves of spleen, has made it seem. His vision in *An Essay on Man* of man's position in the universe is as comic as Sterne's fond look at Uncle Toby in his bowling green:

> Chaos of Thought and Passion, all confus'd;
> Still by himself abus'd, or disabus'd;
> Created half to rise, and half to fall;
> Great lord of all things, yet a prey to all;
> Sole Judge of Truth, in endless Error hurl'd:
> The glory, jest, and riddle of the world!   (III.13—18)

The contradictions in human nature that Pope so precisely points to in this passage are reflected in his own tendency to see the world sometimes with joy, sometimes with pain. On the one hand, his mockery of Belinda betrays at least equal amounts of affection and admiration barely concealed behind his amusement; on the other, the sport he makes of the dunces, while vigorous, is essentially joyless: his horror and disgust for the senseless fools are as deep as his wit is sharp. His concern for public morality, like Swift's, is on the whole greater than his capacity for accepting private folly. (However, like *A Tale of A Tub*, *The Dunciad*'s liveliness has the peculiar effect of endowing the "nameless Somethings" with a

17

vitality and attractiveness of their own.)

It is only later in the century that one finds a satirically oriented writer consciously refraining from vindictive mockery. Richard Owen Cambridge's comments in the Preface to his *Scribleriad*, "an Heroic Poem" published in 1752, show that he expects to be praised for his restraint: "I flatter myself I have shown throughout my Book that the Follies of Mankind provoke my Laughter and not my Spleen; and so long as they have this effect on me, I cannot have any great quarrel against them. It may plainly be perceiv'd that I have industriously kept clear of much strong satire which naturally presented itself in a work of this nature."[26]

Verse satire was still, in the words of Robert Whitford, "vigorous and eager for combat" well into the last decades of the century.[27] Johnson's "Vanity of Human Wishes," while untainted by splenetic lampoons, has in common with less pure examples of the satiric mode a sharpness of tone which expresses the dissatisfaction of the author, in this case his distress with the pride of mankind in general. Proof of satire's continued commitment to the spleen may be seen in Charles Churchill's *Rosciad*, which shows no more generosity towards its victims—actors and playwrights—than did *The Dunciad*, upon which it was closely modeled. Cambridge's conscious abstention, therefore, is evidence of the pressure that was exerted even on a form so wedded to severity as this one. Epitomizing this pressure is the verse satire on ridicule, in which the writer chastens the authors of conventional satire for their splenetic motives and at the same time demonstrates the method of composing good-natured satire:

> Then let Good nature every Grace exert
> And, while it mends it, win th'unfolding Heart,
> As in some stream the Bank's projected Force
> Not stops the Current, but directs its Course,
> So let Good nature o'er our Mirth preside,
> Divert, not check; without impelling, guide.[28]

Severely critical authors of previous ages who had long been favorites were not exempt from the operations of newly "sensible" audiences. Their works were subjected to reassessment and if their illiberal origins could not be ignored or denied, they were rejected in favor of more flexible masterpieces. The process by which Shakespeare replaced Jonson in the affections of the English people has been analyzed in considerable detail by Stuart Tave, beginning with the transformation of Falstaff from a "humours" character into a humorous character. Like the meaning of the word "humour," which took on favorable connotations some time between Dryden's criticism and Dennis's, Falstaff came to be representative not of affectation and obsession but of mere weakness offset by sufficient virtues to be worthy of love, if not esteem. Reflecting the extent to which good-nature has become a powerful recommendation by 1744, Corbyn Morris praises Falstaff by declaring "it is impossible to be tired or unhappy in his Company."[29] In 1753, Arthur Murphy dismisses Jonson's "disagreeably odd" men of humor using the same criterion: "[T]here is hardly anything in any of them, that would induce a Gentleman to spend an Evening with them."[30] While the standards of Morris and Murphy would seem to derive from the ancient preference for the "liberal" jest, it is clear that Falstaff could hardly qualify as a "liberal" jester in the classical sense. Far from being an ironist who shows good taste, tact, and propriety, he is rather the buffoon who is "more concerned to raise a laugh than to keep within the bounds of decorum."[31] Whereas the gentleman to Aristotle is one whose actions are guided by reason and sense, to these critics he is simply one who is cheerful and good at heart, if coarse in mind.

As one could not easily turn Jonson's sly and witty manipulators into openhearted or, as Morris describes Falstaff, "Evergreen" companions, it is not surprising that Jonson was demoted from his high place in the ranks of English comic writers, remaining in low esteem for most of the eighteenth century. Confirming this distaste in a later issue of the *Gray's Inn Journal*, Murphy spurns Jonson's comic characters using Morose as an example, whom he considers to be a "surly, ill-natured, absurd Humorist, whom we can hardly laugh at, and he soon becomes very bad Company."[32] As Tave comments, "the harshness of [Jonson's] humor became a mere foil to Shakespeare's sweetness,"[33] although ironically, it was Jonson's elevation of the humor from a delicate fluid to a ruling passion that led to the more generous attitude towards humorous characters.

Don Quixote was subjected to the same kind of scrutiny with considerably more success both from the point of view of the audience and the work. The eighteenth-century reader was pleased to find that the knight was not meant merely to be ridiculed and the work was in turn pleased to reveal some of its previously unnoticed subtleties. Thus Sarah

Fielding, in 1754, exemplifying the new sympathetic reader, notes that the "strong and beautiful representation of human nature exhibited in Don Quixote's madness in one point and extraordinary good sense in every other, is indeed very much thrown away on such readers as consider him only as the object of their mirth."[34] That madness does not necessarily entitle a person to ridicule, that it may actually demonstrate the strength and beauty of human nature, is a startlingly different attitude from the one which assumed that the Don was no worthier than the works which made him mad. Here is evidence not only of generosity towards foibles, the kind of indulgence that Addison and Steele show towards their companions, but of an actively delighted interest in the struggles of mankind to overcome the handicaps of being human. Foibles and the struggles they give rise to are seen as contributing to the worth of life rather than detracting from or having no bearing upon it. Falstaff, according to this manner of thinking, is admirable not simply because he is openhearted and strangely virtuous but because he manages to be openhearted and kind while catering to his vanity, love of idleness, and tendency to exaggerate (as opposed to lie). The comic character is relished rather than scorned or pitied; he is laughed at without being mocked, and admired without being wept over.

The balance between mockery and tears is held only with determination and alertness. Once scorn is deemed inappropriate, weeping becomes a constant threat to comic delight, for sympathy and affection lead easily into sentimentalism: one need only deny the ridiculous aspects of human weakness and the absurdity of the spectacle presented by a flawed man trying to pass himself off as one of the great miracles of creation for laughter to turn to tears. Thus, while the writings of David Hartley and Adam Smith contributed to the general softening of comic responses by encouraging a sensitivity to the humanity of others, their ideas also nurtured the anticomic response of gravity. Sympathy, a passionate recreation of another's passions, precludes, in its purest form, laughter at the unconscious absurdity of human beings.[35] The tendency of critics towards the end of the century to expect comedy to be blurred by the gravity of sympathy did more damage to Swift's reputation as a comic genius than did Corbyn Morris's redefinition of comic standards. Whereas Fielding was able to perceive the comedy in Swift's satire, and commend him along with Cervantes and Lucian for sending his satire "laughing into the world," James Beattie in 1776 finds fault with Swift's mind for being unlike that of "the amiable Thomson," for having "little relish for the sublime and beautiful."[36]

In the revaluation process that accompanied the appreciation of good cheer for its energizing properties, it is not surprising to find that *Don Quixote* was among those productive of continued delight. Américo Castro identifies the source of both its energy and good cheer in his discussion of the book's powers of "incarnation":

The basic theme of *Don Quixote* is life as a process creative of itself—the onrush of incitements (the written or spoken word, love, wealth, possibilities of amusement, etc.) into the riverbed of the life of each individual. . . . The style of *Don Quixote* rests on the assumption that all reality is something transitory, "transient," something that is inundated by effluvia emanating from some individual life, or that is already stylized in literature. The consciousness of feeling oneself living is the foundation upon which this oscillating world of constant flux finds stability.[37]

The sense of life that a novel can induce makes it equally not surprising that "the new species of writing" was finding such immediate popularity at the same time as *Don Quixote* was first admired for its ability to express all the feelings of being alive. The novel's expansive form, with its possibilities of context and tone, is peculiarly suited to establishing the balance that is essential to "restorative" comedy. By embracing both pity and scorn without contradiction within its wide span, the novel can fuse together these emotions and generate a powerful spirit of mirth. This mirth in turn gives comic novels their value, their power to refresh mankind with invigorating evidence of man's ability to survive and flourish in spite of the obstacles he encounters along the way.

The prose narrative first began to examine the possibilities of its form when sunniness began to prevail over the episodic thunderclaps of satire. The earliest novels were written as much as any other literature of the time to offer correction—even *Don Quixote* surely owes its creation in part to Cervantes' wish to correct fossilized attitudes towards nobility —and followed the traditional method of satire in presenting its material. Ronald Paulson traces the episodic descriptions of fool-knave relationships found in the picaresque narratives back to Juvenal and comments on the "spectrum of satiric subject matter" that may be presented through this conventional device.[38] What distinguishes these works from formal satire and prepares the way for the novel is the sense of realism, of life

21

going on, that is maintained throughout the separate "thunderclaps" and serves to link them for the reader, usually by arousing interest in one particular character.

Even *Lazarillo de Tormes*, the prototype of most picaresque works, suggests the concern for the individual which today is the main criterion for differentiating between the novel and the satirical narrative. When Lazaro reverses the normal procedure and supports his starving master out of affection for him, emotion expressed in the prose softens any satiric edges that happen to intrude. The relationship between Lazaro and the impoverished squire takes precedence over the relationship between the hungry rogue and the evils that society forces him to learn:

I often reflected upon the Capriciousness of my Destiny that had taken me out of the Hands of two churlish Masters who let me die of Hunger, to put me into the Hands of a Third, who was so far from being able to maintain me, that he was glad to get me to mump a Morsel of Bread for him.

However, I wish'd him well; and since it was not in his Power to do otherwise heartily lamented his miserable Condition; and many time I pinch'd my own Gut to bring home something to him.[39]

The tact and delicacy with which he handles the tender matter of being his master's provider transforms Lazaro from a mere satirical observer into a human being:

Will you please to try, Sir, said I (putting the Ox Foot in his Hand, with two good Morsels of Bread) *when you have tasted it, you will be convinc'd that 'tis a Treat for a King, 'tis so well dress'd and season'd.*

However, rather than exploring the differences in their temperaments throughout a variety of experiences, as Cervantes does with his master-servant pair, the author of *Lazarillo de Tormes* disposes of the master in order to progress: the squire "forgets" the way home in an effort to avoid the rent collector and Lazaro is left free to encounter new experiences.

It was the *Roman comique,* as Paulson points out, that first suggested the possibility of a unified whole by introducing a romantic framework:

The *Roman comique* casts a long shadow on the eighteenth-century English novel, a much longer one than on the French. We can detect in it the general plan of Fielding's *Joseph Andrews* and the novels of Smollett—a Quixotic fool and a pair of lovers, both parties pursued and persecuted, with at least one partly guilty and with ridiculous reactions to his persecution, the other innocent and dignified in adversity. In the second place, the *Roman comique* produces a satire set off by the romantic story of Etoile and Destin and shading off from the folly of Ragotin to the roguery of La Rancune, to the foolish knavery of La Rapinière.[40]

Like Cervantes, who invokes the aid of a Dulcinea del Toboso (whose nonexistence is irrelevant) to explore fully the qualities of the knight's character, to make him much more than simply the "fool" in a fool-knave relationship, Scarron turns his *Roman* into a matter of human rather than satirical interest by weaving the threads of an emotional experience into the fabric of his observations about society. This attention to the details of characters' emotional as well as physical lives becomes increasingly comprehensive as the novel continues to develop: the gap between *Lazarillo* and *Joseph Andrews* may be measured by how little we know about the little servant's true feelings and how much we know about Joseph's.

By the time Defoe turned his attention to the prose narrative, the English novel may be judged to exist. Deloney and Nashe, building on jest-book character types, had already captured the flavor of English life in as lively a prose style as the Spanish works of the period; the cony-catching pamphlets recorded the English version of rogueries with an equally satirical bite. In *Moll Flanders,* Defoe brought together a wide range of characters and incidents in a focused and realistic account of human life (however extraordinary), at the same time preserving the comic liveliness of the Elizabethan works.

Yet just as eighteenth-century readers later recognized the difference between the comic moments that lighten the moral gravity of *Pamela* and the comedy that is central to the morality of *Tom Jones,* so they felt too the difference between the liveliness of Defoe's works and the remarkably bracing spirit that Fielding breathed into his novels. *Moll Flanders* must be distinguished from the "new species": for even more than the picaresque works, Defoe's novel comes close to expressing a cynicism about life that is deadly to the comic spirit. His insistence on Moll's naiveté, which we must accept along with his lectures on Christian morality, makes the facts of her life seem a cause for distress rather than delight. When Gil Blas is coerced into becoming a thief, his adjustment, while difficult, is nevertheless cheerfully achieved, whereas Moll has to learn a resignation, a sufferance which makes her life seem joyless. Gil Blas learns to make choices between different kinds of experience, preferring always those most likely to be pleasant and pleasurable; Moll seems to swing back and forth with events making excuses about necessity and engaging in her chosen actions with an underlying guilt unknown in the little rogue heroes. She is put through the trials of experience, one episode after another, with no change to explore the intricate workings of the internal life which extenuate the disquieting facts of the external one.

In his thesis on "The Tradition of the Comic Novel," Ernest Simon describes the process by which the novel converts the raw materials of life into comic substance: "In order to be comic, [the] fundamentally threatening facts of human existence must appear in a context where their meaning is preserved while their ominousness is blunted and their destructivity nullified. The comic novel creates such a context through its inclusiveness, which admits within the work positive facts to counterbalance the negative and threatening ones."[41] The positive facts need not be strokes of fortune; they may emerge from within the characters themselves. When the prose narrative began to use its breadth to plumb the depths of its characters, when the characters became detached enough from the individual episodes to offset the evils of circumstance with the force of their personalities, the novel began to realize its potential for comic vision. Incidents worthy of satire, evil people, ravages of fortune —all these were then absorbed into the stream of the novel without affecting the comic integrity which lay in the characters who survived these ills, and often in a narrator as well, who extended the context to include his own detached vision of the events.

The encouragement to extend the context of a literary work and to consider the complex motives behind actions and reactions was offered by English society in the mid-eighteenth century. This society expressed its acute consciousness of human variety in its taste and showed its determination to be generous towards unusual instances of this variety in an almost systematic devaluation of satirical works. The demands on people were no less than they were on literary works to be agreeable and cheerful. No longer did an Addison have to coax his readers into good-nature; it was a requirement of society:

The most allowable as well as agreeable kind of laughing is that which proceeds from cheerful good-humour; the person that laughs is pleased, and no body is offended; the satisfaction even runs through the whole company. On the other hand, the laughter that proceeds from contempt, argues a disturbance of soul, and gives a quite different air to the countenance: 'tis really an effect of the spleen, nature taking that way to relieve itself.[42]

The attitude behind these pronouncements is that behavior arising from a faulty spleen (and similarly, writing that reflects an excess of bile) is unpleasant and, even worse, infecting. Ill-nature is a disease which must not be spread.

The widespread suffering from the vaguely named and poorly diagnosed disease known as "the spleen" has perhaps more than an incidental relation to the change in comic tastes and tones in the century. Noting that in this period "spleen attained the dignity of a national affliction," Tave remarks that "English comedy and even English farce and comic epilogues had a function that went beyond the conventional instruction of ridicule, and beyond mere amusement. They were a vital national bulwark against the ever waiting terrors of lunacy, melancholy, spleen."[43] That these waiting terrors were responsible for the composition of the great comic novels of the period has been jocularly suggested by Oswald Doughty, who comments that "we might indeed, with but little exaggeration, seek to show that the necessity for distraction from spleen was one of the influences leading to the creation of the modern novel."[44] But the critical implications of Tristram's provocative claim to have written "against the spleen" have never been considered: the vitality of these novels has never been traced to their courageous battles against melancholy or to the force of laughter that was their most valuable ammunition. Tave's fine study concerns itself primarily with the development and critical reception of amiable humorists rather than dealing with the effect their presence has on particular works. Most other critical studies still explain the greatness of these works in terms of the vestigial bits of satire or hints of coming sentiment, while ignoring or simply acknowledging the invigorating spirit which not only enlivens the very satire or sentiment they admire but, more important, enlivens the lives of readers regardless of changing tastes.

It is certain that the physical and psychological benefits of a good laugh were not lost on medical theorists or the spleen-sufferers themselves. In differentiating between the false, almost hysterical laugh brought on by "black choller" and the genuine laugh that relieves the splenetic condition, Timothy Bright, in his late sixteenth-century "Treatise of Melancholie" shows that he appreciates the refreshment that true laughter offers:

The heart is always affected in true laughter, and not alwayes in a fained kind, which is only a shaking of the chest, and retraction of the lippes, without the liuely and chearfull eye, fraught with the ioyfull spirites, which replenish the merie countenaunce. This kinde is that which melancholicke persons without obiect break out into . . . the heart receaueth no contentment.[45]

Robert Burton (in his inimitable way) gives proof that such appreciation goes back to ancient times. Quoting biblical proverbs and ancient physicians' writings which attribute long life to a merry heart and a merry heart to mirthful companions, he notes that "for these causes our physicians generally prescribe this [mirth] as a principal engine to batter the walls of melancholy, a chief antidote, and a sufficient cure of itself."[46] At the same time the purgative powers of laughter are recommended by Burton in a quoted observation that bad health is contracted from and increased by sadness and therefore offset by high spirits *("Mala valetudo aucta et contracta est tristitia, ac propterea exhilaratione animi removenda")*.

Trust in the powers of laughter did not diminish in the eighteenth century. Dr. Stukeley affirms the value of laughter for cleansing the system of splenetic matter:

A fit of laughter has often cur'd a fit of the spleen. Laughter is a passion proper to the human race, and certainly is assisted by the spleen; as in that convulsion, the diaphragmatic and phrenic branches give and receive blood readily to it. The spleen only in human bodies is fastned to the diaphragm, and its concussions reciprocally assist the spleen, whence mirth at meals must be very useful towards a good digestion.[47]

He goes on to comment on the folly of reading prayers at mealtimes rather than engaging in mirthful conversation, for maintaining cheerfulness is one of the best ways of maintaining health.

That this method of cure and prevention was not only widely held to be valid but also widely used is attested by the proliferation of jest-books that began in the late seventeenth century, the popularity of one spawning many others and many editions. Jests became identified as "pills to purge melancholy"; the stationer who sent forth his collection of songs, ditties, and rude poems with an assurance to his readers of the medical value of the contents seems to express a common attitude:

> *Paracelsus* wanted skill,
> When he sought to cure that ill;
> No Pectorals like the Poets Quill.
> Here are *Pills* of every sort,
> For the *Country City Court,*
> Compounded and made up of sport.
> . . . .
> Cures the *Spleen,* Revives the *Blood,*
> Puts thee in a Merry Mood,
> Who can deny such *Physick* good,
> Nothing like to Harmless *Mirth,*
> Tis a Cordial on earth,
> That gives Society a Birth.[48]

John Dunton, who had to justify his own excessive mirth, recommends his work with a similar reference to the good of the body, foreshadowing Tristram's own reasons. " 'Tis plain enough that what's so pleasant as this must needs be profitable too another way to the *Body,* by chearing the spirits, sweetning the Blood, dispelling black melancholy Fumes and making it as *brisk as a Prentice just out of his Time,* a Crack't Tradesman newly Set-up again, a jolly young Bridegroom on the Wedding night, or a fair Bride the next morning."[49]

Feeling similarly compelled to "apologize" for his propensity to mirth, Colley Cibber rallies behind the forces of creation, citing nature's obvious genius as evidence of laughter's value to mankind. "If I am misguided, 'tis nature's fault, and I follow her from this persuasion, that as nature has distinguished our species from the mute creation by our risibility, her design must have been, by that faculty, as evidently to raise our happiness, as by our *os sublime,* our erected faces, to lift the dignity of our form above them."[50]

Even Addison who "would not willingly laugh, but to instruct," chooses to substantiate his plea for good-nature by alluding to its physical benefits, though equally notable is the faintly contemptuous attitude that still hounds comic writers today:

> Laughter is indeed a very good Counterpoise to the Spleen; and it seems
> but reasonable that we should be capable of receiving Joy from what is
> no real Good to us, since we can receive Grief from what is no real evil. . . .
> Laughter, while it lasts, slackens and unbraces the Mind, weakens the
> Faculties, and causes a kind of Remissness, and Dissolution in all the
> Powers of the Soul: And thus far it may be looked upon as a Weakness
> in the Composition of Human Nature. But if we consider the frequent
> Reliefs we receive from it, and how often it breaks the Gloom which is
> apt to depress the Mind, and damp our Spirits with transient unexpected
> gleams of Joy, one would take care not to grow too Wise for so great a
> Pleasure of Life.[51]

The contempt probably springs in part from the marked inclination in
the female sex to get carried away with laughter; the usefulness of even
silly mirth is, however, granted by a writer who is clearly amused by the
feminine trait: "The giggle is peculiar to girls, and is owing to a certain
petulancy in the muscles of laughter, to dance away without a fiddle.
However, it is a very good preservative against the green-sickness."[52]

The burden of providing amusement for a drooping public was in
many ways a real one for the authors of novels to take upon themselves,
just as satirists had felt the necessity to instruct a decadent public in the
years of moral and political reversals. References to victims of melancholy abound in eighteenth-century works, ranging from the archetypal
Crabtrees to the countless Belindas who took refuge in the malady to win
sympathy and whatever else might be gained. Real-life heroines apparently resorted to the same method, cultivating the symptoms of this at
once fashionable and dreaded disease for their own ends, at once reveling
in the ailment and yet, like Belinda, suffering no less than those who
came by their attacks naturally:

> As the Ladies rival us Men in most things, and outshine us in all Things,
> they have run away with an elder Brother's Part, even of the Spleen. It
> seems to have taken a liking to their Constitutions. . . .
> But they bear this Distemper, not only with Contentment, but Tri-
> umph; for *it is the Mode*; and a *hoop'd Petticoat*, a *Monkey* and a
> *pretty Fellow*, are not more fashionable.[53]

The element of fashion had been complicating and aggravating the ailment since Elizabethan times; Lawrence Babb discusses the far-reaching effects of Aristotle's problem beginning with the provocative question, "Why is it that those who have become eminent in philosophy or politics or poetry or the arts are clearly of an atrabilious temperament?" Renaissance scholars pondered the question with great interest and account for the prevalence of the disease. According to Babb, "If there had been no Aristotelian problem, the melancholic attitude would never have won the popularity which it enjoyed during the Renaissance. No man would have cared to confess himself melancholy if that had been to confess himself blockish and silly. But Aristotle lent melancholia a philosophic and artistic glamor, and many men were more than willing to declare themselves affected."[54] The Aristotelian notion obviously prejudiced the observations of medical men. Dr. Cheyne, in his influential work of 1734, *The English Malady,* confidently generalizes that the disease "never happens or can happen to any but those of the liveliest and quickest natural Parts, whose Faculties are the brightest and most spiritual, and whose Genius is most keen and penetrating."[55] The willingness to declare oneself a victim of the spleen lasted well into the eighteenth century, when medical treatises identifying melancholia as a mental disease related to mania (as in the manic-depressive cycle) seem finally to have had an effect on the number of fashionable cases. Johnson, for one, in 1776 did not ascribe to the "foolish notion" of Dr. Cheyne that "melancholy is a proof of acuteness."[56]

Melancholy had always been closely associated with madness and a great deal of the nosological work in the eighteenth century, by which time medical theorists had detached themselves from their pertinacious belief in the humors, was devoted to sorting out the different species of the disorder that went variously by the names of spleen, vapors, mania, hypochondria (a disorder of the stomach producing great perturbations of the spirit), and hysteria (the female version of hypochondria, emanating from the womb). Debates of classification filled medical treatises, generally resulting in the grouping of melancholy with mania and hypochondria with hysteria; the term "spleen" is not common in medical writings, except in passing reference to the popular name which served as a catch-all for all of these related ailments.

By mid-century, consensus seems to have established that there are two types of madness, both being "a constant disorder of the mind without any considerable fever; but with this difference, that the one is attended with audaciousness and fury, the other with sadness and fear: and that they call *mania*, this melancholy. But these generally differ in degree only. For *melancholy* very frequently changes, sooner or later, into maniacal madness; and, when the fury is abated, the sadness generally returns heavier than before."[57] Popular belief, if we may judge from Johnson's own fears (disputed however by Boswell) supported the alliance of madness and melancholy.

Indeed, the Galenic conception of melancholy as a terrifyingly gloomy state of mind exerted at least as powerful an influence as that of the Aristotelian problem. The dangerous effects of melancholic vapors upon the brain, as described by physicians of the day, would present a fearful prospect even to those who occasionally induced a faulty spleen for fashion's sake:

[W]hat Emotions of Mind and Body ensue ... is incredible to speak; the former is often crowded with the darkest scenes of Horror and Distrust, with sad and melancholy Reflections on their own dismal and gloomy State; from which often they shut out all hopes of Recovery and fall into an incurable Despair; ... they reflect deeply on their present woeful Condition, and exaggerate to themselves the miserable Effects of their Distemper, never never to be cur'd; and thus, by frequent, and almost continual Reflections, those dark, gloomy Ideas fix so deep an Impression on the Brain and Seat of the common Sensorium, that the least Motion of the Nerves, ever after shall revive the Memory of these dark and despairing Thoughts.[58]

Dramatic images of the progress of melancholy into madness appear in medical writings throughout the century. In 1755, Sir George Baker notes that "melancholy encroaches slowly, step by step, like that poison which the barbarians are reported to prepare so skillfully that they can gradually waste away a man's vital stamina and consume him by degrees in a slow death."[59] Thus, while one might pretend to be troubled by melancholy in order to authenticate one's wit, true melancholy was conscientiously avoided, even by indulging in a false case, which had the benefit of amusing oneself as well as others. To preserve the flow of animal spirits, the wondrous fluid which looked after the nervous system and acted as a liaison between the brain and the body's organs, or later in the century to preserve the flow of blood to the brain, was the concern of every healthy person. To do so one had to preserve one's cheerfulness and guard against a blockage of bile in the spleen or a thickening of the blood (attributable to prolonged gloom and sadness). Johnson's constant behest to Boswell, based on Burton's advice, was "be not solitary; be not idle."[60] Diversion by any means ("except drink," Johnson warns Boswell) is required to offset a gloomy temperament. The national effort to ensure the free-flowing movement of the blood and animal spirits explains a good deal of the popularity of the amiable humorist and of the novel as well, which proved to be peculiarly adaptable to the requirements of a mirth-conscious public.

The comic novel, like the spleen (organ), by drawing in the bitter juices—the harsh uncertainties of life, unpleasant events and characters—and neutralizing them in the context of an expansive tale centering upon amiable characters, contributes to the well-being of the reader, helping to keep the animal spirits moving. The medical imprecision upon which this comparison rests does not detract from its metaphoric validity: "animal spirits" do not circulate and the spleen is a dispensable organ, but pangs of melancholy still trouble the human mind and the hard facts of life which cause them must still be put into a perspective that makes them bearable. The eighteenth-century theorists deduced the symptoms of melancholy to be from "too thick and glewy, or sharp Juices, some great Bowel spoil'd, or strong Obstruction form'd,"[61] giving physical substance to the passions of rage and despair that have the effect of paralyzing the body and enslaving the mind. The business of comic writing is to counterbalance by laughter these passions and thus like the effective spleen to let "the wheels of life" turn fully and actively around.

One may fairly suppose, as Doughty does, from remarks in letters or the comments of characters such as Tristram, that many novels might not have been written if the authors themselves had not been doing battle against the spleen. Smollett was supposed to have suffered acutely from melancholy and we may in that respect look at Matt Bramble as being not only a reflection of Smollett's testy character, but also as a personal cure for his disease: by laughing at Matt's absurd gloom and by putting him through a restorative journey that improves his temper, which in turn improves his health, Smollett must have relieved (in the act of writing) much of his own gloominess of mind. Surely the creation of his lovable nautical characters, who enliven the worlds of Roderick Random and Peregrine Pickle, must have enlivened the author's own mental world. We know for certain that Richard Graves began his *Spiritual*

Quixote "in a pique" and continued writing because it amused him to do so.[62] His intentions were apparently as antisplenetic as Sterne's, though his book turned out to be more genial than mirthful, and therefore decidedly less efficacious in fighting the spleen.

Tristram's full statement on his antisplenetic motives for writing his Life and Opinions may be examined to see how mirth is called upon to stave off the spleen that might arise from satire or from the knobby fact that provoked the satire:

—If 'tis wrote against any thing,—'tis wrote, an' please your worships, against the spleen; in order, by a more frequent and a more convulsive elevation and depression of the diaphragm, and the succussations of the intercostal and abdominal muscles in laughter, to drive the *gall* and other *bitter juices* from the gall bladder, liver and sweet-bread of his majesty's subjects, with all the inimicitious passions which belong to them, down to their duodenums.[63]

The language strikes one immediately as being satirical, though it is much closer to real medical writings than we would at first imagine. Yet what characterizes this passage is the obvious enjoyment the writer—Tristram or Sterne—feels in such a succession of multi-syllabic words, ostensibly the object of his disapproval. We are in turn especially delighted by the way in which sense or nearly sense is made to seem nonsense and the way in which the danger of rhetoric and the distresses of melancholy are nullified by the nonsense. Tristram's words make a seemingly barbed statement against the medical pomp in a parody that is no more odd than the real but a good deal funnier for being supposedly an exaggeration.

His writing also suggests the ravages of "inimicitious" passions, while drawing off one's "bitter juices" by inviting a sense of joy in words, in writing, in the activity of life that is imaged in the activity of the syllable-packed words. As one reads, the content of the passage is verified: the passage itself is antisplenetic, as is the rest of the work, which similarly calls forth an army of mirth to do battle against the gorge of despair that might arise at the thought of an Uncle Toby facing real life. If battle against the spleen is recognized as one of the contributing factors in the development of the English novel, then the particularly mirthful character of these works, the acceptance they express, becomes not only more apparent but also more appreciable as the source of their continuing ability to delight.

Antisplenetic comedy encourages an active delight in the events and characters of the work; it must have conviction enough, which perfunctory sentiment does not, to assure one that life is worth the trouble it causes (the description of which is often mistaken for satire). Christopher Fry, who is one of the few critics to concern himself with the comic spirit as opposed to form, very rightly observes that comedy is "an escape, not from truth but from despair; a narrow escape into faith."[64] The novels of the mid-eighteenth century may be seen as providing various means of escape, all the while suggesting the truth: the especially hearty laughter that is at once aroused by the spleen and acts as ammunition against it carries a recognition of the sorrow and agony it is determined to banish. Its lightheartedness is consciously deceptive and a willing "suspension of acknowledgment" is involved in the very act of laughing. The comedy is all the more vigorous for silently accepting, while consciously not acknowledging, the cruelty and meanness that were so relentlessly exposed in the earlier part of the century, especially by Swift. The necessity to laugh in order to survive happily impels the comedy and increases its force; the comic writer comes to terms with life and recommends that his reader do the same, very much as an early eighteenth-century essayist suggests that the splenetic come to terms with human company: "In order to take off the keenness of his Spleen and ill Nature, he ought to suppose that the World is full of absurd and disagreeable People, that have rough and ill-bred Ways, and know not the Rules of Life; and that he must either habituate himself to the Fooleries of others, or sequester himself from human Commerce."[65]

Thus the novelists of the mid-eighteenth century described with gusto all the disagreeable people and the rough facts of life. Unlike Swift, who did not choose to dispel his own spleen or his readers', because his hope for mankind depended on a universal abhorrence rather than the acceptance of unreasonable behavior, Fielding and his followers and, to an even greater extent, Smollett and Sterne, set out to induce a carefree feeling in their readers, in the hope that mirth would prepare them to face life's inevitably weighty realities with cheerfulness and dignity. It is their evocation of mirth in situations of everyday life that explains the newness and endurance of their "new species."

CHAPTER TWO

" THE NEW SPECIES OF WRITING FOUNDED BY MR. FIELDING "

The new species of writing, first formally recognized by an anonymous pamphlet writer (sometimes believed to be Francis Coventry), distinguished Fielding's novels from the abundant romances of the day not
primarily by Fielding's reliance on nature but by the humor, "without
which the whole performance must be dead and languid."[1] Fielding
himself still gave precedence to the Augustan guiding principle of Nature,
appealing to Genius "to know mankind better than they know themselves."[2] Yet the author and the critic were not really opposed in their
choice of emphasis, for the relationship between Nature, in the sense of
life, and humor is inextricable. Indeed, it is the inherent humor in un-
edited versions of life that the writers of prose fiction who followed in
Fielding's new tradition of the "comic epic poem in prose" tried to bring
out in their edited versions. Fielding established through example the
fact that "life everywhere furnishes an accurate observer with the ridiculous," and his example also served to make the ridiculous seem more a
cause for mirthful appreciation than caustic censure.
　　Scriblerus Secundus, the designation Fielding chose for himself, tells
his true relation to the early eighteenth-century satirists: he is second-
generation stock. His farcical pen transformed the gall and copperas of
his wit into happy works; his mirth softened the hard blows of morality
and turned sermons into inoffensive admonitions. He was charged with
"lowness" rather than viciousness or undue gravity; at his successful
comedies people laughed and were delighted rather than corrected.

That Fielding intended to correct his audiences of both their social and political faults is plain when one reads the texts of the farces, but onstage the frivolity of the vehicle easily disguises the seriousness of the many messages it is asked to carry. In a performance of *Don Quixote in England* Sancho's listening would be active and would have the same depreciating effect that his remark at the end of a particularly weighty speech has: "Oh! Good your worship, proceed: I could fast an hour longer to hear your discourse" (II. i; V, 32). The Don is immediately reduced to the status of a performer, one so entertaining as temporarily to diminish Sancho's insatiable appetite for food. Similarly, one look of fascination on the humble squire's face would be enough to undervalue any sensible speech in the play. Though the message is there, it is hard to take seriously. Fielding's wit sometimes overpowers the force of the implied criticism:

Sancho, when I see a gentleman on his own coachbox, I regret the loss which some one has had of a coachman; the man who toils all day after a partridge or a pheasant, might serve his country by toiling after a plough; and when I see a low, mean, tricking lord, I lament the loss of an excellent attorney. (I. ii; XI, 18)

The utilitarian precepts are clearly stated, but the jest at the end attracts attention to its own cleverness and to the author's private peeve, and thus forestalls any consideration of the real meaning or validity of the ideas. The performance does not stop for the convenience of an audience's thoughts, but rather moves on from jest to jest.

The laughs come thick and fast in *The Tragedy of Tragedies*, every line of which is nonsensical burlesque of heroic tragedies. The nonsense, however, very often masks a sturdy truth. The play's richness comes from just this casual mingling of sense and mirthful gibberish, but its popularity on stage derives almost entirely from the gibberish:

Where art thou, Grizzle! Where are now thy glories?
Where are the drums that waken thee to honour?
Greatness is a laced coat from Monmouth Street,
Which fortune lends us for a day to wear,
To-morrow puts it on another's back.
The spiteful sun but yesterday surveyed
His rival high as Saint Paul's cupola;
Now may he see me as Fleet Ditch laid low. (I.iv; IX, 29)

There is genuine poignancy in the image of greatness, which Grizzle's soliloquizing at once makes more real as he stands there so obviously the recipient of a leased lace-coat and more ridiculous as he so absurdly bemoans the loss of his splendidly-named Huncamunca. Throughout similarly passionate speeches, Fielding manages to insert truly passionate similes, some of which make their point in spite of the general merriment:

> For what's a woman when her virtue's gone?
> A coat without its lace; wig out of buckle;
> A stocking with a hole in't. —I can't live
> Without my virtue, or without Tom Thumb.
> Then let me weigh them in two equal scales,
> In this scale put my virtue, that Tom Thumb.
> But hold! —perhaps I may be left a widow;
> This match prevented, then Tom Thumb is mine:
> In that dear hope I will forget my pain,
> So when some wench to Tothill Bridewell's sent,
> With beating hemp and flogging she's content,
> She hopes in time to ease her present pain,
> At length is free, and walks the streets again.   (I.vii; IX, 33)

While informing us of the acuteness of the Queen's longing for Tom Thumb, the epic simile has its own autonomy and for a brief moment makes the plight of the girl who has been brought up to street-walking acutely felt. That Fielding was able to integrate into his farces such carefully aimed reminders of reality without jarring the essentially mirthful nature of the business at hand, that he could so vividly suggest the pain while reveling in the abundant material for jest, is an achievement which should not be submerged in the general admiration of his skills in burlesque. But neither should one belittle the value of the simply hilarious lines, those that set the moments of pain in the perspective of life, which includes sorrow and joy, high and low, sense and nonsense.

Fielding's defenses against the charges of lowness, in the *Covent Garden Journal* (no. 18) and in the farces themselves, were largely responsible, as Glenn Hatfield points out, for the loss of power that "low" suffered as a critical term. He quotes Colman's verses that attribute the accomplishment to Fielding:

> When Fielding, Humour's fav'rite child appear'd,
> Low was the word—a word each author fear'd!

'Till chac'd at length, by Pleasantry's bright ray,
Nature and mirth resum'd their legal sway.[3]

To connect nature and mirth in a society that was accustomed to associate morality only with gravity, wisdom with a melancholic withdrawal from company, was to make lightheartedness and frivolity as respectable as it had been in the more boisterous days of Elizabeth. Addison's encouragement of cheerfulness had had the effect of somewhat lightening the moral atmosphere, but it took Fielding's shameless laughter to open up a whole "new species" of writing. Though Fielding was quite decisive and right in thinking that he was not writing mere burlesque and encouraging a general revelry at the expense of morality, he was prepared to admit the beneficial effects of that style of writing and in turn to admit the style into his more intentionally serious works: "[Burlesque writing] contributes more to exquisite mirth and laughter than any other; and these are probably more wholesome physic for the mind, and conduce better to purge away spleen, melancholy, and ill affections, than is generally imagined" (Preface to *Joseph Andrews*; I, 20).

While the Licencing Act of 1737, in one stroke, quickly put an end to most of the outright burlesque, his venture into novel-writing was not accompanied by a burial of farce. Indeed, the characters, in spite of Fielding's vigilance with regard to their burlesque features, not surprisingly take on some of the mirthful qualities of the style in which they are described and bring enormous delight to the readers. One must point out, however, that Fielding was careful in the Preface to ascribe the comicality of his created people to their likeness to humankind and would most assuredly deny the presence of Rabelaisian grotesqueries in any of his novels. That is, the mirthful atmosphere does not distort his characters into figures of outlandish or, what would be worse, unrecognizable proportions. Human beings are not transformed into Tom Thumbs or Gargantuas, but in the generous way of comedy human scoundrels are often turned into harmless fellows.

Thus, far from being a despicable figure, Jonathan Wild, like Milton's Satan before him, emerges as a true prince of darkness, as an excellent specimen of vitality and wit. Indeed, Fielding's attitude is purposely ambiguous towards Wild: in setting out to demonstrate that a "great" Walpole is no different from a common highwayman, he goes so far as to assign an essential honesty—in the form of blatancy as opposed to subtlety—and honor—the allegiance one thief bears for another—to the apparently lower order of being. These ironic suggestions, supported by Fielding's lively descriptions of his hero at work, make Wild a formidably attractive character, one who kindly allows his author to satirize at his expense and who is, if anything, the more irresistibly likeable for the satire.

Shenstone is only half-apologetic for his enjoyment of the boisterous and disorderly Squire Western: "You will conclude my Taste to be not extremely *Delicate.* . . . But it is ye only Character y^t made me *laugh;* & y^t is a great Point gain'd, when one is in danger of losing y^t *Faculty* thro' Disuse. Tis moreover a Character better worth exposing than his Landlords & Landladys."[4] We may consider him to be representative of a large group of early readers who were the first to appreciate Fielding's amiable humor and to recognize the antisplenetic possibilities of the "new species" of writing. Having enlisted his works in the ranks of morality, where they are certainly not out of place, Fielding nevertheless appealed largely to those who preferred to be merely entertained, and thus unwittingly opened the way not only for his own followers, but also for the rowdier novels of Smollett and the slap-happier volumes of *Tristram Shandy,* which to early readers were not recognizably moral.

In a letter attributed to Arthur Murphy, the antisplenetic effects of "Mr. Fielding's inimitable comic Romances" are particularly praised, demonstrating the extent to which the mirth of these works has ensured his place in posterity: "A genius like this is perhaps more useful to mankind, than any class of writers; he serves to dispel all gloom from our minds, to work off our ill-humours by the gay sensations excited by a well directed pleasantry, and in a vein of mirth he leads his readers into the knowledge of human nature; the most useful and pleasing science we can apply to."[5] This writer is the first in a long line of critics who have been kind to Fielding, recognizing his genius both as a moralist (as he would wish) and as a laugh-provoking novelist (as his readers insist). That these two views are not unrelated has not always been so scrupulously noted as it was in 1753, and is perhaps the only way in which Fielding has been short-changed by the critics. A look at *Tom Jones,* with a few backward glances at Parson Adams—who unfortunately has no counterpart in the later and richer work—should be enough to reaffirm the justness of associating mirth with nature and thus works of mirth with works of meaning. We may then properly give Fielding credit for making antisplenetic comedy acceptable, for leavening the novel with representatives of human absurdity without detracting from human dignity.

From the Cervantean introduction to the Allworthy household to the author's last declaration of the happiness that was certain to reign in the world of Tom Jones, ease and sunniness are the components of the lightly felt atmosphere. If heaviness threatens the air at any time, caused either by the gloom in Tom's countenance or the harsh words of Mr. Allworthy or the devious evil of Blifil, the threat is brushed away swiftly with a whiff of Fielding's easy words, which preserve the air of well-being and preserve our confidence in the ultimate rightness of things. If Fielding happens to hold himself aloof, some comical character, an innkeeper perhaps or Squire Western in all his glory, is made to wander through the scene at a precarious time, with the same happy effect as Fielding himself. The plot, too, reinforces our complacency, even in a miraculous way when things are getting progressively worse. Though the situation may look bleak, previous emergencies have cleared themselves up, coincidences have rescued Fortune from the clutches of Fate, and, most of all, we have no good reason to suspect that a turn of events is impossible: the very contrivances of the plot seem to beg for reversals to occur at the right moment.

Madness, dire misfortune, despair—all these have little to do with the plot and nothing to do with the world of the novel, unless one relates the Man of the Hill's private universe to that of the other characters. Indeed, *Tom Jones* suggests the existence of genuine pain in life much less than the apparently more lighthearted histories of Tristram Shandy or Matt Bramble. Though R.S. Crane is right to observe that the story is made to unfold against a background that is "potentially serious" and that at the end we are aware that Fortune cannot be counted upon to intervene "in the same gratifying way,"[6] nevertheless, the background is not so much drawn as it is peopled: it is mainly in the characters of *Tom Jones* that the social criticism is contained and they are all composed of comic matter: Blifil is hardly a Modest Proposer, and no one is flayed alive.

So much control does Fielding have over the tone and so much does he want to hold our confidence, that Tom's bastardy becomes a comical accident rather than a significantly crippling misfortune, as in life it would be. By arousing speculation on the possibility of Squire Allworthy's responsibility for the foundling, and by relishing the overly-proper Deborah's disdain and disgust, Fielding makes the whole event seem less a scar on

39

the baby's future life and more an excuse to show how quickly people are ready to believe and circulate rumors that contradict all known facts and to condemn in others crimes which they themselves would (regrettably) never have occasion to commit. Though Tom does suffer because of his low birth—his original suit for Sophia's hand is considered unthinkable and his "ingratitude" severely punished—we are well assured at this point that he is really quite a genteel fellow. Throughout the long novel, Tom is never disgraced by being forced to behave like a bastard; he is consistently genteel, as in fact he turns out to have been all along.

Death is only suffered in a way that is remote from the actual world of the novel; it is as lightly treated as the class system—that is, only villains happen to die, as only good-for-nothings are unrelieved by the charity of either Allworthy or Jones. Death occurs only to those for whom it comes as a just desert:

But while the captain was one day busied in deep contemplations of this kind, one of the most unlucky as well as unseasonable accidents happened to him. The utmost malice of Fortune could, indeed, have contrived nothing so cruel, so malapropos, so absolutely destructive to all his schemes. In short, not to keep the reader in long suspense, just at the very instant when his heart was exulting in meditations on the happiness which would accrue to him by Mr. Allworthy's death, he himself—died of an apoplexy. (I.viii; III, 98)

Violent fights are expressed in the same burlesque terms as violent love-making: the landlady's quite vehement attack on Jones is given no more elevated treatment than is Mrs. Waters' attack on him. Indeed, the landlady's vehemence seems to be directed primarily at Mrs. Waters: Fielding suggests here that a common motive, lust, is behind the two different battles. Even the Rebellion of '45, which is so notably in the background of the novel, is for the most part relegated to the arena of kitchen gossip. One never feels the pressure of political upheaval, certainly not as one feels the pressure of domestic upheaval, as for instance in the Western household. The rambunctious Squire's thunders are frequently heard, whereas all one hears of the rebellion is the "violent thundering" at the gate of an inn by a mass of red-coated merry-makers, and later their dispute over the reckoning.

Even Tom's prison spell is without the usual trappings of prison—the gloom, the damp misery, the plight of fellow prisoners—which Smollett takes such pains to reveal within the comic framework of his novels. The prison is simply a place where conversations that are essential to the plot are held: "Mr. Jones passed about twenty-four melancholy hours by himself, unless when relieved by the company of Partridge, before Mr. Nightingale returned" (XVII.ix; V, 285). Unlike the recent film script version by John Osborne, which managed to bring Tom to the gallows, relying on the camera to make the event laughable, the book starts the uphill course of Tom's fortunes as soon as he has had a few hours to think things out by himself, Fielding thereby ensuring the laughability of the story. This episode in the novel is designed specifically to ease Tom into maturity rather than to comment on the judicial conditions of the time. Whereas Smollett comes dangerously close in his jail scenes to disturbing the mirthful air of *Peregrine Pickle*, preserving the tone only with the aid of some comical inmates and the irrepressible Pipes, Fielding never brings the background so closely into focus that it imposes itself on the central characters or the reader.

Only in the rather substantial exception of the history of the Old Man does Fielding force the reader to consider the alternative to a comic depiction of life; if the rest of *Tom Jones* is almost uninterrupted mirth, The Old Man of the Hill presents clear evidence of the possibility of uninterrupted misery. Even though it is obviously meant to have an emblematic function in the book, to set out a detailed pattern of the world's evils which Tom Jones will have to confront and avoid, the entire section displeases many critics precisely because it is so much a set-piece. It is possibly the only part of the exactingly constructed narrative that would not be missed, except morally. (It is necessary morally as a balance to the history of Mrs. Fitzpatrick for Sophia's benefit.) Yet the artificiality of this section serves the rest of the book well, for on the one hand it allows the facts of the Old Man's tragic city life to be conveyed in a serious manner (though Partridge is occasionally called upon by Fielding to interrupt the gloom) and on the other it keeps the gloom from casting too much of a shadow on the rest of the story: the Old Man's world seems so far removed from Tom's that the misery does not extend beyond the boundaries of the isolated house, or in fact the isolated pages. His case is so extreme as to frighten and at the same time to subvert that fright by being so obviously exaggerated, so much in the tradition of an *exemplum*.[7] Though the tale might seem in many ways to deal more directly with the human condition than do the rather frolicking facts of

Tom's life, by setting the Old Man apart so much and by making his story such a break in the lively pace and tone of the book, Fielding implies that however much the hermit may be valuable as a model or a working study, he is not to be regarded as a living human being. Tom's vitality is more admirable than the man's experience, which leaves him in danger of losing all his humanity (if we may judge from the reception Tom gets from the housekeeper). Gravity is not to be confused with excellence, youthful spirits are not to be condemned out of hand.

If *Tom Jones* remains almost entirely in the lighter regions of the heart, it has still much to say about the heart, about the workings and variations of human nature. In the first chapter of the book, Fielding promises to make his "provision" human nature, and further to satisfy the "keen appetite" first "in that more plain and simple manner in which it is found in the country, and [then to] hash and ragoo it [human nature] with all the high French and Italian seasoning of affectation and vice which courts and cities afford" (I.i; III, 19). This rather presumptuous promise was not lightly undertaken. Fielding was already well skilled in serving up human delicacies for the delight and moral benefit of the reader: the 1749 novel is simply a more luxurious, more polished and subtle version of the feast he offered in *Joseph Andrews* in 1742. While the earlier novel still evinces its relationship to the burlesque stage pieces in many of the characters who appear briefly—Slipslop, Trulliber, Peter Pounce—the creation of Parson Adams, fully clothed in all his complexities and contradictions, and unmatched by any of his author's future offspring, stands as a model for all the other representations of humanity that have since been attempted. Abraham Adams prepared the way, not only for *Tom Jones*, but for all the works that explore life from a comic stance and see the world's inhabitants as essentially humorous, laughable and admirable at the same time.

Adams's excellences have been so completely catalogued that his unique qualities hardly need reviewing. What may perhaps be discussed is the exact way in which his character changed the perspective from which people saw comic characters, how he came as a surprise to the critics and readers of the time and helped to clear the path for the Commodore Trunnions and Uncle Tobies of the following decades. Although by this time Don Quixote was regarded by critics in a rather special light, along with the more vigorously amiable humorist, Falstaff, Parson Adams was not. Corbyn Morris, writing his pamphlet on comedy in 1744, did

not think to include the venerable and absurd parson among the company
in which we now so naturally place him. One would have thought that
the connection between Adams and the "most exquisite and delightful
humour," the kind produced "when the Oddities and Foibles introduced
are not mischievous or sneaking, but free, jocund, and liberal; and such
as result from a generous Flow of Spirits and a warm universal Benevolence" was indeed so obvious that Morris would not have been able so
soon after the publication of *Joseph Andrews* to formulate his definition
without the parson in mind.[8] But Tave notes that surprisingly little early
criticism is found on any aspect of *Joseph Andrews* although evidence of
its wide readership exists in the large number of early editions; those
who did mention it apparently still found it difficult to "adjust themselves to a comic character not designed for contempt." As late as 1753
to 1754, pieces were published on the ridiculous unworthiness rather
than the endearing innocence of the benevolent parson.[9] Critics were
still apt to look upon Don Quixote as a unique figure in literary history,
and Falstaff as still another. When Parson Adams appeared he was not
connected with Don Quixote precisely because he was an ordinary, more
popularized and more possible version of the noble knight errant. When
both his normality and his absurdity were fully appreciated the course
of the English comic character was changed from being a contemptible
figure to an admirable one.

Our first meeting with Abraham Adams does not especially prepare
us to look upon him in any special way, as one would immediately look
comically at Mrs. Slipslop, for instance. He is seemingly engaged in very
ordinary business—that of trying to have his sermons published—and he
is unextraordinarily generous—one expects a parson to offer his ready
funds (admittedly low, but not enough to be comically so) to one of his
own parishioners in Joseph's dire condition. It is not until a few pages
later that we begin to get a picture of his oddities, when he offers his
sermons as security for a loan, and when he settles down to his pipe for
consolation:

He immediately applied to his pipe, his constant friend and comfort in
his afflictions; and leaning over the rails, he devoted himself to meditations, assisted by the inspiring fumes of tobacco.
He had on a nightcap drawn over his wig, and a short great-coat,
which half covered his cassock—a dress which, added to something

43

comical enough in his countenance, composed a figure likely to attract the eyes of those who were not over-given to observation. (I.xvi; I,87)

It becomes clear that our respect for Adams will be in no way proportional to his outer dignity; he is a "low" figure in the sense that he is easily the subject of derision, but our mockery is restrained by the narrator's own restraint and tenderness. Adams is never so foolish as the people who make him seem so are villainous or simply more foolish. The courtroom incident is an excellent example of Fielding's insistence on Adams's worth in relation to other more outwardly respectable people. The justice, the clerk, and the parson in turn each display their own utter ignorance of their purported profession. If we had been inclined to chuckle over Adams's attachment to his Aeschylus, this hilarious scene now forces us to accommodate additional feelings of admiration for the lowly parson along with contempt for the assorted grave men in high position. Adams here is the representative of the common man, grossly misjudged and comically mistreated at the hands of those who should know better.

Even when we are meant to ridicule Adams for his inability to act on the precepts that he preaches, as when he hears the report of his son's death, his helplessness redeems his actions from the accusation of hypocrisy and we cannot feel contempt for this parson who is supremely human and therefore inescapably absurd. Thus, while Maynard Mack is perfectly correct to point out that Adams is the dupe not only of others but of his own "theoretical ideal of conduct that his own nature will not support,"[10] he is exempt from all but the slightest mockery on that account by the frail absurdity he displays and his nobly human attempts in the form of uncontrollable passion to reconcile himself to unreconcilable situations.

Mark Spilka compares our sympathetic reactions to Adams with those elicited by Charlie Chaplin in "City Lights," who would normally be a ridiculous spectacle in his attempt to keep up appearances in the boxing ring; but rather than scorning him, we respect his courage: "We have learned something of this [innate bravery] through time, situation, and the development of character; we are prepared, that is, for his simultaneous display of inner dignity and outer vanity in the boxing ring, and our laughter is accordingly that much richer."[11] Spilka's point is that we are continually prepared throughout the course of *Joseph Andrews* for the "comic resolution," the romping bed-switching night that precedes the marriage of Joseph and Fanny. In a rather too imaginative reading of the farcical events, Spilka establishes the nonetheless valid point that "Adams' faults, like his torn, disordered clothes, are only the outward, superficial aspects of his character," that Fielding wants us especially to see that "the essential Adam, a brave, good man, lies somewhere underneath."

In a footnote to this statement, Spilka reflects pertinently on Partridge, who falls far short of our comic expectations for him: we never feel the "nobility of heart" that is essential to any exemption from scorn. He should be only casually associated with Sancho Panza, whose fulsome warmth he lacks, though Fielding obviously looked to Sancho for his design, and tried halfheartedly to match his noble pattern (and to make us believe in Partridge's worthiness by protesting his loyalty to Tom). Adams's goodness we sense in every ridiculous word he says; Partridge's selfishness is his most salient characteristic. He would not be helping Tom at all if he did not expect some good to come of it in the form of Allworthy's bounty, and unlike Sancho, his crassness is not offset either by his devotion or his conversation. He does not rise above mediocrity in any of his squiring or human capacities, as Sancho so often does so movingly:

I protest Sancho, said Don Quixote, I think thou art as mad as myself. Nay, not so mad neither, reply'd Sancho, but somewhat more cholerick. But talk no more of that: let's see, How will you do for victuals when I'm gone?[12]

If Adams had been cast as a squire to Joseph, we could imagine his understanding and generosity being expressed in such lines as these: it is unfortunate that Partridge is no heir to Adams.

It has been frequently noted that most of Adams's absurdity arises from his unfulfilled expectation of others, based upon his own moral code. That Parson Trulliber will not accommodate his needs simply never occurs to him. He offers his sermons as security in good faith and is unaware that he is comical in doing so. As with all memorable amiable humorists, "the same thing makes [him] admirable and absurd."[13] To recognize the relationship between human frailty and nobility, to see that the worth might arise from the weakness or the weakness from the worth, was what the eighteenth-century readers were being asked, for almost the first time, to do. To make them see that this nobility might be found in all human beings, even those of apparently "low" stature—not only the high-born Don—was Abraham Adams's special task in the novel, and that he so fully succeeded is to the enduring credit of his author.

The number of memorable figures who may be credited to Fielding's imagination is an excellent index of the appreciation he had of the world's variety and of the immense capacity he had for understanding its inhabitants and making them understandable to others. The laughably humanizing treatment to which he exposes the stock character of Square is an example of Fielding's handiwork in making his imaginary characters live. The splendid irony of placing him in the company of "other female utensils" is often praised, but in addition to reducing him to a thing here, Fielding happily and paradoxically transforms him into a man, an ordinary man caught like so many others with his trousers down (figuratively, almost literally). Our first meetings with the philosopher do not incline us to think of him in human terms, especially as he is always associated with the theologian Thwackum, who remains unredeemed by any signs of life to the end. This Tweedledum and Tweedledee image breaks down permanently in Molly Seagrim's bedroom, in which "the man of ideas makes a rather surprising appearance." This embarrassing incident for the staid and upright Platonist serves well to temper our opinion of him, and while we scorn his hypocrisy, we cannot help retaining the sight of his compromised posture and liking him the more for it. More important, this early event is the only way in which his confession at the end is made to seem credible: one feels as if it is just possible for this man to have been lured into repenting by the prospect of a better life after death just as in life he was lured by the charms of Molly Seagrim and the prospect of the immediate joys she offered. A strange but human consistency links the two incidents.

In a similar way, Squire Western's penchant for lively ballads as played by his daughter, whom in his own way he appreciates, helps to offset some of the less pleasing qualities of his character. For all his quickness to pounce on the people around him, whether his sister or his servants, as if they were no different from the unnamed "little animals" who comprise the object of his sport, he is equally quick to be pacified by soothing words and gestures. Though Fielding makes use of his character's tyrannical temperament to condemn the custom of arranged marriages and the indiscriminate regard for fortune at the expense of an evaluation

of human worth, we are nonetheless inclined to like the volatile Squire
and to enjoy the vigor with which he eats, drinks, and generally lives his
life. As Smollett does frequently, Fielding here recommends his vigorous
character with evidence of the openheartedness and childlike guilelessness that accompanies his overabundance of energy. Squire Western is
surely lacking in Commodore Trunnion's amiability, and one would never
offer him as a model of goodness, but he shares with the bearlike uncle
of Peregrine Pickle an engaging lack of self-awareness. Such innocence
helps to turn his ugly behavior into comic comments on human absurdity.
Western's quick reconciliation with Tom on the occasion of his being
pronounced genteel and, more to the point, heir to his uncle's fortune, is
an epitome of his ludicrous inconsistency, almost innocent hypocrisy, if
such a concept may be allowed:

'My old friend Tom, I am glad to see thee with all my heart! all past
must be forgotten; I could not intend any affront to thee, because, as
Allworthy here knows, nay, dost know it thyself, I took thee for another person; and where a body means no harm, what signifies a hasty
word or two? One Christian must forget and forgive another.'

(XVIII.x; V, 351)

Western is clearly not hypocritical in the proper sense; quite the contrary,
he acts in a manner that reflects perfectly what he thinks. But his notion
of "friendship" and the ease with which he swings his loyalties make it
difficult for one to take his word on any matter. Unlike Blifil, who makes
up his mind and acts precisely according to his beliefs so subtly that no
one knows he has those beliefs, Squire Western does not know from one
minute to the next what he thinks, but acts on the conviction of the moment, often contradicting his stoutly-held ideas of a minute ago. Blifil
may be depended upon to carry out a preconceived villainy; Squire
Western may not, and therein lies the charm of his forceful nature.

Mrs. Waters, Black George, and Sophia's aunt Western are among
others whom Fielding has successfully recalled from the ranks of unpleasant people by looking upon them with a tolerant eye. Mrs. Waters
is thoroughly friendly and honest and cannot help engaging in amorous
battles any more than she can help winning them; Black George, we
must believe, is ashamed of his own weakness; Sophia's aunt is understandably crusty in the face of such a nubile and elegant niece. One
would like to include Partridge among these reclaimed characters but,

as he was obviously intended to be a pleasant fellow with a few faults of character, one can only be disappointed that on the whole he is a weak and annoying character with a few surprisingly pleasing qualities. His pedantry does not accord with the rest of him and, further, has the unfortunate result of canceling out the ordinarily endearing effects of the over-concern with bodily comforts which he inherited from Sancho. His lack of sophistication is apparently meant to counterbalance his pedantry and to please us with its humorous side-effects, but Fielding himself is so unsophisticated in his presentation, so heavy-handed as in the set-piece revolving around Hamlet's ghost, that one's pleasure is incidental to one's impression of Partridge's foolishness.

Whereas Fielding fails with Partridge to raise him above the mass of petty human beings, he succeeds very nicely with Tom, who might well have been another spirited rake with genteel manners or a wronged orphan too grateful to be true. Instead he is a brilliant combination of both, his recklessness preserving him from the boring fate of goody-goodihood, his gratefulness saving him from unattractive callousness. Unlike the proud Peregrine Pickle, he manages to make himself as pleasing to the other worthy characters in the book as he is to the reader. When Tom goes into a rage upon the discovery, for instance, of Sophia's muff on his bed at Upton, he is clearly as angry at himself as he is at Partridge, whose tendency to offer information about his companion's activities has led to the unfortunate incident:

The behaviour of Jones on this occasion, his thoughts, his looks, his words, his actions, were such as beggar all description. After many bitter execrations on Partridge, and not fewer on himself, he ordered the poor fellow, who was frightened out of his wits, to run down and hire him horses at any rate; and a very few minutes afterwards, having shuffled on his clothes, he hastened downstairs to execute the orders himself which he had just before given. (X.vi; IV, 220–21)

Fielding's restraint of language, his refusal to describe the momentary madness of his hero even if for artistic reasons only, makes us take lightly this lapse of temper. Smollett, on the contrary, dwells on the evidence of Peregrine's quick madness, wishing to encourage an ambiguous reaction to his well-born main character on the grounds of his birth and to recommend him for more worthy reasons, such as the liberality of spirit that he has in common with Tom. Thus we are given a vivid picture of

Peregrine's violence upon the discovery of Pipe's mismanagement of a love-letter:

> All three were amazed at this confession, the meaning of which they could not comprehend; and Peregrine after some pause, leaped upon Pipes, and seizing him by the throat, exclaimed in an extasy of rage, 'Rascall, tell me this instant what became of the letter I intrusted to your care.' The patient valet, half strangled as he was, squirted a collection of tobacco juice out of one corner of his mouth, and with great deliberation replied 'Why burnt it, you wouldn't have me give the young woman a thing that shook in the wind in tatters, would you?'[14]

Pipes is the hero of this passage, as indeed he has occasion to be elsewhere in the novel. His calm matter-of-factness in the face of his master's formidable anger is Smollett's lesson for Peregrine on the foolish ineffectiveness of a haughty temper.

If much less the object of satire than Peregrine Pickle, Tom was more in danger of being thought of as a low or insignificant figure—a mere foundling—by the eighteenth-century public. Fielding's great achievement was to make him acceptable in his own right, to make his legitimacy unnecessary to his readers' satisfaction, if not to Squire Western's. As Arnold Kettle rightly points out, Tom is a kind of "noble savage" to the eighteenth-century way of thinking: "In Tom the prevailing positive is spontaneity: he acts 'naturally' and therefore the excesses into which his animal spirits lead him are forgiven."[15] As a representative of inherent goodness, Tom is excused rather than scorned; he is naturally comic rather than contemptible, for the whole notion of noble savagery carries with it an "assertion of the capacity of human nature to change itself and the world,"[16] or to put it in comic rather than Marxist terms, an assertion of the resilience and strength of human nature even in the face of life's obstacles and menaces.

Lady Bellaston's fifty-pound note is surely a menace to Tom's conscience, for on the one hand he is in no position to refuse the ready money, and on the other he cannot help being ashamed of its origins. Just as surely, Fielding intends us to commend his hero upon the happy resolution of his embarrassing problem, by which means he at once assuages his conscience and satisfies his charitable urges. Though most readers have not looked upon Tom's selfless disposal of the "guilty" money so kindly as Fielding does, one must nevertheless accept the charity, as the innocent Mrs. Miller does, in the spirit in which it was offered. Nightingale is on hand with his grudging offer of a guinea to demonstrate the alternative approach to charity and to emphasize the fact that Tom was by no means obliged to give away the money that he had originally taken out of great need.

Another instance of Fielding's approval of Tom's "natural" behavior is seen in his description of the battle between his receptive hero and Mrs. Waters. Tom's hot-blooded evaluation of the moment appeals to the reader to abandon inflexible moral codes temporarily and to see the harmless "parley" as proof of his open-hearted generosity:

> And now, gently lifting up those two bright orbs which had already begun to make an impression on poor Jones, she discharged a volley of small charms at once from her whole countenance in a smile. Not a smile of mirth, nor of joy; but a smile of affection, which most ladies have always ready at their command, and which serves them to show at once their good-humour, their pretty dimples, and their white teeth.
>
> This smile our hero received full in his eyes, and was immediately staggered with its force. He then began to see the designs of the enemy, and indeed to feel their success. A parley was now set on foot between the parties; during which the artful fair so slyly and imperceptibly carried on her attack, that she had almost subdued the heart of our hero before she again repaired to acts of hostility. (IX.v; IV, 181)

As one accepts an invitation to fight or dance, Jones accepts what life presents to him, in this case an attractive and amenable companion. The battle vocabulary conveys the force with which the promise of momentary joy imposes itself on the defenseless young man, and the details of Mrs. Waters's specific artillery—"those two bright orbs," her "smile of affection" and "pretty dimples"—add substance to Fielding's claim of irresistibility. Only in the final line of the paragraph, when we are told that the "fair conqueror enjoyed the usual fruits of her victory," does Fielding slightly subvert the sense of life's freshness that he has carefully built up. The let-down is just enough for us to retain our satisfaction while allowing the moral code to reassert its rightful (in Fielding's opinion) position of prominence. Indeed, Fielding's treatment of Tom throughout his apprenticeship in prudence follows the same pattern to the same end: he encourages the reader to enjoy Tom's liveliness while at the same time making us wish that his hero would reconcile his "natural" forces to the sensible teachings of reason or religion. That Tom succeeds in the end, even if only with the lovely Sophia's powerful aid, is a great source of pleasure to us and affirms the rightness of our admiration for him, the positive attraction on which the novel's comic spirit depends.

To cast Tom as a Quixote figure, as Ronald Paulson does, is to turn his human weakness into a madness, an extremity which the tone of the book does not support and which attributes a depth to the comedy that it does not have. Paulson simply overstates the matter, and in doing so makes Tom's essentially healthy activities sound like perverse indulgences: "Tom's Quixotic aberration is his "good nature," his "good breeding," which makes him go to the extreme of giving his body to young or old ladies out of a deep inner compulsion to generosity and love. ... [J]ust as the whirling blades of a windmill became the flailing arms of a giant for Quixote, so the white breasts of Mrs. Waters or the generosity of Lady Bellaston or the appearance of youth and availability in Molly lead Tom to break with both prudence and moral laws."[17] Whereas the mournful Don is ridiculous in spite of the fact that we feel a human attachment to him, Tom is rather normal than mad, rather enviable than ludicrous in his sallies with various bosoms. The resulting tone is invariably happy, lacking entirely the pathos that is associated with the quixotic humorist, lacking as well the richness that the near-tragic knight gives to his history. Fielding must look to his plot and more, to himself to provide the modulation of tone and variation of emotion that any great work must have; the natural parts of his hero are too vigorously in good working order to be the source of artistic fascination or even very much ordinary interest on their own account.

The steady control that Fielding maintains, starting from the preface to each volume, accounts for the comic confidence of the reader all the while that Tom is on the downhill leg of his roller-coasting fortunes. Andrew Wright is inclined to attribute greater importance to the prefaces than most critics, but his point is well taken: "The ornamental status of the prefaces makes us take *Tom Jones* on an ornamental level. Therefore, the probably most arresting structural fact about *Tom Jones* is the series of first-chapters that exhort the reader not to constructive action but to benign amusement."[18] The leisurely pace of Fielding's contributions and the very fact of his presence however have more to do with the soothing of our fear—a fear so soothed that Crane prefers to call it a "comic analogue of fear"—than the incidental or ornamental quality. One has the sense that nothing urgent is happening at the moment or will happen in the future to the suspended characters, for one feels sure that Fielding would not be wasting the reader's time maliciously with his thoughts on love or critics if Tom were shortly to be hanged. We must simply reject the author's call to constructive action, such as rushing for "a first row at Tyburn" and settle back to enjoy his little joke, that of heightening our comic suspense by assuring us that he cannot depend on a *deus ex machina* to extricate his poor hero from the clutches of fate. With this gentle hint, and the accompanying tantalizing fact that the worst has not yet occurred, we delve with eager anticipation into the pages of Book XVII knowing that the twists of the plot are not yet untangled, but that in time, with the help of Fortune, if not a goddess, they will be. And Fortune, we know, must answer to Fielding. Crediting the narrator with the preservation of comedy, Wayne Booth makes an important point about Fielding's mere presence: "[O]ur growing intimacy with Fielding's dramatic version of himself produces a kind of comic analogue of the true believer's reliance on a benign providence in real life. In a fictional world that offers no single character who is both wise and good—even Allworthy, though all worthy, is no model of perspicacity—the author is always there on his platform to remind us, through his wisdom and benevolence, of what human life ought to be and might be."[19]

If not so overtly as in the King of the Gypsies episode, when his didacticism unexpectedly takes precedence over the narrative, Fielding makes known his views lightly but distinctly in the course of relating his story:

It is, indeed, the idea of fierceness, and not of bravery, which destroys the female character; for who can read the story of the justly celebrated Arria without conceiving as high an opinion of her gentleness and tenderness as of her fortitude? At the same time, perhaps, many a woman who shrieks at a mouse, or a rat, may be capable of poisoning a husband; or, what is worse, of driving him to poison himself.

Sophia, with all the gentleness which a woman can have, had all the spirit which she ought to have. When therefore, she came to the place of appointment, and, instead of meeting her maid, as was agreed, saw a man ride directly up to her, she neither screamed out nor fainted away.
(X.ix; IV, 233–34)

First, with a general observation the historian becomes the moralist, without giving up the reins of his story or even disturbing its steady canter; then, with the supporting example of his sprightly heroine, the moralist gives way again to the story-teller. One knows exactly what Fielding thinks about the affected weakness that women are brought up to display, and feels the thrust of his offhand remark about driving a husband to poison—a far more subtle and insidious application of "the many pretty arts" than poisoning him directly. At the same time, one also knows exactly how Sophia went about running away from her father and can compare her favorably with the unspecified artful ladies.

Very often Fielding will turn moralist to maintain the steady comic tone of his story. By drawing our attention from one character, who may be caught up in an unpleasant event, to others or to observable truths about human nature, he saves us from undergoing the character's pain. The reader is not allowed to linger over Tom's unhappiness at his parting from Squire Allworthy, but rather is informed of still another instance of injustice to the benevolent, if mistaken, gentleman's reputation:

The reader must be very weak if, when he considers the light in which Jones then appeared to Mr. Allworthy, he should blame the rigour of his sentence. And yet all the neighbourhood, either from this weakness, or from some worse motive, condemned this justice and severity as the highest cruelty. Nay, the very persons who had before censured the good man for his kindness and tenderness shown to a bastard (his own, according to the general opinion), now cried out as loudly against turning his own child out of doors. The women especially were unanimous in taking the part of Jones, and raised more stories on the occasion than I have room, in this chapter, to set down. (VI.xi; III, 317–18)

We recognize the gross distortion of the rumors in relation to the facts, and must take time out from bemoaning the "rigour" of Tom's sentenced fate to smile at the common human failing of believing the worst about a neighbor or the best about the object of one's lust. Only when Tom is safely out of the house does Fielding continue his tale.

The control Fielding exercises, not only over every character but every word in the novel—very different from the equally tight but seemingly more haphazard watch that Sterne keeps or the more casual, less concerned authority of Smollett—acts as a guarantee that the book will be read as he wishes, that Tom will be accepted on the terms he specifies, that his tone will not be mistaken or his meaning misconstrued. One finds very little argument over interpretation in the criticism of *Tom Jones;* the extent to which Allworthy is flawed by his excess of prudence is a matter of degree rather than principle. The direction of Fielding's satire and the intention of his irony are perfectly clear. One might miss a pleasant subtlety or fail to appreciate a clever foreshadowing, but he makes certain, with his surprisingly delicate heavy-hand, that no one misses the meaning of an action or likes a character one is meant to dislike. By keeping such a careful watch, Fielding achieves the lighthearted, sunny atmosphere that distinguishes the book and makes it immediately pleasant to read. But his government is such that the exclusion of anarchy ultimately lessens the mirth. Fielding's devotion to order and decorum was far too great for him to abandon himself to cathartic revelry, however much he suggests its therapeutic value in the actions of Tom (especially when Allworthy's life is in danger). The gentility of that prudent old man, Allworthy, is an expression of the gentility of the author himself and contributes to the tone of *Tom Jones* at least as much as do the farcical remnants from Fielding's years as a playwright. This gentlemanly geniality was obviously much admired by Fielding's followers, especially Graves, as is apparent from the works which owe their inception and design to the "new species founded by Mr. Fielding." These novels, examined next, show the same delight in human extravagance without giving way to the animal spirits that propelled the mirthful works of Smollett and Sterne.

CHAPTER THREE

FIELDING'S FOLLOWERS

Pompey the Little

Admiration for the spirit of *Joseph Andrews* and the happy inventiveness of *Tom Jones,* along with a hearty contempt for those who scorned
novels as being "empty, trifling and impertinent," led Francis Coventry
to offer his unashamedly mirthful (though anonymously published) work
to the public in 1751. The welcome reception accorded *The History of
Pompey the Little, or, The Life and Adventures of a Lap-Dog,* reflects
the growing number of readers who were willing to accept a book merely
for the hours of enjoyment it promised them. The *Monthly Review*
was disposed to treat the novel with the respect usually reserved for more
substantial volumes, even devoting a portion of the following issue to additional extracts. A total of seventeen pages of choice bits was finally
printed for the amusement of regular readers, and the critical content of
the review was given over entirely to praise, especially for the benevolence
of the wit:

The author, whose name is not to the work, takes for his subject, a
Bologna lap-dog, brought from *Italy* to *England* where he often changes
masters, by several accidents, which furnish the writer with a handle to
introduce a variety of characters and situations; all painted with great
humour, fancy, and wit: and, indeed, he every where displays a perfect
knowledge of the world, through all its ranks, and all its follies. These

he ridicules, with a fineness of edge, unknown to the sour satyrist, or the recluse philosopher. Even his negligences are pleasing. The gentleman, in short, breaths throughout the whole performance, and the vein of pleasantry, which runs through it, is every where evenly upheld, from the beginning to the end. He laughs at the world, without doing it the honour to be angry with it. His lashes, however smart, carry with them rather the marks of benevolent correction, than of the spleen of misanthropy. All his characters are natural. His language easy and genteel.[1]

Though the form of Coventry's little work resembles that of the classic picaresque novel, *Lazarillo de Tormes,* being comprised of casually linked episodes each with its own object of attack, the spirit of the lapdog's adventures is, as the reviewer points out, benevolent and cheerful, closer to the works of Coventry's idol, Henry Fielding, than to the picaresque satires. Like *Peregrine Pickle,* which has essentially the same structure as *Roderick Random* but is a happier work than the earlier novel, *Pompey* retains the elements of satire while manifesting a new leniency towards society's shortcomings.

Coventry does not seek to arouse indignation; in his Dedication to Fielding in the third edition he makes it quite clear that he will be pleased to raise a mere laugh:

To convey instruction in a pleasant manner, and mix entertainment with it, is certainly a commendable undertaking, perhaps more likely to be attended with success than graver precepts; and where amusement is the chief thing consulted, there is some little merit in making people laugh, when it is done without giving offence to religion, or virtue, or good manners. If the laugh be not raised at the expence of innocence or decency, good humour bids us indulge it, and we cannot well laugh too often. (1752: iv)

Indeed, the extensive changes that Coventry made in this 1752 edition seem to be primarily in the interest of even greater amusement, though one may question in some instances the basis of his judgment. William Scott, one of the few modern critics to do more than mention Coventry's work—which in its heyday was regularly linked with Fielding's[2]—feels that "improvement" involved no more than the omission of several interesting chapters and the addition of some "fresh ones which are in general neither better nor worse than those they replace."[3]

A more generous conclusion is possible, however, if one examines the two editions for the quality of pleasure they arouse. Indeed, while considering the narrator still to be essentially satiric in outlook, "a speaker with a bitter and sardonic tone," Toby Olshin finds evidence of Coventry's increasing maturity: "He no longer considers his model [Fielding] a simple satirist who shows his sardonic views on human nature through the use of a picaresque hero."[4] This change is reflected in the narration: there is little reason to distinguish the author from the narrator. The morals that close many chapters in the early editions, a crude satiric device at best, are often shortened or removed in the later. Whereas in the third edition Coventry merely begs the reader's pardon for digressing from the hero's history, in the original version he does not have the confidence to allow a conversation between Lady Sophister and the Doctors Kildarby and Rhubarb to stand without comment. He feels it necessary to conclude with a clarifying note and apologies to Locke. Yet, as he recognized in the later edition, Lady Sophister's sophistry would be evident even to her prototypes among contemporary readers and is far more effectively presented without comment:

'Pardon me, Madam,' said Rhubarb; 'Roses, and peach-trees, and elephants, and lions! I protest I remember nothing of this nature in Mr. Locke.'—'Nay, Sir,' cried she, 'can you deny me this? If the soul is fire, it must be extinguished; if it is air, it must be dispersed; if it be only a modification of matter, why then of course it ceases, you know, when matter is no longer modified—if it be anything else, it is exactly the same thing, and therefore you must confess—indeed Doctor, you must confess, that 'tis impossible for the Soul to be immortal.'   (1752: 60)

Similarly, increased liveliness is the result of Coventry's decision to recast an episode so that a factual account formerly given by the narrator emerges instead in the course of a conversation between servants, which is occasioned by Pompey's careless upset of a dish while in search of food.

Scarce had this happened, when my lady's maid appeared below stairs, and began to scream out in a very shrill accent, 'why who has done this now? I'll be whipped if this *owdacious* little dog has not been and thrown down my lady's backside's breakfast;' after which she fell very severely on the cook, who now entered the kitchen and began to reprimand her in a very authoritative tone, for not taking more care of her dressers; 'but let the 'pothecary, added she, come and mix up his nastiness himself an' he will, for deuce fetch me if I'll wait on her ladyship's backside in this manner: If she will have her clysters, let the clyster-pipe doctor come and minister them himself, and not put me to her filthy offices—O Lord bless us! well, rather than be at all this pains for a complexion, I'd rather be as brown as a berry all my life-time!'

(1752: 77–78)

The lady's inconsiderate attention to her person is at once made more actively real to the reader's imagination and a good deal funnier in the colorful language of the rightfully annoyed maid than the factual sentences of the original narrator, who does not back up his material with the force of Pompey's accident. In addition, Coventry's eye for human frailty has more scope for observation in the tirade that results: the maid who drops the burden of her annoyance on the cook gets an oblique glance cast upon her; the apothecary's part in the business of vanity is disparagingly hinted at.

These little glances are found throughout both versions, but in the later one they seem to be directed more against affectation and less on vicious human beings, in keeping with Fielding's teachings. The man who encourages the untimely death of his first three wives and who appears in the first edition as one of the suitors of Aurora (a worthy young lady) is absent from her drawing-room in the third. Newly developed characters include a "blind" beggar who likes lemon on his sweetbreads (a figure similar to Lazaro's sly, blind master, whose inventiveness supports his avarice) and various members of the scribbling trade. However, one cannot make a positive statement about Coventry's intentions; in one instance a previously humane ostler is turned into an insensitive brute.

Moreover, as much as Coventry softened the general satire, expunging incidental remarks on flatterers, ministers, and the like, the second version includes some new lampoons, including a highly ludicrous and very cutting portrait of Mr. Whitefield, that object of so many eighteenth-century attacks (especially Graves's). The incident is not without humor, but it is humor in the manner of Pope's lampoons, splenetically motivated and outrageously belittling:

All the former part of the time, our hero sat very composed and quietly before the fire; but when they began to chant their hymns, surprized and astonished with the novelty of this proceeding, he fell to howling with the most sonorous accent, and in a key much higher than any of the screaming sisters. Nor was this all; for presently afterwards, Mr. Wh——d attempting to stroke him, he snarled and bit his finger: which being the self-same indignity that Lucian offered to the hand of a similar imposter, we thought it not beneath the dignity of this history to relate it. To say the truth, I believe he had taken some disgust to the exceeding pious gentleman; for besides these two instances of ill-behaviour, he was guilty of a much greater rudeness next day to his works.

(1752: 97)

Today we may laugh at the liberties taken with the normally dignified figure, but in 1810 Mrs. Barbauld still felt compelled to soften some of the remarks for her British Novelists editions.[5] Coventry's offhand attitude towards the dog's impertinence, the casual reference to Lucian and the "imposter," and the flippant suggestion of Pompey's additional crimes are what make the description of the event stinging, yet at the same time funny: the author's amusement both shocks and amuses us in turn. Yet however funny Pompey's rudenesses are, the mirth is paid for with the benevolence that otherwise characterizes the final version of the book.

Inevitably Coventry had to sacrifice some moments of liveliness in excising the satiric episodes that gave rise to them. Thus Pompey no longer gets to demonstrate his masticatory talents or to show off another instance of his admirable sense of occasion:

They were no sooner gone, than his Lordship returned to his Closet, and fell a laughing at the Folly and Impertinence of his Petitioners. 'Curse the Bookies, cries he, do they think I have nothing to do but to make Mayors and Aldermen?' and so saying, he threw down the Petition to the Dog and began to make him *fetch and carry* for his Diversion. Pompey very readily entered into the Humour of this Pastime, and made such good use of his Teeth, that the Hopes of a new Corporation were soon demolished, and the Lord knows how many Mayors and Aldermen in the Moment perished by the unmerciful Jaws of a *Boulogna* Lap-dog.

(1751: 207–08)

One can do without this passage if one must, but the image of Chance that one sees in the description of Pompey's active jaws is typical of the wit that distinguishes Coventry's work from the usual mass of satirically motivated novels.

Unfortunately, too, the little old lady who bore the brunt of the

Methodist satire in the 1751 edition takes her cat with her when she departs into oblivion. The brief friendship between Pompey and Mopsa is the only event in Pompey's life, apart from his accidental separation from Lady Tempest, that the reader is likely to regard with human interest. Regrettably, some of Coventry's most charming descriptive writing shares the fate of the cat:

From this Time their Friendship grew stricter every Day; they used to go upon little Parties of Innocent Amusement together, and it was very entertaining to see them walking Side by Side in the Garden, or lying Couchant under a Tree to surprize some little Bird in the Branches. Malicious Fame no sooner observed this Intimacy than with her usual Malice she published the Scandal of an Amour between them; but I am persuaded it had no Foundation, for *Mopsa* was old enough to be *Pompey*'s Grand-mother, and besides he always behaved to her, rather with the Homage due to a Parent than the ardent Fondness of a Lover.

(1751: 92)

The serious tone is perfectly maintained and made to seem appropriate to the animal relationship. Meanwhile the reader is forced to see likenesses to human behavior and to mock society while feeling compassion for the creatures. The balance between fable and satire is so delicately held that the ludicrousness of the *amour* does not make it any less touching.

Because Coventry does not confine his inventiveness to introductory chapters—indeed, his one rather dull imitation of Fielding's prefaces does not survive his second thoughts—because he does not simply dress a stock novel in the trappings of comedy, as the anonymous writer of *The History of Charlotte Summers* must be accused of doing (his claim to be the natural son of Fielding is not borne out by any demonstrable relationship), one may agree with Edmund Gosse's judgment: "Francis Coventry had gifts of wit and picturesqueness which deserved a better fate than to amuse a few dissipated women over their citron-waters, and then to be forgotten."[6] Even more, one may see that it is his understanding of these very women, his perception of the petrified emotions that pass for human feeling in polite society, and his ability to reveal the foibles of that society at once succinctly and sympathetically that call his novel to our attention.

Coventry knew well that "spleen is the daughter of mortified vanity," and rather than further mortify the sensitive vanities of his readers he set out to ease the affliction by making everyone seem equally afflicted and equally absurd—even the lovely Aurora—in the eyes of a lap-dog. When Aurora's fantasy world, in which only pleasing things can happen, is rudely imposed upon by the frisky puppy, she shows the nature of her vanity by strenuously objecting to the real world and punishing its representative for the destruction of her satisfying dream. One can imagine Pompey's shrug at Aurora's typically human irrationality: "To be interrupted in so critical a minute, while she was dreaming of her beloved peer, was an offence she knew not how to pardon. She darted a most enraged look at him, and resolved never to see him any more; but disposed of him that very morning to her milliner, who attended with a new head-dress" (1752: 196).

Though contributing no more than the occasional bark to the book's action, Pompey has a more unifying effect on the work than a statistical account of his activities would suggest. In spite of his underdeveloped personality and his lack of an animal life of his own, we are conscious of the little creature as a separate character, as a continuous observer in his own right. As one of its most common frivolous possessions, Pompey is a fitting commentator on the artificial society and, as the victim of its frivolity, becomes emblematic of the shiftlessness, the emptiness, and the selfishness that subvert the values of domestic life and turn the faithful hearthside animal into a nomadic beggar. Rather like Dickens's little Jo, whose life is only seemingly tangential to the business of Chancery Lane, little Pompey accepts the world as it is thrust upon him, and in so doing, forces the reader to consider the state of that world. Unlike Jo, however, he is frivolous himself, and dies of old-age after a full and varied life having managed to survive all the comical elevations and depressions in his fortune. In this respect he is a picaresque hero, demonstrating his resiliency and strength as he goes along, either by gnawing through a thick wooden board to escape dissection (by Cambridge students) or simply by adapting matter-of-factly to new and different masters. Even the accidental separation from Lady Tempest, who has fed him on fricassees for a large part of his life, does not affect his equanimity: "He had no sooner dined, and felt himself snug in his new apartment, than he entirely forgot his former mistress" (1752: 71—72).

If Pompey himself cannot express his even-tempered attitude towards life, his creator does it for him in the urbanity of his tone. Though Pompey's eyes are not, for the most part, the medium through which we view society, his presence encourages us to see things with the dispassionate concern of a different species. Coventry's tone is always one of faint amusement, such as we would expect if Pompey were endowed with rational faculties and a speaking voice:

[O]f all the people, who composed this illustrious assembly, Lady *Bab* came the last. They took care to inform the company from time to time, that she was expected, by making the same observation on the arrival of every fresh coach, and, still persisting, that they knew her footman's rap, tho' they had given so many proofs to the contrary. At length, however, Lady *Bab Frightful* came; and it is impossible to express the joy they felt on her appearance; which revived them on a sudden from the depth of despair to the highest exaltation of happiness.

Her ladyship's great toe engrossed the conversation for the first hour, whose misfortune was lamented in very pathetic terms by all the company, and many wise reflections were made upon the accident which had happened; some condemning the ignorance, and others the carelessness of the surgeon, who had been guilty of such a trespass on her ladyship's flesh. (1752: 221–22)

That the joy of the whole company should rest on a title and be hung in suspense by the condition of a large toe is a fact that takes on all its ludicrous implications when set out in simple sentences. Coventry need not try to express their "exaltation": his slightly ironic overstatement of the facts conveys the absurdity of the emotion. His laughter is evident in such phrases as "a trespass on her ladyship's flesh," which at once mimics the tone of the ladies' speech and lowers the diction considerably. Indeed, Mrs. Barbauld was distressed by the unsavory image presented by the word "flesh" and among her many other changes quietly substituted "person."

Even in a clause Coventry's gentle irony works effectively, as when he describes a fastidious gentleman as one "whose embroidery gave a peculiar poignancy to his wit." The use of "peculiar" to modify "poignancy" and "poignancy" to mean a transferable quality of embroidery may be easily appreciated by substituting "polish" for both words. One then loses the sense of this gentleman's immaculate refinement, his complete mastery of polite and meaningless conversation, which one gets from the narrator's overly fastidious choice of words.

When Coventry can refrain from unsubtle sermonizing, which unfortunately he is not always able to do, his style comes close to Smollett's at its most vigorous and cleverly ironic:

A resolution was immediately taken, to make a sally into the streets, and drink champaigne upon the horse at Charing-Cross. This was no sooner projected than executed, and they performed a great number of heroical exploits, too long to be mentioned in this work, but we hope some future historian will arise to immortalize them for the sake of posterity. After this was over, they resolved to scour the streets, and perceiving a light in a cellar under ground, our two heroes magnanimously descended into that subterranean cave, in quest of adventures. There they found some hackney-coachmen, enjoying themselves carousing with porter and tobacco, whom they immediately attacked, and offered to box the two sturdiest champions of the company. The challenge was accepted in a moment, and whilst our heroes were engaged, the rest of the coachmen chose to make off with their cloaths, which they thought no inconsiderable booty. In short, these gentlemen of pleasure and high-life were heartily drubbed, and obliged to retreat with shame from the *cellar* of battle, leaving their cloaths behind them, as spoils, at the mercy of the enemy. Soon after they were taken by the watch, being too feeble to make resistance, and conducted to the round-house; where they spent their night in the manner already described. The next morning, they returned home in chairs, dressed themselves, and then took their seats in parliament, to enact laws for the good of their country.

(1752: 121–22)

Coventry does not quite achieve Smollett's atmosphere of activity, mainly because he parcels the actions into separate sentences. But the contrast between the hurly-burly of the night's escapades and the very quiet mention of the morning's business has a startling effect nevertheless: the narrator's restraint in the face of all the excesses he is describing is sufficiently ironic for his remarks to stand without further comment.

The control that this young and largely inexperienced writer could exercise over his material is epitomized nowhere better than in the final chapter of Pompey's history,[7] which in mock-conformity to similar works gives a general account of the hero's notable qualities:

Let it be remembered, in the first place, to his credit, that he was a dog of the *most courtly manners,* ready to fetch and carry, at the command of all his masters, without ever considering the service he was employed in, or the person from whom he received his directions: He would fawn likewise with the greatest humility, on people who treated him with contempt, and was always particularly officious in his zeal, whenever he expected a new collar, or stood candidate for a ribbon with other dogs, who made up the retinue of the family.

. . . .

[W] hoever considers that he was born in the house of an Italian courtesan, that he made the grand tour with a young gentleman of fortune, and afterwards lived near two years with a lady of quality, will have more reason to wonder that his morals were not entirely corrupted, than that they were a little tainted by the ill effects of such dangerous examples.

(1752: 288–89)

The mingling of satire and fable is consummately carried out here (as in the earlier description of his relationship with Mopsa). Now Pompey is a fawning dependant, no better than a dog; now he is a dog, no better than a typically debauched human. However, by insulting neither humanity nor caninity, Coventry avoids the sinister implications that the *Modest Proposal* so subtly exudes: unlike Swift, he does not suggest that the identification between man and dog (in Swift's case, baby and pig) is frighteningly true and shockingly horrible. Rather, he shows them both to be simply weak and excusably helpless creatures, misled by society and innocently unaware of their own absurdity.

The description of Pompey's death is also applicable to the human event, yet without real sorrow; one cannot expend much pity on creatures who are untouched by their own misery:

For the latter part of his life, his chief amusement was to sleep before the fire, and indolence grew upon him so much, as he advanced in age, that he seldom cared to be disturbed in his slumbers, even to eat his meals: his eyes grew dim, his limbs failed him, his teeth dropped out of his head; and, at length, a pthisic came very seasonably to relieve him from the pains and calamities of long life.   (1752: 290–91)

Only insofar as Pompey's fate is the universal fate can one grieve, for the image of the lazy old dog in retirement from an adventurous life is pleasingly unpathetic.

The scale of the reader's sorrow or outrage is similarly reduced throughout the work: Pompey's misfortunes are a dog's misfortune's, not a young boy's—Lazaro's for instance. The creature's role may be tangential to the major business of the novel, which is to focus on the artificial life of the genteel classes, yet things happen to him which would be intolerable, especially in reference to human life, were he not so able to manage. In turn we would be forced to despise rather than laugh at the unthinking Cambridge scholars who want to mutilate the cheerful animal or the beggar who is addicted to luxury. Only an exceptionally sturdy human hero can soften the satiric blows of a picaresque work and turn bitterness into bitter-sweet. A dog need only be himself, naturally sturdy and nonhuman, to make the crimes against him seem laughable.

An inanimate hero will not do so well: Charles Johnstone's *Adventures of a Guinea*, one of the many imitations to appear in the following twenty years, lacks the warmth of a happily living creature. The passage of the guinea from hand to hand is not reassuring, for the adaptability of the object is never in question, and its relation to human survival is never established. Pompey, on the contrary, tells us as much about the flexibility of individuals as he does about the artificiality of society: marriage may be a financial arrangement and nothing more, but couples come to terms with the fact in their own ways—indeed, the wife may take to lap-dogs. Pompey shares the attitude of his "acceptance world," digesting fricassees and scraps alike, as much as he reveals the essential boredom of its inhabitants simply by being one of the playthings that helps to make acceptance possible.

Coventry puts forth his novel as another kind of plaything, another way of breaking down the artifact by provoking honest mirth. That the "Beaux, rakes, petit-maitres and fine ladies, whose lives are spent in doing the things which novels record," should spurn these works as too low or too familiar is something he laments in his Dedication. His implication is that these people are depriving themselves for reasons of pride of the very amusement that might make their lives as bearable as it seems in comic novels.

Because Coventry is interested in and entertained by his characters, he is able to cancel out the dullness he attributes to them. Using the little animal to convey his interest and amusement, he makes their emptiness seem paradoxically full of life, and invites his readers to enrich their own disappointing realities with the cheerful result. One must not be unduly surprised that the only two novels to be found among Fielding's books after his death in 1754 were *Pompey the Little* and *The Female Quixote:*[8] both authors can fairly claim their own shares of liveliness and imagination, and no doubt were able to provide Fielding with as much mirthful pleasure as he sought.

The Female Quixote

To compare *The Female Quixote* with Cervantes' incomparable original would be an unthinkable offence aginst literary decorum today. Yet in the more casual critical climate of the mid-eighteenth century, Fielding discussed quite freely the likenesses of the two books and, even more surprisingly, managed to come up with several points in Mrs. Lennox's favor —the plausibility and attractiveness of the heroine, the regularity and interest of the story.[9] As the one most responsible for the eighteenth century's new found affection for Don Quixote, Fielding would have been extremely interested in this new variation of the worthy but unworldly knight. For like the Don, Arabella is unfailingly self-redeeming: her charm far overpowers her outrageous blindness; and like *Don Quixote, The Female Quixote* escapes the limitations of burlesque on the open wings of its main character. Indeed, a comparison of the novels is not unseemly when one sees both as burlesques which were betrayed by their author's concern for humanity into becoming comic novels.

The points of similarity between the two works are really quite numerous, if superficial finally in any consideration of their value. Arabella too has had her head turned by a constant and very rich diet of Romances. The seclusion of her family estates makes her delusion seem more natural than the Don's (a nicety much commended by Fielding), but Arabella's belated experiences with the world have as little effect on her understanding as do the knight errant's. She is, we are told many times and occasionally shown, extremely sensible and witty if one can avoid any mention of her favorite topic. Like Don Quixote, she is in a position to surround herself with people who are inclined to go along with her strange ways, so that within the confines of her own world she does not seem extraordinarily ridiculous. Her maid performs the role of squire with great innocence and respect; Glanville, who loves her too dearly to upset her, provides her with the intelligent conversation that the curate and the barber supply in the original. The romantic young girl, like the chivalrous knight, is made to carry the author's satiric messages in her own ridiculous speeches. What Arabella misses in the way of adventures as a house-bound young lady, she makes up for with her imagination and her ingenious ability to implicate the most innocent people in her fantasies. Though she has no occasion to tilt at windmills, she readily supposes that a gardener caught in the act of stealing carp from the pond is a young nobleman in disguise about to throw himself in the pond out of secret love for her.

The fineness of Arabella's imagination is, for all the other similarities of structure and plot, the only meaningful basis for establishing a relationship between the quixotic female and the knight. In both, it is the source of their absurdity and distinction; even more, it is the delicate instrument against which the world must be tuned to make a place for them, to accommodate their ideas of reality that are both right and wrong, silly and sensitive at the same time. In both works the quixotic imagination, by ranging freely between the ridiculous and the grand, is the source of the special comedy that distinguishes them today.

Like Cervantes, Mrs. Lennox had satiric observations to make about society and used her Quixote figure to mock fossils of literature and culture through burlesque writing and didactic episodes as he did (and Fielding after him). In her innocence, Arabella unwittingly acts as chief prosecutor against the Romances: her requirements for life are based on literary models, and in giving her specifications to her maid Lucy for the contents of her "history" she cannot help revealing the absurdity of these works:

Well! exclaimed *Arabella:* I am certainly the most unfortunate Woman in the World! Every thing happens to me in a contrary manner from any other Person! Here, instead of my desiring you to soften those Parts of my History where you have greatest room to flatter; and to conceal, if possible, some of those Disorders my Beauty has occasioned; you ask me to tell you what you must say; as if it was not necessary you should know as well as myself, and be able, not only to recount all my Words and Actions, even the smallest and most inconsiderable, but also all my Thoughts, however instantaneous; relate exactly every Change of my Countenance; number all my Smiles, Half-smiles, Blushes, Turnings pale, Glances, Pauses, Full-stops, Interruptions; the Rise and Falling of my Voice; every Motion of my Eyes; and every Gesture which I have used for these Ten Years past; nor omit the slightest Circumstance that relates to me. (277-78)

Not only does she talk in a high-toned manner that could only be learned from bad fiction—this she always does—but she happily catalogues the coquetries of Romance, which are no different from the ones she spurns in her "real" life. Whereas Arabella is unable to recognize the simple stupidity of numbering the smiles on a girl's face and calling it her history, we see Mrs. Lennox's smile quite clearly.

John Warner, in an unpublished thesis, comments on Mrs. Lennox's skillful use of Arabella's comical deficiencies to pointedly satiric ends. He notes that Arabella's naiveté "allows Mrs. Lennox to make implicit, rather than overtly didactic, contrasts between her heroine's innocent delusion and the sophisticated hypocrisy of society. Without allowing Arabella to assume a satiric pose inconsistent with her romantic role, Mrs. Lennox secures her points by juxtaposing society against her heroine."[10] The contrast is clear when Arabella protects a mistreated prostitute in the mistaken and comical belief that she is a great lady suffering at the hands of a ravisher. The Female Quixote makes us see what society is unable to discern, that it really makes no difference if the ravished woman is a tramp or a lady. Arabella's standard inflexible assumption is as true as if it were a sensible assessment of the situation: "questionless" the man is ravishing the woman and one must be "base" to leave her "in the Power of that Man" (336).

Arabella's blindness necessarily sharpens our vision of reality; her blurry focus must be corrected by our awareness of the true picture. The difference is often satirically instructive, as when the demure young heroine exempts the laws of love from the laws of the land on the strength of the widely followed code of honor, which allows one to "hunt your Enemy thro' the World, in order to sacrifice him to your Vengeance." Her logical deduction that the conventions of love may contradict the conventions of justice rests clearly on the false assumption about honor that was still commonly made in the eighteenth century. Mrs. Lennox uses Arabella's befuddled mind here (a mind which we have seen treats the idea of death more lightly than a kiss on the hand) to deal a humorous but effective blow to the practice of dueling, which was then in the process of dying its own form of slow death.

Though we may still appreciate the aim and thrust of Mrs. Lennox's satiric stabs, many of which are out of date, the book would not still give pleasure without the comedy that so frequently arises from Arabella's addiction to the heroic mode of life. The romantically inclined heroine's habitual insistence on life's conformity with her own imaginative construction is balanced by Mrs. Lennox's equally strong insistence on telling what Aldous Huxley calls the "Whole Truth." Homer is Huxley's model for (and Fielding a later example of) a teller of the Whole Truth, and from his essay one sees that he is simply distinguishing the comic perspective from the more focused vision of tragedy: "[Homer] knew that even the most cruelly bereaved must eat; that hunger is stronger than sorrow and that its satisfaction takes precedence even of tears. He knew that, when the belly is full (and only when the belly is full) men can afford to grieve. In a word, Homer refused to treat the theme tragically. He preferred to tell the Whole Truth."[11]

Arabella's tragic expectations are constantly disappointed by her very human lovers. Glanville's distress could not possibly be genuine in her eyes, since as she says, "that Uneasiness has neither made you thinner, nor paler, I don't think you ought to be pitied: For to say the truth, in these Sort of Matters, a Person's bare Testimony has but little Weight" (80). Although Glanville has not starved himself simply because he has been parted from his lovely cousin for a few months, we know that Arabella's truth is far too demanding to be applicable to the frail beings that human heroes are and that Glanville has, indeed, felt as much distress as is fair to expect on such an occasion.

As often as her innocently arrogant heroine commands her suitors to live or die, Mrs. Lennox counters her commands with the facts of reality. Glanville's fever increases even after Arabella makes known her desire on the matter. Nevertheless she congratulates herself on her lover's eventual recovery, but must then deal with the disconcerting fact of Miss Glanville's indifference to her accomplishment. In fact, throughout the novel, much to Arabella's continual surprise no one gives her due credit for the survival of various lovers and no one actually dies or even suffers extreme discomfort as a result of love—not counting the embarrassment and mortification that Glanville goes through, which Arabella of course does not recognize. Only the Marquis dies, of very natural causes over which his daughter admittedly has no powers. Mrs. Lennox makes it clear that living men do not expire simply to satisfy the rapacities of a lovely young lady's imagination.

The humor, however, is by no means always at the expense of the heroine's flighty mind. The nonromantics become ridiculous in their own way, as they engage in the heroic feat of "educating" Arabella. The adults of the novel always try to force hard reality into Arabella's fantasy world, the domain of which is real enough—her father's sequestered castle. But the castle walls of her mind are more difficult to scale, almost impossible, and the attempts of Glanville's father, Sir Charles, to do so result in the reader's great amusement if not Arabella's enlightenment. Miriam

Small, author of the only full-length book on Mrs. Lennox, judges the humor of *The Female Quixote* to be "most successful when it is obtained by presenting Arabella's idiosyncrasies in their effect upon some stolid and unimaginative person whom they leave in hopeless confusion."[12]

Because the representatives of the real world are so unimaginative themselves, Arabella's sprightliness in comparison allows us to preserve our affection even while laughing at her. When Sir Charles's sceptical question draws a typically positive answer from the authoritative heroine, we laugh at him for taking Arabella so seriously:

> For Heaven's sake, Niece, said Sir *Charles,* How come such improbable Things into your Head? Is it such an easy Matter, think you, to conquer Kingdoms, that you can flatter a young Man, who has neither Fleets nor Armies, with such strange Hopes?
>
> The great *Artaban,* Sir, resumed *Arabella,* had neither Fleets nor Armies, and was Master only of a single Sword; yet he soon saw himself greater than any King, disposing the Destinies of Monarchs by his Will, and deciding the Fates of Empires by a single Word.   (210)

It is somehow pleasing to the reader that Arabella's imagination can supply her with such splendid facts about man's ability to accomplish what he sets out to do. Her conviction is of course absurd, but her optimism is contagious. Obstacles, physical or mental, do not exist in a heroic realm, for the imagination amends them, accounting for the ease with which heroes carry out their lives. The tales are unintentionally comic, for while they deal exclusively in large and noble happenings and are peopled with impossibly courageous heroes, all of which has nothing to do with the comic universe, the expedition with which the hero reaches his goal is naturally comic and is what makes the romantic genre so appealing to ordinary mortals. Even death is reduced to inconsequential proportions by the very frequency of its occurrence (indeed, the true hero will eschew suicide because it is so easy, choosing instead to pine away in a forest unbeknownst to his loved one). One cannot help being charmed by the world of heroic tragedy; how very stolid Sir Charles sounds and how much more preferable are the absurdities of Arabella. Just as the inn becomes, for the reader as for Don Quixote, a real castle, so when Arabella answers her uncle's objections we admire her and wonder why he is not able to see things so imaginatively.

The very figure of Arabella serves the comedy of the work, for even while she is exposing the affectations of the fashionable world, she is drawing attention to her own naturally fine qualities. Admitting to Miss Glanville that her observations of society might be construed satirically, she nevertheless shuns the character of a satirist: "When Actions are a Censure upon themselves, the Reciter will always be consider'd as a Satirist" (280). She is right to reject the label, for her manner is such that the recitation always impresses the reader more with her own modesty and natural sense than with its barbed implications:

What room, I pray you, does a Lady give for high and noble Adventures, who consumes her Days in Dressing, Dancing, listening to Songs, and ranging the Walks with People as thoughtless as herself? How mean and contemptible a Figure must a Life spent in such idle Amusements make in History? Or rather, Are not such Persons always buried in Oblivion, and can any Pen be found who would condescend to record such inconsiderable Actions?   (279)

This speech is not so much satire as a more mundane statement of Keats's assertion that "a man's life of any worth is a continual allegory." In the same way, Arabella's extraordinary appearance at the ball in a dress styled after the "gallant" Princess Julia's, a dress that suits her own features perfectly, is not a slap in the face to the other ladies present (though they take it as one) but a recommendation of good taste and individuality. In turn, our admiration for Arabella, a comic response, overshadows our scorn for the empty-witted ladies, a satiric response.

Only when Arabella herself becomes tiresome, stubbornly positive of her superior understanding, does the comedy fail. When she imposes endlessly on the sensible and loving Glanville, the reader stops appreciating her fantastic visions and starts wishing that she would venture out of her fortified mind long enough to see the lively possibilities of reality. Her arrogance becomes as unbearable to the reader as it is to the other characters, especially when in the eighth book (of nine) she is still quick to assume that a beau, whose taste is more for her fashionable cousin, must have chosen to fall upon his sword to "put an End to his Life and Miseries at once" after she denied him the favor of loving her: "How, Sir, interrupted *Arabella,* is he dead then already? Alas! why had he not the Satisfaction of seeing me before he expir'd, that his Soul might have departed in Peace! He would have been assur'd not only of my Pardon, but Pity also; and that Assurance would have made him happy in his last Moments" (317). Like Sir Charles, one wishes to cry out in despair in the middle of the endlessly long discourse that follows:

> I am very sorry, Madam, said Sir *Charles,* to hear you talk in this Manner: 'Tis really enough to make one suspect you are—
> You do me great injustice, Sir, interrupted *Arabella,* if you suspect me to be guilty of an unbecoming weakness for this Man: If barely expressing my Compassion for his Misfortunes be esteem'd so great a Favour, what would you have thought if I had supported his Head on my Knees while he was dying, shed Tears over him, and discover'd all the Tokens of a sincere Affliction for him?—
> Good God! said Sir Charles lifting up his Eyes, Did any body hear of any thing like this? (317)

Arabella's self-assurance allows her to make assumptions that support her peculiar cast of mind; she habitually interrupts with her own version of a person's thoughts. In the past she has even convinced herself that the elder Glanville was violently in love with her and trying to usurp his son's place, when in fact he was trying to advance it. It is maddeningly inconceivable to her on this occasion that Sir Charles might want to suggest that she is out of her wits. That he grows peevish along with the reader is what saves the comedy from degenerating too much. With a rapid transfer of loyalties, the reader makes answers for Sir Charles that will end the matter before Arabella has a chance to misconstrue his words again. If Mrs. Lennox had not given us the company of reluctant listeners within the book, we would not have been able to bear not only Arabella's nonsense but also the fact that those around her were tolerating it. Throughout the novel we are reassured by the down-to-earth people who surround the Female Quixote that there is a limit to even the most creative and liberating imaginings, that improbabilities are boring when they have no enlightening relation to real life. Yet as we sense that Sir Charles still respects Arabella's intelligence and admires her character as much as ever, we do not like the extravagant heroine any less.

In addition to Arabella's occasionally tiresome character, there are faults of timing which impair the usually smooth narrative: the repetition of an observation in different forms, the protraction of an event that is only mildly amusing, the inclusion of an unnecessary speech are all misjudgments that disturb the comedy on occasion. Yet Mrs. Lennox's control over the tone of her work is apparent in her handling of the burlesque material. The long central section in which Sir George, a friend of Glanville's, sets out to win Arabella from him by indulging her heroic predilections with a "history" of himself as a young prince, might well have been only a satiric digression were the tone not so perfectly suited —more affectionate than mocking—to the whole novel. Mrs. Lennox's inventive imagination, which is at least as extravagant as Arabella's, together with her ear for the portentous gravity of the Romance style, serve both the originals and her parody well.

One has the chance in this section to get inside a romantic tale, to become as involved with the fantasy as Arabella perpetually is, to be enchanted as well as diverted. Mrs. Lennox has managed to combine the ludicrous aspects of the stories—the dungeons, the wicked brothers, the exiles—with their appealing qualities—the nobility of the heroes, the variety and excitement of the storybook world—and thus to make us laugh and keep us fascinated at the same time. A brief extract is all that is needed to convey the peculiar flavor of both the original and the parody:

Then, taking leave of me with much Tenderness, she went out of the Prison, leaving *Toxares* with me, who assisted me to dress, and conducted me out of that miserable Place, where I had passed so many sad, and also joyful Hours. At a Gate to which he brought me, I found a Horse waiting; and, having embraced this faithful Confidant, with many Expressions of Gratitude, I bestowed a Ring of some Value upon him to remember me by; and, mounting my Horse, with a breaking Heart, I took the first Road which presented itself to my Eyes, and galloped away, without knowing whither I went. I rode the whole Night, so totally engrossed by my Despair, that I did not perceive my Horse was so tired, it could hardly carry me a Step farther; At last the poor Beast fell down under me, so that I was obliged to dismount; and, looking about me, perceived I was in a Forest, without seeing the least Appearance of any Habitation. (238)

The striking features of romantic prose are its humorlessness, its verbiage, its concentration on extremities of emotion, its grim determination to carry the reader along with the hero and reproduce in him identically heightened feelings. Mrs. Lennox matches the luxuriousness of the style, dwelling on the exact quality of the action or emotion as lovingly as the writer of genuine Romance. Rather than lightening the prose with obvious burlesque, she has, like Pope in *The Dunciad*, harnessed the self-parodying features of the original to do the job for her; in this way the reader

has the experience of both. We meditate upon the knight's mixed emotions, the "sad, and also the joyful" hours spent in that "miserable Place"
—paradox sustains the lively imagination. We appreciate that the value
of the ring was considerable, but not unseemly—all this is carried in the
word "some," which is given force by one's notions of heroic beneficence.
We feel the discomfort of the "poor Beast" and understand the urgency
of the situation that necessitated the neglect of that animal. Yet, at the
same time, our image of the teller, the careless and frivolous Sir George,
and our consciousness of the context, which is maintained by the sceptical questions of Sir Charles (who has understandably been thrown into
a state of confusion by the sudden elevation of his son's friend to the
post of "young prince of Kent"), make the sentiment and the ominous
air of Fortune and Fate that hangs over the tale seem palpably ridiculous.
The Female Quixote is both enlivened and enriched by Mrs. Lennox's
sensitive ear, which was able to reproduce accurately the absurd and yet
captivating works of the Romantic imagination.

The nonburlesque narration perpetuates the lightheartedness that is
aroused in the parody. The ironic teller of Arabella's history manages
her business so gently as to be almost unnoticeable; indeed, Ronald
Paulson insists she is not there: "There is no ironic observer like Fielding's
narrator to distance Arabella; she is merely described."[13] One may have
to refer to Meredith's highly literate definition of irony to appreciate
Mrs. Lennox's delicate treatment of her character, which has been adjusted
to the temperament of her Female Quixote and to the understated jest of
the work as a whole. According to Meredith, "if, instead of falling foul
of the ridiculous person with a satiric rod, to make him writhe and
shriek aloud [as Fielding and Smollett often do to their minor characters],
you prefer to sting him under a semi-caress, by which he shall in his anguish be rendered dubious whether indeed anything has hurt him, you
are an engine of Irony."[14] In *The Female Quixote,* the caress almost
fully relieves the sting:

Having said this, with one of her fair Hands she cover'd her Face, to hide
the Blushes which so compassionate a Speech had caus'd—Holding the
other extended with a careless Air, supposing he would kneel to kiss it,
and bathe it with his Tears, as was the Custom on such melancholy Occasions, her Head at the same Time turned another Way, as if reluctantly
and with Confusion she granted this Favour.—But after standing a Moment in this Posture, and finding her Hand untouch'd, she concluded

that Grief had depriv'd him of his Senses. (313)

Mrs. Lennox's restraint amounts to irony; her very lack of commentary is a comment when supported by the suggestions concerning Arabella's state of mind, the "supposing" and "as if reluctantly" revealing the degree to which she deludes herself. The reader sees clearly that she is not so innocent as to be entirely without guile and vanity. In addition, the "so compassionate" and "such melancholy Occasions" are straightforwardly ironic descriptions that make Arabella's exaggerations seem absurd. Although the author does not stop to mention that she is sorry to have to inform us of the weaknesses in her favorite character, the loving mockery is as clear as it is in Fielding's novels.

In general, the evidence of a narrator's genuine affection for a character conduces to annul any frailties and to heighten the charm. An author's humorous thoughts, his remedy for the splenetic view of human nature, are carried most effectively in the tenderness of his tone, in his conscious abstention from satire when satire is temptingly appropriate. That one may be lightheartedly malicious and turn mirth into a weapon of spleen is quickly confirmed by Butler's portrayal of the quixotic Hudibras. Miriam Small makes a distinction between the figures in *Hudibras* who "come nearer in time to Don Quixote" and the large group that "looms in the distance of the eighteenth century, gentler and more gracefully whimsical than the figures that gallop vigorously but sometimes awkwardly through the octosyllabics of Butler; for that reason to many a little more in the tradition of the sentimental fantastic old knight himself."[15] The distinction is valid primarily because in reading *The Female Quixote,* we never sense any ironic betrayal by the author of her characters; there are no poisoned darts to shape our opinion. Mrs. Lennox takes care to suit the tone to her subject, and as the only real villains in *The Female Quixote* are the invisible writers of Romance, not even the Romances themselves, the narration is gentle throughout and provocative of the kindly smiles one senses to be always present on the face of the author herself.

Only towards the end of the novel does the prose seem to reflect an occasionally humorless expression. Mrs. Lennox is almost as successful at resisting the temptation to moralize as she is at refraining from satire and on the whole maintains a nice distance both from sermon and scorn. But just as her timing once or twice slips, her ear is guilty of similar insensitivities (or possibly her admiration for Johnson leads her at times to misappropriate his style). Arabella's diatribe against satire, so far from being satirical itself, is too evidently a sermon presented by the author:

> The Ugliness of Vice, reply'd *Arabella*, ought only to be represented to the Vicious; to whom Satire, like a magnifying Glass, may aggravate every Defect, in order to make its Deformity appear more hideous; but since its End is only to reprove and amend, it should never be address'd to any but those who come within its Correction, and may be the better for it: A virtuous Mind need not be shewn the Deformity of Vice, to make it hated and avoided; the more pure and uncorrupted our Ideas are, the less shall we be influenc'd by Example. (277)

Even the echo from Swift's Preface to *The Battle of the Books* has been couched in morality at the expense of its irony. The straightforward declarative sentences, dull unless handled by a master of diction, fall flat upon the audience as well as the company: we are forced to agree entirely with Miss Glanville's observation, "You are so very grave, and talk upon such high-flown Subjects."

The gravity and subject of the penultimate chapter, however, prove a far greater threat to the humor of the work as a whole. A serious suggestion made in 1843 attributing this chapter to Johnson himself has been accepted by many scholars since then as plausible.[16] The least one can say, on the evidence of the style, is that Mrs. Lennox was writing what she thought would please and compliment her eminent and gracious friend. Thus the corrections of the "good Divine" are all offered in the sweeping sentences of Johnsonian truths:

> The only Excellence of Falsehood, answered he, is its Resemblance to Truth; as therefore any Narrative is more liable to be confuted by its Inconsistency with known Facts, it is at a greater Distance from the Perfection of Fiction; for there can be no Difficulty in framing a Tale, if we are left at Liberty to invert all History and Nature for our own Conveniency. When a Crime is to be concealed, it is easy to cover it with an imaginary Word. When Virtue is to be rewarded, a Nation with a new Name may, without an Expence of Invention, raise her to the Throne. (378)

The weight is almost too much for the comedy to bear: the ending simply does not spring naturally from the delightfully light story that

FIELDING'S FOLLOWERS

precedes it. Only the efficiency with which it is accomplished is comical about Arabella's cure, and one would not comment on that fact except as a justification, for, Mrs. Lennox's need to be efficient (to avoid excessive length—a specific recommendation from Richardson, no less[17]) accounts for the chapter's jarring artificiality and sententiousness.

However, the substance of Mrs. Lennox's last chapter, even more troubling to the comedy than the tone, is finally the most regrettable feature of the concluding section. It is here that the fragile connection between the sublime original and the clever offspring is most endangered. Throughout the novel we nurtured Arabella in our affections on the basis of the understanding that Mrs. Lennox displayed of Arabella's romantically turned intellect. We accepted Arabella's pronouncement on Indifference as the author's vindication of her heroine's weakness, which is that of a strong and imaginative mind: "I am persuaded that Indifference is generally the inseparable Companion of a weak and imperfect Judgment. . . . [For] certain it is that this lukewarmness of Soul, which sends forth but feeble Desires, sends also but feeble Lights; so that those who are guilty of it, not knowing any thing clearly, cannot fasten on any thing with Perseverance" (311). When set against her earlier statement, the purport of this speech in reference to her own weakness is clear: "To say the Truth, I am inclin'd to conceive a greater Hope of a Man, who in the Beginning of his Life is hurry'd away by some evil Habit, than one who fastens on nothing" (310). Yet at the end the evil of her former habits of thought is stressed and the greatness of mind that such extravagance reflects is nowhere reasserted. Whereas in Don Quixote, the deathbed recantation is accompanied by the narrator's reaffirmation of his character's worthiness, mad or sane, in *The Female Quixote* Arabella's shame at her past is so great as to repudiate all that we found charming. No one speaks in honor of the childlike heroine now newly grown-up as Cervantes does of Don Quixote now the ordinary Alonso Quixano. He notes that whether as a knight or a plain man, Quixote "had always shew'd himself such a good natur'd man, and of so agreeable a behavior, that he was not only belov'd by his family, but by every one that knew him."[18] Charlotte Lennox neglects to praise her sprightly heroine for the entertainment she has offered along with the vexation. She does not contradict Arabella's cries about having "trifled away" her time. The omission is a sin against the very comedy she has so imaginatively engendered from the hearty stock of Cervantes' incomparable

77

(Fielding's opinion notwithstanding) work. Fortunately, the reader does not require any justification for the facts of Arabella's life; her quixotic imagination is provocative of a comic pleasure that raises the novel from the realm of the "historically interesting" to one which merits the consideration given to works that accurately record, with cheerfulness, the complexity of human nature.

The Vicar of Wakefield

When the evidence put forward is *The Vicar of Wakefield*, Goldsmith's avowed devotion to mirthful comedy is seriously questioned. Recently, in an attempt to rescue the work from the critical dumps, Robert Hopkins put forth a case for recognizing Goldsmith's novel as a piece of "amiable satire."[19] However, in focusing on the satire rather than the amiability, Hopkins has not explained the source of the easy pleasure which so many generations of readers have felt, even while protesting loudly the faults of construction. In his effort to acquit the book from the charges of sentimentalism, he has often confused comedy and satire, using characters' absurdities and humorous burlesque passages as evidence of satiric intention, when in fact they show nothing more than Goldsmith's desire to entertain his readers with instances of human and stylistic folly. The faults of construction are obviated by Hopkin's interpretation, but so is the Vicar's charm, and without the main character's redeeming personality (one surely modeled after Parson Adams's), the amiability of the ironic tale is lost.

The argument for satire rests on an exposition of the Vicar's materialistic hypocrisy, by which is implied his knowing deception of his family and parishioners with regard to his motives and aspirations. Rather than seeing the Vicar's desire to marry his daughters to men of moderate fortune as a desire to ensure their happiness (a middle-class aspiration perhaps, but not inappropriate to non-Wesleyan clergymen), Hopkins sees his concern as proof that "for the Vicar marriage is more a business investment than a sacred spiritual bond."[20] That the Vicar undoubtedly deceives *himself* as to the extent of his snobbishness, Hopkins is right to point out, and that this deception is underlined by the terminology he uses and the actions of other characters is also true. But self-deception is a matter for mirth as hypocrisy is one for satire. If the Vicar were more than a thirty-five-pound-a-year country parson at the height of his career, if he were a bishop with pretensions to power, Goldsmith might have made him the vehicle for "one of the most savage indictments of *bourgeois* values in eighteenth-century literature" as another recent critic describes him.[21] Instead he created a rather simple figure, whose virtue is somewhat undermined by his vanity and whose vanity is somewhat offset by his self-mockery. He created a very human figure with strengths and weaknesses, the fit subject for comedy rather than castigation.

The easy humor of the novel lies primarily in the characters, though D.W. Jefferson is right to demonstrate the comic reduction of tragedy into absurdity that is effected by Goldsmith's choice of stock words and phrases (similar to Smollett's descriptions of fear and rage) and by the farcical speeding-up of events that leaves one breathless rather than worried.[22] It is essential of course to the comedy that nothing drastic be allowed to harm "a family so harmless" as the Primroses or to humiliate very painfully a family already so humble by nature. Comic events, however, do not sustain the cheerful spirit as they do in the much more imaginative action of *She Stoops to Conquer* or *Joseph Andrews*. But for the naive reactions of the main character, the source of *The Female Quixote*'s strength as well, the events of the book would not be worth retelling, even in Goldsmith's sprightly manner. Moreover, unlike those in *The Female Quixote,* the burlesque passages are not ludicrous enough to sustain mirth.

The recognized success of the first half of the novel may be traced to Goldsmith's characterization of the Vicar as a good-natured man in the same tradition as the hero of his first play. The author deals with his character in the same gently ironic manner (albeit through his character's own words) as Sir William Honeywood deals with his nephew in the play; he chooses to overlook the little failings in order to recommend the essential goodness: "We must touch his weaknesses with a delicate hand. There are some faults so nearly allied to excellence, that we can scarce weed out the vice without eradicating the virtue." The virtue in both the nephew and the vicar-narrator is a sweetness that springs from guilelessness, an unfailing belief in the prevailing morality of mankind which their experiences refuse to support, an acceptance of traditional values long after their fashionable demise. The same naiveté that allows the Vicar to be duped by a Thornhill with due warning allows him to undertake the reformation of prisoners using the simple expedient of tobacco stoppers as therapy; it allows us to mock him but even more to admire him and to wish him success however much we remain dubious about his prospects. This guilelessness is a characteristic of all the worthy characters in the novel and Goldsmith's admiration of this trait is evident in the delicacy of his irony.

The book is ironic enough so that the Vicar does not make us believe in the benevolence of humanity, but the irony is so mitigated by Goldsmith's delight in his creations as to make us want to believe in such goodness. Simplicity is recommended throughout the novel in the Vicar's easy-going style of narration, which is thoroughly uncomplicated and unpretentious—qualities as long-wearing as Mrs. Primrose's wedding dress. Through his prose, the simplicity and sturdiness of his family are conveyed with great conviction. The introductory paragraphs leave the reader with a strong impression of the Primroses' unspoiled virtue, and of the unity and happiness that derive from it:

[W]e loved each other tenderly, and our fondness encreased as we grew old. There was in fact nothing that could make us angry with the world or each other. We had an elegant house, situated in a fine country, and a good neighbourhood. The year was spent in moral or rural amusements; in visiting our rich neighbours, and relieving such as were poor. We had no revolutions to fear, nor fatigues to undergo; all our adventures were by the fire-side, and all our migrations from the blue bed to the brown. (IV, 18)

Goldsmith graces his little family with the peace and contentment that are always associated with pastoral life; the rhythms of his descriptions reinforce the suggestion, especially in the sentence where an emphatic "no" and "nor" are swiftly balanced by the positive assertions of "all" and "all." He avoids making their happiness seem entirely dull by using such words as "adventures" and "migrations" in a way that ironically denigrates what is usually meant by those activities and at the same time attributes the excitement of them to the family's homely occupations.

Until Mr. Thornhill so rudely imposes the worldly variety of adventure upon them, the Primroses' nonhearthside activities (even after they are considerably reduced in circumstances) extend only as far as the neighboring fair. If the fair turns into a real adventure, it is only because of their unworldliness. Moses' gross of green spectacles is an emblem of his simplicity, the blindness that occurs when one's eyes are open too wide to see what is going on. The entire family is in need of protection from the blinding light of innocence: the Vicar's foresight does not arm him against the sharpers at the fair—in fact the same sharper who victimized Moses. Their awareness of Thornhill's reputation does not save them from his intrusion. Such frailties are more admirable than absurd because like the "good-natured" man's and Parson Adams's, they are related to strengths.

Other frailties are more absurd than admirable, but still far from despicable: their consciousness of the pitfalls of vanity does not prevent them from falling into them—cosmetic washes, family portraits, susceptibility to flattery and pomposity. Goldsmith carefully includes the Vicar in the family's displays of pride and gives him his own share of vanity concerning the Primroses' gentility: on the occasion of their change in fortune the Vicar notes that the family has not had the education to "render them callous to contempt," and he observes "for the honour of the family" that his daughters never went without money in their pockets though they were enjoined never to spend it. These unconscious vanities (which would not be recognized as vanities by most eighteenth-century readers) are balanced in the novel by the Vicar's cheerful admission to sharing the faults of pride that he so often attributes to his wife and daughters. The quality in himself to which he would seem to be most blind—that is, his weakness for producing and delivering sermons, he actually sees quite clearly; besides noting that "as an author" he could "digest no small share of flattery" he refers to his "long and painful lectures upon temperance, simplicity, and contentment" and to his "deliver-[ing] an observation."

Just how much Goldsmith directs us to admire the simplicity and openheartedness of the Primroses is perhaps best demonstrated by the rare instances in the book of a sudden guardedness, the result of Goldsmith's accurate dramatization of class attitudes. When Burchell metamorphoses into Sir William, we are told that he "assum[ed] all his native dignity," though we had never noticed any lack of that quality when he was the plain and kindly, if somewhat eccentric, Mr. Burchell. This sudden change is not so attractive as Goldsmith intended it to be; not an aristocrat himself, he naturally had the deference that was proper to an Englishman of his time and consequently chose to transform all the qualities of common humanity that we had grown to admire into those more fitting a lord. Instantly, Burchell is all condescension:

"Ah, Sir," cried my wife, with a piteous aspect, "how is it possible that I can ever have your forgiveness. . . ."

"My dear good lady," returned he with a smile, "if you had your joke, I had my answer: I'll leave it to all the company if mine were not as good as yours. To say the truth, I know no body whom I am disposed to be angry with at present but the fellow who so frightened my little girl here. I had not even time to examine the rascal's person so as to describe him in an advertisement. Can you tell me, Sophia, my dear, whether you should know him again?"   (IV, 168)

We have had hints before of Burchell's tendency to speak in a manner apparently above his station, including the Vicar's especially revealing remark "that though he was a money-borrower, he defended his opinions with as much obstinacy as if he had been my patron." Just as in that case Goldsmith automatically assumed the natural superiority of the upper class, so here Burchell is given the offhand confidence that derives from a consciousness of one's superiority—he can afford to grant Mrs. Primrose her joke, because he knows he had the last laugh; he can afford to waive his right to be angry because his honor is unquestionable, and if he is not angry it is because he can afford to fall in love with someone who is below his station, which the Primroses cannot do: his assurance allows him to refer to Sophia as "my little girl" and "my dear"—liberties he would not so quickly have taken in his former character.

One cannot help resenting his patronizing tones, for the essential worthiness of the Primroses is insulted by these insinuations of their lowliness: Burchell all but reprimands Mrs. Primrose for her openness, which she herself is horrified to recall. Yet Mrs. Primrose is likeable precisely because she is a little too pushy, a little unsubtle, but as a result not at all underhanded or petty, not at all like the coy ladies of the town (who turn out to be prostitutes). Indeed, Mr. Burchell also is likeable primarily because Goldsmith had him pitch in with the family chores so cheerfully and sit in their modest parlor-kitchen relishing their unfashionable conversations. His sudden elevation at the end does not do justice to the natural unassuming man who was fit company for the Vicar and whose evaluation of high-sounding talk was "Fudge!"

His bluntness, the full force of which we experience in our reading, is especially endearing. Goldsmith immensely improved the comedy and effectiveness of the "Fudge" scene by actually placing the word at the end of each paragraph of society chat, rather than simply telling us, through the Vicar, that Burchell indulged in this disconcerting undercutting. The Vicar himself is not unbearable from the start because his ironic comments have the lively immediacy of asides in a play:

"Ay," returned I, not knowing well what to think of the matter; "Heaven grant they may be both the better for it this day three months!" This was one of those observations I usually made to impress my wife with an opinion of my sagacity; for if the girls succeeded, then it was a pious wish fulfilled; but if any thing unfortunate ensued, then it might be looked upon as a prophecy. (IV, 65)

At a stroke, Goldsmith undercuts all the Vicar's "wise" platitudes and makes him engagingly self-aware and openhearted.

Yet we must consider it a failure in Goldsmith's comic art that the Primroses are not more laughable than they are, and therefore not as human as they should be: in trying to make them into good people, Goldsmith smoothed them out of existence, with the exception perhaps of Mrs. Primrose, who is at least slightly stupid. Because most of the action is indirectly described, except for the less comic events of the second half, *The Vicar of Wakefield* lacks the vigor that is essential to any truly comic work. Moses brings home the green spectacles, and we are able to reconstruct the humorous situation in our minds, but we are not presented with the dramatic, or rather lively evidence of his absurdity. Goldsmith is so anxious to please that he is entirely too generous towards his characters' shortcomings. Because he wished to recommend Moses' credulity more highly than his pedantry, he is less delicate in his handling of the latter trait; Moses is thus more memorably comical as a pedant than as a simpleton.

In *The Good-Natur'd Man* Goldsmith gives us the opportunity we miss in *The Vicar* both to laugh at and love the credulous man, to observe directly as the unworldly hero disavows another's truths simply because those truths are inconceivable to him. Lofty has managed to acquire the reputation of a benefactor and has allowed his name to be connected with Honeywood's sudden rescue from bankruptcy:

Honeywood: The world, by what I learn, is no stranger to your generosity. But where does it tend?
Lofty: To nothing; nothing in the world. The town, to be sure, when it makes such a thing as me the subject of conversation, has asserted,

that I never yet patronized a man of merit.

Honeywood: I have heard instances to the contrary, even from yourself.

Lofty: Yes, Honeywood, and there are instances to the contrary, that you shall never hear from myself.

Honeywood: Ha, dear Sir, permit me to ask you but one question.

Lofty: Sir, ask me no questions: I say, Sir, ask me no questions; I'll be damn'd, if I answer them!

Honeywood: I will ask no further. My friend, my benefactor, it is, it must be here, that I am indebted for freedom, for honour. Yes, thou worthiest of men, from the beginning I suspected it, but was afraid to return thanks; which if undeserved, might seem reproaches.

(IV.i; V, 58)

Lofty tells nothing but the truth throughout the conversation; therein lies the humor of the situation. He will genuinely be damned if he answers any searching questions. Honeywood's inclination to see the best in people deafens him to the irony of his own observation—"even from yourself"—which the audience hears and laughs at. Lofty is indeed nothing, nothing in the world, but the good-natured man steadfastly refuses to accept such a poor opinion of another man, a noble but ridiculous refusal. In making the scene at once hilarious and heartwarming, Goldsmith makes us accept the weakness and the virtue of such generous credulity.

Goldsmith's kind treatment of Lofty, the truthful villain in this play, is incidentally instructive of the way in which he rewards and therefore recommends openheartedness in all his works. The redeemable rogues are the ones who always act as if they never really expect to get away with what they are doing (like Tony Lumpkin, though roguery is far too strong a word for his playful mischief-making). Jenkinson in his own way is as credulous as the Primroses, because his vanity persuades him to trust in his cleverness; he is always clever rather than insidious and is rewarded at the end for his generosity and frankness; whereas Thornhill is left in the rather ridiculous position of mastering the French horn to overcome his melancholy. Goldsmith likes those who wear their frailties and faults on their sleeves, where all who are not quite so blind as the Vicar or Moses may see them and take care.

What we miss so much in the latter half of the novel is the Vicar's cheerful irreverence towards himself and his mockery of his own shortcomings. Too often we are allowed to feel the full weight of his sermons.

Not only in the set-piece that Goldsmith inserted for our benefit but also in the pious little speeches to the Vicar's wife and family does the burden of his morality crush the comic spirit of the novel. Only occasionally does Goldsmith offset the Vicar's absurd optimism with a bit of action that contradicts his cheerful hopes. When George enters the jail, all "bloody, wounded and fettered with the heaviest irons," the Vicar's thankfulness for his son's happiness and innocence is shown to be much too premature and unrealistic. More often, however, the Vicar's sanguine thoughts are allowed to stand unchallenged by reality: "If we are to be taken from this abode, only let us hold to the right; and wherever we are thrown, we can still retire to a charming apartment, when we can look round our own hearts with intrepidity and with pleasure" (IV, 139). Indeed, the Vicar actually converts the jail into a charming apartment at the expense of the book's comedy; when the prisoners put away their jest-books in favor of cribbage—that ever so polite card game—our belief in the likeness of the characters to ordinary earthly people is finally snuffed. Even the comical speed with which this transformation is accomplished, which Hopkins points to as evidence of Goldsmith's satire of the Vicar's optimism, is unfortunately not enough to offset the impression that the Vicar's unlikely methods have worked.

In contrast, Fielding makes certain that we never forget the absurd limitations of even his worthiest characters, Parson Adams in particular. If one compares the scene in which Adams learns of his youngest son's "drowning" with the one in which the Vicar learns of his younger daughter's abduction, Fielding's comic and loving appreciation of human frailty is evident whereas Goldsmith's is submerged in a mass of comforting observations. Both prepare their readers for the scene by engaging their virtuous characters in pious conversation, which is suddenly interrupted by news of the disaster. However, whereas Adams is exaggeratedly earnest in his teaching on this occasion, spouting biblical references that turn out to be embarrassingly relevant, Dr. Primrose is simply himself, referring his problems, as is his wont, to the "heavenly Father." Though like Parson Adams, the Vicar is unable emotionally to practice always what he preaches, that is, though he is Job-like when his injuries are personal but as miserable as poor sinning folk when his family is attacked, Goldsmith fails to capitalize on the comic implications of the Vicar's weakness. Rather than "stamping about the room" the Vicar laments in rather pathetic terms (but not with the comic formality of a Walter

Shandy) and allows himself to be comforted by his son and wife. Fielding only relieves his parson to embarrass him further with tangible evidence of his excessive grief, the appearance of his wet, but living son. Our opinion of Adams's godliness is not diminished by his comically immoderate behavior, but our sense of his humanity is heightened, as is our sense of man's ridiculous inability on the one hand to control life's events and his remarkable ability on the other to cope with sudden changes in fortune by indulging in useless but forgivable passion—the parson's joy at his son's "resurrection" is no less excessive than was his grief.

The Vicar's listless surrender to comfort and Goldsmith's surrender to pathos represent a defeat for the mythical Comic Spirit who hovered actively over the first part of the novel. If Dr. Primrose had managed to retain his fine sense of irony throughout his troubles, or if Goldsmith had invited the reader more often to cast an oblique eye upon him, the Vicar would have been a more human and memorable character than he turns out to be. He would have been the first Mr. Bennet, not merely a working model for him. That Goldsmith intended to create a full-fledged ironist, a gentle one like Mr. Bennet who has no inclination toward satire, seems as evident as his failure to do so. William Gallaway, who strives with clarity and reason to clear Goldsmith's name from the charges of sentimentalism, is rightly forced to retrace his steps after bringing Goldsmith to the brink of satire and concede the "indulgence of the novelist to his own heart and to the hearts of a sentimental reading public."[23]

Indulgence not only in sentiment, but also in formal sermonizing dampens the comic spirit of the novel. Goldsmith was virtually forced to drop his comic tone in order to take advantage of his character's authority as an upright vicar to give force to his own tracts (once he had decided to include them in his novel) on the monarchy, the penal system, and Christian forgiveness. If he had encouraged the reader to make jests at the doctor's expense after he himself had stopped, he would have suffered his pieces to be discounted as lightly as the Whistonian dispute, which he did not wish to do. Thus the pomposity of the Vicar's language is not undercut by unusual extravagance as one would expect if the Vicar's optimism were being mocked:

I cannot tell whether it is from the number of our penal laws, or the licentiousness of our people, that this country should shew more convicts in a year, than half the dominions of Europe united. Perhaps it is owing to both; for they mutually produce each other. When by indiscriminate penal laws a nation beholds the same punishment affixed to dissimilar degrees of guilt, from perceiving no distinction in the penalty, the people are led to lose all sense of distinction in the crime, and this distinction is the bulwark of all morality: thus the multitude of laws produce new vices, and new vices call for fresh restraints.   (IV, 151)

The rhetoric suits the subject of his tract perfectly, and the cadences are designed to emphasize the main points—"the multitude of laws produce new vices, and new vices call for fresh restraints." Indeed, the only extravagance is Goldsmith's for supposing that he could slip in a full-length essay without endangering the tone of his comic novel.

Fortunately, it is not impossible for us to lend a serious ear to Goldsmith's ideas and at the same time to deride his character for his inability to withhold virtuous ideas from a possible audience. One has the feeling that Goldsmith was no more able to refrain from delivering his observations than the Vicar was, and was similarly aware of his weakness though he regularly let it get the best of him and, in this case, his novel.

For the novel does have as many faults as Goldsmith disarmingly concedes in the Foreword. It is only our willingness to make good Goldsmith's debt to comedy, to call forth our own resources of mirth when his seem to be overcome by didactic motives or pathetic feelings, that accounts for our easy pleasure. Yet a firm belief in the guilelessness of the book's composition, in the similarity between the Vicar's helplessness and the author's allows us to delight in the novel as much as Goldsmith obviously delighted in his character. They are both charming, if slightly weak, creations.

The Spiritual Quixote

To judge from the casual, happy air of *The Spiritual Quixote,* the "pique" brought on by itinerant preachers which impelled Richard Graves to begin his novel in 1757 was effectively dispelled by his pleasure in composing the work, which is subtitled "The Summer Rambles of Mr. Geoffry Wildgoose." He extended the pleasure over many years before finally publishing the novel in 1773.[24] His quiet and gentle style, which evokes the warm and sunny prospects of summer, precludes the possibility of a satirical hailstorm, and distinguishes his efforts from the headier

comic works on which he modeled his writing. The comedy of this
Quixotic tale lies in its geniality, not in witty irony or energetic fantasy;
indeed, readers expecting the liveliness associated with the "new species
of writing" or with tilting against windmills are bound to be disappointed
by the tameness of the characters and the naturalness (excepting perhaps
the entirely rainless summer) of the events. The motivating anger at
Methodism results not in satire but a slight jest aimed at the sect and a
pleasant novel that occasionally mocks Methodist extravagances. Graves
himself is aware of the book's predominantly mild tone:

Now though the courteous reader should be as fond of humour as this
facetious bookseller [who was sorry there was no humour in the Life of
Mohamet] was; yet, if, in travelling through a flat country, he should
now and then meet with a picturesque prospect, sometimes with a bit of
galloping ground, and sometimes with a droll object upon the road, he
must patiently submit to jog on some parts of the way, without any
thing to entertain or amuse him; for such probably will be the fate of
the gentle reader of this various history.   (30)

"Flat," "picturesque," and "droll"—with a little bit of "galloping":
these adjectives describe Graves's style and characters as well as the world
of the book. The defenders of Graves's tenuously maintained reputation
usually offer a similar list of ingredients to account for their pleasure in
reading his novels: "Graves had keen powers of observation and an exact
memory, and from these two endowments he made his novels. The charm
they possess is the charm of their age, in the country among quiet folk,
kindly gossips, leisurely travellers, honest toilers, generous squires and
clergymen and ladies bountiful."[25] "Leisurely," "kindly"—one may
apply these modifiers (and add those offered by Havelock Ellis—"wayward ease" and "genial")[26] indiscriminately to the tone and the action
of *The Spiritual Quixote* and in so doing explain why the overall effect
of the novel is so soothing, almost too soothing to be comical.

In presenting a picture of the two "pilgrims" about to set out on their
mission, Graves shows clearly the romantic inclination of his imagination:

The harmless red-breast, with his solitary note, began to break in upon
the stillness of the dawn; and, from the sweet-briar that grew around
the lattice, to interrupt the gentle slumbers of Jeremiah Tugwell, when
Mr. Wildgoose arrived under his window; and, by the signal agreed upon,

summoned him to the place of rendezvous. Jerry soon appeared at the cottage-gate, in his short jerkin, (being somewhat between a coat and a waist-coat) his jelly-bag linen cap upon his head, with his oaken staff under his arm, and his wallet on his shoulder. (42)

We have already been instructed to consider the solitary tooth "in his upper mandible" as giving Wildgoose's squire a picturesque, rather pleasing appearance, and set here against the background of birds, flowers, and the dawn, Tugwell seems more rustic than ludicrous. Graves's poetic appreciation of the Malvern scenery becomes almost a blessing in praise of their journey, making the "pilgrimage" less mirthful than the sally of an enthusiast would ordinarily be: "The whole scene was enlivened by the music of the birds; the responsive notes of the thrushes from the neighbouring haw-thorns, and the thrilling strains of the sky-lark, who, as she soared towards the heavens, seemed to be chanting forth her matins to the great Creator of the universe" (43).

Yet this preoccupation with the natural beauties of the world, if it works against the mirth of the novel, does not work against its comic purpose. Clarence Tracy, in his recent Introduction, is right to see the entire excursion as an ironic commentary on the lesson Wildgoose preaches along the way: "All about them the sun shines on the grass in the meadows, the fish swim in the streams, the huntsman's horn echoes across the hills, and good ale is on tap in the inn—calling men out of themselves, if only they would hear the call. This is the artistic purpose of the sight-seeing digressions, to be a symbol of a more healthy and less introspective way of life" (xix). The sharpness of the irony generally found in didactic works—which *The Spiritual Quixote* surely is—has been toned down to preserve the gentle air of joy that carries with it the book's moral. Graves's attacks on the Methodists are no more violent than the remarks he jestingly directs against the new practice of using message cards, a trivial nuisance rather than cause for outrage.

The whole business of Methodism is reduced to a foolish case of intellectual indigestion, a minor irritation causing at worst some extravagant behavior:

Such a multifarious body of divinity indeed quite unsettled Mr. Geoffry's mind; and filled his head with such a farraginous medley of opinions, as almost turned his brain. It produced at least, to speak candidly of the matter, that sort of phrenzy, which we ascribe to enthusiasts in music, poetry, or painting; or in any other art or science; whose imaginations are so entirely possessed by those ideas, as to make them talk and act like madmen, in the sober eye of merely rational people. (20)

Graves sees the Methodist literature in terms of animal feed, referring to it variously as "crude trash," "crabbed food," and in this case as a "farraginous medley." But the Methodists themselves are rather mildly portrayed as overstimulated artists: only the barbed remark about "merely" rational people indicates his resentment of their self-righteous attitude.

The likeness of itinerant preachers to quack doctors is stressed on several occasions. Graves implies that one visits a Methodist meeting when one is afflicted with hypochondria of the mind. Thus, Lady Sherwood, whose "uncommon genius and lively fancy" failed to be satisfied by the "plain rational scheme of the established Religion . . . listened with the same attention to the enthusiastic doctrines of these itinerant Preachers, as a person labouring under an hypochondriacal distemper does to the extravagant pretensions of a Mountebank" (174). Methodism is an alternative social pastime to mountebankery. Tugwell clarifies the equation when Wildgoose mounts the horse-block following a tirade by a medical vendor: " 'Yes, yes,' cries Tugwell; 'here is the true spiritual Mountebank, Gentlemen: here is the Quack Doctor of your souls' " (358). Just as no one allows mountebanks to arouse their spleen, for the occupation is mostly harmless and successfully exposes the laughable gullibility of human beings, so the Methodists do not suffer greatly at the hands of Graves for being likened to these quacks.

Similarly, those who fall under the spell of their local preacher are shown to be weak (or like Lady Sherwood simply bored) rather than mad or heretical. Indeed, often down-to-earth considerations make succumbing to the cant a sensible course of action, for a multitude of misdeeds may be excused by so doing. Graves undermines the supposed conversion of sinners by pointing out the absurd consequences of one such highly-charged meeting. Here the zealous worshippers accept Whitefield's interpretation of the rain as a blessing from heaven and naturally become thoroughly wet in the course of the outdoor meeting; whereupon many a "pious soul" was furnished with "a good pretence for taking a cordial; and the brandy-bottle and ginger bread were plentifully distributed by the suttlers, that always attended on these occasions"

(234). By mentioning the professional victualers, Graves slyly indicates that another excuse would have been found if the rain had not so conveniently provided one.

That more sinning than reforming takes place under the auspices of the New Birth is Graves's thesis, and he proves it comically throughout the book: Wildgoose's neglect of his mother, who becomes ill with distress (in true eighteenth-century fashion) comments upon the nature of his concern for the health of human souls; Mrs. Sarsenet becomes impoverished and can no longer support her mother and sister, though she provides breakfasts for worshippers; the honest barber becomes a thief. After a ludicrous attempt to rob Wildgoose, which Graves seems to have modeled on the desperate young man's abortive attempt to rob Tom Jones, the barber reveals the unhappy results of his association with the Methodist preacher:

'You yourself [he says to Wildgoose], however, (without intending it) have been the principal cause of bringing me to this distress. My neighbour Fillpot, at the public-house, out of spite, paid off a year and a half's rent, which I owed my Landlord, seized upon my goods, turned me out of my house; and now my wife, who has just lain-in, is destitute of the necessaries for a woman in her condition; and my children are, at this instant, crying for bread.' (313)

Tugwell offers the sensible observation that perhaps the barber did not benefit from his conversion, whereupon the quixotic evangelist plumbs the depth of Methodist folly in his reply:

Wildgoose was not pleased with being reminded of this unlucky instance; but said, 'the Barber's was a particular case; that he was persecuted by his neighbours, and driven by necessity to one wicked attempt; and that, he made no doubt, the Barber was still in a state of Grace, though appearances were against him.' (319)

The state of Grace is the voluminous cloak under which sinners may hide, and Graves makes clear how inviting such an easy conversion is to the most profligate members of society. The jargon (what Tugwell calls the "gospel lingo") is easily acquired, and the advantages of speaking the pious language are seen to be many. The manageress of a brothel demonstrates her skill to Wildgoose and informs the reader in the meantime of the many benefits involved:

'Sir, I keep as good orders in my house as any woman in England; and though (I thank God!) I have always had good custom, and have had twenty couple at a time, taking their recreation, in my house, yet (I bless God!) I never had any murder, or riot, or daggers-drawing, since I have been in business. Then I make my poor Lambs read the Bible every Sunday, and go to church in their turn; and, in short, though their bodies may be polluted, I take great care of their souls; and I hope God will wink at my poor Lambs that *sport themselves together.*' (256)

Once the heart is relieved of responsibility for the body's actions, as Graves implies it is in Wildgoose's answer—"our outward actions are indifferent in themselves; and it is the heart that God chiefly regards"—society and religion no longer enjoy the fruits of their interdependence and, as Graves suggests, even murder may be casually dismissed as an offence of the body only. In his novel, however, no murders are committed with the sanction of the new religion: Mrs. Wildgoose recovers in time; Mrs. Sarsenet does not starve; the barber goes back to his honest ways. Some uncondemned drunkenness and prostitution are the worst results of the conversions.

Misguidance rather than evil is shown to be at the root of Methodist folly. Thus, "Mr. Wildgoose also bestowed an handsome gratuity upon a poor woman, who had been used to retail Gin about the streets, but who pretended to have lost her trade, and to be reduced by poverty, by so many of her customers having been converted by Mr. Whitfield" (240). Wildgoose is obviously not wrong to be liberal with his charity, but Graves clearly notes the unworthiness of the recipient along with the gullibility of his hero. Misguidance, of course, is what leads Wildgoose to abandon his common-sense and trust to miracles for his daily nourishment: fortunately, he provides himself with an earthbound companion who performs the requisite miracles very unmiraculously by stowing away at each stop a sufficient amount of food and drink in his capacious wallet.

Wildgoose's denial of bodily needs stems, however, from a firm adherence to basic principles; if misguided, he is at least free of Whitefield's hypocrisy. Indeed, Whitefield is portrayed by Graves as one whose foolishness is not redeemed by any generosity or genuine piety. The plate of muffins (well-buttered) and the basin of hot chocolate at his side when Wildgoose enters is an emblem of his spiritual weakness, and an ironic contrast to the prayer book which Wildgoose expected to find. Though Graves makes it plain that even his hero will put aside spiritual considerations when confronted with a succulent "calve's head," chocolate and muffins smack of frivolous luxury in a way that Geoffry's "devout" feastings do not. Whitefield emerges as a petty, illiberal leader, and his success is seen as the greatest evidence of the foolish gullibility of ordinary men.

By building on facts that appear in Whitefield's journal and by dramatizing the recorded events and turning them into comic events, Graves is able to expose the claims upon which many of the conversions rest. First we are introduced to a little girl, "not above thirteen years old," who cries out in the novel as in the journal that "she was pricked through and through by the power of the word" (250). Shortly after, her hysterical fit, which Wildgoose ascribes to the powerful effect of the "new birth," is properly traced to the imminence of an actual "new birth." By carrying the words in Whitefield's journal to their implied extremes, Graves makes comment unnecessary and fortunately refrains from adding any.

The descriptions of religious meetings contribute greatly to the mirth of the novel. Graves was most original and most humorous when dealing with "popular" humanity; their simplicity and susceptibility provided him with material both for laughter and affection. Perhaps the most successful incident in the book, certainly the most lively and engaging, concerns the unfortunate collier who fails to draw a distinction between the "black and bloody design" that Wildgoose cautions his audience against concealing and the black-pudding he had thrust into his bosom before entering the meeting:

The Collier still persisting in his mistake, began to sweat, and to wipe his face, and to pull his coat still closer together. Wildgoose, observing his confusion, proceeds with greater vehemence—

'But let us not, through false shame, still harbour this black and poisonous serpent in our breasts; which will sting us to the very soul: —Let us confess our sins to one another—let us drag the accursed thing from our bosom. . . .'

The poor Collier wriggled about in great agonies, and the Preacher was still more urgent—

'Out with it! Cast it from thee! and trample under foot every vile lust and carnal appetite that thou hast harboured in thy bosom!—'

The poor fellow, now convinced that he was discovered, and yet vexed at the importunity of the Preacher, cries out, 'The devil take the hog's-pudding!'—threw it amongst the crowd; and made his escape from this imaginary persecution. (251)

93

Graves traces the progress of his superstition, observing effectively in the present tense how it takes root and on what grounds it is fed. Given the essential misunderstanding, only slightly far-fetched, the rest follows the normal course of human error. By making the mistake seem plausible and its results farcical, Graves not only draws attention to the kind of mistakes upon which the Methodists thrive but also shows us the natural pitfalls that human beings face in their everyday life. He makes us feel sorry that the man has been deprived of his supper, even while we laugh at his unfounded terror.

When Graves is observing rather than thinking, describing rather than preaching, he sees the mirthfulness of people and events, and reproduces the cheer he feels in his quietly amused style. By referring to the collier repeatedly as "the poor fellow" or by dubbing Wildgoose and Tugwell "the two pilgrims," he becomes a fireside narrator in the manner of Fielding, encouraging his readers to share his feeling of warmth. When his head stakes a claim in the narrative, however, the didacticism that results is too impersonal—even worse, too uninteresting—to sustain the happy ease he arouses in the galloping or droll passages. Graves never misses a chance to champion the cause of the Church of England, though he also suggests some reforms in clerical practices. If he has occasion to find fault with the attitude of one vicar, who is somewhat rigorous in his collection of tithes, he quickly balances the account by portraying a man of "the old-fashioned piety," one who keeps his parishioners happy and who is himself a worthy person. The portrait unfortunately is merely an outline, and is too obviously a theoretical figure (or perhaps an exaggerated compliment) to be true: "Griskin was a man... that shewed his Faith by his Good Works. He gave much in charity, prayed often, and fasted now and then. Having the tithes in his own hands, it enabled him to keep a plentiful table, to which every sober honest man was welcome. He every Sunday invited by turns some of the Parishioners to dine with him; one or two of the most substantial in the parlour, and as many of the oldest and poorest in the kitchen. . . . By this means he kept up his dignity" (350). The facts are set out, but the figure fails to come alive. As happens too often for the good of the comedy, the reader is taught rather than enticed, told rather than made to feel the superiority of a system that supports its faith with actions appropriate to its object.

Striking one as artificially as the essays in *The Vicar of Wakefield,* the sporadic demonstrations of "good works" do not suggest the goodness

of the hearts behind the deeds, as the demonstrations of Methodist follies persuade one of the nonsense at the heart of the religion. Graves
seems unable to dramatize amiability in any but the lowest classes, who
are actively comical as well as good. Most of his Allworthies are as unreal as Allworthy himself, unredeemed by even the suggestion of foolishness that Fielding offers to relieve his character from the burden of goodness. In the case of Lady Forester, one is meant to scorn the poor souls
who turn up their noses at the quality of her charity, who ask for more
meat in their soup, who have the audacity not to take the medicines she
recommends. In contrast, and for our admiration, Graves shows us a
pretty scene of twenty children, happily employed and grateful for the
munificence of their Lady Bountiful. But Graves fails to make her as
pleasant as he sees her, mainly because he fails to give her a sense of humor about herself. She self-righteously considers herself "sufficiently
rewarded" by the many ungrateful poor folk "in the consciousness of
having discharged her duty" and towards her obedient little children she
preserves an air of "visitorial authority." She is simply too stuffy to be
very nice. Though the eighteenth-century audience probably viewed her
attitude towards charity with more sympathy than we do, readers in any
age do not take kindly to faultless human beings (such as Mr. Burchell,
and even he has a speckled reputation to offset some of his present perfection).

As in *The Female Quixote,* much of the dialogue at the end of the
novel, following Wildgoose's awakening, suffers from the subversive effect of stilted language and style. Indeed, the discussion that takes place
between Dr. Greville and the recovered pilgrim is not a discussion at all
but rather a continuous sermon dealing with the reforms necessary for
upholding the virtues inherent in organized spiritual activities. Whereas
some mild irony in the long prosaic passages would have preserved the
comedy of the work, Graves's unsubtle lessons bring the novel to a deadening close, which is only partially enlivened by the marriage between
the sensible Miss Townsend and the newly sensible Wildgoose. If some
foolish preacher had come on the scene and challenged Geoffry's turn
of heart, perhaps causing him to waver again in his conviction, the same
ideas might have been conveyed with equal emphasis and far more cheerfulness. If, in ending the episode involving the rapacious Widow Townsend and her lover, Graves had not fallen back on the easy moralistic
summary, but instead had slyly suggested that their fortunes did not

bring them everlasting happiness, the whole tale might not have seemed such a set-piece, inserted for the improvement of young ladies. Graves's air of indulgent amusement, carrying with it his approbation of the human race, is seriously dampened by his unresisted impulses to preach his own sermons while making fun of Wildgoose's.

The fun he makes of the Spiritual Quixote is not enough to sustain the comic spirit; his hero lacks the vitality from which most amiably humorous works in turn get their life. One may apply the same criticism to Geoffry Wildgoose that Tave raises against Smollett's rather dull Quixote figure, Sir Launcelot Greaves: "[His] benevolence lacks amiability, chiefly because he is not a mixed character: his aberrations, for that matter, are neither laughable nor likable."[27] Unlike Uncle Toby's delicacy, Tom Jones's imprudence, or Matt Bramble's impatience, Geoffry's enthusiasm does not make us cherish him for his comicality. One may claim that Wildgoose's aberration is related far more to the satirical ends of the book than is usually true of an amiable defect, but Peregrine Pickle's pride does not stop him from commanding our affection. Wildgoose is simply too undistinguished a character to be remarkable either for his madness or his goodheartedness. He speaks too often for Graves himself to be considered very mad; the satire is frequently transferred to stuttering bumbling vicars, as it is in *Joseph Andrews* as well, but neither the vicars nor Wildgoose are very entertaining:

'Pray, Sir,' says Wildgoose, '(if I may take the freedom) what do you mean by the cure of souls?'—'By the cure of souls? Why, I mean burying the dead—baptizing children, and marrying—and—and—reading prayers, and preaching—and the like.'—'Why, as to burying and marrying,' replies Wildgoose, 'those functions seem rather to belong to the care of the body, than to the cure of souls. And as for preaching (though I don't doubt, Sir, but your doctrine is an exception) yet, from what I have observed from the generality of preaching, whatever becomes of our souls, Christianity cannot long subsist among us, unless it should please God to send some better labourers into his vineyard.' (62)

Because Graves was so anxious to show that Methodism was not wholly without merit, especially as it was practiced by its sincere adherents (Wesley, not Whitefield), he made his quixotic figure seem not very quixotic at all. Wildgoose inherits Wesley's sensible beliefs and worthiness, and thus becomes wooden when he should be comical:

—'Sir,' says Rouvell, 'if you knew the honour and happiness of being upon an agreeable footing with people of distinction, you would not scruple a little artifice, to conceal any trifling circumstance that might disgust them; or grudge an expence a little beyond one's income, to enable one to appear in some measure upon a level with them.'—'Sir,' replies Wildgoose, 'I apprehend, it is neither dress, birth, nor fortune, but *education* and *behaviour*, that puts all gentlemen upon a *level*, even in the opinion of the world.' (172)

All this is very fine, but not in Wildgoose's mouth; Graves unduly loaded his comic butt with parcels of his own philosophy, and crippled him further by not allowing him any measure of independence as a ridiculous figure.

Geoffry's relations with Miss Townsend might have been developed so as to fill out the hero's character, if not to heroic proportions, at least to those of a recognizable human being. One does not expect the lady to have a life of her own, though Graves succeeds here to a greater extent than Smollett did. But the presence of a sweetheart should do more to enlist our interest in the gentleman than Julia's is allowed to do. Most of her part is given over to the relation of her history, which is quite unoriginal (indeed, it closely resembles one of the many told in Sarah Fielding's *David Simple)* and is certain to end up happily. Whereas Charlotte Lennox has Arabella spout out evidence of her simplicity during Bellmour's "history," thus transforming the tale into a conversation, a part of the action, Graves allows Julia to speak almost wholly uninterrupted by questions or requests for clarification. Her tale remains a freely associated episode, along with those of Mr. Rivers and Captain Johnson. On two occasions throughout the long narrative Wildgoose injects a thought; one time he merely makes a pious observation that is not extreme enough to be comic and yet too extreme to be agreeable—"Providence rarely deserts us"—and another time, he almost succeeds in being quixotic:

'I am afraid then,' says Wildgoose, 'you had not many religious books put into your hands by your good father?'

'No,' says Miss Townsend; 'but I had a few by my good mother, which I made a point of reading every Sunday; such as Tillotson's Sermons, the Whole Duty of Man, and the like.'

'Why,' replies Wildgoose, 'you might as well have read the Seven Champions or Jack the Giant-Killer, as either the Whole Duty of Man or Tillotson, who knew no more of Christianity than Mohamet.' (81)

Comments such as these add a light and pleasant touch both to the immediate narrative and the whole novel, but Graves does not often let his hero indulge in humorous hyperbole.

The grave preacher's companionship with Jeremiah Tugwell offers him many more occasions to show his humanity than does his romance. Indeed, the perpetually thirsty, perpetually cheerful squire redeems many of the book's weaknesses. Much of the novel's geniality for which it has been justly praised derives from the pleasing consequences of the democratic alliance between the Spiritual Quixote and his faithful companion:

The Keeper had but one spare bed, which Tugwell could not be prevailed upon to partake with his Master; but took up his lodgings with the Groom in the hay-loft; and Wildgoose, making it a point of conscience, not to indulge himself in the softness of a down-bed, when his fellow labourer fared so coarsly, wrapt himself up in the coverlet, and lay upon the floor. So, though they were both thoroughly tired, through the complaisance of the one, and the quixotism of the other, a very good feather-bed remained useless and unoccupied. Wildgoose, however, slept tolerably well on the floor; and Tugwell would have slept better in the hay-loft, had not the Groom, who chose to lie in his boots and spurs, given Jerry now and then an involuntary titillation.   (113)

Though Graves had no need to tell the reader that it was their complaisance and quixotism that caused the absurd waste, for the action amply demonstrates this, yet the description is warm and lively. The addition of the Groom is a happy stroke, for the bed seems even more ludicrously empty than it would have done had both slept reasonably well and Jerry's experience of the "involuntary titillation" increases the merriment.

It is the involuntary titillation of Jerry by Wildgoose's notions, however, that provides most of the merriment. Jerry bows to his master's judgment and trusts his opinion on most matters, but at the same time he cannot refrain from divulging his own way of looking at things, which is invariably the way of common sense. Any pretensions that the novel may have to being spiritually related to the original *Quixote* are founded on the conversations that take place between the master pilgrim and his squire:

'Gad-zookers!' says [Tugwell], 'these Welsh people are all mad, I think; I never heard such rantipole doings since I was born; a body cannot sleep o'nights for 'em.'

'Ah! Jerry,' replies Wildgoose, 'this is a glorious time! these are the triumphs of Faith! these are the true symptoms of the New Birth! People are never nearer to the Kingdom of Heaven than when they are *mad*, as you call it. . . .'

'But come Jerry,' says he, 'a poor sister is labouring under the pangs of the New Birth, and wants our assistance. We must walk a mile or two before breakfast.'—'Walk a mile or two before breakfast!' says Tugwell; 'why I had no supper last night; and my stomach is so empty, that I can hardly walk at all without my breakfast. If the young woman is in *labour*, she has more need of a midwife than our assistance.' (295)

Sancho himself could not have come up with a more accurate assessment of the true state of events nor could he have elicited more quixotic remarks than Wildgoose's celebration of madness—"[people] have never better reason to hope for Salvation, than when they are ready to hang and drown themselves." Tugwell's speech is lively and in character. He has no use for figurative pregnancies when his stomach is empty. Graves shows Jerry's impatience by having him echo his master's unpleasant idea of a walk in the same paragraph, a device of timing which Graves uses quite often to quicken the pace.

The down-to-earth squires who accompany enthusiastic knights by their very presence cast an oblique light on their masters and yet in accompanying them provide effective images of the cohabitation possible among the seemingly irreconcilable representatives of a ridiculously varied species. Like Sancho, Tugwell has a comic perspective on life and encourages the reader to see the novel's events and characters in the same way. On the one hand, he offers practical comments which clash with Wildgoose's quixotic ones, making them seem even more quixotic than if they stood alone; on the other, he accepts his master's quirks for what they are, even though he does not share them, making his oddities seem not very remarkable in the context of varied human behavior. In the same blunt way as Sir Toby Belch, he reminds us that there is no single correct way to go about living. For cakes and ale he substitutes plum pudding: " 'Odsbodikins!' (cries Tugwell as soon as he could empty his mouth) 'cannot a man have true Faith, that loves plumb-pudding?' " (335).

His practical mind is satisfied easily by apparent realities and apparent relations between things, and because he is so easily satisfied, the realities are as he sees them and the relations exist in the random manner he conceives of them:

'I believe I understand what the gentleman means by the *New Birth.* It is no longer ago than last October, we had been grinding apples, and making cyder, for Madam Wildgoose, your Worship's mother; and all the next day I was mortal sick, and troubled with the gripes and the belly-ach; and I thought I should have *sounded away.* Old Madam gave me some *Higry-pigry;* and our Dorothy, who is the best wife in England, would have had me eat some bacon and eggs; but I could not bear the smell of victuals; and I thought I should have died. But at night, as soon as ever your Worship began to preach in our chimney-corner, I found comfort; and, from that time to this, I have never drunk a drop of cyder, nor been at an ale-house, till we came this journey, nor at any merry-making, nor *sich* like; as your Worship very well knows.' (231–32)

Tugwell's comfort is no less actual and the effects no less real because his deductions are not strictly logical; we see that a case of colic may do in place of a religious trauma if one is willing to think of the one as the other. Though Graves is most concerned here with mocking the absurd foundation of the Methodist conversions, one may fairly say that Tugwell's stomach pains provide him with a perfectly legitimate reason for believing in the effects of faith, which so far as he knows have been conclusively demonstrated.

Tugwell conveys the advantages of an innocent acceptance of what life presents as real and true by enjoying the pilgrimage so heartily. In contrast to Wildgoose, whose mind is distracted by abstractions such as Conscience and Faith, he relishes his experiences on the road and is quick to join in the community whenever he can. Rather than preaching to fulfill a preconceived notion of Duty, Tugwell calls out "Tallio!" in his enthusiasm for the hunt and guzzles strong beer. Whereas Wildgoose can only allow himself to value Miss Townsend's handkerchief as the emblem of a "very good girl," Tugwell comes to the real point: 'Odsbobs! Master,' (says Tugwell) 'you seem to be as fond of the young woman's handkerchief, as I am of plumb-pudding. One would think it was a love-toy; and that it was given you by your sweetheart' " (336). Wildgoose's theoretical approach to the world's delights leads him to topple the statues in Shenstone's gardens, even while admitting the elegance of his host's taste. Here too Tugwell invalidates his master's ideas with reference to actuality:

'Why, Jerry,' (says Wildgoose) 'a person may be guilty of Idolatry by
setting his affections too much upon any thing; . . . it is an act of friendship . . . to wean them from those objects. . . .'
    'Why, to be sure,' (says Tugwell) '. . . if one *man* was at liberty to take
away from another, whatever he had *set his heart* upon, they might take
away one's wife, or one's cow, or one's dog, or one's cat; and then there
would be no living at peace in the world. Now, there is my dog Snap;
I *loves* him almost as well as I do my wife; and, if the best man in
Gloustershire were to steal my dog, I would take *the law on him.*' (332)

By his constant and contagious delight in earthy, simple things—food,
drink, love—Tugwell shows that Providence is best served not by "wean-
ing" other people from the things they love but by an active appreciation
of what it offers. He carries the comic message of his author in every
gulp of beer that he takes for every one of Wildgoose's pious expressions.
    Without Tugwell, *The Spiritual Quixote* would be unthinkable, unless
the Quixote himself were extended in breadth and was able to see himself the way Tugwell sees him, sceptically as well as respectfully. The
author's indulgent attitude towards humanity finds its fullest expression
in the character of the squire, who is both tolerant and begs toleration
from others. It is not enough to trace the spirit by which *The Spiritual
Quixote* transcends its many mediocrities—of form, of character, of
event—to Graves's "artistic liberty, his freedom from professional concern, his irresponsibility to anything but his own impulse to write"[28];
one must also recognize the pervading influence of Graves's comic vision,
which granted him the license to mitigate his satire, gave warmth to his
didacticism, and produced a character so admirably and laughably human
as Tugwell is.
    The comedy that is characteristic of the "new species of writing"
springs from the source of all comedy, the sense of Nature's fitness. The
easiness of the language, the wit of the burlesque, and the moral under-
pinnings of the plots (excluding perhaps *Pompey the Little*'s) convey a
confidence in life's order, as they do in the fantastic works of Aristophanes on the one hand and in the darkly apprehensive, more elegant
comedies of Swift and Pope on the other. How these mid-eighteenth-
century novels differ in particular from the satiric comedies is in their insistence on the contribution of even the most wayward oddballs to this
order. From their author's appreciation of the *discordia concors* found
in nature derives the lighthearted tone, the willingness to entertain man-

kind with evidence of his own folly. Yet, in distinction to the works to be considered next, the entertainment rarely becomes evidence itself of folly—that is, the comic writers maintain a control over themselves and their work that acts as a standard against which the oddities of nature may be set. Thus while they provoke mirth, they do not become Masters of the Revels themselves.

CHAPTER FOUR

SMOLLETT AND STERNE
AND ANIMAL SPIRITS

Animal spirits, not genteel geniality, brought forth the most truly antisplenetic novels in the mid-eighteenth century. It was left to Smollett and Sterne, two gentlemen not nearly as sure as Fielding was of the gentility of their own natures, to encourage readers to purge life's troubles by sporting with them freely and to take heart in their own oddities by owning them joyfully. Perhaps because the comic faith of Smollett and Sterne lay not in a belief in the order and fitness of life's variety but, less morally, in the fitness of delight in the variety, their comedy was not partially offset by decorousness (though the Augustan ideals are still present, more or less ironically, in all their novels).

Peregrine Pickle

Despite the ebullient chaos that marks, in particular, *Peregrine Pickle* and *Tristram Shandy*, these works merit Hazlitt's designation along with *Tom Jones* as those novels which promote the greatest feeling of happiness.[1] Yet an easy heart and careless happiness are not the effects one would expect from reading the energetic and often violent work that *Peregrine Pickle* most decidedly is and that Smollett apparently intended it to be. The activity of the syntax, which has been described as "deployed for surprise, exuberance, extravagance, and shock,"[2] would seem to preclude the relaxed sense of comic well-being that one feels. And yet, comically enough, the great energy, the "expedition" of events, the extremity of language, are precisely what account for the easy heart.

Peregrine himself acts as an emblem of this strange relationship between action and well-being: throughout the novel he is constantly on the move, constantly acting upon wild, often cruel plans and whims, constantly at the height of spirits, except for the period of his jail confinement, a period of utter inactivity (when he loses even the desire to write) and utter dejection. So long as the novel moves, and it does even during Peregrine's brief lapse, our spirits are high and our feeling of life's fullness is at once exciting and reassuring. Sterne in *Tristram Shandy* summarizes the happy effect of activity in answer to Bishop Hall's words in favor of inertia:

—So much motion, continues he, (for he was very corpulent)—is so much unquietness; and so much of rest, by the same analogy, is so much of heaven.

Now I [says Tristram] (being very thin) think differently; and that so much of motion, is so much of life, and so much of joy—and that to stand still, or get on but slowly, is death and the devil—. (493)

The Bishop seems far more likely to suffer from the spleen than Tristram, who is at this point running merrily across France, giving the chase to Death. Dr. Stukeley would agree with Tristram's assessment. In a statement which may well have been the source of Tristram's own, he notes that "it's notorious enough how the hysteric train of ills has gain'd ground, since action in both sexes is difus'd, which with chearfulness is one great method of preventing and curing the vapors. The wheels of life grow rusty without continual motion, death is no other than a cessation of motion."[3] Indeed, the energy and variety of the mid-eighteenth-century novelists are their major weapons against the spleen, and, together with a comic tone which implies that the activity and range of experience are what make life fun and rewarding, account for the reader's joy and ease.

The tone is, of course, at least as important as the energy: Swift is surely even more violent and extravagant than Smollett and is just as surely successful in not promoting a feeling of security and happiness. The elements of adventure and farcical comedy are all present in *Gulliver's Travels* (its unfortunate reputation as a child's story springs from its fantastic, outlandishly imaginative events) but the effects are far from whipped-cream-in-the-face laughter. Fine distinctions must be drawn from the tone between the outrageously funny and outrageously tragic, distinctions upon which the whole of the *Modest Proposal*, for instance, depends. The usual elements of comedy—that is, the unusual exaggeration of certain human characteristics, actions, or language, may with a slight twist in tone or emphasis make the funny seem suddenly very unfunny. Life may seem suddenly "[not] a farce, [but] a ridiculous tragedy, which is the worst kind of composition," as it did to Swift.[4]

But in *Peregrine Pickle* the feeling that life is a farce or at least a mirthful comedy is maintained in spite of the satirical excursions into the realm of ridiculous tragedy. In fact, Smollett caught the spirit of LeSage more truly than he intended, to judge from the Preface to *Roderick Random*, for the same mirth that he believed prevented the reader of *Gil Blas* from feeling "that generous indignation which ought to animate [him] against the sordid and vicious disposition of the world," more often than not in *Peregrine Pickle* works against his own satire. While he has no targets that come close to matching the sordidness and viciousness of the naval conditions described in *Roderick Random*, he does attempt to make some serious observations on the prevailing methods of dealing with debtors. Peregrine's chats with the inmates of the Fleet reveal the severe restrictions of liberty which debtors suffered under the bailiff system. But the prisoners' tales are so entertaining and good-natured that, for all that the bailiffs are made to seem unscrupulous, one cannot help being amused at their enterprising methods and the perseverance of both parties:

"You must know, Mr. Pickle, I was one day called into my chapel, in order to join a couple in the holy bands of matrimony; and my affairs being at that time so situated, as to lay me under apprehensions of an arrest, I cautiously surveyed the man through a lettice which was made for that purpose. ... He was cloathed in a seaman's jacket and troussers, and had such an air of simplicity in his countenance, as divested me of all suspicion. ... and [I] had actually performed one half of the ceremony, when the supposed woman, pulling out a paper from her bosom, exclaimed with a masculine voice, 'Sir, you are my prisoner, I have got a writ against you for five hundred·pounds' " (689).

The somewhat shocking situation of a priest being threatened by imminent arrest in his own church is completely offset by the surprising appearance of the phony woman, who pulls the pertinent papers from her equally phony bosom, at the same time speaking in an authentically male voice. The humiliation suffered by the offenders and the absurdity of imprisonment which makes any rectification impossible are suggested in the various tales, but the acceptance of the experience as just another event in life in the end makes a more lasting impression on the reader than the necessity for reforms.

Indeed, Smollett's acceptance of the world as he finds it, which is reflected in the pace and tone of the narrative, is what makes *Peregrine Pickle* a comic, as opposed to satiric, novel. The acceptance includes even the outrageous behavior of the hero himself, whose satirical streak tends toward the vicious and whose pranks require large allowances from the reader to swallow with equanimity. Yet, because Smollett conveys in his prose his own enjoyment in describing the events of Peregrine's life, the happy and the nasty ones, the reader shares his delight.

The taming of Hawser Trunnion is accomplished with great expedition, and it is by the pace of the narrative that Smollett makes it comical rather than pathetic; in one short paragraph the imposing figure of the Commodore is greatly imposed upon by a mere wife, who happens to be an equally imposing figure:

This unexpected declaration, together with the behaviour of his wife, who in his hearing desired the carpenters to resume their work, filled the breast of Trunnion with rage and mortification. He pulled off his woollen night-cap, pummelled his bare pate, beat the floor alternately with his feet, swore his people had betrayed him, and cursed himself to the lowest pit of hell, for having admitted such a cockatrice into his family. But all these exclamations did not avail; they were among the last essays of his resistance to the will of his wife, whose influence among his adherents had already swallowed up his own; and who now peremptorily told him, that he must leave the management of every thing within doors to her, who understood best what was for his honour and advantage. She then ordered a poultice to be prepared for his eye, which being applied, he was committed to the care of Pipes, by whom he was led about the house like a blind bear growling for prey, while his industrious yoke-fellow executed every circumstance of the plan she had projected; so that, when he recovered his vision, he was an utter stranger in his own house. (46)

What makes the whole scene so comical is the helpless rage of Trunnion, who pulls, pummels, beats, swears, and curses in consecutive clauses and then quietly submits in the space of a sentence with a low growl or two. The bear image is both appropriate and ironic, for his rage is loud and terrible but his submission is mouselike in comparison, especially set against the strength of Mrs. Trunnion's will, which is conveyed in the indirect quotation of her peremptory statement. The rapid succession of active verbs traces the rapid mental process by which Trunnion comes to terms with the turn of events and then, in order to maintain his self-respect, comes to terms with himself and becomes a tractable husband.

The pace of the narrative succeeds too in conveying Hatchway's personal triumph in the face of a ridiculous handicap, one which threatens his legs with inaction when his trunk is already far ahead of its buttresses and his mind already at his destination: "Such was his impatience, that he would not give himself the trouble to disengage the fractured [wooden] member; but unbuckling the whole equipage in a trice, left it sticking in the crevice, saying a rotten cable was not worth heaving up, and, in this natural state of mutilation, hopp'd into the room with infinite expedition" (754–55). The accomplishment of his goal within a single clause impresses us with his buoyancy, which is expressed in his philosophical dispatch of the leg just one clause beforehand.

The extended action that Smollett packs into a single sentence contributes along with the pace to the comic life of the novel; the compressed energy of these incrementally stretched sentences lies in the remarkable variety of motion and gesture that Smollett forces together to form a single event:

Finding the door unlatched, his suspicion was confirmed, and he made no scruple of creeping into the chamber on all-fours; so that the painter having stript himself to the shirt, in groping about for his Dulcinea's bed, chanced to lay his hand upon the shaven crown of the father's head, which by a circular motion, the priest began to turn round in his grasp, like a ball in a socket, to the surprize and consternation of poor Pallet, who having neither penetration to comprehend the case, nor the resolution to withdraw his fingers from this strange object of his touch, stood sweating in the dark, and vented ejaculations with great devotion, till the friar tired with this exercise, and the painful posture in which he stooped, raised himself gradually upon his feet, heaving up at the same time the hand of the painter, whose terror and amazement increased to such a degree at this unaccountable elevation, that his faculties began to fail; and his palm in the confusion of his fright sliding over the priest's forehead, one of his fingers happened to slip between the Capuchin's teeth, with as firm a fixture, as if it had been screwed in a blacksmith's vice. (288–89)

A good deal of the comic effect undoubtedly arises from the mechanical nature of the action, reinforced by the choice of similes, "a ball in a socket" and "screwed in a blacksmith's vice." But this Bergsonian explanation, so simple to apply to so many comic passages, does not fully account for the reader's pleasure, which would not be the same if all these actions were told in separate sentences. The breathless quality of the one sentence, with successive participial clauses suspended from the opening "finding," resembles that of a silent movie with its hurried but not quite connected actions; the exhilaration of following the alternate movements of the painter and the priest with one's eyes or imagination while relating the separate pieces of movement to the whole action constitutes much of the fun. Smollett's appeals to the senses of sight and touch emphasize the comic stealthiness of the two characters and give the scene a tangible liveliness.

"Vigorous" is the word most often used to describe and praise Smollett's style, and from the passages already quoted one can justify the choice. But color and imagery also enrich the narrative, by adding suggestive depth to the "fairly uncomplicated events and unidimensional emotional states" which, in Stevick's estimation, comprise the bulk of the action. Smollett is a far more skilled technician than one would suppose from most of the accounts of his narrative method, and his comedy benefits from his imaginative descriptions. He constantly adjusts images to the surroundings of his novel, adding color without disturbing the intimate tone of a comic history (as Fielding also does so successfully).

Smollett brings the entire sensuous experience of a public fair to bear upon a fight between Peregrine and a country squire by casually suggesting the likeness rather than setting up a formal comparison: "With this view he returned the salute, and raised such a clatter about the squire's pate, that one who had heard without seeing the application, would have mistaken the sound for that of a salt-box, in the hand of a dext'rous Merry Andrew, belonging to one of the booths at Bartholomew Fair" (132). The sight and sound of Bartholomew Fair (even though only the sound evokes the image) give one a sense of the comic wildness of the fight, and the absurdity of the whole event is moreover brought out by the image of Peregrine as the Merry Andrew—his cockiness and nimbleness become that of a clown. Also suitably metamorphosed is Pallet at the remarkable dinner "in the manner of the ancients" when the delicacies cause him to resemble "the leaden statue of some river god, with the liquor flowing out at both sides of his mouth" (237). Here the ironic contrast between the elegance of the occasion and the resulting nausea of the guests is captured in the suggestively flowing "liquor."

Smollett conveys the entertainment and excitement of the world's events not only in the pace and color of his language but also in the pulses of the characters he created. Only one who was sensitive to the endless range of humanity could make such a thoroughly dull character as Gam Pickle seem not only likeable, but rather interesting. All that is wrong with him and at the same time all that is right is expressed in his courting message to the future Mrs. Pickle:

Madam,
    Understanding you have a parcel of heart, warranted sound, to be disposed of, shall be willing to treat for said commodity, on reasonable terms; doubt not, shall agree for same; shall wait of you for further information, when and where you shall appoint. This the needful from
                                                             Yours, &c. (14)

The efficiency with which Gam is inclined to dispatch his love affair is highly amusing, though we may have some doubts about his terminology. Yet, Gam's "parcel of heart, warranted sound," however much it neatly packages the young lady—who turns out to be most unpackable—into a "commodity," is not without its note of friendliness and desire: it is, after all, her heart he is bargaining for, and he puts the matter to her with all due respect. One has only to turn to the *Modest Proposal* to note the difference between this rather kindly manner and a truly sinister way of disposing of women: "It is true a Child, *just dropt from its Dam,* may be supported by her Milk, for a Solar year. . . ." Rather than perversion, Gam's style reflects his solid mercantile mind; if it suggests too that he will always act according to his head's dictates rather than his heart's, such a quality was not considered undesirable in an eighteenth-century husband.

The comical humanity of all of Smollett's characters is conveyed in their own words, spoken and written. Through their speech, Smollett gives his many varied representatives of the human race both breath and breadth. Thus, Cadwallader Crabtree (an earlier version of Matt Bramble) speaks like a misanthrope and yet reveals a humanizing vulnerability to insult (Peregrine's) in his sputtering fury: " 'Sblood! why didn't nature clap a pair of long ears and a tail upon me, that I might be a real ass, and champ thistles on some common, independent of my fellow-creatures? Would I were a worm, that I might creep into the earth" (628). The vivid self-portrait, expressing his shame as much as his misanthropy, evokes sympathetic mirth from the reader. Similarly, Emilia, the model of perfection, speaks like a modest young lady and yet shows, to the reader's delight, that she is flesh and blood too:

'Heigh ho! who would imagine that a sprightly girl, such as I, with ten thousand pounds, should go a begging? I have a good mind to marry the next person that asks me the question, in order to be revenged upon this unyielding humourist. Did the dear fellow discover no inclination to see me, in all the term of his releasement? Well, if ever I can catch the figitive again, he shall sing in his cage for life.' (773)

Smollett did not have Congreve's genius for women's speech but Emilia's suitability for Peregrine and her capability to be his wife are demonstrated on a few such occasions when the author allows his heroine to emerge from her cardboard pattern.

Smollett's nautical characters are always selected for praise, as well they should be: Tom Bowling (of *Roderick Random*) is naive, blunt, sensible, and generous; Hatchway is all these things and perhaps slightly more good-humored besides; Pipes has his loyalty and simple goodness to distinguish him. Smollett's special talent for translating these universal qualities into the peculiar expression of seamen allows these men to demonstrate their uniqueness at the same time as they reveal their humanity. If the nautical language is comically unusual, even absurd, Smollett makes it also completely natural and acceptable in the mouths of his seamen, especially in the most fully developed and comical of these characters, Commodore Trunnion. The Commodore's self-respect, which came to his rescue upon his marriage to Mrs. Grizzle, and his natural good-humor, which withstood the various stresses that this marriage placed upon it, combine to overcome the reader's inclination to mock such an outlandish creature. That Trunnion's famous dying speech has often been considered worthy of Falstaff is because, like Falstaff, he does not sacrifice his character when he is defeated (by death if not by a king). Trunnion's final monologue, bordering always on the absurdly pathetic, maintains itself in the realm of the comically heroic:

'Swab the spray from your bowsprit, my good lad, and coil up your spirits. You must not let the top-lifts of your heart give way, because you see me ready to go down at these years; many a better man has foundered before he has made half my way. . . . Here has been a doctor that wanted to stow me chock-full of physic; but, when a man's hour is come, what signifies his taking his departure with a 'pothecary's shop in his hold? Those fellows come along side of dying men, like the messengers of the admiralty with sailing orders; but, I told him as how I could slip my cable without his direction or assistance, and so he hauled off in dudgeon.'   (392)

The sensibility of his ideas far outweighs the extravagance of his vocabulary, while it is this very choice of words that gives his speech its characteristic integrity. These are not pious platitudes, but the genuine expressions of a proud man who has come to terms with death as he had with all the other events of his life. Indeed, this end confirms the absence of pettiness, small-mindedness, and "extravagance of breath" that are evident in his first words, " 'Here, you Tunley, there's the hand of a seaman, you dog.' " With the skill of a playwright, Smollett turns his minor caricatures into unique human beings and serves the comedy of his novel well by encouraging delight in their differences rather than mockery at their obvious peculiarities.

Although everyone agrees that Peregrine is essentially unpleasant, few readers would find it possible not to like him, faults and all. One wonders if the rights and privileges of being a hero carry with them the guarantee of being favored, or if there is something in Smollett's particular characterization that redeems his rascality. Just how much the vitality of a character can affect our attitude towards him is evident in the excuses we are willing to make for the wicked Count Fathom's outrageous behavior. Smollett's clearly satirical intentions with regard to his outlaw hero, as set out in the Dedication, are entirely subverted by his lively descriptions of Fathom's rogueries. Morally we cannot abide the character, but until Smollett abruptly transfers our attention to Renaldo, who is truly worthy of our affections (and slightly dull as a result), we are happy to accompany the unworthy hero on his escapades and share the excitement with him. In the same way, Peregrine surely benefits from the vivacity Smollett attributes to him and from the general pace and activity of his history as well.

The role that he has to play as Emilia's lover, contradictory though it may be, serves to keep us on his side while he goes about his satirical business as well as the business of growing up. Our sympathetic feeling may also arise from the fact that, as Ronald Paulson notes in a different context, "every time Peregrine punishes a person, however unjust his motive, his satiric analysis of that person is true."[5] This peculiar combination of hero and antihero, high-mindedness and meanness, angel and devil, is precisely what allows Peregrine to contribute as much as he does to the comedy of the book: he is both laugher and the laughed at, and is missing only the ability to laugh at himself to be the perfect comic hero, as Gulley Jimson is, or indeed, Tristram.

Peregrine's immense capacity for experience serves him well in his self-appointed position as society satirist. He lives up to all the implications of his full name, those of outlandishness, mischievousness, and the especially suitable nautical meaning of "pickle," to rub salt (maliciously) on wounds incurred from flogging. Peregrine, of course, does both the flogging and the rubbing, and enjoys every minute of his victim's punishment. Because, as it has been stated, the ones who are punished usually deserve the rough treatment they receive, and because Smollett describes that treatment with his customary gusto, the reader cannot help enjoying the violence and admiring the evil genius behind it. In this adventure designed to humiliate "grave characters," a group of political enthusiasts, Peregrine's satirical appetite is gratified and the reader's pleasure is no less than his:

They had already broke their glasses in consequence of his suggestion, drank healths out of their shoes, caps and the bottoms of the candlesticks that stood before them, sometimes standing with one foot on a chair, and the knee bent on the edge of the table; and when they could no longer stand in that posture, setting their bare posteriors on the cold floor, they huzza'd, hollowed, danced and sung, and in short were elevated to such a pitch of intoxication, that when Peregrine proposed that they should burn their perriwigs, the hint was immediately approved and they executed the frolick as one man; their shoes and caps underwent the same fate by the same instigation, and in this trim he led them forth into the street, where they resolved to compel every body they should find to subscribe to their political creed, and pronounce the Shibboleth of their party. (115)

Peregrine's part in leading this revel through the street shows the subtlety with which he fits the punishment to the crime: their enthusiasm is exposed as mere intoxicated hysteria and shown to be aroused by any idea that catches their momentary fancy—a political creed or periwig burning. Smollett's use of the incremental sentence and catalogue of verbs again reinforces the frantic quality of the action and makes the increasing pitch of their intoxication seem increasingly ridiculous.

Peregrine himself, however, is not immune from hysterical enthusiasm or histrionic gravity. Smollett has his laugh at him as Peregrine the Despairing Lover (who despairs for Emilia after he has failed to rape her). In a wild goose-chase undertaken in pursuit of the fleeing lady, Peregrine discovers that his object is not Emilia, but some other poor gentlewoman in flight, who believes she is being followed by her father. His reaction to discovering that he has diverged considerably from his intended path is in the best ludicrously melodramatic style: "His eyes rolled about, witnessing range and distraction; he foamed at the mouth, stamped upon the ground with great violence, uttered incoherent imprecations against himself and all mankind, and would have sallied forth again he knew not whither" (417). His expression upon seeing the unknown lady is equally exaggerated and comical: "The Gorgon's head, according to the fables of antiquity, never had a more instantaneous or petrifying effect, than that which this countenance produced upon the astonished youth. His eyes were fixed upon this unknown object, as if they had been attracted by the power of inchantment, his feet seemed rivetted to the ground" (419). When Emilia had rebuffed him for attempting to rape her, he "raved like a Bedlamite." Smollett's stylized use of similes and formal constructions ("he knew not whither," "that which this countenance produced") precludes our taking seriously any of Peregrine's distress: we are disposed to look upon him as a clown, acting out various classic poses of stupefaction, madness, frenzy, those poses of heightened emotion that undermine the feeling while exaggerating the manifestation of it.

Peregrine's excessive pride is also put through Smollett's stylistic centrifuge and separated into its harmless but laughable elements of youthful overreaction and spirited self-defense. In a letter to his uncle, Peregrine's diction is so much more formal than the diction of all but the most haughty nobleman that it is preposterous when addressed to anyone but such a person; to his uncle Trunnion it is so patently absurd as to destroy the effect he had obviously intended it to have:

Sir,
    Tho' my temper could never stoop to offer, nor, I believe, your disposition deign to receive that gross incense which the illiberal only expect, and none but the base-minded condescend to pay; my sentiments have always done justice to your generosity, and my intention scrupulously adhered to the dictates of my duty. Conscious of this integrity of heart, I cannot but severely feel your lady's unkind (I will not call it ungenerous) recapitulation. . . (136)

We might well have been shocked by the disrespect of Peregrine's sentiments or thrown up our arms in disgust, if Smollett had not created the letter along with its own automatic warning device, advising the reader to attend to the absurdity more than the contents. Peregrine, at this point, is only a school boy and nowhere more plainly shows himself to be one, especially in contrast to his uncle, who replies in characteristic fashion, "Heark ye, child, You need not bring your fine speeches to bear upon me. You only expend your ammunition to no purpose" (136). Peregrine's weakness as a nephew and a lover as opposed to his success as a satirist offsets much of the force of his satirical jibes and makes him more a character than simply a satiric spokesman. While David Evans is right to point out that Peregrine's appeal is not that "of a complex personality whose moral development we follow," he does not sufficiently recognize the fun Smollett has with his character's shortcomings. To say that Peregrine "spends his career observing human nature with a detached view and growing in the arts of exposing and exploiting the human race"[6] is to underestimate the extent to which his relationships with other characters prevent him from seeming as detached as he perhaps sees himself.
    Pipes, for example, is one of Smollett's agents in the humanization of his hero. Peregrine's aloof pride seems hardest to take when it is directed against the faithful Pipes, who is his misjudged and mistreated companion and servant. On each occasion, though, Pipes himself steps in and saves the comedy, saves us from dismissing the imperious Peregrine from our affections. Either with his particular brand of sea-talk or a piece of drastic action, such as throwing his life's savings into the fire, Pipes rescues the tone of the incident by forcing Peregrine's pride to turn to sudden mortification and remorse when faced with Pipes's greater pride.

Smollett ensures the comicality of the money incident by turning it into an epic mockery of both proud characters, but especially Peregrine: "Nor was the proud heart of Pickle unmoved upon this occasion" (684).

The elevations and deflations that we distinguish in the hero's character, and the ups and downs that he feels himself, are not surprising in the comic context of the novel. Were *Peregrine Pickle* to have been a tragedy, Smollett would probably have let his petty hero fall once, with a thud, or he might have prepared him first with a minor shock to his vanity. As it is, he chooses instead to send him down comedy's bumpy road, and forces him to encounter the many little traps on the obstacle course that comedy loves to set up for all human heroes. The energy with which Peregrine is made to reel down the awkward course of his youth, and the nature of the obstacles—their relation to the larger landscape of life, their variety, the range of reactions they induce—determine the spirit of the comedy. The more energetic, the more outlandish the obstacles, the greater the resulting mirth and the reader's "heart's ease."

The sheer abundance of incidents that occur within the broader events of Peregrine's childhood, schooling, travels, fashionable internship, and disgrace, including as well the extraneous matter that is introduced for Peregrine's diversion (such as the notorious Memoirs and the Annesley trial case), contributes to the comic atmosphere—"so much of motion is so much of life." Critics are very quick to criticize the rambling "diffused" unstructured quality of Smollett's novel, though Rufus Putney's article has undoubtedly forestalled much comment by revealing an underlying "plan," the plan of Peregrine's development from a petty to a worthy hero, and by demonstrating the extent to which Smollett had control over the diffusiveness.[7] What Putney does not discuss is the positive contribution to the comedy that Smollett's rambling narration makes, his casual attitude towards mixing the momentous with the frivolous, the extraordinary with the everyday. That Trunnion dies heroically in the same work as the transformed nymph makes her unexpected and unconventional gesture (generally assumed to be the model for Eliza's Ascot blunder) is comic; Peregrine's attempt to rape Emilia is comic only because it is described with no more or less attention than are Peregrine's various pranks on his schoolmasters, friends, enemies, and relations.

In the world of comedy, brushing one's teeth may have as much significance as consummating one's marriage—though writers admittedly favor the latter—for what counts is whatever happens to strike one at the moment as an event, not what one knows in the perspective of time to have been an event worthy of mention. The activity that is constantly occurring taken collectively is what comprises most of all events, though the separate parts may be slighted in preference to the momentousness of the whole in our later recollections. Comedy does not belittle these little parts that are usually lumped into "youth" or "marriage," "failure" or "success." Rather, it is often at its most perceptive when examining the would-be trivialities, the irrelevant dregs that noncomic art must filter out for the sake of the form and focus of the whole. Thus, to the immense benefit of comedy, many of Peregrine's adventures are relevant to nothing at all, except life in general. Peregrine gobbles the episodes that Smollett creates for him, dutifully turning them into exemplary and comic bits of life.

One could easily excise the whole sequence of events concerning the Capuchin and his fair charge, and the tangential affair between the lady of pleasure and the Hebrew gallant. Peregrine's character with respect to women is quite clear from his behavior to Mrs. Hornbeck, and the existence of such characters as the Capuchin is too well known to be effective material for satire. What one would lose by extracting it therefore is some delightful farce and the introduction of some assorted humorous characters in the Diligence who broaden the panorama of the novel's view of life still further.

A thumb-nail sketch, quickly whisked before our eyes for no special reason, often adds to the comedy by suggesting secondary scenes, panels that are not strictly necessary to the finished panorama, but which add to our appreciation of the whole. Such is the effect of a little paragraph describing the reactions of Trunnion's former mates to the guns announcing Peregrine's return to the garrison:

The landlord observed, that in all likelihood the commodore was visited by hobgoblins, and ordered the guns to be fired in token of distress, as he had acted twenty years before, when he was annoyed by the same grievance. The exciseman, with a waggish sneer, expressed his apprehension of Trunnion's death, in consequence of which, the patereroes might be discharged with an equivocal intent, either as signals of his lady's sorrow or rejoicing. The attorney signified a suspicion of Hatchway's being married to Miss Pickle . . . upon which Gamaliel discovered some faint signs of emotion, and taking the pipe from his mouth, gave it as his opinion, that his sister was brought to bed. (356)

One cannot help recalling Sterne's fully painted portrait (written ten years later) of the Shandy household staff caught in the act of digesting the news of Bobby's death. Here, too, though on a modest scale, the commentary offered by each character tells more about the particular character than about the incident in question. Indeed, Gam's pricelessly inaccurate opinion is worthy of Uncle Toby himself, as is his careful attention to his pipe. One could surely do without such miniatures in the novel, but their addition is more than decorative. Collectively they provide a background that is both faithful to the life and the comedy of the work, against which the more extravagant happenings, such as the Bacchanalian party at the Garrison, may be shown with significance.

To extend the background of the novel and its significance from a family history to a study of society is surely the only justification for the rudely long intrusion of Lady Vane's memoirs. Smollett must have known that, although it would add nothing to his particular story of Peregrine Pickle and his Pride, it would add its own racy vitality to his account of life's types, follies, occurrences—that is, of comedy's supporting role in life. The Lady of Quality's naughty adventures are singularly suited to the tone of Smollett's story, and the style, though decidedly not Smollett's, has its own energetic virtues. (It is quite possible and even likely that Smollett was responsible for polishing and tightening the insertion.) The tale of Lady Vane's transcontinental flight from her impotent husband is a lively, if not economical way for Smollett to suggest that real life is just as full of outlandish events as fictional histories make it seem. He himself must have been as fascinated by the character of the bold and strong-willed lady as Peregrine was, enough perhaps to have suggested its inclusion in one of his novels. Whatever the actual circumstances, this long digression is no more out of place than many of the other equally dispensable, equally lively episodes: it exposes another bit of life, and has the additional virtue of being within the realm of actuality, rather than merely possibility.

Verisimilitude counts for a great deal in a comic novel, for no matter how outrageous a farce is, to be funny it must still consist of possible extensions from real life. What is wanting in the probability of the matter must be supplied by the ease of the manner in which it is passed off as genuine. Smollett's great genius lies in his ability to make the outrageous seem ordinary, in the easy glibness with which he describes a "Feast in the Manner of the Ancients" or a meeting of the College of Authors.

Fielding too has the same facility for describing mad scrambles, the grand battle at the inn of Upton being a classic example. Like Smollett, he invites his readers to relish the absurdity of the doings and to admire the craft with which he murders reality, yet at the same time to bear in mind the likeness to human beings that his characters show and the relation their actions have to real life. When lesser authors take the liberty of farce, their self-consciousness usually betrays them into dullness, which in turn destroys the comic fabric of life that farce is dedicated to revealing for our appreciation and delight.

The bustling activity in expansive novels such as *Peregrine Pickle* often promotes comedy by its very bustle. In a work of sustained satire, the focus must be relentlessly on the object of derision, whereas in a work full of incidental satire, the consequent diffusiveness lessens the thrust of each attack, leaving the reader with the sense of a series of affectionate pokes. Moreover, in *Peregrine Pickle,* by linking the innumerable types of the world in the same volume, so innumerable as to render typecasting ridiculous, and by placing an alert young man whose appetite for new experience is endless in the middle of them, and even more by creating a hero as foolish and weak as his own victims with yet his particular share of redeeming characteristics, Smollett advances the comic principle of universal acceptance. The mirth aroused equally at the expense of Peregrine and all the odd characters who come into his life serves to recommend a wide-mindedness, an approach to life that is unhampered by the prejudices and self-righteousness that combine to induce a chronic disturbance of the spleen.

Smollett's followers, often in spite of themselves, enriched the comedy of their period simply by catching the fascination with "low-life" and the world's variety from their master. J.M.S. Tompkins sees the virtue in their choice of subject matter and its range, and expresses it admirably:

The authors shared Smollett's journalistic and experimenting temper . . . and stuffed out their disconnected narratives with the most multifarious materials, real or fictitious. They are often exceedingly coarse in a good-humoured, heavy-handed way, and they are full of lively touches, of real things seen and heard, dresses and street-cries and smoking puddings and the talk of the servants' hall. They are muddy enough, but the mud is more fertile than the etherealized substance of the sentimental novel, and it is the merit of these books that they are, in the full sense of the word, vulgar, that they nourished the democratic, realistic and humorous elements in the basement of English fiction, while the majority of respectable novelists were taking tea with the ladies in the drawing-room above.[8]

Such praise may be applied to Smollett himself, although he is one of the "respectable" novelists. All the energy and the sense of life that is contained in the vast expanse of *Peregrine Pickle*—indeed, all the mud—accounts for the antisplenetic effect it has upon readers. Peregrine's nastiness, the incidents of violence and satire, rather than offsetting the happiness that is generated, are subsumed into the comic atmosphere through the medium of Smollett's spirited style and story, and are exhibited in their most presentable guise. It is not, as Robert Spector would have it, that "the satiric intention of the novel justifies Smollett's methods of characterization and accounts for the coarseness, vulgarity and violence of his world"[9]; rather, it is the very coarseness, vulgarity, and violence as encountered by Smollett's capable hero that counterbalances the implied criticism of life with mirthfulness. Smollett does not try to hide the Peregrines, Capuchins, or Hornbecks of the world, he mocks them, enjoys them, and does everything to make their company acceptable. Our delight is ample testimony to their acceptability and to the acceptability of all that is at once shocking, wondrous, pitiful, and absurd in life, of all that would nourish the spleen if we did not maintain a careful vigilance against it with the indispensable help of laughter.

Tristram Shandy

The tenacious resistance of *The Life and Opinions of Tristram Shandy, Gent.*, to the stroke of Posterity's hatchet-man, Oblivion, is striking testimony to the special strength and resilience of this great comic work. Ever since Johnson made his famous pronouncement on its fate, "Nothing odd will do long. *Tristram Shandy* did not last," distrust and amazement have been voiced by critics who begrudge the presence of Sterne's work alongside the other great productions of the eighteenth century. Praise for the many handles that Sterne so obligingly offered the critics "to suit their passions, their ignorance or sensibility"—the satire, the sentiment, the wit—is tempered with astonishing frequency by a suggestion that the walking stick itself is rather slight, a frail object incapable of supporting the wonderful variety of shapes and styles that it has apparently been de-

119

signed to do. That is, the comedy that informs the whole work has been
duly recognized and noted in passing, and Sterne has been given credit as
a humorist, but the comedy has rarely been appreciated as the source of
its endurance and special character.

Until recently, much of *Tristram Shandy*'s uniqueness, and Sterne's
comic freedom, has been mistaken for mere eccentricity and accordingly
judged as trivial. The value of everything that Sterne found "Laugh-at-
able" in his own way has been found wanting in exact proportion to the
heartiness of Sterne's laugh. Even Ernest Dilworth, in attempting to
counter Sterne's reputation as an eminent sentimentalist, comes to the
unfortunate conclusion that he is a great, if typically shallow, jester:
"It was part of the genius and limitation of Sterne that he saw best what
was within a few feet of his nose; if he knew no dimensions in depth, he
was master of the subtleties of the façade; his only interior was a hearthside one, and the firelight made a merry place, miles from the dark corners of the room. . . . The difference between Sterne and other shallow men
is that he made comic art of what is called a disability."[10] If Mr. Dilworth
did not aspire to being somewhat of a jester himself, one could only gasp
incredulously at his final distinction. A comic genius simply may not,
like the Tale Teller's "wise" man, be content with the "films and images
that fly off one's senses from the superficies of things," one cannot be
Swift's gullible fool and be alive to the irony of man's inherent absurdity
and nobility, as the great jester is. Dilworth did not appreciate Sterne's
comedy any more than did his predecessors.

The more recent critical trend, however, has been to disparage comedy
that is not rooted in a satirical criticism of life. Thus, admirers of Sterne's
novel have been defending his reputation with evidence of his corrective
intentions and corrosive wit. John Stedmond was among the first to put
forward the suggestion that Tristram's Life and Opinions might be a satiric appeal to the audience for discrimination and taste, similar to Swift's
Tale. In such an assessment, the comic appeal for tolerance and amusement of Tristram's self-made mess is apparently judged to have insufficient
significance. In a later work, however, Stedmond indicates his disapproval
of "apologists for comic works [who] often cite their satiric elements,
their 'thoughtful' laughter."[11] Yet the critical attitude that colored Stedmond's early views is no less in evidence today. A powerful temptation
to see *Tristram Shandy* as a satire of the same order and potency as *Tale
of a Tub* has led Melvyn New to misunderstand the essential comedy of

the work, to reject Sterne's humorously oriented intellect. He sees *Tristram* as Sterne's attack "against human pride, which creates out of its own barrenness magnificient edifices to its own passions and follies and complex systems bearing no relationship to reason and reality." [12] By not allowing himself to feel the force of Sterne's delight in man's passions, follies, and systems, which are some of the ways open to man to fight against the natural shocks of life, New fails to see that Sterne's portrayal of the Shandy family is not at all bitter or corrective in intent. While mocking the hopeless attempts, either through reason or sentiment, to triumph over illness, impotence, death, and all the other hazards of life, Sterne is also positively admiring the perseverance of mankind in the face of all-too-certain failure. It is this admiration that New fails to set against his interpretation of Sterne's mockery. In *Tristram Shandy*, Sterne looks at the world critically and yet tenderly, and while making the nature of life's perplexities painfully clear, he is, above all, concerned with endorsing man's struggle with those perplexities: therein lies the richness of the comedy and the novel.

The strange mixture of satire and admiration that gives rise to comedy in *Tristram Shandy* is imaged in the character of Yorick, whose own outlook is partly satirical, partly sentimental, and who is described by Tristram with an indulgence that is both ironic and loving. In this attempt to describe him, Tristram repeats the self-mocking words of Yorick with affection:

At different times he would give fifty humourous and opposite reasons for riding a meek-spirited jade of a broken-winded horse, preferably to one of mettle; . . . in all other exercitations, he could spend his time, as he rode along slowly,—to as much account as in his study;—that he could draw up an argument in his sermon,—or a hole in his breeches, as steadily on the one as in the other;—that brisk trotting and slow argumentation, like wit and judgment, were two incompatible movements.—But that upon his steed,—he could unite and reconcile every thing,—he could compose his sermon,—he could compose his cough,—and in case nature gave a call that way, he could likewise compose himself to sleep.   (20)

Yorick's lighthearted yoking of the hole in his breeches with the argument in his sermon, or the composition of his sermon with the composure of his cough serves as verification of Tristram's earlier observation that the parson "loved a jest in his heart—and as he saw himself in the true point of ridicule, he would say, he could not be angry with others for seeing him in a light, in which he so strongly saw himself" (19). We are made to feel very kindly towards this country parson, and yet to see him as a ludicrous figure. Knowing that Yorick is meant to embody Sterne's account of himself, and that Tristram acts simply as Sterne's puppet in publishing the characterization, increases our sense of the self-mockery and self-adulation in Sterne's joke on himself. Also evident is Sterne's ability to see himself with the same comic eye out of which he sees the rest of the world and, in turn, his ability to regard the world with the same tenderness as he regards himself. His image of himself is the image he has of man in general; like Eliot's Prufrock, his Yorick is both an ironic self-portrait and a more universal composite of a pitiful, comic, helplessly self-conscious human being, whose irony is his greatest charm.

Sterne's Yorick is at all times the Fool, and was purposely and aptly named for him. As a Fool, both laughable and lovable, he lets himself get involved in such hopeless situations as the one concerning his horse. Yorick loved a fine horse; his neighbors loved riding his horse; Yorick loved his neighbors and therefore hardly ever rode his own horse, "the upshot of which was generally this, that his horse was either clapp'd, or spavin'd, or greaz'd;—or he was twitter bon'd, or broken-winded, or something, in short, or other had befallen him which would let him carry no flesh;—so that he had every nine or ten months a bad horse to get rid of, —and a good horse to purchase in his stead" (21). Yorick's solution to this problem is none other than the comic solution to life as a whole; rather than worrying about a new horse all the time, or fretting about the worsening condition of the old, he was "content to ride the last poor devil, such as they had made him, with all his aches and infirmities, to the very end of the chapter" (21). If things are so bad that they cannot get worse, one may as well laugh at them and enjoy them. That Tristram confirms the value of this philosophy is apparent not only in his approval of Yorick's behavior, but in the very act of writing his own history, which is at once a hopeless task and very entertaining. Moreover, we may deduce that Sterne concurs with these views from our own affection for the two characters, an affection which is grounded equally in derision and delight.

Yorick's death scene is one of the most complex entanglements of jest and earnest, satire and sentiment, mockery and sympathy in the book. On the one hand, Yorick dies, and is a stark reminder of the moral borne by his namesake, that of inevitable mutability: "Where be your gibes now, your gambols, your songs, your flashes of merriment, that were wont to set the table on a roar." On the other, Sterne makes us do what Hamlet knows the Queen is unable to do, "Laugh at that."[13] Grief multiplied to proportions far more grand than its cause, as Sterne shows figuratively in the countless plaintive voices reciting "Alas, poor Yorick," is comic; the overwhelming blackness of the page inserted as a symbol for death, a giant sob caught within the pages of a book, is by its tangible presence comic as well. It is as if a clown walks across the stage at this moment with a placard that reads, "Weep." That the death is Yorick's, and that Yorick is a representation of Sterne, and that the page thus represents self-pity for an event which has not happened—as if the clown were mourning his own death as he walked across—is comically ironic: here is grief without any cause at all, the grief at one's own eventual death that is most comically and pitifully felt by all human beings.

Sterne's humor and eccentricity are deliberate and carry within their deliberateness a perception of the world which gives *Tristram Shandy* its meaning. The implications of this consciously comic vision have only rarely been considered, first by Nietzsche and more recently by critics who have begun to explore the nature of Sterne's comicality.[14] Nietzsche expanded Goethe's praise of Sterne's liberating effects in a paragraph subtitled, "The Freest Writer," and paid tribute to his remarkable nobility of spirit, his ability to "be right and wrong at the same time, to interweave profundity and farce":

May he be satisfied with the honour of being called the freest writer of all times, in comparison with whom all others appear still, square-toed, intolerant and downright boorish! . . . He was—if language does not revolt from such a combination—of a hard-hearted kindness, and in the midst of the joys of a grotesque and even corrupt imagination he showed the bashful grace of innocence. Such a carnal and spiritual hermaphroditism, such untrammelled wit penetrating into every vein and muscle, was perhaps never possessed by any other man.[15]

Nietzsche's extravagance is matched only by Sterne's own, and his language is only fitting to describe an author who playfully writes "SPLEEN" after mentioning the word "gay" in order "to keep up a good understanding amongst words . . . not knowing how near [one] may be under a necessity of placing them to each other" (502).

Fluchère considers the importance of accident in Sterne's style and explains his casual freedom in terms of his sense of the unfettered nature of the world: "The incoherent, the rhapsodic, the baroque—everything that is included in the word eccentricity and all that in traditional criticism calls forth the word disorder, arises in Sterne . . . from the recognition of the fact that the world is an immense field of experience, and man a being curiously determined by countless contingencies each of which exists in a very personal relation to him."[16] The structure of the book Fluchère traces to Sterne's desire "to translate the processes of the mind, operating on a given human situation, into a verbal representation that will completely render both its substance and its potentialities."[17]

These intricate and incomprehensible processes also account for much of the comedy of the work. The wit that is a by-product of the mind's strange activities joins forces with the pathos that arises from our sense of the helplessness of the mind to control its own process, its inability to make sense of the world with the material provided, and produces comedy: the wit and the pathos help us to accept and appreciate the puzzles that continually trouble the intellect by making the effort seem worthwhile in itself and the accomplishment, however incomplete in the face of the facts, splendid in the face of the obstacles. Sterne makes us see that the eccentric is really the normal, or as B.L. Reid incisively observes: "*Tristram Shandy* is the absurd made comically programmatic. The formalizing of the artifice conduces both to comedy and to philosophical statement. By so intricately manipulating the anarchy of experience, Sterne asserts a tyrannizing control that at once renders the absurd laughable and declares it representative, philosophically normative."[18] To bring alive his own comic vision of the real world, to show that the absurd is the normal—both comically and pathetically so—and to dramatize the need for tolerance and courage and lightheartedness in dealing with such absurdity, Sterne created the world of Tristram Shandy, a world in which evidence of grotesque incompatibility—of people with other people, of people with the world—is everywhere.

The curious inclusiveness of this world, which is really quite exclusive—consisting of a very limited number of characters who meet in an even more limited number of places—may be traced to the haphazard occurrence of events and thoughts which give, as Smollett required, a "large, diffus'd picture of life." Whereas writers of the "new species" usually designated certain events and then looked at the portion of life attached to those events, Sterne chose rather to designate Shandy Hall and look at the portion attached to that small enclosure, which becomes a microcosm in the process, not a microcosm of people but of life, with all its illogical, unexpected events and contingencies.

The comedy one senses in a world where the unexpected is the everyday occurrence is intertwined with a sense of tragedy as well, as both Reid and Rufus Putney have perceptively discussed.[19] There is a fatality in the absurdity that is inescapable and frightening, a fatality which is responsible for crushed noses, dissolved arguments, irrelevant digressions, and other misfortunes which are for the most part comic to the outsider and tragic to the human being involved. Sterne intimates the presence of terrors that lurk in the backgrounds of destiny, waiting to ambush us, but he does so not to frighten but to prepare and protect: the preparation and protection he offers is comedy, a comic vision strong enough not to ward off impending evils but to allow one to live with them when they turn up. Thus, the deliberate eccentricity, the deliberately anarchic view of a world in which individuals must manage, each in their own way, to overcome private adversities. Laurence Sterne offered the world his comic work avowedly in the hope that he could arm his readers with his own consciousness of the need for laughter: "I humbly beg, Sir [he wrote in his Dedication to Pitt] that you will honour this book by taking it . . . into the country with you; where, if I am ever told, it has made you smile, or can conceive it has beguiled you of one moment's pain—I shall think myself as happy as a minister of state" (3).

It would seem that Sterne "paints his face" and puts on "his ruff and motley clothes" to higher purpose than Thackeray was able to comprehend; beguilement is the business of the jester and underlying his display of merriment is the need for such beguilement and the need for the display to end in laughter. Sterne shows his genius in being able to plead the necessity and carry off the jest at the same time:

But mark, madam, we live amongst riddles and mysteries—the most obvious things, which come in our way, have dark sides, which the quickest sight cannot penetrate into; and even the clearest and most exalted understandings amongst us find ourselves puzzled and at a loss in almost every cranny of nature's work; so that this, like a thousand other things, falls out for us in a way, which tho' we cannot reason upon it,—yet we find the good of it, may it please your reverences and your worships—and that's enough for us. (293)

Tristram's deference to "madam" and his formal address to the various dignitaries give this passage an ironic tone that leads one to assume at first that he means not one jot of what he says. Yet if one bears Tristram's history in mind, and remembers specifically that Tristram, not Sterne, is speaking, the source of the irony becomes clear; it is not that Tristram is saying a thing which is not, it is rather that he is acutely aware of the truth of his assertion—that life is an insoluble puzzle—having had so much occasion to escape from the riddles and mysteries of life; it is irony directed at himself for being in such an unfortunately excellent position to offer his opinion. We are not meant to reject Tristram's observations, but rather to see how ludicrously true they are, how pitiable a thing man would be if he did not escape our pity by the wonderfully irrational contrivance of finding the "good of it." The irony does not detract from the real cheerfulness with which Tristram notes that Nature, the "dear Goddess," provides us with the necessary impulses and gestures to overcome provoking shocks.

Sterne, too, in real life called upon irrational spirits to make his escape. In the later volumes of *Tristram Shandy* we may consider Sterne himself to be speaking when Tristram describes his encounters with Death:

Now as for my spirits... I have much—much to thank 'em for: cheerily have ye made me tread the path of life with all the burdens of it (except its cares) upon my back; in no one moment of my existence, that I remember, have ye once deserted me, or tinged the objects which came in my way, either with sable, or with a sickly green; in dangers ye gilded my horizon with hope, and when DEATH himself knocked at my door— ye bad him come again; and in so gay a tone of careless indifference, did ye do it, that he doubted of his commission—
"—There must certainly be some mistake in this matter," quoth he.
(479)

This description is such a thinly disguised account of Sterne's own struggles to stay alive that one feels the pathos of it acutely. But Sterne's "careless indifference" or rather his determination to be carelessly indifferent does not allow us to pity him; we may admire his courage and laugh at his self-characterization, but we must recognize fully that he is alive to make fun and therefore not deserving of pity.

That Sterne places life over death, the present over the past, comes out especially in the supposedly sentimental passages, especially LeFever's death scene. Over the years he has infuriated readers with his inability to refrain from the last spoiling word (if one sees him as a helplessly shallow jester) or disturbed them with his demand that they not give in to the comfortable pathos he has aroused (if one sees him as a writer with a comic purpose). Sterne does not "go on," in reply to his own question, but chooses to start another chapter both for the stated reason that he is "impatient to return to [his] own story" (426), and for the more important reason that sorrow for the dead is too easy and satisfying a feeling, too much like self-pity, and the time could be better spent in actively living. Thus Tristram continues his rhapsodical work, having inserted the black page following Yorick's death as a symbol of his genuine grief and his determination to mock it. Take advantage of the moment, greet life with an open-house reception, such are the real lessons of his "sentimental" passages. Feed an ass for curiosity, measure Janatone right now:

[H] e who measures thee, *Janatone,* must do it now—thou carriest the principles of change within thy frame; and considering the chances of a transitory life, I would not answer for thee a moment; e'er twice twelve months are pass'd and gone, thou mayst grow out like a pumkin, and lose thy shapes—or, thou mayst go off like a flower, and lose thy beauty—nay thou mayst go off like a hussy—and lose thyself.   (490)

Despite the lighthearted references to "shapes" and to aunt Dinah who went off like a hussy, Sterne feels deeply the sad inevitable changes that occur to living things in the course of living. But his response is not to mourn but to appreciate what there is at the moment; his flippancy does not deny the essential pathos of mutability, it insists on it and consequently on the need to act while one has the opportunity.

Because Sterne sees an individual lifetime as a "fragment," spleen and anger, the bilious and saturnine passions, both of which clog up the channels of the blood that make "the wheel of life run long and chearfully round," are crimes against nature. Thus Sterne takes on the vital job of jester and shows, in the book that is his jest, the effectiveness of deliberate mirth in ridding the system of its wasteful passions. Tristram's personal fight against disillusionment with life is the impetus behind his writing; and in turn, his writing is his salvation, or as Fluchère sees it, Tristram's efforts are an answer to the challenge that the facts of his life present him with: "Autobiography thus becomes a sort of revenge for a wasted life, an absurd and farcical revenge it is true, but one which can restore the balance."[20] Tristram himself asserts the probable success of such a plan: "I will answer for it the book shall make its way in the world, much better than its master has done before it—Oh *Tristram! Tristram!* can this but be once brought about—the credit, which will attend thee as an author, shall counterbalance the many evils which have befallen thee as a man" (337).

The whole character of Tristram, the misdirected Homunculus grown into the image of a man, is dedicated to demonstrating the value of his battles against his unfortunate past, against despair or, on the petty everyday level, the spleen. The careless tone in which he informs us that he has been "the continual sport of what the world calls fortune" evinces the comic view of the world that lies behind it:

[T]hough I will not wrong her by saying, She has ever made me feel the weight of any great or signal evil;—yet with all the good temper in the world, I affirm it of her, that in every stage of my life, and at every turn and corner where she could get fairly at me, the ungracious Duchess has pelted me with a set of as pitiful misadventures and cross accidents as ever small HERO sustained. (10)

Fortune is here transformed into a big bully, tormenting the small figure of Tristram with the likes of pebbles and a few stones; Tristram forgives her with the slight grudge that a helpless young boy bears towards his more powerful companion who has on the whole amused him but who has hurt him somewhat in doing so. The knowledge that he has lived through the experience unscathed and has thus perhaps earned a bit of respect from the rough-playing Duchess helps him with his forgiveness and prepares him to accept the next attack with relative equanimity.

Critics, the everyday counterparts of the ungracious Duchess, get the same good-natured reaction from Tristram: "If any one of you should gnash his teeth, and storm and rage at me, as some of you did last MAY . . . don't be exasperated, if I pass it by again with good temper,—being determined as long as I live or write (which in my case means the same thing) never to give the honest gentleman a worse word or a worse wish, than my uncle *Toby* gave the fly" (162). Spleen might prevent Tristram from writing, which would be tantamount to dying, so he has his little joke in equating the "honest" critics with Uncle Toby's fly and then continues merrily on his way.

Faith, not resolve, may provide the necessary defense against life's sudden shocks. Walter and Toby Shandy are Sterne's representatives of this equally effective means of bearing the burdens of existence as well as possible. A conversation between them, or rather a discourse by Walter on the occasion of his son's unfortunate delivery, shows the differing nature of their faiths:

> Though man is of all others the most curious vehicle, said my father, yet at the same time 'tis of so slight a frame and so totteringly put together, that the sudden jerks and hard jostlings it unavoidably meets with in this rugged journey, would overset and tear it to pieces a dozen times a day—was it not, brother *Toby*, that there is a secret spring within us— Which spring, said my uncle *Toby*, I take to be Religion.—Will that set my child's nose on? cried my father... the spring I am speaking of, is that great and elastic power within us of counterbalancing evil, which like a secret spring in a well-ordered machine, though it can't prevent the shock—at least imposes upon our sense of it.   (277–78)

Walter's secret spring in this case turn out mirthfully to be the all-powerful name, Trismegistus, an unparalleled product of his hobby-horse-dominated mind. The contrast between Walter's concept of a "great and elastic power" and the absurd generation of that power is comic, and the comedy in turn reinforces the notion of man's great resilience. Any little thing will do to counterbalance evil provided one believes in its power to do so. Uncle Toby's simple faith in Religion is not any more practical, as his brother is quick to point out, than choosing a high-sounding name. What is important, for the characters and the readers, is the conviction that all is not lost, that the family will survive this crisis and that one may laugh at the whole event.

One might fairly suppose that Sterne is advocating a world of fools in the happy state of being well deceived. Being in a perpetual state of deception however is not to be confused with the conscious decision to disavow evil, misery and death. The one is based on the Panglossian error that this is the best of all possible worlds, the other is closer to the Spinozistic idea that it is best to "keep one's pecker up," no matter what is coming. If one refuses to grant recognition, to give cruelty and death their due, however much one knows they are a part of life, then one is in a stronger position to appreciate the kindness and goodness in life and get on with the business of living. Gulliver, most would agree, could have managed life much better without his voyage to the land of the Houy-hnhnms and his sudden apprehension of human weakness. If Gulliver changes from a fool to a knave in the course of his travels, from an innocent and alert observer of humanity to an embittered flayer of mankind, one can see that Swift clearly hopes that he will find his way to the sane and reasonable state that lies between them, the one in which observation leads to useful correction, not outrage. Though Sterne is not as concerned with the correction of society as is Swift, both would grant that the achievement of individual generosity and gentility, both dependent on personal happiness, is a contribution towards a corrected society that every person should be able to make. Because Swift's emphasis is more on the necessity for the contribution than on the personal achievement alone, his plea is the more impassioned for having the more to accomplish, and at the same time the more embittered for the unlikelihood of its being heard. Sterne would be satisfied with a more fanciful result, a "kingdom of hearty laughing subjects," being convinced that "disorders in the blood and humours, have as bad an influence . . . upon the body politick as body natural" (338). The implication is that if each one takes care of his own spiritual health, that of the country will come naturally.

Not everyone is able to laugh, especially not, like Laurence Sterne, in the "same tender moment" as they cry. Hobby-horses may substitute for outright laughter; indeed, they are but different, personalized forms of the comic vision. A man is characterized as much by his hobby-horse as his head, Sterne asserted, for it delineates the special path along which he chooses to make his way in the world. Their value to the characters of *Tristram Shandy* is that of all comedy: they make the world navigable if not quite conquerable. Uncle Toby's allows him, as Stanley Eskin observes, to organize and understand the chaos at Namur and to make sense of the rest of life by connecting it with his military experience.[21] Walter is able to categorize and intellectualize all the troublesome stray bits of emotion or chance that might interfere with his previously laid-out plans.

The frustration and anguish felt by Toby as a result of his complete puzzlement by words, and in turn his inability to express the exact nature of his wound to other people or himself, is relieved to a great extent by Trim's happy suggestion of a tangible replacement for mere words—the bowling green. Not only do the models remove the ambiguity from his military vocabulary, they also scale the events which gave rise to the original confusion down to an unfrightening size. It is this combination of tangibility and smallness that makes the fortifications comic, or rather Uncle Toby comic, just as any gentleman who acclimatized himself to riding on trains by playing with electric models would be. The bowling green is essentially a giant playground, and Uncle Toby, guilty by association, is no more than an overgrown child. But the suggestion that Toby's guilt is forced upon him by the baffling nature of real life and the overwhelming size of the world outside the bowling green gives the comedy a serious heart and makes Uncle Toby as noble as he is comic. The bravery of his attempt to make sense of an apparently nonsensical situation—that is, life—redeems any failure in his attempt. There is a real need to bring life down to size and to clarify with objects the ideas that govern it; the fulfilment of this need is therefore natural and commendable, even though the fulfilment is only a substitution, a makeshift apparatus rather than an actual achievement. The achievement consists, of course, in accepting the substitution and going on with life.

Toby's brother Walter is not really very different from himself. Whereas the one uses models to understand the facts of reality, the other uses words, uses them indeed as if they were models, to make the facts of reality fit a neat and pleasant pattern, which they do not naturally do. Both Uncle Toby and Walter Shandy are rather dignified characters, and believe implicitly in the dignity of man; they both depend upon their hobby-horses to keep them neatly mounted and to keep the road they follow free from possible pitfalls. To Toby, no military maneuver is too complex for comprehension once it has been imitated exactly and no fact of life is too incomprehensible if it can be related to its military counterpart. Just so, to Walter, no fact is unbearable if one can express it in words, which are not themselves inimical, but rather reasonable and orderly. One can work with words as one cannot with emotions, which are apt to change suddenly or be illogical. Words serve as well as models for reducing events down to a manageable size, and have the advantage over Toby's toys of being reasonable, and even—if necessary—generously ambiguous. Walter uses his theories to uphold his view of the order of reality and the nobility of man, and need only reject as arrant nonsense any expressions that do not affirm his assumptions:

As for that certain, very pale, subtle, and very fragrant juice [affirmed] to be the principal seat of the reasonable soul . . . my father could never subscribe to it by any means; the very idea of so noble, so refined, so immaterial, and so exalted a being as the *Anima,* or even the *Animus,* taking up her residence, and sitting dabbling, like a tad-pole, all day long, both summer and winter, in a puddle,—or in a liquid of any kind, how thick or thin soever, he would say, shock'd his imagination; he would scarce give the doctrine a hearing. (148–49)

His dismissal is as ridiculous and magnificent as Uncle Toby's bowling green activities are. His narrow-mindedness is absurd, especially in a philosopher, and yet his protection of man's dignity from unworthy explanations, from ignominious hypotheses, is touching and says more for the frailty but also the reality of that dignity than any noble explanation could. Man's determination to make the best of himself and of life takes the comical form of a hobby-horse, and Sterne in his dramatized dissertation on hobby-horses demonstrates both the comedy and the nobility of man, who is no more than a homunculus with props, but who manages nevertheless.

The value to Tristram of a hobby-horse is perhaps greatest of all, for his enables him to see comically on his own, to laugh outright; that is, the need in Tristram for a prop, a mount with which to overcome hurdles is replaced by a readiness to laugh that is derived from his rides on his hobby-horse. His sitting down to write represents a conscious search for an explanation, a justification for his life, and by mounting his hobby-horse, by attempting to order his life into the neat and logical pattern of My Life and Opinions, he succeeds in overcoming the need for justification and logic by laughing at it and himself, by stumbling on the road and enjoying it. Tristram becomes a true comic hero, whose heart is as "determined as the phoenix." The image is Christópher Fry's and rests on his notion of the unswerving concentration of the mythical bird to bring about his own rebirth: "What burns must also light and renew, not by a vulnerable optimism but by a hard-won maturity of delight, by the intuition of comedy, and active patience declaring the solvency of good."[22] That Tristram does not chase away his hobby-horse, but continues writing his book after the first few exhilaratingly muddled pages, is because he does not choose to, for the little filly turns out to be amusing for itself:

What a rate have I gone on at, curvetting and frisking it away, two up and two down for four volumes together, without looking once behind, or even on one side of me, to see whom I trod upon!—I'll tread upon no one,—quoth I to myself when I mounted—I'll take a good rattling gallop;

but I'll not hurt the poorest jack-ass upon the road. . . .

Now ride at this rate with what good intention and resolution you may,—'tis a million to one you'll do some one a mischief, if not yourself—He's flung—he's off—he's lost his seat—he's down—he'll break his neck—see!—if he has not galloped full amongst the scaffolding of the undertaking critics! (298)

Tristram's frisky rides are as exhilarating to us as to him. Our feeling of pleasure is similar to that aroused by Smollett's energetic sentences: in both cases the author's zest for experience is contained within the writing.

Norman Holland sees the hobby-horse as central to the comedy of the work, and explains its double-value: "On the one side of the paradox, Sterne pokes fun at his characters by making silly (but real) things suddenly pop onto this personal road and topple over both hobby-horse and rider. On the other side of the paradox, Sterne pokes fun at the serious obstacles of reality by having the characters jump his hobby-horse triumphantly over them."[23] One must see, though, that in writing *Tristram Shandy* Sterne surely concentrates on the latter virtue of the hobby-horse, for the silliness of the character almost always goes unnoticed in the light of his triumphs. What Holland refers to as a paradox is simply comedy's normal method of dealing with human beings: characters are created with such ludicrous proportions and shortcomings that one cannot be surprised if they fail to surmount an obstacle or two, and one laughs at their shame (while delighting in their energy); if however, they manage, in spite of their ludicrous make-up, to conquer a hurdle unexpectedly, one laughs all the more at their surprising dexterity. We may note that it is the characters who are not equipped with effective hobby-horses who are most often seen to get splashed by the mud in the road—most notably and literally, Dr. Slop. Because he lacks the ability to laugh at himself, and because he cannot fall and get up again without displaying his lack of resiliency—physical and mental—we laugh at his silliness and shame much more than if he did it for us and we feel no sense of his having triumphed over his short, squat, human body. But comedy never entirely deprecates its subject, for he is invariably a member of the human race, which is comedy's true subject and darling. Our laughter is not entirely at the shame of Slop; a good deal of it may be attributed to our pleasure in the exaggeration, the vitality of the scene. Moreover, our laughter at the farcical elements of the incident makes us feel more kindly towards the foolish figure, for as Sydney Smith rightly pointed out after Sterne's time, but in a passage especially applicable to his kind of humor, "contempt accompanied by laughter, is always mitigated by laughter, which seems to diminish hatred, as perspiration diminishes heat."[24] Our laughter makes us remember his humanity, man's proneness to stumble, and we forgive his silliness as much as we delight in it.

Sterne has indicated in a more straightforward manner than the pages of his novel permit that affectionate comedy is the only acceptable kind. Setting up for a man of wit "on the broken stock of other people's failings" is, according to his sermon, what "has helped to give wit a bad name, as if the main essence of it was satire." He goes on in "The Levite and His Concubine" to distinguish between nasty and kindly humor:

Certainly there is a difference between Bitterness and Saltness,—that is,—between the malignity and the festivity of wit,—the one is mere quickness of apprehension, void of humanity,—and is a talent of the devil; the other comes down from the Father of Spirits, so pure and abstracted from persons, that willingly it hurts no man; or if it touches upon an indecorum, 'tis with that dexterity of true genius, which enables him rather to give a new colour to the absurdity, and let it pass. (I, 214)

Sterne surely intended *Tristram Shandy* to be utterly without bitterness, and one may determine his success by using Dr. Slop as a touchstone. The supposedly vicious lampoon of Dr. Burton (apparently a relic of the "Yorkshire epic" that *Tristram Shandy* originally was) would have no life for us today if it were simply a splenetic creation. So many of the characters in *The Dunciad* are merely dead names to us because they are based so closely on people who died and were not worth remembering (except perhaps to explain some of the jokes in the poem). *The Dunciad* triumphs over the bulk of its ghostly subjects mainly because of the incomparably alive creation that Dulness herself is: had Pope written his epic and left out his goddess (an impossible assumption) our interest in it would surely be dulled in proportion to its subject. What saves the caricature of Dr. Burton from being bitter and gives it life today is that Sterne's abuse of the overstuffed doctor is, Work rightly notes, "as ludicrous as rancorous" (lxv). If we are to believe Sterne, his portrait is Cervantic rather than satiric, and Slop's fall was not meant maliciously but comically: the humor arises not from the image of the would-be Burton besmirched with mud and *"unwiped, unappointed, unanealed"*

(107), but rather from "describing silly and Trifling Events, with the Circumstantial Pomp of great Ones."[25] Of course we laugh actually at a combination of Sterne's jest at the expense of the Roman Catholic doctor and at the enlargement of the trifling event, but it is well to note that other barbs aimed at the Church, such as those in the sermon scene, are not nearly so funny as this, which is supported by the humorous description of the fall. Sterne does not deal in lampoons, though he may incidentally lampoon—the test is whether or not the passage is comic even if we are unaware of an existing original. He is concerned rather with characters who are so uniquely absurd that they may be mistaken for representations of real people, but are more fittingly taken as general representatives of the human race, comic types of a comical species.

These representatives suggest the appropriateness of tolerance and openness in one's relationships with human beings. Sterne sees to it that the relationship with his characters is that of one person to others, not of a reader to fictitious creations. One feels quite certain after reading *Tristram Shandy* that one has never met anyone quite like either of the Shandy brothers. Yet just as certainly one feels that they serve very well as models of the human race; we would not be surprised if we met a Walter or a Toby in the street tomorrow. Like all great comic characters, especially Falstaff, they are made to seem outlandish and ordinary at once. Just as Falstaff, who manages to sum up every human characteristic ranging from sophistication to naiveté, roguery to honesty, churlishness to gentility, is still miraculously life-sized, not larger, so the Shandy brothers—one with an oversized sensibility, the other with an oversized mentality—are loved for their very grotesqueries, which prove them to be ordinary fallible human beings. By emphasizing that the ordinary is made up of separate pieces of the extraordinary, comedy fulfills one of its primary functions, which is paradoxically to make the ordinary seem not especially outlandish, to make us understand that incongruity must be reconciled with our prejudiced notions of the regular and the typical.

Sterne's ability to make his characters' oddities obvious without straining our sense of the possible distinguishes him as a comic artist. Only Walter Shandy would choose to define the right end of a woman—which only Toby Shandy would need to have defined for him—by comparing "all the parts which constitute the whole of that animal" not anatomically, but "analogically" (102). Yet in the context of the discussion, and of Uncle Toby's extreme modesty, Walter's approach is perfectly sensible, if nonetheless unusual and peculiar to himself. Uncle Toby more often than his brother surprises and delights us with his interpretations of the topic under discussion, but one can never faithfully say that his way of looking at things is illogical or unbelievable; on the contrary, his remarks are often remarkably to the point and no more absurd than what has passed for sense from the other speakers:

But what are these, continued my father . . . to those prodigies of childhood in *Grotius, Scioppus, Heinsius* . . . and others—some of which left off their substantial forms at nine years old. . . . But you forget the great *Lipsius,* quoth Yorick, who composed a work the day he was born;—They should have wiped it up, said my uncle *Toby,* and said no more about it.

(410-12)

All the naïveté and compassion that characterizes Uncle Toby is summed up in this one statement, which is delightfully laughable and yet eminently sensible. The conversation has been bordering on the incredible and Toby's down-to-earth observation is needed to offset the spur that Yorick has given to Walter's hobby-horse. The same is true of Toby's firm intervention in the argument concerning the duchess of Suffolk: "Let the learned say what they will, there must certainly, quoth my uncle *Toby,* have been some sort of consanguinity betwixt the duchess of Suffolk and her son—" (331). That Toby should need to state such an obvious point is not entirely his fault; the fact has been somewhat obscured by the findings of the learned. Nevertheless, Sterne teases him for his innocent acceptance of nonsense in the line that follows: "The vulgar are of the same opinion, quoth Yorick, to this hour." These little scenes may be admired for their wit, but should be valued for their comedy, for the understanding they show of the way in which sense and nonsense may cohabit happily in the human mind and the way in which odd individuals are indeed unique in their oddities but are typical in being odd.

Tristram's assessment of the wonderfully assorted members of his family accurately accounts for the loving reception bestowed upon them by readers of each successive generation: "I believe in my soul . . . the hand of the supreme Maker and first Designer of all things, never made or put a family together . . . where the characters of it were cast or contrasted with so dramatic a felicity as ours was" (236). We are not tempted to look for an ironical undertone, for the statement only confirms what we feel.

Separately, but most delightfully together, the Shandy household enter-
tains us with the miracles of oddity to be found among the human race,
casually collected under one roof. A brief look at the famous kitchen
scene shows the mastery with which Sterne sketches in whole characters
with a few lines of dialogue. The gatherings in the kitchen are dramatically "parallel" we are told to the ones in the parlor of the family; the
servants of Shandy Hall show the same kind of peculiarities, the same
sort of individualities in their reactions to a piece of news as the members
of the family do. If there is a sameness in this kitchen group not found
in the other, it is the selfishness that seems to override all their other
passions. All but Trim, who stands above the group with his oratorical
authority, accept the news of Bobby's death according to the differences
it will make to their lives. Susannah, with the vanity of a maid, instantly
envisions the colored dresses of her mistress; she speeds the burial in
her imagination so that the period of mourning will begin all the sooner
and accordingly passes the news along with a small addition: "Master
Bobby is dead and *buried.*" The "fat foolish" scullion adopts a simple
attitude toward the death; with a kind of animal sense of self-preservation, "So am not I," she responds to Obadiah's excited, "He is dead!
he is certainly dead!" (360). Obadiah's own reaction consists of the
thought that the household staff "shall have a terrible piece of work in
it in stubbing the ox-moor," now that the alternative of Bobby's trip
abroad is ruled out.

Their acute concern with themselves is in no way cause for satirical
chastisement in Sterne's eyes. Rather than being corrosive in his wit,
he seems to admire the poor dropsical scullion's forthrightness above all:
Bobby is dead, as surely as she is alive, and the fact that she was not the
one to die cannot help pleasing her, regardless of any affection she might
have felt. What succeeds, however, in moving her as well as the rest of
the group is Trim's timely reminder of human mortality: "Are we not
here now, continued the corporal, (striking the end of his stick perpendic-
ularly upon the floor so as to give an idea of health and stability)—and
are we not—(dropping his hat upon the ground) gone! in a moment!"
(361). As Tristram wisely notes, none of us are "stocks and stones."
Even the fat foolish scullion melts at the thought of her own inevitable
weakness. The selfishness does not disturb Sterne because he feels so
poignantly the enormity of the knowledge of death that each human
being must overcome. Much more than in the carefully set up apostrophe

that follows may Sterne's true sentiment be felt at this moment, for the apostrophe turns out to be nothing more than a jest on Trim's old hat. But, in ending with a jest, he also reveals the depth of his own feeling and his need to laugh it away.

To all the strange creatures who people the world of *Tristram Shandy* Sterne extends honest feelings of affection and pathos; these feelings are deeply grounded in his comic vision, in his unflagging delight with life and his awareness that the delight may be tinged with pain. That he is most effective in conveying the honesty and depth of his feelings when he is most humorous may be verified by a comparison of the two Maria episodes in his novels. If Sterne truly meant us to feel his great sorrow for the hapless Maria in *A Sentimental Journey*, he does not succeed with such blatant appeals to our refined and elevated feelings: "I sat down close by her; and Maria let me wipe [the tears] away as they fell, with my handkerchief. I then steep'd it in my own, and then in hers, and then in mine, and then I wip'd hers again, and as I did it, I felt such indescribable emotions within me, as I am sure could not be accounted for from any combinations of matter and emotion" (270). He describes the acuteness of Yorick's feelings, but we are left only to doubt the quality of such pathos which we cannot share because he has given us no more cause than a wet handkerchief. Even the self-parodying Shandean remark that follows—"I am positive I have a soul; nor can all the books with which materialists have pestered the world ever convince me to the contrary"— does not convince us of his soul's sympathy with humanity, for Sterne turns our attention to Yorick's soul not to rebuke his or our natural impulses towards too easily felt tenderness, but to celebrate his own such impulses.

Tears are conspicuously missing from the parallel account in *Tristram Shandy*:

MARIA look'd wistfully for some time at me, and then at her goat—and then at me—and then at her goat again, and so on alternately.
—Well, *Maria*, said I softly—What resemblance do you find? (631)

By directing the humor at himself, and continuing to do so for the rest of the incident even while protesting that he will refrain from mirth for the rest of his days to honor the "venerable presence of Misery" that Maria represents for him, Sterne reveals much more truly his genuine pity and makes the reader feel his emotion. Here he is not causelessly blubbering at the sight of tears, he is trying to follow the thoughts and feelings of a helpless young girl, he is trying to understand what she feels about life at that moment. All his sympathy is contained in his apparently thoughtless remark, for it shows his awareness at that moment of the absurdity of life and, in turn, his consciousness of the pain to which Maria is therefore exposed.

That his pathos is so unsatisfactory without his humor is not surprising when one traces the source of his refined feelings to his sense of absurdity. The sounds of human dissonance that are everywhere heard in a theoretically harmonious world impress Sterne with the need for a sensitive adjustment to reality, a comic adjustment that takes the discord into account while deriving pleasure from the whole composition. Nothing amuses Sterne more than the unlikely match between Walter Shandy and his wife, though his understanding of the submerged tragedy of their foolish relationship—Walter's consuming vexation, Mrs. Shandy's inconceivable placidity—shows clearly in his depiction of their marriage. There is no satire in his account of Walter's perpetually puzzled despair at having wound up with such an unphilosophical mate, one who is unable to distinguish between "a point of pleasure and a point of convenience." His situation becomes emblematic of the entire human experience: one may be perfectly well-equipped, so one thinks, to get on top of considerations of fate and forture, and still be floored by stray bits of irrationalism, in the form of emotion or chance, that constantly get in the way. One feels, along with Sterne, the terrible uncertainty of human relationships, and therefore the terrible uncertainty of each human being about his own life. Mrs. Shandy's ability to floor her husband to the point of making him doubt the soundness of his rational conclusions simply by mindlessly agreeing with him is perfectly shown in the comical "bed of justice" scene, in which the make-up of Tristram's breeches is being discussed:

—They should be of leather, said my father, turning him about again.—
They will last him, said my mother, the longest.
But he can have no linings to 'em, replied my father.—
He cannot, said my mother.
'Twere better to have them of fustian, quoth my father.
Nothing can be better, quoth my mother.—
—Except dimity—replied my father:—'Tis best of all,—replied my mother.

(438)

139

Mrs. Shandy's compliance is matched only by her husband's increasing exasperation at that compliance. Sterne catches the placidity of the one and the annoyance of the other in the timing of their lines and the punctuation. Mrs. Shandy speeds up her replies in the same proportion as Mr. Shandy speeds up his suggestions. When he interrupts her with "—Except dimity," she replies in the same paragraph, and her remark is prefaced with a dash and appears as a clause following the colon that concludes his. Sterne's observation of speech here is no less perceptive than his attention to gestures, with the same intent: to reveal the struggle involved in carrying on a simple conversation. Mrs. Shandy's automatic responses are no different from Uncle Toby's automatic pipe-smoking or "Lillabullero" whistling. Both of them do not wish to be troubled by ideas or opinions that do not match their own or in any way threaten the serenity (or in Mrs. Shandy's case, vacuity) of their minds. The precisely recorded conversation reveals how dangerous it would be for Mrs. Shandy to consider the matter of the breeches seriously, which would mean having a genuine opinion in opposition to her dogmatic husband's. In the face of opposition, we know, Walter would not have faltered. The humor of the scene lies in the apparent stupidity of the one and the corresponding distress of the other, but the true comedy arises from our realization that neither can truly assert himself—Mrs. Shandy because it would be to no avail, Mr. Shandy because he is foiled by a lack of opposition and thus wavers, which is the true cause of his distress.

A hobby-horse may provide the courage required to meet a world that is too big or too puzzling, as the Shandy characters show, but it may have the unfortunate side-effect of aggravating the ordinary estrangement of people. An enormous amount of affection and bravery is required to overcome the normal jeopardy of misunderstanding that plagues the different forms of human communication, and hobby-horses, so necessary to making one's way in the world, increase the amount of effort that is needed to make one's way with people. If the hazards of human relationships are symptomatic of the world's jest-swollen belly, then Sterne suggests that wit and instruction may be found out from the admirable attempts of the Shandy family to understand each other and make themselves understood. The brothers have each developed their own methods of contending with the misfiring of the other's thoughts. Walter goes into a passion; Uncle Toby smokes his pipe or whistles. Precisely because they are armed against the possibility of spleen and rage in their meetings together, they are not afraid to try once again to communicate and thus they succeed on an emotional if not a literal level. Unlike Gulliver, who changes from a responsive human being into a bitter, reserved madman as a result of his disillusioning attempts to understand his position in relation to other people, the Shandy brothers offer an optimistic resolution to the problem.

The two brothers are endlessly comical and at the same time touchingly admirable because they do not avoid the risks of conversation, no matter how painful the attempt may prove at the time. Walter is decidedly anguished at the renewed proof Toby offers of his unalterable simplicity in their discussion of—or rather Walter's dissertation on—truth and the study of noses:

'Tis a pity, said my father, that truth can only be on one side, brother *Toby*,—considering what ingenuity these learned men have all shewn in their solutions of noses.—Can noses be dissolved? replied my uncle *Toby*.—
—My father thrust back his chair,—rose up,—put on his hat,—thrust his head half way out,—shut the door again,—took no notice of the bad hinge,—returned to the table. . .   (239)

Toby meets this performance with his usual good nature:

'Twas all one to my uncle *Toby*,—he smoaked his pipe on, with unvaried composure,—his heart never intended offence to his brother,—and as his head could seldom find out where the sting of it lay,—he always gave my father the credit of cooling by himself.—He was five minutes and thirty-five seconds about it in the present case.   (240)

Superficially the comedy of this scene may be attributed to the ridiculous wit of Toby's answer and to the gestures so analytically and dramatically exposed by Sterne. But neither the wit nor Bergson's mechanistic explanations get at the heart of the scene, which lies in the failure and the ultimate success of the two brothers to share their lives with each other. The success is comic success, that of accepting the fact that they are intractably opposite and must begin again as best they can. The process of acceptance is seen both as disturbing and rewarding. That it is reanimating as well is attested by Walter's relaunching of his deep philosophy into the ever-shallow waters of his brother's mind, and by his brother's ever-patient admission of the vessel:

—Why, by the *solutions* of noses, of which I was telling you, I meant as
you might have known, had you favoured me with one grain of your
attention, the various accounts which learned men of different kinds of
knowledge have given the world, of the causes of short and long noses.
—There is no cause but one, replied my uncle *Toby,*—why one man's
nose is longer than another's, but because God pleases to have it so.—
That is *Grangousier*'s solution, said my father.   (240)

Despite the apparent consensus, the two are clearly back to where they
started in understanding one another verbally, yet the comic point has
been made: the attempt is what counts in establishing human relationships.

Toby's ability to make himself understood by Trim is directly related
to the absence of words in their most remarkable communications. The
memory of shared activity leads to new action, while their common
hobby-horse allows them to participate equally. The directness with
which they are able to fall into step with one another stems from the
essentially childlike faith that each understands the other. Indeed, the
only time the possibility of mutual incomprehension arises is when Trim
describes his adult passion for the fair Beguin, and tries to do so in adult
terms. Toby refuses to admit the facts of Trim's experience, or to allow
Trim to admit them in words, the effect of which he knows will not be
erased by any amount of whistling. The division between them never
really occurs, though, for Trim offers no contradiction to Toby's version
of what happened when Trim seized the hand of the fair Beguin. Rather
than permit a misunderstanding to arise between them, they resort to
their usual faith in the other to understand what is going on, just as Toby
does whenever he begins to whistle. This faith is both comic in itself
and basic to comedy: Toby and Trim, and Toby and Walter, are funny
in their successful attempts to respect the oddities of the other; they
are also reassuring in a world where less valiant attempts, less openness
and tolerance, can result in coldness and permanent despair.

Tristram, too, it is apparent from his narrative, respects—even more,
cherishes—the quirks of the people who are so much a part of his life,
and one feels that he equally well loves the entire human race (as Sterne
would have us believe of himself). To approach *Tristram Shandy* as
satire is to be required to see the story that Tristram tells as "one great
anatomy of the fools and knaves who affect him," and his recollections
as "a long list of consequences to himself."[26] Yet his many apostrophes

acclaiming the merits of various people may mock false sentiment, but
they do not mock the characters themselves. Even when faced with the
ludicrous picture of his uncle decked out in pursuit of the Widow Wadman, Tristram eschews the opportunity to raise a malicious laugh:

> Had SPLEEN given a look at [the wig], 'twould have cost her ladyship
> a smile . . . he could as soon have raised the dead.
> Such it was—or rather such would it have seem'd upon any other
> brow; but the sweet look of goodness which sat upon my uncle *Toby*'s,
> assimilated every thing around it so sovereignly to itself, and Nature had
> moreover wrote GENTLEMAN with so fair a hand in every line of his
> countenance, that even his tarnish'd gold-laced hat and huge cockade of
> flimsy taffeta became him. (601)

Her ladyship still smiles at the extravagance of the outfit, but not mock-
ingly at Uncle Toby's simple-mindedness. Nor is there any note of resentment mixed with the affection in Tristram's voice when he explains
his father's peculiar penchant for theories: "In truth, there was not a
stage in the life of man, from the very first act of his begetting,—down
to the lean and slipper'd pantaloon of his second childishness, but he
had some favourite notion to himself, springing out of it, as sceptical,
and as far out of the high-way of thinking, as these two which have been
explained" (145). Tristram's fondness is expressed in the Shakespearian
description and in the note of admiration for his father's achievement
at having ambled along such strange paths so consistently throughout
his life.

His concern, for the most part identical with Sterne's own, for his
imagined audience's happiness is more than a mere formality, or so we
are made to believe by his attentiveness. His command that we laugh
at him or do anything, only keep our tempers, shows a wish for our well-
being that is related to his announced reason for writing his book—to
drive away the spleen. The thing that strikes one above all is that he is
trying to make the choicest experiences of his family come alive so that
we may receive the same amount of delight from them as he still does.
That he enjoys the absurdity of many of the events is obvious from his
warm mockery at such great length of the marriage settlement, the visit-
ation dinner, the great curse, and his own continuing efforts to make
some order out of his haphazard family history. Indeed, Tristram's
readiness to include himself among the odd creatures of his family serves

not only to make him truly a part of that family and therefore more than simply an ironic narrator of a mixed-up tale, but also to soften any rough satirical edges.

He bears no grudges, makes no serious accusations, for he is one of them, and they are all members of the same comical human race. The ironic remarks that he makes at the expense of his father or his uncle are gentle and understanding of the anomalies imposed upon them by Nature, some of which have been accidentally passed on to himself. The extravagance of his father's *Tristrapoedia* is surely equal to that of his uncle's great wig, and Tristram in this case is affected directly by its profound uselessness (whereas the wig harmed no one who did not die from laughing at it). He does not deny the foolishness of his father's wisdom:

> [H]e was three years and something more, indefatigably at work, and at last, had scarce compleated, by his own reckoning, one half of his undertaking: the misfortune was, that I was all that time totally neglected and abandoned to my mother; and what was almost as bad, by the very delay, the first part of the work, upon which my father had spent the most of his pains, was rendered entirely useless,—every day a page or two became of no consequence.— (375)

But rather than blaming his father for neglecting him, he generalizes his observation so that Walter seems merely the victim of a common human failing:

> —Certainly it was ordained as a scourge upon the pride of human wisdom, That the wisest of us all, should thus outwit ourselves, and eternally forego our purposes in the intemperate act of pursuing them. (375)

Tristram pities his father rather than himself and he pities mankind in general for being susceptible to the tricks of Time and other natural laws, as he is himself both directly and indirectly: his own inability to supply a minute of reading time for a minute of his life is a curiosity of Time that he must accept, and the cause of his having to order his life into reading matter is a result of his father's having been duped by Time into neglecting him.

The law of Chance exercises similar control over his life, so that he finds himself accidentally circumcised at the age of five, having directly encountered the chance effects of a loose window sash. Tristram identi-

fies the culprits who were indirectly responsible for the accidental occurrence, his uncle having directed Trim to find some weights for the
battlefield equipment—a request that is in turn related to the chance
occurrence at Namur—but he focuses the reader's attention on the wonder of the coincidence, not on the foolishness of his uncle's hobby-horse.
He dismisses the whole disaster with a " 'Twas nothing."

Tristram's propensity to overlook or rationalize the shortcomings of
the people around him has, not surprisingly, a comic effect on "his"
work. Like Sterne's his comic vision makes a joke of the world and a
miracle of the human race that somehow manages to make the world
its home. A lament for man that Tristram makes at the beginning of
Book Five is subverted by a jest at his own expense, an expense which
Sterne himself shares, for the charge concerns the method by which
Tristram Shandy is composed:

Who made MAN, with powers which dart him from earth to heaven in a
moment—that great, that most excellent, and most noble creature of the
world—that *miracle* of nature, ... the *image* of God ... the *ray* of divinity ...
the *marvel* of *marvels* ... to go on at this pitiful—pimping—pettifogging rate?

(343)

If one takes the whole statement as ironic, then man is not "the most
excellent, and most noble creature" and Tristram does not really go
sneaking on at a pitiful rate, that is, one must conclude from previous
references that his work is a brilliant and original work of art that will
contribute to the "stock" as well as the "bulk" of man's learnings. If
once accepts the assertion of man's nobility, then Tristram, and in effect
Sterne, is indulging in a characteristic bit of conscious and comic self-
pity in the hopes of winning our sympathies. Either way, the image of
human species does not suffer, for an individual may triumph over
his pitiful condition or else humanity is noble in spite of his apparently ig-
noble ways. One is left with the inevitable conclusion that on the one
hand man is ludicrous and paltry, the inhabitant of a world that imposes
pettiness upon him, and on the other, man's belief in his own nobility
allows him to triumph over his birthright by acting with stature and becoming truly noble.

Unlike Swift, no matter how much Sterne reduces the scale of mankind in order to dramatize the difficulties man has in making his way

145

through life, he maintains his capacity for admiration and amusement. Swift's whole purpose in Book Two of *Gulliver's Travels* is to demonstrate "how contemptible a thing [is] human grandeur" and he does so by dramatizing with terrifying minuteness the insults that Gulliver is forced to endure. Our admiration for Gulliver's efficiency in dealing with the flies, for instance, is offset by our sense of his false pride: he does not accept the ludicrousness of his position among giants any more than he rejects the value of the honor bestowed upon him by the Lilliputians, the title of "nardac" for his bravery and strength. For all his objectivity, Gulliver is blind to his own absurdity. The objective observer in *Tristram Shandy,* who like Gulliver is himself an object of observation, is as acutely aware of his own inadequacy to life as Sterne and the readers are. One certainly has the sense of man's physical and mental insufficiency in *Tristram Shandy*—the impotence of both mind and body apparently afflicting the Shandy men has often been noted—but one does not feel as if the magnitude of the soul is diminished by the body's failure to house it properly or the mind's to protect it from the shocks of the world. The bravery of all three—Walter, Toby, and Tristram—in attempting to cope with the demands of the world more than replaces the dignity lost by their homunculean drawbacks and their use of hobby-horsical props. Moreover, their bravery is admirable because, unlike Gulliver's, it is grounded in the knowledge of their own smallness and inefficiency and in a faith in the great and elastic power within them to counterbalance their own absurdity.

The faith, which is expressed in hobby-horsical activities or simply in a self-mocking jest, arms its possessor against the clashes of other absurdities and allows him to act with tolerance and courage. The faith itself becomes the means by which man triumphs over his characteristic puniness. Tristram's book, Fluchère rightly claims, is "a dazzling testimony to his victory over words and things, a proof of his vitality and vigilance."[27] Toby would have been basely betrayed into solitude and despair, first by his wound, were it not for his whole-hearted commitment to his bowling green war, and second, by the peace of Utrecht, were it not for the likeness between love and war that Mrs. Wadman happily encourages him to discover. He valiantly forges ahead with a siege at her doorstep, thus maintaining the dignity and orderliness that soldiering gives to his life and that he so painstakingly preserved on his green. Walter's fruitless mental voyages into the realm of auxiliary verbs in search of the Northwest passage of the intellect is counterbalanced by the equanimity—that is, the real fruit of his mental voyages, with which he is then able to meet the irrationalities of other people. His puzzlement is no less than Toby's many times, and his idolatry of reason makes puzzlement a difficult thing to bear. Nevertheless, Walter triumphs consistently over his demands for rationality by rationally absolving his helplessly befuddled brother of any intentional crime and acting tenderly and affectionately towards him. Each of the three manages his little stock of understanding and ability with husbandry, and turns the potential cause for ridicule—his life on earth—into a call for celebration.

Whereas Smollett, in *Peregrine Pickle,* urges the acceptability of Fortune, Chance, and Evil in life by making their dangers seem challenging and stimulating, Sterne offers the possibility of triumph over these dangers. Of all Smollett's characters, only Commodore Trunnion would find himself at home in *Tristram Shandy,* for he alone has a fully developed comic faith in man's ability to live happily and peacefully, which arms him with the necessary power to do so. Sterne demonstrates the necessity and value of the comic imagination by showing us that the public outrages of Nature are nothing to the private ravages of despair and the concomitant ills of spleen and aloofness, and by showing us that we may overcome these with determination and affection, with conscious mirth that protects the mirthful against the forces of despair and loneliness.

A Sentimental Journey

Beckoning his readers once again to ignore their spleens and take joy in their affections, however absurdly they might be led astray, Sterne launched a new Yorick shortly after the publication of the final volume of *Tristram Shandy* on a wildly extravagant and thus inevitably comic grand tour as the heart experiences it. The invitation to join the flighty hero has been received and accepted with alacrity in each succeeding generation even by those whose doubts about Sterne and the holiness of his heart's affections have been nurtured on the innuendos of the notorious *Life and Opinions.* Indeed, the volatility of both the hero and prose of *A Sentimental Journey* accounts for the charm of the work and (paradoxically) its endurance.

147

From the first words, Yorick delights the reader with his impulsive footloose attitude towards life:

—They order, said I, this matter better in France—
—You have been in France? said my genleman, turning quick upon me with the most civil triumph in the world.—Strange! quoth I, debating the matter with myself, That one and twenty miles of sailing, for 'tis absolutely no further from Dover to Calais, should give a man these rights— I'll look into them: so giving up the argument—I went straight to my lodgings, put up half a dozen shirts and a black pair of silk breeches—'the coat I have on, said I, looking at the sleeve, will do'—took a place in the Dover stage; and the packet sailing at nine the next morning. . .   (65)

We get caught up in the rapidity of the events, and even more in his ordering of the matter ("the coat I have on . . . will do"); we are aroused by his careless dispatching of everyday obstacles. The joy of the work lies in allowing oneself to be wafted along by the splendid breeziness of tone and timing, which give a sense of Yorick's comic triumph over the mundane limitations of distance—both mental and spatial—and everyday contingencies. Yorick is not so much footloose as heartloose; in his casual disregard for life's conventions he spreads the comic gospel to those whose hearts are not hardened to his charm.

His capacity to draw the reader along with him depends less on one's assessment of his sentimentalism and more on a sympathy with his ebullient personality, and in turn that of his creator's, than critical disputes have made it seem. Yorick's sincerity is not the crucial question: one can like Yorick and agree to be carried along on his whirlwind journey whether one sees him as a highly admirable human being, a bumbling fool, or a sly knave. Early critics, who were enchanted by the exchange of snuff-boxes and who had no reason to find fault with Yorick because for them the sentiment involved in offering his box made up handsomely for his initial reluctance to part with a sou, were encouraged to accompany the traveler and to feel the force of his emotional experiences, the tidal "ebbs and flows" of his passions. In contrast, Rufus Putney, who in his 1940 article was one of the first to intimate that Yorick's sentiments were of dubious quality, responded to Sterne's playful irony, to the way in which the grounds for Yorick's sentiments were continually mocked by his manner of pursuing them. More recently, Gardner Stout in his Introduction has insisted on Yorick's awareness of his own impulses and reactions, and has taken heart in the susceptibility he shows "to all the venial imperfections of human nature" despite his vigilance against them and his efforts to hide them from others. The sentimental reader's delight in the emotional energy is the modern reader's delight in the emotional equivocation, a different form of the same energy.

Yet interpretations of the equivocation differ and affect one's reading of the novel. Wholehearted participation in the *Journey* and appreciation of its comic excesses ultimately depend upon one's faith in Sterne's ability to see his character objectively, while presenting him to the reader for subjective approval. In glinting his eye noticeably only to those who will not be offended by the suggestive glances, Sterne has shaded this sign of his awareness from some who look for it and cannot be sure it is there. Virginia Woolf failed to be assured of Sterne's control over Yorick's pettinesses and, being inclined to attribute them to his creator instead, failed to be charmed by Yorick. In her Introduction to the *Journey*, she characterizes them bòth as hypocrites who have no intention of sharing the secret of their vanities with the reader. Yet the most serious charge against Sterne and the most damaging to his comedy is not that he is a hypocrite, but that he is genuinely blind to the weaknesses that Yorick continually evinces, that he does not recognize the dangers of Yorick's whimsical misuse of advantage, either in disposing of his charity or befriending a young girl. Such a reading makes the breezy tone of the work seem as ominous as that of the Modest Proposer. However, it is the very breeziness of the *Journey* that gives confidence in Sterne's control and works against a portentous interpretation.

The capriciousness of Yorick's sentiments, rather than making him seem devious, enhances his air of forthrightness, of directness:

—Base passion! said I, turning myself about, as a man naturally does upon a sudden reverse of sentiment—base, ungentle passion! thy hand is against every man, and every man's hand against thee—heaven forbid! said she, raising her hand up to her forehead, for I had turned full in front of the lady whom I had seen in conference with the monk—she had followed us unperceived—Heaven forbid indeed! said I, offering her my own— (89-90)

Yorick's unembarrassed acquiescence to the call of his impulses is attractively spontaneous; there is little in it of the base passion which he finds himself courting literally and comically with his hand. He has a kind of impish naïveté, which invites us to see how, in the circumstances, his acceptance of the challenge that chance offers is the only fitting way to act. Taking the hand of the lady is merely completing the step that he had started in innocence: to contemplate the dangers of the move would be to lose the rhythm, miss the beat that life is constantly sounding to those who listen (and which is reflected in the punctuation of the encounter: as is so often the case in this work, dashes replace full stops, signifying the continuous action and reaction that is taking place). Yorick's action, we are made to feel, has no more method in it than did his journey across the channel, which was undertaken on account of similarly accidental provocation. Madame L—— questions the basis of his current thoughts very much as the gentleman who doubted Yorick's authority to expound upon French characteristics did.

Sterne's method throughout the *Journey* is to give substance to casually felt sentiments, to make tangible those vaguely defined abstractions upon which common sentiments are based, in order to reveal their superficiality but at the same time to commend the underlying impulses that give rise to such sentiments. Thus, toying with lofty thoughts of generous allowance towards the seller of the post-chaise, Yorick is forced by the reality that Sterne abruptly forces upon him to lapse back into his normal selfish frame of mind. Yet he reverts in a way that mocks his former elevated strain without casting aspersions upon the openheartedness that brought such effusion to his lips. The shallowness of his cultivated gentility is shown at the same time as his "ungentle" passions are seen to be no more base than is any spontaneous gesture of friendliness.

Real sentiments are those which spring from communication, from the moment, and are found in those who approach life with an open heart and mind. It is very easy for Yorick to feel as if he could give away his portmanteau until he is faced with the immediate choice of giving away a sou or nothing. Then to give away nothing turns out to be the way he truly feels. Sympathy, as Kenneth MacLean notes in relation to the *Sentimental Journey*, is an automatic and satisfying activity of the imagination, which tends to recreate another's pain as if one were suffering oneself. "Such imagination may be indulged without pain to the purse or heart: at the same time, and on the contrary, it may fill one with pleasure."[28] Merely thinking kindly thoughts is no more morally commendable than actively refusing to give a sou. Indeed, Yorick's refusal would have been acceptably polite and simple had he not indulged

in flights of idealized sentiment a moment before. The discrepancy between the way he would like to act and the way he actually does is what
makes his action noteworthy and ungenerous.

That Yorick feels the presence of this gap even before he meditates
upon his refusal and, more important, before he tries to repair it for the
benefit of Madame L——'s good opinion, is apparent from his ungracious
outburst at the monk's request. Arising not from the fact that he sees
his virtues becoming the "sport of contingencies" but rather that he sees
that his virtues do not really exist at all, this outburst has the effect not
of excusing but of chastising him with evidence of his meanness and the
uselessness of his high-sounding sentiments. However, this self-chastise-
ment has the effect of partly excusing his actions in the reader's eyes.

Yorick's journey through France presents him with repeated opportunity to compare the grandeur of the word with the truth of the action:
his emotions at the outset are on the scale of the barber's claims—"You
may immerge it, replied he, into the ocean, and it will stand"—and if
they are not any less extravagant at the end, they are at least put into
the perspective of reality, the same perspective in which the barber's
words are seen to be meaningless—"Paris being so far inland, it was not
likely I should run post a hundred miles out of it, to try the experi-
ment" (159).

Far more admirable than the barber or Yorick, who says conventional
phrases of *politesse* to hide the true nature of his thoughts, is the grisette,
who makes no offers and has no thoughts but those she is prepared to
act upon: "Feel it, said she, holding out her arm." Her "civility" is
marred somewhat by the mercenary considerations that in part explain
her forthcoming friendliness, but the honesty of her "attack," an attack
in the style of Mrs. Waters or the Widow Wadman, makes Yorick's embarrassment seem an unworthy response. The genuine enjoyment she
seems to derive from this method of sale, and the moment of true "communication," both mental and physical, that results from her civility
transforms her act of seeming prostitution into a worthwhile experience
both for her and Yorick, one that transcends language and artificial emotion:

There are certain combined looks of simple subtlety—where whim, and
sense, and seriousness, and nonsense, are so blended,that all the languages
of Babel set loose together could not express them—they are communi-

151

cated and caught so instantaneously, that you can scarce say which party is the infecter. I leave it to your men of words to swell pages about it—it is enough in the present to say again, the gloves would not do; so folding our hands within our arms, we both loll'd upon the counter—it was narrow, and there was just room for the parcel to lay between us.

(168)

Sterne may be laughing at the phrases and sentiments that are meant to disguise lust, but he has only appreciation for the accidental gestures that express true feeling—even lust. He is surely laughing at Yorick for not admitting the attractions that keep him lolling upon the counter, but the distinction Yorick implies between "your men of words" and those of action is not part of the joke. In mocking the coyness of his Sentimental Traveller, Sterne coyly suggests that he is not to be reprimanded for his natural inclinations.

One's feelings about Yorick as he posts his way through France undergo the same alterations as his erratic temper does, but one senses generally the underlying goodness of his vulnerable heart and therefore agrees to be delighted by his joyous, if bumbling capers. One can easily fault him for the entirely irresponsible disposal of the small sum he has self-righteously set aside for charity; yet the same selfish disregard for the consequences of his decisions and actions leads him to choose La Fleur and almost justifies his selfishness. His reasons for wanting a servant are as vain as his reasons for being charitable and his method of choosing La Fleur is as whimsical as his selection of the charity recipients. But no one would wish that Yorick had been more reasonable or clearheaded about the lively applicant for the valetship:

[La Fleur] had all the dispositions in the world—It is enough for heaven! said I, interrupting him—and ought to be enough for me—So supper coming in, and having a frisky English spaniel on one side of my chair, and a French valet, with as much hilarity in his countenance as ever nature painted in one, on the other—I was satisfied to my heart's content with my empire; and if monarchs knew what they would be at, they might be as satisfied as I was. (125)

The "festivity" of La Fleur's temper, which "recompenses" Yorick's own frivolity in choosing him, "supplies" all the missing requirements one could hope for in a human being. The obvious rightness of Yorick's

152

choice (perhaps sexually motivated, if one considers the suggestions of La Fleur's foppery and his name), goes far to confirm the feeling we have that his own festivity, which often takes the form of frivolity, supplies many of his wanting virtues and much of his deficiency in reasoning. One justly overlooks the vanity or sensuality that propels the mirth which any monarch—as Sterne suggests in *Tristram Shandy* as well—should encourage; for mirth or love, both forms of selfish satisfaction, in turn produce mirth and love in others.

If one believes that circumstance in its haphazard way does more to subvert the natural virtue of cheerfully impulsive actions than does the egocentricity which in varying degrees is responsible for them, it becomes difficult to accept Arthur Cash's argument that "for Sterne, virtue is never sanctioned by a sensation or moral sense; it is sanctioned only by reason."[29] Cash turns Yorick into the teller of an incriminating tale, one who is not redeemed by the cheerfulness of his narration any more than Swift's Teller is. He considers Yorick's "hobby-horsical quest" for virtue to be a complete failure, rather than seeing it as an illustration of "the perplexities, and the possibility of fulfilling the eighteenth-century moral imperative to *Know thyself*" as Gardner Stout does (Intro., 43). Cash does not see that, for Sterne, reason can be as abstract and ineffective as high-sounding phrases turn out to be. In acting without thinking out the implications, Yorick stands a better chance of doing some good than if, like the rational Walter Shandy, he never acted at all. Circumstances may confuse his impulses by presenting sixteen candidates for eight pieces of charity or by twisting and double-twisting the wires of a cage, but one must not condemn the original spirit in which the actions were undertaken at the same time as one laughs at the bungled actions.

That Yorick is a bungler Sterne would not have us doubt, though the nature of his emotional clumsiness is just ambiguous enough for the polite ladies of the eighteenth century to accept him on innocent terms. The reader is not allowed to judge the weaknesses of Yorick without implicating himself: just as the Widow Wadman's portrait is left for the reader to paint as his imagination wishes, Yorick's sexual indiscretions cannot be committed without the consent of the reader, who must make certain assumptions about human nature in order to accuse Yorick of improper behavior. Also he must supply the definitions of the "crimes": just as he must insist in *Tristram Shandy* on supplying a new meaning for "nose," in *A Sentimental Journey* he must insert a word other than the logically natural "hand" to fill in the details of Yorick's final escapade. The italicized "fairly" in "all he can *fairly* lay his hands on" does not naturally suggest feminine attractions unless one gives physical substance to the otherwise innocently metaphoric remark. The reader finds that his own imagination must have salacious tendencies in order to accuse Sterne and Yorick of having an unseemly meaning in mind. To this extent he shares Yorick's human tendencies to act more coarsely than he would like to do; he is teased by Yorick as Yorick is teased by chance or circumstance. But in implicating the reader, Sterne does not force him to be ashamed of himself; his purpose is to allow the conventionally moral reader to feel the same delight in momentary occasions as Yorick does, to accuse himself in order to be able to exonerate himself and Yorick in turn. By encouraging the reader to fall into the same human trap as Yorick does, Sterne provokes the laughter that Coleridge traces to "a certain oscillation in the individual's own mind between the remaining good and the encroaching evil of his nature, a sort of dallying with the devil."[30] Thus, when Yorick is incapable of chasing away the lustful thoughts that parade as fatherly interest in his encounter with Madame R——'s serving girl, the reader is inclined to laugh at his own recognition of Yorick's ambiguous deportment, a recognition that carries a tacit approval. Coleridge's use of "dallying" explains the reader's willingness to be drawn into the situation; he does not need to commit himself to a course of action, any more than Yorick does. He can enjoy the flirtation and the emotions that accompany such dalliance, and move on as freely as Yorick to the next occasion of feeling.

Yorick's airy manner of unconcern ensures that one is always detached. One cannot consider weighty consequences because the event is over before any cause for alarm arises. Even the starling cannot be taken seriously (though many critics have tried). One might wish, as Rufus Putney and others do, that Yorick had freed the bird once it was in his possession. But as soon as one begins to condemn him for his thoughtlessness, Yorick moves on to the real point of the incident: the bird loses its reality almost as soon as it acquires it and becomes once again a prop, a symbol temporarily given substance in order to mock the human tendency to attend more to one's own interests in espousing another's cause than to the cause itself: "But as all these wanted to *get in*—and my bird wanted to get out—he had almost as little store set by him in London as in Paris" (205). Yorick's telescopic observations concerning the bird's fate quickly shift the irony at his own expense to society's.

Throughout the work, Yorick's irony, if we accept that the italics and winks are as much his as Sterne's, encourages amusement rather than castigation (of himself or society). The frustrating business of trying to keep in step with the world and at the same time trying to set the pace of others to conform with one's immediate feelings and needs cannot help resulting in indefensibly inconsistent actions. Yorick's ironic analysis of his efforts shows that he does not attempt to defend his impulses, but his account is also designed to make clear that his inconsistency arises from the inevitable clash between the immediate emotions of the world's occupants. At Nampont, Yorick would like to love the postillion as much as the peasant loved his ass, but the postillion unavoidably parches the flowering tenderness by being himself of a contrary disposition, caring not in the slightest about Yorick's potential affection for him as a fellow creature. One sees, of course, that Yorick is more annoyed at not being able to luxuriate in the fine feeling he has discovered in the peasant than he is at not finding it possible to love the postillion: "The deuce go, said I, with it all! Here am I sitting as candidly disposed to make the best of the worst, as ever wight was, and all runs counter" (144). Yet his own recognition of the artificiality of his sentiment-making carries with it a recognition of the absurdity of his behavior, which in turn forestalls any possibility of our condemning him. Absurdity, especially self-confessed, can be relished or pitied, but it is not admissible evidence of malice or cruelty or anything other than natural human weakness.

Only when Yorick's selfishness—that is, his desire to indulge in elevated emotion, overpowers his fine sense of irony, as it does in his encounter with Maria, does his absurdity make us impatient rather than mirthful or sympathetic. One feels on this occasion as if Sterne's comic strength, which A. Alvarez has identified as arising from the fact that "no matter how wholeheartedly he pursues high feeling, unredeemed reality keeps breaking in,"[31] fails him. This episode in the *Journey* is begging to be relieved by a Tristram, who under similar circumstances, remarks, "What an excellent inn at Moulines!" One cannot help being disappointed as well by Yorick's rather smug conclusion, so disparagingly described by Virginia Woolf, to the charitable exercise at Montriul. If Yorick was basking too much in the gratitude of the beggars, Sterne might have indicated that the philanthropist's pleasure was greater than actually merited.

These are, however, small indulgences in a work that understands the special joy of feelings that are disproportionate to their causes, however much it may urge us to laugh at them. The exhilarating sense of carefree delight which the tone of the *Journey* evokes in us is sustained by the weightlessness of the events rather than their significance, by their momentum rather than their momentousness. Alvarez sees this work as "perhaps the most bodiless novel ever written," and indeed the term "novel" seems far too full-bodied to describe the flighty series of brief encounters that comprise the *Journey*. If Fielding's works are leisurely excursions and *Tristram Shandy* a progressive course of digressions, the *Journey* may be seen as a slalom run, in which the artificial obstacles of life—the processes involved in acquiring passports, coaches, directions—and the natural ones—the distrust and fear of strange people and strange customs—are approached and surmounted on the strength of the emotional energy which propels the Traveller lightly on his way. The work breathlessly recreates that energy and thus has the same recreative effect on the reader as Yorick's skip through France has on him.

This analogy, however, does not take account of the irony which gives the *Journey* a dimension more complex than that of a ski run. Gardner Stout's comparison of Yorick's ironic narration and self-appraisal with the parables of the "early instructors of mankind," implies a seriousness that the book does not have, but it also serves to point out that Yorick's view of the journey is of as much interest and value as the journey itself. In his sermon on Self Knowledge, Sterne discusses the use of parable as a device for struggling against the forces of self-love which inevitably distort the objectivity of the judgments one makes about oneself; Stout sees the *Sentimental Journey* accordingly as "a kind of 'parable' or 'fable' " describing Yorick's private attempts to know himself (Intro., 43). His ironic commentary is the means by which he remains detached from his self-analysis as he both struggles and learns to come to terms with his feelings.

In calling the work a parable, Stout does not mean to imply that it is an emblematic history in the sense that *Tom Jones* is. For the *Journey* (to use Stout's terms) is more about the perplexities and the ultimate possibility of knowing oneself than the history of a man's progress towards self-knowledge. Yorick's struggles are more productive of equivocation than resolution and genuine change. That is, the excitement and interest in the work lie not in observing the development of a character in relation to his experiences but in feeling the varying and opposing forces of momentary emotion that affect a character whose main business is to leave himself open to them. Fluchére makes this point, and in so doing explains the *Journey*'s deficiency as a novel: "Yorick is at the centre of the book, but alone. Apart from LaFleur, an amused and amusing accomplice in his master's revels, he has no one about him but passers-by, not real characters. His grisettes are almost interchangeable. Always full of the present—but his own present, not that of a vast intellectual activity—he has no other purpose but to see that his sensibility is always free and available."[32] Additional characters might have saved the *Journey* from plunging headlong down the course of Yorick's trip and allowed it to accrue the substance, the context, "the vast intellectual activity," that justify such expenditure of energy. One is carried away by Yorick's carefree jaunt, but the recreation is not as sustaining as it would be if Yorick's loose heart had led him as tangibly to his goal of self-knowledge as his loose feet carry him across France. To ask this of the book, however, is to ask for another *Tristram Shandy*. In that work Sterne shows Tristram using the characters and experiences that affect his life to make sense of himself and his position in the world. His strangely successful attempt conveys a spirit of hope for the odd human species that lasts longer than the intoxicating spirit of Yorick's runaway emotions.

Yet one must take heart from the constant cheerfulness of Yorick's heart, which takes joy in as much as possible, however little and unfounded a source may be, and one may see hope for the human race in one for whom the intensity of melancholy is as great a source of delight as it was for Keats. Indeed, if the method of *A Sentimental Journey* is that of a parable, its spirit and message are those of the "Ode on Melancholy": "Then glut thy sorrow on a morning rose. . ." Sterne's sermons provide a more prosaic statement of the necessity for joy and a strenuous engagement with life, and the *Journey* may be seen as a dramatic commentary on this text:

I pity the men whose natural pleasures are burdens and who fly from joy, (as these splenetick and morose souls do) as if it was really an evil in itself.

If there is an evil in this world, 'tis sorrow and heaviness of heart—The loss of goods,—of health,—of coronets and mitres, are only evil, as they occasion sorrow;—take that out—the rest is fancy, and dwelleth only in the head of man.   (II, 13)

The narrative of Yorick's travels is enduringly comic, not because it is made up of parables or is one itself, but because it invites the reader to join in its joyful celebration of Yorick's disregard for life's spleen-provoking obstacles, while recognizing the selfish pitfalls of such an attitude.

Humphry Clinker

The spleen that motivated Smollett's energy and comically expelled itself in *Peregrine Pickle* is more gently but decisively purged in his last novel, *The Expedition of Humphry Clinker*. The mellowing of his mood and the easing of his style result in a more thoughtfully comic work; this "pleasant gossiping novel" (as Hazlitt described it) bears the weight, though lightly, of Smollett's antisplenetic sermon to himself. The whole book is like the relaxed Lismahago, a plump raisin, but the marks of its soured and shriveled origins show in the consciousness with which Smollett smoothes out the furrows in his characters' tempers. All the more interesting for being on the one hand so evidently good-natured, for being occasionally placed by critics into the porridgey mass of sentimental literature, and on the other for having a characteristic bite and the same satirical wrinkles apparent in Smollett's earlier works, *Humphry Clinker* is most notable for the acidic tenderness of its comedy.

The energies at work in this novel, in contrast to Smollett's earlier ones, are directed toward modulation, adjustment, and temperance. Characters are changed, tempered by the force of the action as against forcing the action to fit their own extremes, either satirically or sentimentally. In a strange way, this work that seems on first consideration to be least a novel of all Smollett's fictional works is most one, especially if character development is what is required of a novel. The Expedition accomplishes what Smollett's Adventures failed to do: the characters change their natures rather than simply growing older and slightly wiser. Stances and perspectives are modified; differences are reconciled, not removed by violence. Keats's observation, which David Evans quotes with reference to the moral values of *Humphry Clinker*, is actually much more appropriate to *Peregrine Pickle*: "Though a quarrel in the streets is a thing to be hated, the energies displayed in it are fine."[33] One might choose instead to summarize the values of *Humphry Clinker* with a playful converse of another remark from Keats's letters: "The knowledge of contrast, feeling for light and shade, all that information (primitive sense) necessary for a poem are great enemies to the recovery of the stomach." Matt Bramble, in acquiring a first-hand knowledge of the world's variations and being responsive to them for the first time, develops the awareness and gusto of the chameleon poet and promotes the recovery of his stomach at the same time. The other characters, if they do not increase their capacity for sensitivity quite so much, change in their relations towards each other, from maintaining a constipated aloofness to encouraging a comfortable closeness, so that each one seems healthier both physically and spiritually. By being exposed to the separate personalities contained in the letters and thus increasing our own "knowledge of contrast" and "feeling for light and shade" we too are more easily purged of our splenetic prejudices; the united group of "originals" promotes most effectively our comic health by making us value their differences while delighting in their collection.

The achievement of a healthy comic sense, a strength which allows one to accept one's own infirmities or another's foibles, to extend oneself rather than withdraw, is the destination towards which the action moves, as the little traveling party unwittingly directs itself towards spiritual health in the journey undertaken for Matt's bodily health. Individually they "case-harden" their constitutions by exposing themselves to each other and to the natural shocks of new experiences. As a group they benefit from their new understanding of themselves and each other, and offer mutual support so that retreat or defence, the coatings of misanthropy or liberality (Jery's concern with his gentlemanly image which prevents him from giving charity) are no longer necessary.[34]

It is not accidentally that Smollett echoes Sterne's Shandean message: "We should sometimes increase the motion of the machine, to *unclog the wheels of life*" (399). That the mind can dangerously affect the body as well as the body affect the mind, that the relationship between the spirit and its physical organism is fully reciprocal, is what the travelers learn from each other and demonstrate to us. Like *Tristram Shandy*, *Humphry Clinker* is a dissertation upon laughter, dramatically presented; it restates imaginatively what essay writers asserted plainly:

Let them laugh, for it is a most healthful exercise, gives briskness to the blood's motion, makes a proper and lively distribution of the animal spirits, and is a more powerful exorcism of those blue devils, which too often possess our poor mortal fabric, than what can be performed by a conclave of cardinals.[35]

For outright laughter may be substituted, as Sterne substituted hobbyhorses, the excursion itself, which loosens the constricted nerves of the travelers and enlivens their spirits so that they are able to laugh when necessary; they achieve the "easy and happy state in which [according to Hutcheson] we are most lively and acute in perceiving the ludicrous in objects," the perception of which in turn "tends to dispel fretfulness, anxiety, or sorrow."[36] That is, by opening themselves up to the comedy which life presents, by being responsive to the rich and ludicrous variety which their excursion opens up to them, they become truly healthy.

If Matt Bramble's disorders of mind and body dominate the attention of the other travelers and take precedence over any of theirs in our minds, it is because his sufferings are not only of the greatest magnitude, but also the most complex in nature. His is the true melancholy acted upon by humor, as described by the authors of *Saturn and Melancholy*:

The most perfect synthesis of profound thought and poetic wistfulness is achieved when true humour is deepened by melancholy; or to express it the opposite way, when true melancholy is transfigured by humour—when a man whom at a superficial glance one would judge to be a comic, fashionable melancholic is really a melancholic in the tragic sense, save that he is wise enough to mock at his own Weltschmerz in public and thus to forge an armour for his sensitivity.[37]

In turn, of all the characters, Matt has the most potential to develop a generous sensitivity towards his fellow inhabitants of the world; he has the greatest capacity for a working comic sense, as he has the greatest capacity for both suffering and relishing. Of the travelers, he is the most fit to become the subject of a work with serious moral pretensions. One can almost see *Humphry Clinker* as a possible sequel to *Gulliver's Travels*. Gulliver's journey has made it impossible for him to serenely maintain his innocent and passionate belief in man's goodness and reason, and his rage and disappointment, all the more acute for his sensitivity, force him to turn away from the species entirely: not so much out of hate as out of pain and impossible idealism. He is left at the end, like Matt at the outset of his journey, a man "without a skin," vulnerable to the slightest insults of nature and man. But as Gulliver is not "altogether out of

Hopes" that he may "in some Time" learn "to suffer a Neighbour Yahoo in [his]Company without the Apprehensions . . . of his Teeth or his Claws," so Matt undertakes a journey in active search of his health, opening himself up to the unknown insults and attacks from the very source of his "infection," the outside world. But Gulliver's only real hope, as Swift surely wants us to see, lies in his shedding his horselike veneer and accepting his wife and children for what they are, human beings like himself, perhaps smelly, even proud, though no more so than he. So, too, the Expedition truly ends when Matt sheds his false and ineffective covering, and accepts his place as a somewhat flawed human being in a somewhat flawed world.

The humble Humphry Clinker's place in the novel is clarified if one sees him as the character who most of all helps, or impels, Matt to remove his cloak of self-righteousness and distress and to turn his forced gaiety into genuine mirth. Robert Donovan offers a convincing account of Humphry's heroic designation in the title:

Humphry is a living reminder that Matthew is involved in mankind by his own sin, and Humphry's presence deprives him of the right to despise the follies and absurdities of other men, or draw credit from the disinterestedness of his own benevolence. The relation of mutual dependency and obligation is one that begins to develop from the moment of Clinker's first appearance in the novel and culminates fittingly in the overt recognition of the ultimate basis of the relation.[38]

Smollett's preoccupation with Scotland begins to make sense as well if one sees that country as the embodiment of heartiness and generosity: Matt first begins to realize here that deficiencies of climate and comfort may be more than offset by the warmth and succor that people have to offer: "[F]or a man is as apt to be prepossessed by particular favours as to be prejudiced by private motives of disgust. If I am partial, there is, at least some merit in my conversion from illiberal prejudices which had grown up with my constitution" (231).

That Matt was riddled with illiberal biases and affected by complacent pride, like Gulliver, Smollett makes clear from his first letter to the apparently endlessly patient Doctor Lewis:

I have told you over and over, how hard I am to move; and at this time of day, I ought to know something of my own constitution. Why will you be so positive? Prithee send me another prescription—I am as lame and as much tortured in all my limbs as if I was broke upon the wheel: indeed, I am equally distressed in mind and body—As if I had not plagues enough of my own, those children of my sister are left me for a perpetual source of vexation—what business have people to get children to plague their neighbours? (5)

Far from displaying Augustan passivity, as David Evans suggests, Matt shows here that he is full of nervous energy, energy that is misdirected into selfishness. One can hear his peevish sputtering and must laugh at the irony of his own positiveness in asking, "Why will you be so positive?" Other ironies (not apparent to the first-time reader) indicate his sorry condition. He feels as if he is broke upon the wheel because he does not let the wheel of his life run cheerfully round. He berates others for having children who become a plague upon their neighbors while Humphry Clinker is trying to make his way in the world without the benefit of the man who is most properly his closest neighbor—his father Matt. Although one is never allowed to dislike Matt—he does take care of the poor even if he glorifies himself in the process—one has decidedly mixed feelings about him in the beginning, as Jery has as well. The reader has to grow to understand Matt better and he has to learn to understand himself.

Jery has his own set of prejudices, but his are such that we may nonetheless rely on the accuracy of his observations. He is Peregrine Pickle's representative in *Humphry Clinker,* a sprightly young gentleman, much taken with himself and easily roused to feelings ranging from anger to generosity, an acute observer of the world who is very interested in establishing his position in it. His concern with his position colors his values but not his raw observations, whereas Matt's values stem in great part from his distorted way of looking at things. Jery's openmindedness is in keeping with his cultivated liberality, but is a commendable trait nevertheless. We cannot help being pleased by his temperate reaction to his uncle's unpleasant humor:

My uncle is an odd kind of humorist, always on the fret, and so unpleasant in his manner, that rather than be obliged to keep him company, I'd resign all claim to the inheritance of his estate.—Indeed his being tortured by the gout may have soured his temper, and, perhaps, I may like him better on further aquaintance. (8)

162

Acting as a standard against which Matt's squinty critical vision may be tested, Jery's comic vision might serve as an ideal were it not evidence of his naiveté more than his sensitivity:

Yesterday morning, at the Pump-room, I saw a broken winded Wapping landlady squeeze through a circle of peers, to salute her brandy-merchant, who stood by the window prop'd upon crutches; and a paralytic attorney of Show-lane, in shuffling up to the bar, kicked the shins of the chancellor of England, while his lordship, in a cut bob, drank a glass of water at the pump. I cannot account for my being pleased with these incidents, any other way than by saying, they are truly ridiculous in their own nature, and serve to heighten the humour in the farce of life, which I am determined to enjoy as long as I can.— (49)

His appreciation is a bit too flippant, too callous; it lacks the depth of the true comic hero, who enjoys the farce of life because he has no choice. While it is true that he matures on the journey and has almost as much potential for sensitivity as his uncle, his most important function in the novel is to help his uncle attain the stature of a comic visionary by laughing at what normally excites Matt's spleen. He is on hand to show Matt (and the reader as well) that the chaos of the world, as epitomized by the crowds at Bath, may be "a source of infinite amusement."

Though Smollett quite clearly feels the need to vent his spleen at the excesses in which "satiety" (Win's wonderfully metaphoric word, based on current pronunciation) indulge, and does so at great length in Matt's letters, he just as clearly recognizes that his bitterness is based on prejudices similar to Matt's. To see the novel simply as a splenetic emanation is to fail to understand its motivating forces. If Smollett finds himself in his ill-health becoming increasingly sympathetic to Gulliver's account of mankind, he works out his feelings in the dialectic that emerges from the opposing letters of Matt and Jery. The disdain Matt—and presumably Smollett—feels for humanity in an assembled form is reminiscent of Gulliver's after his final voyage:

Imagine to yourself a high exalted essence of mingled odours, arising from putrid gums, imposthumated lungs, sour flatulencies, rank arm-pits, sweating feet, running sores and issues, plaster, ointments, and embrocations, hungary-water, spirit of lavender, assafoetida drops, musk, hartshorn, and sal volatile; besides a thousand frowsy steams, which I could

not analyse. Such, O Dick! is the fragrant aether we breathe in the
polite assemblies of Bath. (66)

But as Don Pedro is present to undermine Gulliver's harsh impressions,
so Jery gives his version of his uncle's experience:

A few days ago we were terribly alarmed by my uncle's fainting at the
ball. He declares, he will sooner visit a house infected with the plague,
than trust himself in such nauseous spital for the future and that he would
never desire a stronger proof of our being made of very gross materials,
than our having withstood the annoyance, by which he was so much dis-
composed. For my part, I am very thankful for the coarseness of my
organs, being in no danger of ever falling a sacrifice to the delicacy of
my nose. (66–67)

Though Matt seems unable to delight in the democratic collection of
human society, as we see especially in his reaction to a Methodist meeting
led by Humphry, one must not assume that Smollett does not appreciate
or at least wish to appreciate the rights and privileges of the "mob." It
is a private shortcoming that he regrets enough to correct with Jery's observations (and Lydia's romantic ones as well) and Humphry's simple-
minded but honest actions; similarly Swift corrects his possible connection with Gulliver by the addition of the sensibly charitable Portuguese
Captain. Matt, too, softens some of his testier remarks by disparaging
his ability to be objective. Even though Matt and Gulliver have an extravagant delicacy in common, they are distinguished by Matt's ironic sense
of his own extravagance, which Gulliver lacks. Together with all the
other viewpoints, his latent self-mocking ability serves to remove all but
the suggestion of a sting from *Humphry Clinker:* "I know you will say . . .
I am rankled by the spleen—Perhaps you are partly in the right; for I
have perceived that my opinion of mankind, like mercury in the thermometer, rises and falls according to the variations of the weather" (77).
Smollett has the reader conclude that Matt's problems are more in need
of attention than those of mankind, though the hint that human ludicrousness may be the cause of Matt's discontent is pointedly made.

Rather than seeing *Humphry Clinker* as a pettier *Gulliver's Travels,*
as might be suggested by the comparison,[39] one may take Matt's sense
of humor, underdeveloped though it may be, as an indication that Smollett wishes to dissociate himself from his character's satire—indeed, even

his character perceives that his sputtering is an immediate effect of the spleen. Smollett allows the reader to deny Matt's conclusions because he himself, through Matt's remarks, undermines their authority, whereas the responsibility to conclude that Gulliver is mad rests entirely on the reader—even Don Pedro comes to have a reasonable opinion of his "veracity." If *Humphry Clinker* were intended as satiric rhetoric, we might regret that it lacks the richness of Swift's ambiguity, but as it is rather a novel primarily about a man who journeys from a satiric to a comic point of view, who loses his spleen (disease) as he collects his animal spirits, we cannot fairly say that Matt is a small Gulliver and that Smollett's concerns are not so noble as Swift's. Rather we must simply conclude that Smollett wants us to feel comfortable about life and Swift does not.

The travelers, including Matt, are all amiable humorists; they do not make us despair at human ignorance, folly, pride, greed, or pettiness, though they are by no means free of these weaknesses. Indeed, the novel ends when they are transformed from humorists into amiable human beings, with their originalities and frailties so muted and corrected as to make them no longer interesting subjects for a comic novel. Like Sterne, Smollett conceives his characters comically, as much admiring as mocking, as much laughing as appreciating. Humor is not allowed to dwindle into sentimentalism and wit is not allowed to corrode the humor. The comic attitude prevails throughout the book, most of all upheld in the characterizations.

Liddy is a sweet and gentle creature whose romantic notions derive from her goodness and innocence; yet rather than being a heroine or wholly an object of admiration, she is humorously treated. We are pleased with her sweetness not because it makes us think benevolently of sinlessness but rather because it is the source of her comic fragility. Matt's gently critical but appreciative assessment is shown to be true throughout the novel: "She is a poor good-natured simpleton, as soft as butter, and as easily melted—not that she's a fool—the girl's parts are not despicable, and her education has not been neglected . . . but, she's deficient in spirit, and so susceptible—and so tender forsooth!—truly, she has got a languishing eye, and reads romances" (11—12). Her vulnerability affects her senses, so they are at once heightened and unreliable; her vision of Ranelagh is her private vision of an enchanted land, only partly based on reality, as we note from her uncle's equally prejudiced but more specific account. Whereas the warbling of a singer makes Liddy feel as though she is "in paradise," Matt notes that "it is well for the performers that they cannot be heard distinctly" (89). As easily as she imagines herself in paradise, she is sunk to the depths of despair; her nerves are completely upset by an accidental glimpse of her lover, who is fittingly a sentimental hero disguised as a traveling actor to avoid a match, which in his parodying opinion, "must make him miserable for life."

The effect Liddy's tender sensibility has on the other members of the traveling party, with the exception perhaps of her jealous aunt, is to bring out their own matching feelings. Jery's distress at her "unworthy" love affair arises more from his desire to protect her from the world than from his conception of a gentleman's responsibility: in refusing to bind Wilson over as a vagrant, he acts with genuine gentility that shows he is thinking of his sister's feelings as well as her lover's. Matt's brusque reaction to Humphry's preaching is softened by Liddy's fear of his displeasure: "Mr. Bramble, perceiving Liddy in great trepidation, assumed a milder aspect, bidding her be under no concern, for he was not at all displeased at any thing she had done" (137). The perception and understanding of a sensibility as sensitive as his own, yet as sweet as he is bitter, has a healing effect on his wounded temperament. At once an object both of affection and amusement for the characters and the reader, Liddy is a comic creation, a little compliment to human nature in the same way that Uncle Toby grandly is.

Maintaining a humorous tone, precariously balanced between satire and sentiment, is a delicate task that Smollett performs with great skill. Satire is betrayed into comedy by the humorous affection of the author and his other characters for the objects of their contempt. It is only half true to say of Win and Tabby, as Mary Wagoner does, that "these characters, whose self-esteem depends most heavily on physical vanity and presumption, the cardinal sins of the neoclassical satirists, are treated with particularly vehement laughter that explodes their presumption by demolishing their claims to dignity."[40] While it is impossible to maintain the same fine picture of Tabby that she has of herself, especially when she asks for her "litel box with [her] jowls" or her "bumdaffee," we do not necessarily feel that she is without her own special kind of dignity. Her determination to get a husband and the efficiency with which she acts are truly remarkable; her very vanity is seen to be no more than the offspring of her determination, for she must believe in her own eligibility before she can hope to impress men with it. She brow-

beats her brother rather to make him feel her presence, to make herself
indispensable—as she oddly is—than to make him uncomfortable, though
she very often does so. Jery declares himself convinced that "she has . . . a
most virulent attachment to his person; though her love never shews itself but in the shape of discontent; and she persists in tormenting him
out of pure tenderness" (62). When she is in danger of being banished by
her brother for her ridiculous weakness with regard to her lap-dog, her
sudden meekness belies her former show of power. And then, the family
is overjoyed not at her defeat, but at the declarations of mutual esteem
which Tabby's unusual humility brings forth.

Unlike the classically ridiculous characters, as defined and memorably
created by Fielding, Tabby is a character to be reckoned with, a part of
the family unit. She is not Mrs. Tow-wowse, whose appearance in *Joseph
Andrews* is incidental and designed for the satirical purposes of one episode. If Tabby were expelled from the book for ridiculous behavior,
Matt would be without his "thorn" and would not have the same occasion
to fume and sputter, Jery would lose a source of diversion, Win would
be without a model to imitate. The oddity of Tabby's personality is not
primarily a target for satire but rather is an essential ingredient in the expedition's compound. James Foster recognizes her importance to the extent that he subtitles the novel, "The Journey of an Odd Sentimentalist
and his Unsentimental Sister."[41] The contrast between the two Brambles
is vital to the ferment of the novel, which ends when their differences are
resolved, Tabby's vinegary qualities being somewhat diluted by the prospect of marriage and Matt's tolerance for vinegar being proportionately
increased by his new companions and interests.

Similarly, Lismahago is more than simply a "grotesque," a representative of "Hogarthian caricature" as Lewis Knapp too easily dismisses him
in the Introduction to his edition of the novel. He participates in the
comic life of the work more than by arousing obvious mirth, mirth that
would be more contemptuous than cheerful if it were not for his larger
role. David Evans properly sees this incredible figure as an additional
grindstone acting upon Matt Bramble, one who is more effective than
Tabby in managing to smooth down Matt's prejudiced exterior: "In
Lismahago, with his irascible but experience tested opinions, Bramble
meets a character who, largely because of the comically grotesque nature
of his background and appearance, can upset much of Bramble's dogma-
tism."[42] After our first impressions of this incomparably conceived

"original," our first supercilious feelings of amusement change to gentler
ones mixed with admiration for his tenacity and honesty, his simple but
determined method of coping with life. He may lack the ability to laugh
at himself or at life, but he does not require the strength that laughter
provides, for he is never in danger of despairing; he has the courage of a
wild animal and like one is fiercely committed to survival at any cost to
himself. Rather than one who sees his own preposterousness, a comic
hero in his own right, Lismahago is proof for the comic hero of the possibility of survival against the enormous odds of fate. By being laughable
and at the same time wonderfully alive, he allows one to see the essential
relationship between absurdity and nobility.

That he is at once absurdly undemanding of life and yet appreciative
of essential human dignity, his defense of the way he runs his life shows:

Sir, (replied the Scot, with great warmth) you are the man that does me
injustice, if you say or think I have been actuated by any such paltry
consideration [as money]—I am a gentleman; and entered into the
service as other gentlemen do, with such hopes and sentiments as honourable ambition inspires—If I have not been lucky in the lottery of life, so
neither do I think myself unfortunate—I owe no man a farthing; I
can always command a clean shirt, a mutton-chop, and a truss of straw;
and when I die, I shall leave effects sufficient to defray the expence of
my burial.   (190)

The enthusiasm with which he throws himself into a marriage that might
be merely an arrangement of convenience is thoroughly consistent with
his attitude towards life and is evidence in addition to what we have
gathered from his Indian experience of his talent for making the best of
a bad bargain. The most impressive result of his determination to do so
is that he actually does turn a potentially disastrous affair into a miraculously successful relationship. Matt lets us know that he expects the two
odd creatures to "be as happily paired as any two draught animals in the
kingdom" (339) and we know from Lismahago's previous experience
with the squaw that these expectations are not unreasonable. Matt also
comes to appreciate the Scotsman for himself: "I make no doubt but
that he will prove a valuable acquisition to our little society, in the article
of conversation, by the fire-side in winter" (339). In a sense Lismahago
is the embodiment of all the experiences to which the travelers expose
themselves; he is Scotland's representative; like the people of that country,

he is simple, bold, generous, and above all, tough-minded and tough-sinewed, unspoiled by luxury. Having been through his own expedition, he gathers together in his person all the virtues that this expedition is designed to teach and helps to effect the change in spirit that the novel is all about.

Win, too, is more a representative than a caricature. She is Smollett's incarnation of good-nature—in a more honest and appealing way than Jery is—and simplicity. Her presumption, far from being exploded by laughter as Mary Wagoner asserts, is the cause of the only pathetic feeling we have for her, for that weakness is the natural liability of both her good-nature and her naiveté. In trying to oblige her superiors or lovers she is caught in the highly risible occupation of imitating those of a higher station in life. To say though that she is afflicted with an excess of pride contradicts the absolute lack of malice and self-assurance she expresses in her letters. Indeed, her presumption is no different from her religion; they are both "infections" caused by an overexposure and oversusceptibility to the events and people connected with them. She is alert to all the life-styles around her, and if she temporarily favors that of the "wally de shamble" to honest Humphry's, it is because it offers her a new and interesting way of life. The example of her mistress does not provide her with the strength she requires to avoid falling prey to her own foolishness: Tabby has chased after every man who might possibly be persuaded to marry her, and Win, who is without the ability to discern the nature of Tabby's foolishness, is inclined to follow her lead. Smollett makes the reader like her for her weakness; her explanation of the affair seems touching rather than contemptible:

God help me! I have been a vixen and a griffin these many days—Sattin has had power to temp me in the shape of Van Ditton, the young squire's wally de shamble; but by God's grease he did not purvail—I thoft as how, there was no arm in going to a play at Newcastle, with my hair dressed in the Parish fashion; and as for the trifle of paint, he said as how my complexion wanted rouch, and so I let him put it on with a little Spanish owl; but a mischievous mob of colliers, and such promiscous ribble rabble, that could bare no smut but their own, attacked us in the street, and called me *hoar* and *painted Issabel,* and splashed my close, and spoiled me a complete set of blond lace triple ruffles, not a pin the worse for the ware. (219)

The very simplicity of her detailed confession, complete with feminine regrets for her spoiled ruffles, attests to its sincerity and her surprise assures the reader of her ignorance of the impropriety. Gall and presumption are not her crimes, only vanity and good-natured foolishness.

Win's presence makes very little real difference to the travelers and it was not to effect changes in them that caused Smollett to include her in the letter-writing group; nor was it to show any change in her—only her station undergoes alteration. Rather, her letters and recorded remarks affect the disposition of the novel itself. Smollett created her as a spokesman for alert naiveté, to describe things with a freshness—even coarseness—that contributes to the comic atmosphere by giving the reader still another perspective from which to view the characters and events.

That there is a "genuinely creative gusto" in her language, "a recognition of ambiguities, a deliberate fusion and telescoping of words and hence of meanings," Walter Allen rightly notes and comments on the result: "Incongruities are linked together and found to be congruous."[43] Her simple mind necessarily makes the abstract into comprehensible concretions, and makes the remarkable seem ordinary and the ordinary remarkable:

Lord knows, what mought have happened to this pyehouse young man, if master had not applied to Apias Korkus, who lives with the ould bailiff, and is, they say, five hundred years ould, (God bless us!) and a con geror; but, if he be, sure I am he don't deal with the devil, otherwise he wouldn't have sought out Mr. Clinker, as he did, in spite of stone walls, iron bolts, and double locks, that flew open at his command. (155)

In trying to make sense of the sometimes peculiar administration of justice, she makes the reader aware in a new way of the extraordinary power of law, of words handed down for centuries that acquire supernatural authority as it were. Even those usages which are intended to be simply funny carry metaphoric messages from Smollett to the reader, while amusing us with their simplicity: "My parents were marred according to the rights of holy mother crutch, in the face of men and angels—Mark that, Mary Jones" (338). Mary Jones would mark if she were able, apart from the bawdy humor, the fact that a holy ceremony is no guarantee of a happy and binding marriage: "marred" here has the same effect as "marriage hearse" has in Blake's poem. Antimonarchists may find support for their attitude in Win's description of Saint "Gimses": "the sweet young princess, and the hillyfents, and pye-bald ass, and all the rest of the royal family" (108).

Win's undiscriminating naiveté makes her a fitting reporter of Humphry Clinker's activities, and she acts very often as his liaison with the reader, beginning with her observation concerning the whiteness of his posteriors. Through her we hear of Humphry's Methodist efforts from one who is not biased against them or merely amused: "Oul Scratch has not a greater enemy upon hearth than Mr. Clinker, who is, indeed, a very powerfull labourer in the Lord's vineyard. I do no more than yuse the words of my good lady, who has got the infectual calling; and, I trust, that even my-self, though unworthy, shall find grease to be expected" (155). Though Smollett undermines the value of these remarks by originating them with Tabby and showing Win's natural humility to be somewhat wanting (the joke is more on Methodism, however, than on Win), her faith in Humphry Clinker's industriousness may be taken at face value. The pride she takes in repeating the vocabulary of others assures us we are getting a fairly ac-curate report of Humphry's teachings, and the large portion of her letters devoted to moral lessons and to vaguely acquired notions of the "new Gerusalem" testifies to Humphry's religious assiduity. Together with Matt's more wary view and Jery's humorously indulgent view, Win's re-spectful and loving account gives us a complete picture of this comical catalyst who joins the excursion in its early stages and remains to en-courage the chemical reaction that takes place.

Other yeasty figures appear along the way, adding to the general fer-ment. Their business is mainly to stir up reaction, from the characters and the reader; like the many Trullibers and Hornbecks of the eighteenth-century novels, they were created with specific didactic functions, as well as to arouse mirth. Micklewhimmen provides some diversion for Jery, while demonstrating for Tabby's benefit the outrageous selfishness of charity that begins at home. Thrown back at her when she least expects it, Tabby hears her own favorite principle uttered with as much vehemence by the fleeing lawyer—"Na, na, gude faith, charity begins at hame!"—as she herself has ever shown. The lawyer is too busy saving himself from fire to worry about any others, just as Tabby is usually too interested in her vain acquisitions to spare any sustenance for the needy people her brother often seeks to relieve. "Fire is a dreadful calamity," offers Micklewhimmen in self-defense; Tabby "bridles" we are told, replying, "Fire purifies gold and it tries friendship" (176). The jest might have been at the expense of both, if Tabby's temper had not already been showing signs of improvement, and her nature seen to be not wholly mean. As it is, she loses a prospective suitor and gains a little understanding, while we have a good laugh.

In contrast, our hilarity finds no release when Mrs. Baynard makes her appearance. The emblem Matt assigns to her person—"faded fruit and iced froth"—expresses the emptiness and frigidity of the luxury she is designed to represent. A more sinister character than most of the other figures of ridicule, mainly because she has such a devastating effect on everything—the people and the land—around her, Mrs. Baynard is Swiftian in conception. Judging from her coldness and insensitivity to others, this fashionable woman would be capable of approving the Modest Proposal, if it seemed fashionable to do so. Matt's description of her "improvements" to the farm cannot help recalling the experiments of the creative projectors of Laputa:

To shew her taste in laying out ground, she seized into her own hand a farm of two hundred acres, about a mile from the house, which she parcelled out into walks and shrubberies, having a great bason in the middle, into which she poured a whole stream that turned two mills, and afforded the best trout in the country. The bottom of the bason, however, was so ill secured, that it would not hold the water, which strained through the earth, and made a bog of the whole plantation: in a word, the ground which formerly paid him one hundred and fifty pounds a year, now cost him two hundred pounds a year to keep it in tolerable order. (292)

Evans is reminded, not surprisingly, of Pope's "Epistle to Burlington," the moral of which is precisely Smollett's: " 'Tis Use alone that sanctifies Expense./ And Splendour borrows all her rays from Sense" (ll. 179–80). The characters would hardly have to meet this useless woman to condemn the damage she has done, but her appearance in the novel along with her spoiled son has the remarkable effect of rousing Liddy's spirit to check the young boy's rudeness. Her main purpose in the novel is, however, an indirect one. The necessity for Matt to step in and actively extend true charity, that is, his friendship, arises when Baynard's attachment to the termagant fails to diminish after her death. In helping his friend mitigate the harmful influence of his wife, Matt also helps to correct his own uselessness. Mrs. Baynard's shameful addiction to luxury is too evil to be very amusing at close range, but from the happy perspective of the sensible Dennison home, where the journey finally ends and

Matt renounces the sedentary (and luxurious) sport of splenetic letter-writing, Mrs. Baynard's contribution to the comedy of the novel is perfectly clear.

James Quin is responsible for a different kind of fermentation, stirring the action by his merit rather than his fault. In introducing Quin into the travels, Smollett is at once using the occasion to compliment the actor whom he regretted having criticized in his two earliest novels and to teach Jery the same lesson about prejudice that he apparently had to learn in real life, though his bias was professional rather than social in origin.[44] In the *Expedition,* Quin is the perfect urbane gentleman that Jery would like to be and whom Smollett sets forth as a good example for him: "He is not only a most agreeable companion; but (as I am credibly informed) a very honest man; highly susceptible of friendship, warm steady, and even generous in his attachments; disdaining flattery, and incapable of meanness and dissimulation" (50). Going on to admit his predisposition, Jery shows that he is aware of but not yet the master of his youthful tendency to make hasty assessments based on appearance or reputation:

Were I to judge, however, from Quin's eye alone, I should take him to be proud, insolent, and cruel. There is something remarkably severe and forbidding in his aspect; and, I have been told, he was ever disposed to insult his inferiors and dependants.—Perhaps that report has influenced my opinion of his looks—You know we are fools of prejudice. (50)

This early experience provides him with reason to be more conscientious about his opinions of other people, and prepares him for his openhearted reception of Wilson.

Smollett also tests his own prejudices, as held by Bramble, against the democratic notions put forth by Quin, whose profession has exposed him to a wider and more typical slice of life than Matt's. Though Quin proves his point about polite assemblies by showing they are not very different from what one would expect at Billingsgate, his urbane acceptance seems callous in comparison to Matt's wounded sense of delicacy. Indeed, the comic tone is slightly disturbed here by the note of regret and reproach sounded by Matt and Smollett at the evidence of human grossness to be found even among the most privileged members of the race. But comedy is restored in Jery's letter with the description of Tabby's conversation with Quin. In reply to her query about his relationship to Nell Gwyn,

173

Quin informs Tabby "with great solemnity" that his mother was "not a whore of such distinction" (53). His irreverence not only is mirthful but serves to emphasize the comic rule that distinction may not be attached to any select group, but is found rather to reside in individuals who may claim it for a surprising variety of reasons.

One may wonder at times about Smollett's true feelings about humanity—he has been variously described as unpleasantly egotistical, hot-tempered, and intolerant—but his comic integrity may not be questioned alongside the redeeming characters of Quin and Clinker, and the redeeming nature of the journey itself. The very abundance of types and opinions one encounters in *Humphry Clinker* inevitably contributes, as in *Peregrine Pickle,* to the comic spirit of the work. The energy that coursed through Smollett's earlier works is not lacking in this one: the great variety that was noted and commended by the first reviewers gives *Humphry Clinker* its great vitality, the vitality of people, places, and events.

What Putney says with reference to *Peregrine Pickle* is especially relevant to the *Expedition*: "From Smollett we learn most fully how the mid-eighteenth century looked, tasted, and smelled."[45] Indeed, in *Humphry Clinker,* we do not learn about the quality of life incidentally: the travelers' exposure to sensation comprises the greatest part of the action, and in their different modes of appreciating their experiences lies the interest of the action. Edinburgh's smells, Mrs. Baynard's ragouts, Bath's crowds, and London's white bread all provide material for incidental satire, but are much more important as agents for the central business of the novel, the acquisition of tolerance by the characters, the author and the reader. Indeed, the whole Scottish section is Smollett's plea to the reader to refrain from the satire arising from prejudice. He does here for the reader what he does throughout the novel for the benefit of Matt; he shows the lively attractions of things and places that seem at first notice to be uninviting or spleen-provoking.

Matt's first letter from north of the Tweed carries news of his healthier attitude towards life: "I now begin to feel the good effects of exercise—I eat like a farmer, sleep from mid-night till eight in the morning without interruption, and enjoy a constant tide of spirits, equally distant from inanition and excess" (219). In gaining his spirits, he loses his bent for criticism, and starts seeing things with a freshness and pleasure that has hitherto been characteristic only of Liddy's vision. His description of Loch Lomond might be his niece's were the true author not apparent

in the usual catalogues of precise details that require his maturity to perceive and record;

Nor are the banks destitute of beauties, which partake of the sublime.
On this side they display a sweet variety of woodland, corn-field, and
pasture, with several agreeable villas emerging as it were out of the lake,
till, at some distance, the prospect terminates in huge mountains covered
with heath, which being in the bloom, afford a very rich covering of
purple. Every thing here is romantic beyond imagination.   (248)

In his next letter he admits he has no desire to be critical, and where he
might have found fault, he praises instead: "The Lowlanders are generally
cool and circumspect, the Highlanders fiery and ferocious; but this violence of their passions serves only to inflame the zeal of their devotion
to strangers, which is truly enthusiastic" (253).

His new easiness does not escape the notice of his nephew, who comments that he "never saw [his]uncle in such health and spirits as he now
enjoys" (262). Scotland pleases Jery as well; the people, whose civility
appeals to his sense of propriety, provide him with a source of admiration rather than amusement. The satirical edge in his letters is replaced
by an expository appreciation of the Scottish people and way of life, as
he finds himself "insensibly sucked into the channel of their manners
and customs" (221). Liddy notes that "an amiable young lady" even
manages temporarily to "subdue the stubborn heart" of her brother,
while Jery contents himself with observing that he "never saw so many
handsome females together, as were assembled" at the hunters' ball in
Edinburgh. He is clearly taken with the social acitivities available to him
here, which are peculiarly suitable to his own gentlemanly inclination.
The recurring phrase, "I never saw such," indicates that his college-blind-
ed eyes are opening to the fact that strange and different things may be
just as acceptable and pleasurable as the familiar. His feeling at home
here is a tribute to his adaptability and receptiveness to the new ideas
and customs. Smollett's personal regard for his own homeland, and his
intention to praise it for the benefit of Englishmen, does not detract
from this tribute. Jery might easily have disagreed with his uncle's enthusiastic approval of the country without undermining that approval: that
he does not attests to the growing agreement between them and the continuing movement of the plot during the homiletic tour of Scotland.
Indeed, the whole Scottish expedition shows the increasing concord

within the family, though the excursion across the Firth demonstrates how easily still the harmony may be disrupted (until true family ties and marriage bind them together indissolubly). On this disastrous voyage Tabby rejects Humphry's "spiritual consolation"; Jery is engrossed in his own discomfort; Matt's improvement is so marked, however, that he laughs, in spite of his sea-sickness, at his sister's obstinate insistence that he direct the boatman in his official capacity as a justice of the peace.

If Tabby's delight in the northern nation is found to be relatively deficient, it is easily explained by the absence of eligible men; fresh air and civility that do not end in matrimony are no cures for her frustration and crustiness. She requires her private representative of Scotland, the inimitable Lismahago, who has the power to change her status as well as enliven her life.

Liddy too has a temporary set-back while in Scotland; the sudden appearance of a young man who resembles her mysterious Wilson and asks her to dance weakens her spirits and her health. However, she is receptive to the strengthening air and enchantment of Loch Lomond. Evidence of her increased maturity and ability to compose herself after a shock is found in the rather subdued and factual account of the incident that she writes after her restorative spell in the Highlands. A good portion of her letter is taken up with reflection upon female inconstancy and coyness. She shows quite clearly that she has given the behavior of her aunt and the love-stricken Win Jenkins, as well as all the fashionable women of Bath and London, serious consideration and if she is not flattering in her judgments, it is because she is now thoughtfully perceptive:

My dear Willis, I am truly ashamed of my own sex—We complain of advantages which the men take of our youth, inexperience, sensibility, and all that; but I have seen enough to believe, that our sex in general make it their business to ensnare the other. . . . My poor aunt, without any regard to her years and imperfections, has gone to market with her charms in every place where she thought she had the least chance to dispose of her person. . . . As for Jenkins, . . . she has also her heartheavings and motions of the spirit; and God forgive me if I think uncharitably, but all this seems to me to be downright hypocrisy and deceit. (259–60)

Liddy is well on her way to becoming an honest and loyal wife; even more, a sensible one. The expedition prepares her for her future life by testing her innocent notions of goodness and sweetness against experience, against Lady Griskin and Mrs. Baynard, and enabling her to strengthen them into convictions upon which to act.

Not so serious or lasting a benefit is reserved for Win Jenkins in Scotland; her naiveté remains her most endearing quality, despite the concomitant faults of character to which it exposes her, as pointed out by the newly critical mind of Liddy. If the benefit to Win derives more from her happy state of self-deception, especially with regard to the "wholesome" vapors of Edinburgh, than from any advantages inherent in the Scottish way of life or method of sewage disposal, the benefit to the reader is that of cheerful mirth. The simplicity and directness of her reactions, especially to the famed supernatural phenomena of Scotland, tend to allay the slight stodginess that comes over the novel in the Scottish interval. Because Jery's natural fondness for seeing the ludicrous in things is abated by his awe of the country, we look to Win to provide us unwittingly with the more comical aspects of their experiences and to maintain the lightness of tone that is so remarkable throughout the novel.

Throughout *Humphry Clinker*, Smollett invites his readers to participate in the general cure, either by laughing at the characters or themselves or by relishing the extent to which the laughable or simply odd contribute to the pleasure and value of life. Humphry, who has the air of a ragamuffin even in his ruffles and is the designated emblem of the novel's moral, is such a cheerful figure because he is so touchingly silly, whether he is bashfully apologizing for some unintended blunder or jumping up and down with joy, and at the same time, he never loses the dignity he displays when he responds to Matt's simple request for a list of his qualifications:

"An please your honour, (answered this original) I can read and write, and do the business of the stable indifferent well—I can dress a horse, and shoe him, and bleed and rowel him; and, as for the practice of sowgelding, I won't turn my back on e'er a he in the county of Wilts—Then I can make hog's-puddings and hob-nails, mend kettles, and tin sauce-pans. . . . I know something of single-stick, and psalmody, (proceeded Clinker) I can play upon the Jew's harp, sing Black-ey'd Susan, Arthur-o' Bradley, and divers other songs; I can dance a Welsh jig, and Nancy Dawson; wrestle a fall with any lad of my inches, when I'm in heart. . ."
(83–84)

What Smollett has him say is that he is qualified for life, for the unexpected, the ordinary, the big, the little, the necessary, the joyful: he is prepared to deal with any permutation that arises in life's lottery and he goes on to show how happily capable he is of managing those that do.

In learning to live with him and appreciate all his varied virtues, and in learning to live with themselves by exposing themselves to the hazards and benefits of unknown people and places, the other characters of the book become similarly capable of managing life, and become in turn similarly healthy and joyous. The final test of the family's concord, its acceptance of the variety that exists within its midst, and of Matt's triumph over the encrusted biases that had stopped up the natural flow of his heart's feelings, comes at Humphry's revelation of his parentage. The event follows his heroic rescue of Matt during the symbolic dousing which marks the rejuvenation of Matt's spirits, an event which is also a kind of communal bath, a final cleansing which removes the remnants of prejudice that had estranged the travelers from each other. In place of the disorder and distemper that accompanied Humphry's introduction into the novel, when the carriage overturned, cooperation and concern bring the family through the disaster of the flood. Liddy expresses the new sense of communion that has imperceptibly tied them together when she gasps in a great upheaval of passion upon discovering the safety of her uncle: "My dear uncle!—My best friend! my father!" (315). Matt is obviously touched at her avowal of affection, but the reality of his position as father of the household does not really occur to him until he finds out for how long he has unknowingly avoided his responsibility: he is "really shocked" at his old carelessness which has left Humphry so long an orphan. However, that he corrects his mistake without any further ado is no surprise to the reader; what is surprising and pleasing is the equally immediate acceptance of the others, especially Tabby. Their openheartedness corresponds to the warmth that their new sense of family generates and to the understanding in general of humanity that has been fostered by this warmth: Tabby instantly sees signs of a family resemblance, hitherto unnoticed; Liddy is proud; Jery refers to him as his "new-found cousin" and extends his hand as if to a gentleman; only Win is somewhat flustered by the new turn of events, which might deprive her of a lover. That Win is not disappointed in her hopes, that she too is allowed within the ranks of the family, is further proof of the tolerance and sympathy that have developed in each of them. Jery understands Humphry's feelings and obligations; Matt considers the "nymph's happiness"; Tabby is reluctant only because she will have to reward Win for past services—her hesitation is mercenary rather than personal. The action thus progresses towards its comic conclusion, owing in large part to the simplicity and charm of Humphry Clinker.

In her forthright way, Win records the "matthew-murphy'd" state of the Bramble party by the end of the novel. In contrast to the "sad taking here at Glostar," she reports the happiness at the "Dollison" estate and describes the atmosphere: "I want for nothing in this family of love, where every sole is so kind and courteous, that wan would think they are so many saints in haven" (338). Providence—or so Win says—goes on to provide a properly comic ending, by being "pleased to make great halteration in the pasture of our affairs.—We were yesterday three kiple chined, by the grease of God, in the holy bands of mattermoney" (352). The "picklearies" of Tabby are still in evidence, but are nothing to the striking harmony of the family gathering. Their furrowed tempers are all smoothed out; they have survived the journey and its trials with energy and grace; moreover, they have all "laid in a considerable stock of health" and serenity with which to enjoy actively the fruits of their new appreciation of life.

Delight in the unpredictable variety of life's adventures and the world's inhabitants has perhaps never been more energetically and exhilaratingly proclaimed than in the novels of Sterne and in Smollett's *Peregrine Pickle* and *Humphry Clinker*. In these works, the antisplenetic process is seen most clearly: crimes are transformed into pranks, misfortunes into minor mishaps, illnesses into curable disorders, madness into lovable disorders. Heroes abound, elevated to this stature in spite of their frailties by virtue of their boldness and bravery in taking on the challenges of life. They are helped along by a hobby-horse perhaps but more generally by the companionship of other human beings facing similar trials. The tone of the novels, which is largely responsible for the transformations and elevations, is one that holds the balance between mockery and sentiment, one that encourages an active joy in ordinary life.

CHAPTER FIVE

PERPETUAL MIRTH

The man who chuses never to laugh, or whose be-
calmed passions know no motion, seems to me only
in the quiet state of a green tree; he vegetates, 'tis
true, but shall we say he lives?[1]

The attitude underlying Colley Cibber's defense of himself was undoubtedly shared by all the comic writers of the eighteenth century.
Pope himself, who laced into Cibber's character quite wickedly in *The
Dunciad*, could hardly have helped subscribing to these views: gravity
and dullness are only slightly different forms of the same spiritual immobility. Indeed, mobility of spirit is ultimately what distinguishes a
living work from the multitude of heavy-lidded ones. In so far as works
that do not set out to be tragic are lively and energetic, evocative of
life, they are comic, even though they may also be satiric or, more unlikely, sentimental. Comedy turns satiric when its energies are directed
towards correcting, reforming society; when, however, all the activity,
all the excitement is busy cheering, rejuvenating the reader, the comedy
may be considered primarily antisatiric, even if it contains whole chunks
of corrective material within it.

It is this good-tempered, restorative comedy that the eighteenth century began to favor in its middle years, and it is by good-tempered
standards, the standard of the healthy spleen, that the works of this
period ought to be judged. The vital questions are not, "What is being
mocked?" "What positive alternatives are suggested?" They are, "How
much of real life is included?" "How much hope for humanity is a-
roused in the laughter that is provoked?" Tristram's kingdom of hearty
laughing subjects is an ideal in any age, but one which the comic writers
of the mid-eighteenth century, with their concern for the reciprocal

health of mind and body, and their persuasion that the health of society would follow from the health of its individuals, sought especially to bring about in their comic works by actively promoting hearty laughter.

Shaftesbury's disapproval of men "diseased" with the spirit of satire, whose "chief passion" was to "find fault, censure, unravel, confound, and leave nothing without exception and controversy,"[2] set the tone for the shift from brilliantly derisory wit to comfortably mirthful humor. His preference for the cheerful expressions of a healthy spirit proved to be contagious and encouraged writers to seek a more generous style of composition than the incisive verse satire. Thus Fielding presented the gregarious "new species" of writing, the "comic epic-poem in prose," a form that was capable of balancing implied criticism against an unabashed delight in all that was being criticized. The English comic novel showed itself, like *Don Quixote,* to be happily suited to displaying the frailties of mankind without rancor and the troubles of life without gloom, to dealing with realities without sacrificing the excitement that the popular romances had attributed to the most ordinary events. To a reading public acutely aware of the unpleasant symptoms of the spleen, the novel brought great relief, demonstrating the possibility of navigating through the rough course of life with one's spirit emerging unruffled by the arduous journey.

In reflecting on Christopher Fry's comments on comedy and faith, Nathan Scott elucidates the relationship between comedy and spiritual health: "The comic *katharsis* does, I think, essentially involve such a restoration of our confidence in the realm of finitude as enables us to see the daily occasions of our earth-bound career as being not irrelevant inconveniences but as possible roads into what is ultimately significant in life."[3] What gives the eighteenth-century novel—"wrote against the spleen"—its comic value is its unflagging concern with daily occasions, with the seemingly "irrelevant inconveniences." The resilience of human beings, their ability to adapt to their own shortcomings and misconceptions about the world, is tested and proved in the laughable course of events by the peculiarly eighteenth-century characters, the humorists, who combine the dignity and foolishness of Don Quixote with the forthright earthiness of his squire. The pangs of growing up, so humiliatingly suffered especially by those who sally into the world unprotected by the armor of trial and error, susceptible to every extravagance, are shown to be painful but essentially valuable wounds to the tender-footed heroes of these novels (including Matt Bramble, whose trials and errors had rendered him so sensitive as to require the assistance of Humphry Clinker to attain both maturity and health). The novelists, by using words as spiritedly as the temperaments and movements of their characters demanded, by catching the rhythms of actions and gestures in their prose, were able to demonstrate and encourage the flexibility of spirit that is the true contribution of comic literature to society.

The power of a work to enliven its readers will ensure its reception in any age by counterbalancing weaknesses or eccentricities that might otherwise be prominent. In the eighteenth-century works of such disparate orders as *Tristram Shandy* and *The Sermons of Mr. Yorick*—the one open to hostility on account of its bawdiness, the other to neglect on account of its subject matter—were welcomed for the cheerfulness they have in common, the cheerfulness with which their author, not at all one to write in the "quiet state of a green tree," endowed them:

Let the narrow-minded bigot persuade himself that religion consists in a grave forbidding exterior and austere conversation; let him wear the garb of sorrow, rail at innocent festivity, and make himself disagreeable to become righteous; we [the Critical Reviewers] for our parts, will laugh and sing and lighten the unavoidable cares of life by every harmless recreation: we will lay siege to Namur with uncle *Toby* and *Trim,* in the morning, and moralize at night with Sterne and Yorick; in one word, we will ever esteem religion when smoothed with good humour, and believe that piety alone to be genuine which flows from a heart, warm, gay, and social.[4]

The desire of the reviewer to laugh and sing and lighten the cares of life is by no means an exclusively eighteenth-century feeling, and his literary criteria have been more universally applied than is generally acknowledged. An explanation for the failure of a particular work to endure any longer than topicality or timeliness make it entertaining lies very often in the failure of the author to promote cheerfulness, or to arouse at least the comforting sense of familiarity that comes from recognizing life in an imaginary account of it.

The "Memoirs" of Lady Vane survive only because they are attached to the perpetually breathing *Adventures of Peregrine Pickle,* though at the time the long confession was sustained (and to an extent sustained Smollett's novel) by virtue of its undeniably fascinating bits of current gossip. The life of *John Buncle* was extended well into the nineteenth century only because the critics of the romantic period sensed the humor of the individual who was responsible for yoking together discussions on mathematics and seashells, and descriptions of romantic encounters. They were amused by the odd design and attributed a liveliness to the book that was probably true of its author. Readers in later years, however, were not sufficiently patient to be entertained by the pages of technical material inserted between the tales of romance, and today they are happy to dismiss the work with a mere reference to its eccentricity.

Tristram Shandy, too, might well have been dismissed (Johnson thought it was) were its eccentricities not paradoxically so faithful to the ordinary patterns of life, patterns that Sterne, by being alert to their natural oddities, was able so vigorously to reproduce. Similarly the other novels of this period that endure do so on the strength of their capacity for suggesting a complex yet manageable reality, one which is extraordinary and exhilarating and yet, after all, only ordinary. The didactic, emotional, or purely whimsical intentions of the truly antisplenetic writer are incidental (or contribute) to his creation of life out of words; for it is the cheerful bustle of life, in all its improbable, incomprehensible, and endlessly shifting appearances, that gives the substance and validity to his comedy that comedy in turn tries to give to life.

NOTES

Introduction

1. Paulson, p. 10.
2. Swabey, p. 159.

Chapter 1

1. *The Spectator*, no. 23.
2. Stukeley, p. 2.
3. Hooker, p. 366.
4. Aristotle, *Poetry*, p. 34.
5. Locke, I, 528.
6. Houston, p. 56.
7. Lengthy excerpts from Wotton's 1705 essay on the *Tale* appear in *Swift: The Critical Heritage*, ed. K. Williams, pp. 37–46.
8. Tave, p. 24. I am greatly indebted to Professor Tave's work for innumerable references and insights into the comic history of the period.
9. The full passage is worth quoting: "There is more of Humour in our English Comick writers than in any others. I do not at all wonder at it, for I look upon Humour to be almost of English Growth; at least it does not seem to have found such Encrease on any other Soil. And what appears to me to be the reason for it, is the great Freedom, Privilege, and Liberty which the Common People of England enjoy. Any man that has a Humour is under no restraint or fear of giving it Vent; they have a Proverb among them, which, maybe, will show the Bent and Genius of the People, as well as a longer Discourse: *He that will have a May-pole, shall*

have a May-pole." Congreve in a letter to John Dennis, 10 July 1695.
10. Hutcheson, p. 11.
11. Locke, II, 373.
12. Morris, pp. 3, 20–21, 24–25, 31.
13. Dunton, I, 46.
14. Dunton, I, 142.
15. Blackmore, p. 203.
16. Lewis, p. 146.
17. Farquhar, *Constant Couple*, I.i.
18. Farquhar, *Recruiting Officer*, I.ii.
19. C.J. Rawson joins Arthur Sherbo and others in cautioning against the easy generalization that sentiment drowned out all satire on the stage. He deals at length with Kelly's satiric impulses in "Some Remarks on Eighteenth-Century 'Delicacy'."
20. Quoted in Nicoll, II, 207.
21. Goldsmith, III, 213.
22. Nicoll, II, 269.
23. *The Beggar's Opera* III.i (Air XLI).
24. Hooker, pp. 361–62.
25. Hooker, p. 367.
26. Cambridge, p. xvi.
27. Whitford, p. 172.
28. Whitehead, *ll.* 377–83.
29. Morris, p. 29.
30. *Gray's Inn Journal*, no. 38.
31. Aristotle, *Ethics*, p. 245; IV. viii.3.
32. *Gray's Inn Journal*, no. 96.
33. Tave, p. 135.
34. Sarah Fielding, *The Cry*, II, 169.
35. For a discussion of sympathy and laughter, see Tave, pp. 202–09.
36. Williams, p. 195.
37. Castro, p. 176.
38. Paulson, p. 25.
39. *Lazarillo*, pp. 72–73.
40. Paulson, pp. 35–36.
41. Simon, p. 255.
42. Pitsligo, p. 178.
43. Tave, p. 187.
44. Doughty, p. 262.
45. Bright, pp. 162–64.
46. Burton, p. 370; II.2.vi.4.
47. Stukeley, p. 72.
48. Preface by the Stationer in *Wit and Mirth*.
49. Dunton, II, 9.
50. Cibber, p. 19.
51. *The Spectator*, no. 249.
52. "Dissertation Upon Laughter" in *Repository*, ed. I. Reed, II, 10. This piece was originally published in 1741.

53. Gordon, pp. 14–15.
54. Babb, p. 66.
55. Cheyne, p. ii.
56. Boswell, p. 782.
57. Mead, "Medical Precepts and Cautions," *Three Hundred Years of Psychiatry,* ed. Hunter and Macalpine, p. 387.
58. Robinson, pp. 230–31.
59. "De Affectibus Animi" in Hunter and Macalpine, p. 401.
60. Boswell, p. 1043.
61. Cheyne, p. 193.
62. Letter from Graves to Dodsley, 3 February 1758, quoted in Hill, p. 18.
63. Sterne, *Tristram Shandy,* p. 301.
64. Fry, "Comedy," in *Comedy: Meaning and Form,* ed. R. Corrigan, p. 15.
65. Morvan de Bellegarde, p. 168.

Chapter 2

1. *Essay on the New Species of Writing,* pp. 16–17.
2. Fielding, *Complete Works,* V, 33. All references to this edition will contain a set of numerals corresponding to the act and scene or book and chapter of the particular work, and a set (following the semicolon) to the volume and page in Henley. Thus, this quotation from *Tom Jones:* (XIII. i; V, 33).
3. Hatfield, p. 66.
4. Quoted in *Henry Fielding: The Critical Heritage,* ed. Paulson and Lockwood, p. 164.
5. Paulson and Lockwood, p. 357.
6. Crane, p. 638.
7. Andrew Wright makes a similar point in *Mask and Feast,* p. 89.
8. Morris, p. 31.
9. Tave, p. 142.
10. Mack, p. x.
11. Spilka, p. 14; the quotations immediately following are from p. 15.
12. Cervantes, I, 229.
13. Tave, p. 149.
14. Smollett, *Peregrine Pickle,* p. 128.
15. Kettle, I, 73.
16. Kettle, I, 74.
17. Paulson, p. 138.
18. Andrew Wright, p. 72.
19. Booth, p. 217.

Chapter 3

1. *The Monthly Review,* III (1751), 316–17.
2. As late as 1772, a reviewer in *The Monthly Review* (XLVI, 263),

included Coventry in the "first Rank" of humorous novelists. A
fifth edition of *Pompey* was printed in 1773.
3. Scott, p. 218.
4. Olshin, pp. 118, 123.
5. Volume XXIII in the series. Mrs. Barbauld butchered the work to
her taste, frequently changing words and omitting clauses and
sentences. Scott draws attention to several of these alterations.
6. Gosse, p. 211.
7. Very little is known about Coventry's life. A letter from Gray to
Walpole, 3 March 1751, is one of the few sources of information:
"Pompey is the hasty production of a Mr. Coventry . . . a young
clergyman; I found it out by three characters which once made
part of a comedy that he showed me of his own writing [when
they were together at Cambridge]." Gray, *Correspondence*, I, 344.
8. According to Ethel Thornbury, p. 8. The catalogue of the sale of
Fielding's library has, however, been missing from the shelves of
the British Museum since 1955.
9. Fielding, *Covent-Garden Journal*, I, 280–82.
10. Warner, pp. 115–16.
11. Huxley, p. 98.
12. Small, p. 72.
13. Paulson, p. 277.
14. Meredith, "An Essay on Comedy," *Comedy*, ed. Sypher, p. 42.
15. Small, p. 93.
16. In an appendix to the Oxford edition (pp. 418–27), Duncan
Isles discusses the relationship between Mrs. Lennox, Johnson,
and Richardson. He feels that the evidence of Richardson's help,
contained in two letters recently found, discounts any possibility
of Johnson's having written the chapter. Margaret Dalziel, however, indicates in her notes (pp. 414–15) that the suggestion,
first put forth by the Rev. John Mitford, should not be too
quickly rejected.
17. Letter from Richardson to Mrs. Lennox, 13 January 1752, quoted
by Isles, p. 423.
18. Cervantes, IV, 316.
19. Hopkins, p. 236.
20. Hopkins, p. 188.
21. Jaarsma, p. 339.
22. Jefferson, pp. 623–24.
23. Gallaway, p. 1181.
24. Letter from Graves to Dodsley, 3 February 1758, quoted in Hill,
p. 18.
25. *Times Literary Supplement*, 11 May 1922, p. 298.
26. Ellis, p. 854.
27. Tave, p. 159.
28. Hill, p. 47.

Chapter 4

1. "On Novelty and Familiarity." In the essay "On Reading Old Books," Hazlitt remarks: "My father Shandy solaced himself with Bruscambille. Give me for this purpose a volume of *Peregrine Pickle* or *Tom Jones.*"
2. Stevick, p. 717.
3. Stukeley, p. 73.
4. Letter from Swift to Pope, 20 April 1731. The same letter carried this advice to the pain-ridden poet: "Sweeten your milk with mirth and motion."
5. Paulson, p. 184.
6. Evans, " 'Peregrine Pickle'," pp. 259–60.
7. Putney, "The Plan," p. 1057: "One can see now that Smollett did not blindly confuse a blackguard and a hero; nor did he degrade Peregrine's character without a purpose."
8. Tompkins, p. 44.
9. Spector, p. 82.
10. Dilworth, p. 108.
11. Stedmond's suggestion was first made in "Satire and *Tristram Shandy*," *SEL* I (1961), 53. A revised version of this article appears in the later work, *The Comic Art of Laurence Sterne*. The quotation is from p. 6.
12. New, p. 2.
13. Norman Holland comments on these lines (*Hamlet* V.i.212–215) in his article, p. 422.
14. See Richard Lanham, *'Tristram Shandy': The Games of Pleasure* (Berkeley: University of California Press, 1973), which appeared after the completion of this study. His chapter entitled "Games, Play, Seriousness" is of particular interest.
15. Nietzsche, VII, 60–62.
16. Fluchère, p. 268.
17. Fluchère, p. 77.
18. Reid, pp. 110–11.
19. Reid, pp. 124–27; Putney, "Laurence Sterne," pp. 159–70.
20. Fluchère, p. 73.
21. Eskin, p. 274.
22. Fry, p. 17.
23. Holland, p. 422.
24. Quoted in Tave, p. 86.
25. Sterne, *Letters*, p. 77; 1 January 1760.
26. Paulson, p. 252.
27. Fluchère, p. 72.
28. MacLean, p. 408.
29. Cash, p. 113.
30. *Coleridge's Criticism*, Lecture IX; quoted by Stout, Intro., p. 40n.
31. Alvarez, p. 595.
32. Fluchère, p. 437.
33. Evans, " 'Humphry Clinker'," p. 266.

34. For similar discussions of *Humphry Clinker,* to which I am indebted, see Reid, pp. 78—99 and Evans, " 'Humphry Clinker'," pp. 257—74. Also of interest is Robert Uphaus, "Sentiment and Spleen: Travels with Sterne and Smollett," *Centennial Review* XV (1971), 406—421, which was published subsequent to the completion of the research for this study.
35. In Reed, II, 10. This piece originally printed in 1741.
36. Hutcheson, pp. 26—27.
37. Klibansky et.al., p. 235.
38. Donovan, p. 137.
39. Reid comes close to suggesting this, p. 89, but puts forth a strong case for reading the novel as comedy, not satire.
40. Wagoner, p. 112.
41. Foster, p. 128.
42. Evans, " 'Humphry Clinker'," p. 268.
43. Allen, p. 71.
44. Evans, " 'Humphry Clinker'," p. 271.
45. Putney, "The Plan," p. 1065.

Conclusion

1. Cibber, p. 17.
2. Shaftesbury, II, 223.
3. Nathan Scott, Jr., in Corrigan, p. 107.
4. *Critical Review* IX (1760), 405.

LIST OF WORKS CONSULTED

Primary Sources:

[Amory, Thomas]. *The Life of John Buncle, Esq.* London, 1756–66.

Aristotle. *The Nicomachean Ethics*, translated by H. Rackham. London: Heinemann, 1926.

———. *On the Art of Poetry*, translated by I. Bywater. Oxford: Clarendon Press, 1920.

Blackmore, Sir Richard. "An Essay Upon Wit" in *Essays Upon Several Subjects*. London, 1716, pp. 186–235.

Boswell, James. *Life of Johnson*, edited by R.W. Chapman. London: Oxford University Press, 1953.

Bright, Timothy. *A Treatise of Melancholie*. New York: Facsimile Text Society, 1940.

Burton, Robert. *The Anatomy of Melancholy*. London, 1845.

Cambridge, Richard Owen. *The Scribleriad, An Heroic Poem*. London, 1752.

Cervantes Saavedra, Miguel de. *The History of the Renowned Don Quixote*, translated by Motteux and Ozell. 9th ed. 4 vols. London, 1749.

Cheyne, George. *The English Malady*. London, 1734.

Cibber, Colley. *An Apology for the Life of Mr. Colley Cibber*. London, 1822.

Coventry, Francis. *The History of Pompey the Little, or, The Life and Adventures of a Lap-Dog*. London, 1751.

———. *The History of Pompey the Little*, 3rd ed. London, 1752.

———. *The History of Pompey the Little*, edited by Mrs. Barbauld. British Novelists Series, no. 23. London, 1810.

Critical Review, The. IX–XXXV (1760–1773).

Dissertation on Comedy, A. London, 1750.

Dunton, John. *A Voyage Round the World, Or, A Pocket-Library*. 2 vols. London, 1691.

Essay on the New Species of Writing Founded by Mr. Fielding, An. London, 1751.

Farquhar, George. *Complete Works*, edited by C. Stonehill. 2 vols. London: Nonesuch Press, 1930.

Fielding, Henry. *The Complete Works of Henry Fielding*, edited by W. Henley. 16 vols. New York: Croscup and Sterling, 1902.

——. [Sir Alexander Drawcansir, pseud.] *The Covent Garden Journal*, edited by G.E. Jensen. 2 vols. New Haven: Yale University Press, 1915.

Fielding, Sarah. *The Adventures of David Simple*, edited by M. Kelsall. London: Oxford University Press, 1969.

Fielding, Sarah, and Collier, Jane. *The Cry: A New Dramatic Fable*. Dublin, 1754.

Gay, John. *The Poetical Works of John Gay*, edited by G.C. Faber. London: Oxford University Press, 1926.

Gentleman's Magazine, The. XIX–XLIII (1749–1773).

Goldsmith, Oliver. *The Collected Works of Oliver Goldsmith*, edited by A. Friedman. 5 vols. Oxford: Clarendon Press, 1966.

Gordon, Thomas. *The Humourist: Essays Upon Several Subjects*. London, 1730.

Graves, Richard. *The Spiritual Quixote*, edited by C. Tracy. London: Oxford University Press, 1967.

Gray, Thomas. *The Correspondence of Thomas Gray*, edited by Toynbee and Whibley. 3 vols. Oxford: Clarendon Press, 1935.

Gray's Inn Journal, The. Dublin, 1756.

History of Charlotte Summers, The. London, 1749.

Hutcheson, Francis. *Reflections Upon Laughter*. Glasgow, 1750.

Johnstone, Charles. [An Adept, pseud.] *Chrysal; Or, The Adventures of A Guinea*. London, 1760.

Lennox, Charlotte Ramsay. *The Female Quixote*, edited by M. Dalziel with Appendix by D. Isles. London: Oxford University Press, 1970.

Le Sage, Alain-René. *The Adventures of Gil Blas of Santillane*, translated by T. Smollett. Oxford: Limited Editions, 1937.

Life and Adventures of Lazarillo de Tormes, The. London, 1726.

Locke, John. *An Essay Concerning Human Understanding*, edited by A.C. Fraser. 2 vols. Oxford: Clarendon Press, 1894.

London Magazine, The. XX–XLII (1751–1773).

Monthly Review, The. I–XLVIII (1749–1773).

Morris, Corbyn. *An Essay Towards Fixing the True Standards of Wit, Humour, Raillery, Satire and Ridicule*. London, 1744.

Morvan de Bellegarde, Jean Baptiste. *Reflexions Upon Ridicule*. London, 1706.

Pitsligo, Alexander Forbes, Baron. *Essays Moral and Philosophical on Several Subjects*. London, 1763.

Reed, I. ed., *The Repository*. 2 vols. London, 1777.

Robinson, Nicholas. *A New System of the Spleen, Vapours, and Hypochondriack Melancholy*. London, 1729.

Scarron, Paul. *The Comical Romance,* translated by J.B. London, 1665.
Shaftesbury, Anthony Ashley Cooper, Third Earl of. *Characteristics of Men, Manners, Opinions, Times,* edited by J. Robertson. 2 vols. London, 1900.
Smollett, Tobias. *The Adventures of Peregrine Pickle,* edited by J. Clifford. London: Oxford University Press, 1964.
——. *The Adventures of Roderick Random.* London: Oxford University Press, 1930.
——. *The Expedition of Humphry Clinker,* edited by L. Knapp. London: Oxford University Press, 1966.
The Spectator Papers [by Addison and Steele], edited by D. Bond. 5 vols. Oxford: Clarendon Press, 1965.
Sterne, Laurence. *The Letters of Laurence Sterne,* edited by L. Curtis. Oxford: Clarendon Press, 1935.
——. *The Life and Opinions of Tristram Shandy, Gent.,* edited by J. Work. New York: Odyssey Press, 1940.
——. *A Sentimental Journey Through France and Italy by Mr. Yorick,* edited by G. Stout, Jr. Berkeley: University of California Press, 1967.
——. *The Sermons of Mr. Yorick.* 2 vols. Oxford: Basil Blackwell, 1927.
Stukeley, William. *Of the Spleen: Its Description and History.* London, 1723.
Whitehead, William. *An Essay on Ridicule.* London, 1743.
Wit and Mirth: An Antidote Against Melancholy. London, 1684.

SECONDARY SOURCES:

Allen, Walter. *The English Novel: A Short Critical History.* London: Phoenix House, 1954.
Alvarez, A. "The Delinquent Aesthetic" *Hudson Review* XIX (1966), 590–600.
Babb, Laurence. *The Elizabethan Malady.* East Lansing: Michigan State College Press, 1951.
Booth, Wayne C. *The Rhetoric of Fiction.* Chicago: University of Chicago Press, 1961.
Buck, Howard Swazey. *A Study in Smollett, Chiefly 'Peregrine Pickle.'* New Haven: Yale University Press, 1925.
Cash, Arthur H. *Sterne's Comedy of Moral Sentiments: The Ethical Dimension of the 'Journey.'* Pittsburgh: Duquesne University Press, 1966.
Castro, Américo. "Incarnation in *Don Quixote*" in *Cervantes Across the Centuries,* edited by Flores and Benardete. New York: Gordian Press, 1969, pp. 146–88.
Coleridge, Samuel. *Coleridge's Miscellaneous Criticism,* edited by T. Raysor. London: Constable, 1936.
Corrigan, R., ed., *Comedy: Meaning and Form.* San Francisco: Chandler Publishing, 1965.

LIST OF WORKS CONSULTED

Crane, Ronald S., "The Concept of Plot and the Plot of *Tom Jones*," in *Critics and Criticism*, edited by Crane. Chicago: University of Chicago Press, 1952, pp. 616–47.

Dilworth, Ernest Nevin. *The Unsentimental Journey of Laurence Sterne*. New York: King's Crown Press, 1948.

Donovan, Robert Alan. *The Shaping Vision: Imagination in the English Novel from Defoe to Dickens*. Ithaca: Cornell University Press, 1966.

Doughty, Oswald. "The English Malady of the Eighteenth Century," *RES* II (1926), 257–69.

Ellis, Havelock. "Richard Graves and 'The Spiritual Quixote'," *Nineteenth Century* LXVII (1915), 848–60.

Eskin, Stanley. "*Tristram Shandy* and *Oedipus Rex*: Reflections on Comedy and Tragedy," *College English* XXIV (1963), 271–77.

Evans, David L. "*Humphry Clinker*: Smollett's Tempered Augustanism," *Criticism* IX (1967), 257–74.

——. "*Peregrine Pickle*: The Complete Satirist," *Studies in the Novel* III (1971), 258–74.

Fluchère, Henri. *Laurence Sterne From Tristram to Yorick*, translated by B. Bray. London: Oxford University Press, 1965.

Foster, James R. *History of the Pre-romantic Novel in England*. MLA Monograph no. 17. New York: MLA, 1949.

Gallaway, William F. Jr. "The Sentimentalism of Goldsmith," *PMLA* XLVIII (1933), 1167–81.

Gosse, Edmund. *Gossip in a Library*. London, 1892.

Hatfield, Glenn. *Henry Fielding and the Language of Irony*. Chicago: University of Chicago Press, 1968.

Hill, Charles Jarvis. "The Literary Career of Richard Graves," *Smith College Studies in Modern Languages* XVI (1934), 1–148.

Holland, Norman. "The Laughter of Laurence Sterne," *Hudson Review* IX (1957), 422–30.

Hooker, Edward Niles. "Humour in the Age of Pope." *HLQ* XI (1948), 361–85.

Hopkins, Robert. *The True Genius of Oliver Goldsmith*. Baltimore: Johns Hopkins Press, 1969.

Houston, Beverle Ann. "*A Tale of a Tub* and *Tristram Shandy*: Continuity and Change in Persona, Structure and Style." Unpublished doctoral dissertation, UCLA, 1969.

Hunter, R., and Macalpine, I. eds., *Three Hundred Years of Psychiatry 1535–1860*. London: Oxford University Press, 1963.

Huxley, Aldous. "Tragedy and the Whole Truth," in *Collected Essays*. London: Chatto and Windus, 1960, pp. 96–103.

Jaarsma, Richard J. "Satiric Intent in *The Vicar of Wakefield*," *Studies in Short Fiction* V (1968), 331–41.

Jefferson, D.W. "Observations on *The Vicar of Wakefield*, " *Cambridge Journal* III (1950), 621–28.

Kettle, Arnold. *An Introduction to the English Novel*, I. London: Hutchinson, 1967.

Klibansky, R., Panofsky, E., and Saxl, F. *Saturn and Melancholy*. London: Nelson, 1964.

LIST OF WORKS CONSULTED

Lewis, C.S. "Addison," in *Eighteenth-Century English Literature: Modern Essays in Criticism*. Edited by J. Clifford, New York: Oxford University Press, 1959, pp. 144–57.

Mack, Maynard. Introduction to *Joseph Andrews* by Henry Fielding. New York: Holt, Rinehart, Winston, 1948.

MacLean, Kenneth. "Imagination and Sympathy: Sterne and Adam Smith," *JHI* X (1949), 399–410.

New, Melvyn. *Laurence Sterne as Satirist: A Reading of "Tristram Shandy."* Gainesville: University of Florida Press, 1969.

Nicoll, Allardyce. *A History of English Drama*, II. Cambridge: Cambridge University Press, 1952.

Nietzsche, Friedrich. *The Complete Works of Friedrich Nietzsche*. Translated by O. Levy. Edinburgh, 1911.

Olshin, Toby. "*Pompey the Little*: A Study in Fielding's Influence," *Revue des Langues Vivantes* XXXVI (1970), 117–24.

Paulson, Ronald. *Satire and the Novel in Eighteenth-Century England*. New Haven: Yale University Press, 1967.

Paulson, Ronald, and Lockwood, Thomas, eds. *Henry Fielding: The Critical Heritage*. London: Routledge, 1969.

Putney, Rufus. "Laurence Sterne, Apostle of Laughter," in *The Age of Johnson: Essays Presented to C.B. Tinker*. New Haven: Yale University Press, 1949, pp. 159–70.

——. "The Plan of *Peregrine Pickle*, " *PMLA* LX (1945), 1051–65.

Rawson, C.J. "Some Remarks on Eighteenth-Century 'Delicacy,' with a Note on Hugh Kelly's 'False Delicacy,' " *JEGP* LXI (1962), 1–13.

Reid, B.L. *The Long Boy and Others: Eighteenth-Century Studies*. Athens, Ga.: University of Georgia Press, 1969.

Scott, William. "Francis Coventry's *Pompey the Little*, 1751 & 1752," *N&Q*, n.s. XV (1968), 215–19.

Sherbo, Arthur. *English Sentimental Drama*. East Lansing: Michigan State University Press, 1957.

Simon, Ernest. "A Tradition of the Comic Novel: Sorel, Scarron, Furetière, Sterne, Diderot." Unpublished doctoral dissertation, Columbia, 1963.

Small, Miriam Rossiter. *Charlotte Ramsay Lennox: An Eighteenth-Century Lady of Letters*. Yale Studies in English, no. 85. New Haven, 1935.

Spector, Robert. *Tobias George Smollett*. New York: Twayne, 1968.

Spilka, Mark. "Comic Resolution in Fielding's *Joseph Andrews*," *College English* XV (1953), 11–19.

Stedmond, John M. *The Comic Art of Laurence Sterne*. Toronto: University of Toronto Press, 1967.

Stevick, Philip. "Stylistic Energy in the Early Smollett," *SP* LXIV (1967), 712–19.

Swabey, Marie Collins. *Comic Laughter*. New Haven: Yale University Press, 1961.

Sypher, Wylie, ed. *Comedy*. Garden City: Doubleday, 1956.

Tave, Stuart, M. *The Amiable Humorist: A Study in the Comic Theory and Criticism of the Eighteenth and Early Nineteenth Centuries*.

Chicago: University of Chicago Press, 1960.

Thornbury, Ethel. "Henry Fielding's Theory of the Comic Prose Epic," *University of Wisconsin Studies in Language and Literature* XXX (1931).

Times Literary Supplement, unsigned article on Richard Graves, 11 May 1922, p. 298.

Tompkins, J.M.S. *The Popular Novel in England, 1770–1800.* London: Methuen, 1961 (first published 1932).

Wagoner, Mary. "On the Satire in *Humphry Clinker,*" *PLL* II (1966), 109–16.

Warner, John M. "Smollett and the Minor Comic Novel, 1750–1770." Unpublished doctoral dissertation, Harvard, 1964.

Whitford, Robert C. "Satire's View of Sentimentalism in the Days of George the Third," *JEGP* XVIII (1919), 155–204.

Williams, Kathleen, ed. *Swift: The Critical Heritage.* London: Routledge, 1970.

Wright, Andrew. *Henry Fielding: Mask and Feast.* London: Chatto and Windus, 1965.

INDEX OF AUTHORS

This index lists authors only. Allusions to titles and characters have been incorporated into the respective author's listing. The author of a quotation identified in the notes but not the text has an entry for the page on which his words appear. Anonymous works and articles are entered under the titles of the books or periodicals.